PUBLIC SPEAKING
for Personal Success

PUBLIC SPEAKING
for Personal Success

Michael S. Hanna
University of South Alabama

James W. Gibson
University of Missouri — Columbia

wcb
Wm. C. Brown Publishers
Dubuque, Iowa

Book Team

Editor Stan Stoga
Developmental Editor Edgar J. Laube
Designer Kay Dolby
Production Editor Gloria G. Schiesl
Photo Research Editor Shirley Charley
Permissions Editor Vicki Krug
Product Manager Marcia Stout

wcb group

Wm. C. Brown Chairman of the Board
Mark C. Falb President and Chief Executive Officer

wcb

Wm. C. Brown Publishers, College Division

G. Franklin Lewis Executive Vice-President, General Manager
E. F. Jogerst Vice-President, Cost Analyst
George Wm. Bergquist Editor in Chief
Beverly Kolz Director of Production
Chris C. Guzzardo Vice-President, Director of Sales and Marketing
Bob McLaughlin National Sales Manager
Marilyn A. Phelps Manager of Design
Julie A. Kennedy Production Editorial Manager
Faye M. Schilling Photo Research Manager

PN 4121 H234 1987

Cover photograph of *Buffalo II, 1964*, by Robert Rauschenberg, from the collection of Mrs. Robert B. Mayer.

The credits section for this book begins on page 424, and is considered an extension of the copyright page.

Library of Congress Catalog Card Number: 86–72075

ISBN 0–697–00829–0

Printed in the United States of America
10 9 8 7 6 5 4 3 2 1

This book is fondly dedicated to Loren Reid, Professor Emeritus at the University of Missouri, Columbia— teacher, colleague, and friend.

CONTENTS

PART 2
Planning the speech: Getting started

PART 4
Common types of speeches

14   *Speeches for special occasions 306*

Outlines the expectations and approaches for preparing and presenting speeches for gatherings designed to honor, to pay tribute to, or to inspire groups of listeners.

15   *Speaking in groups 322*

Explains how to become an effective participant in group decision making and how to present the group's findings in a public setting.

PREFACE

This text, *Public Speaking for Personal Success,* is written for students enrolled in an introductory public speaking course. We have tried to present a thorough blend of theory and practical application so that students will find this book both informative and useful. Our teaching experience and our ongoing research into the basic speech communication course convince us that this is a desirable approach, because it maintains intellectual integrity while showing students precisely how to prepare and deliver a speech. Throughout this text, our suggestions are based on the research literature of our field. In addition, each chapter includes many illustrations and real-life examples to help our readers understand and apply those suggestions.

The title of this text, *Public Speaking for Personal Success,* conveys our primary reason for writing this book. We believe that there is a direct relationship between a person's verbal ability—especially in one-to-many settings—and how that person is perceived by others. If others perceive a person as articulate and competent, then that person's chances for achieving success in personal, civic, and professional endeavors increases dramatically. As one of our former students (now a successful executive in a major corporation) put it, "In the real world of industry and commerce, it doesn't matter how much you know if you can't easily put it into a coherent and persuasive presentation." The title of this text is intended to convey the book's applicability. Students will encounter many occasions when they will have to organize their ideas and present them to others. The knowledge and skills presented herein offer students a valuable tool that will last a lifetime. The time and energy invested now will yield dividends for years to come.

Students learn to give speeches most easily when they see how the ideas they are studying actually apply. For this reason, we have included a large number of carefully developed examples and illustrations. We have deliberately drawn many examples from the classroom because we believe that students must be able to relate to the examples and perceive them as models of attainable performance. We have also included a number of examples from business and professional settings. In chapter 4 on audience analysis, Mark Williams, a computer engineer, fails to communicate effectively with his listeners because he wrongly assumes that their knowledge is comparable to his own. A young government worker's speech falls short of its goal in chapter 12 because the message does not meet the criteria of competence and appropriateness for informative speeches. These examples, framed in settings beyond the public speaking classroom, impress upon students the relevance and applicability of their work in this course.

Specific Features

Our coverage of the material and sequencing of the chapters is designed to fit public speaking classes as they are generally taught today. Our composite understanding of the basic course draws on two major sources. First, we have participated in the "Survey of the Basic Course," a longitudinal survey first conducted in 1970 and subsequently performed three times. This research, the only such study in existence, has afforded us a clear understanding of the topics and the amount of coverage that instructors across the country think are important in the basic speech course. Second, Wm. C. Brown Publishers has conducted both quantitative and qualitative market research in the basic public speaking course. We are confident that the organization and coverage presented here are compatible with most basic courses. However, because the chapters are self-contained and cross-referenced, an instructor can present these materials in a different pattern.

We also carefully reviewed our own experience with teaching public speaking—nearly fifty years in all—to discover what has helped our students become effective speakers. This fund of experience often served as a reliable guide because both of us have tried over the years to think of the student first: which approaches clarify content, reduce anxiety, and generally facilitate the acquisition of public speaking skills, and which do not. The features of this text are designed to respond to student needs based on this fund of experience.

Content Features

Chapter 1. We are convinced that effective public speaking is an important skill that can contribute to a person's personal and professional success. Such skill derives from a knowledge of the components of public speaking and from self-confidence. The first step in acquiring a knowledge of public speaking is to understand the communication process. In chapter 1 we introduce a process model of communication for that purpose. This model does not allow, however, for the fact that public speaking is more structured and formal than conversation. These attributes of public speaking often produce anxiety in the speaker, anxiety that must be controlled for the speaker to be self-confident. We go on to reassure students that nervousness is normal and it can be controlled.

Chapter 2. This chapter provides an overview of the essential steps in preparing a speech. We chose this position in chapter 2 because many instructors want students to give speeches as early in the term as possible. While we take up many of the same themes in greater depth in subsequent chapters, there is plenty here to get students started.

Chapter 3. The topic of effective listening is attracting increasing attention in our society because so many people are poor listeners. We approach this concern by describing the problems that commonly distract us and undercut our listening attention. This understanding will, in turn, afford students an awareness of how to plan and deliver speeches that make it easier for listeners to pay attention.

Chapter 4. Perhaps the most difficult concept for students to learn is that the speech must be related to the listeners. A speech that listeners do not attend to is a waste of time. Here we emphasize the need for effective audience analysis. Every student who reads this book will know that the audience is the most important part of the speech setting and that careful attention to the listeners is the most effective means of ensuring a successful speech.

Chapter 5. Students often seem to want to include everything they know about a subject in a single speech. Consequently, clear and careful focus on a single idea and a single purpose has often been among the most difficult concepts to teach. We emphasize this point in chapter 5, but only after describing proven guidelines for developing both the quantity and quality of the ideas.

Chapter 6. Often the nature of the topic and the audience will suggest a particular pattern of organization. A planning outline imposes structure on the presentation. This structure helps students assemble their ideas and assists the audience in following the speaker's train of thought. The speaking outline is the final manifestation of this process of organizing and outlining. This is the focus of chapter 6.

Chapter 7. A good introduction prepares the audience for what is to follow, and it confers upon the speaker the confidence that the speech is off on the right track. A good conclusion summarizes the main points of the speech while signaling to the audience that the speech is over. This chapter is filled with suggestions and illustrations of ways to "frame" a speech.

Chapter 8. Effective delivery cannot be taken for granted. Using notes, attending to verbal and nonverbal concerns, and dealing with unwanted surprises are all aspects of delivery. Because effective delivery can make the difference between a good and a mediocre speech, we have tried to anticipate and answer a wide range of questions related to delivery.

Chapter 9. Over the years we have found that most of our students have no idea how to go about developing or using evidence. Chapter 9, on supporting ideas with evidence and argument, presents what we believe to be most helpful to students. We suggest ways that students can strengthen their speeches through attention to the idea of credibility.

Chapter 10. Our students—and most of the adult learners in the business and industrial community whom we have trained—often have difficulty judging, developing, and using visual materials. Students who follow the suggestions in this chapter will be able to develop useful visual materials easily. We are confident that this is the most complete and helpful chapter of its kind among introductory public speaking texts.

Chapter 11. Language provides the building blocks of thought and communication and is, therefore, a tool that can be shaped to serve us better. Our language will work more effectively for us if we understand its nature and the problems inherent in its use. We offer suggestions for improving language use, because we feel strongly that language, if chosen carefully, can be the key to successful presentation.

Chapter 12. Informative speaking involves the transmission of ideas and information from a speaker to an audience. Because the goal of an informative speech can be either to expand upon or clarify what the audience already knows, the nature and appropriateness of a topic are important. We stress the positive aspects of a good informative speech—clarity, simplicity, and concreteness—and reinforce the student's understanding by emphasizing that opposing aspects—vagueness, abstraction, and apparent complexity—are problems that must be avoided.

Chapter 13. Moving listeners in the desired direction is, in a sense, the essence of leadership and is, therefore, an important tool for people who want to achieve personal success. A successful persuasive speaker understands the motivations of the audience, and thus uses logic and emotion to change the attitudes of the listeners. In this chapter students will also learn about the importance of speaker credibility and about the fallacies that must be avoided in order to achieve credibility in the minds of listeners.

Chapter 14. Students need to understand speeches for special occasions because such speeches play an important role in the ritual life of American society. Whether it is a speech of introduction at the Rotary Club, a keynote speech, or a speech of tribute at a retirement ceremony, the special occasion speech places certain demands on the speaker and constraints on the content of the speech. Chapter 14 will make students more aware of this kind of speech and its important role in our society.

Chapter 15. Because decision-making groups are so much a part of our civic, governmental, and business subcultures, effective participation in such groups can make an important contribution to personal success. Decision making, because it is a cooperative process, requires sensitivity to the concerns of others and the effective use of leadership skills. Our final chapter on small groups affords students insight into the nature of groups and provides advice on successful group participation. Many of the principles of effective communication discussed in earlier chapters are shown to apply in a group context. The results of effective decision making often take the form of a proposal that must be advocated. This special persuasion problem implies that the student must learn to handle a variety of public group contexts. Chapter 15 ends with a discussion of these important contexts.

Learning Aids

Chapter-Opening Pedagogy

Each chapter opener is designed to give students the clearest possible impression of the nature and purpose of the chapter. The chapter **outline,** which includes three levels of headings, shows students the chapter organization at a glance. The **objectives** point toward the most important themes within that organization, and the **preview** surveys the essential elements of the chapter. These three elements will acquaint the student with the content of the chapter and effectively serve as the basis for review.

End-of-Chapter Pedagogy

At the end of each chapter the student will find several helpful learning tools. The **summary** aids review by providing only the gist of the chapter. The **key terms,** defined in the *glossary* as well as in the text, provide the essential concepts that students should retain. **Discussion questions** enhance understanding by asking students to apply what they have learned in concrete situations, and encourage students to practice the analytic and performance skills we describe. Following the **notes** are **suggested readings,** an annotated bibliography that gives students suggestions for further reading material. Our end-of-chapter sequence is complete but not burdensome, didactic but not prescriptive.

To help reinforce in students' minds the relationship of public speaking skills to success in later life, we have selected **quotations** from successful people. These quotations appear in boxed inserts in chapters 1, 6, and 11. For example, students will read comments from Senator John Danforth on organizing a speech and from Edwin Newman on the value of effective language use. Gloria Steinem talks about stage fright and Shirley MacLaine about reducing her dependence on lengthy notes. In each case, students will be led to understand that what they are learning now can serve them later.

Boxed Inserts

Students will find the end-of-book material equally helpful. In selecting the nine **sample speeches,** we used instructional value and topic interest as the most important criteria. We also felt it was important to expose students to various levels of speaker experience. Therefore, we have presented speeches by Mario Cuomo and Pat Schroeder, political figures whose success has been based partly on their ability to speak effectively often. In contrast, we have included three speeches by students whose only training has been a one-term course in public speaking. Between these extremes are two speeches by experienced student speakers and two speeches by professional people who speak occasionally. This range of speaker experience should convey to students the notion that growth in public speaking ability is a process that is applicable now, in the classroom, *and* in future pursuits. As a further study aid, we have included *marginal notations* that point out the strengths and appropriateness of the major sections of each speech.

End-of-Book Pedagogy

Student speakers often need to use the library to find information and supporting evidence. We have included a section on **using the library,** which many students will find helpful. Professional librarians have reviewed and provided constructive comments for helping us refine and improve this section of the book. We are confident that students will find it a valuable reference.

The **glossary** is a compilation of the important terms used in the study of public address.

Unique to this text is the **troubleshooting guide.** We think that students ought to be able to find answers to questions *that are couched in student terms.* This guide is organized around the questions most commonly asked by our students. Then the page on which the answer to the question can be found is given. For example, the question might be, "When should I use visual supporting materials?" or "How can I help my group become a stronger team?" The pages on which the answers to these questions can be found are then listed—in this case, on pages 203–8 and 332–33, respectively. We believe that this guide will give students wider access to this text by providing a different approach to organizing and classifying the information.

These end-of-book materials, like the body of the text, have been created with the student in mind. Our overriding concern has focused on students and how we can assist them in acquiring the knowledge and skills of public speaking. We want to serve them well. *Public Speaking for Personal Success* should be much more than a text that gathers dust on the shelf after one term of use. We hope we have created a book that will provide guidance long after students have completed the course. Personal success is, after all, an endeavor that should continue beyond the classroom.

Acknowledgments

The following reviewers have provided valuable suggestions in the progress of our work. We are grateful and want to express our sincere appreciation for their contributions.

Martha Atkins *Iowa State University*
Martha Cooper *Northern Illinois University*
Roseanne Dawson *University of Southern Colorado*
Thurman Garner *University of Georgia*
Kathleen German *Miami University*
Larry Hugenberg *Youngstown State University*
Linda Medaris *Central Missouri State University*
Kathleen Morgenstern *California State University, Fresno*
Mary Pelias *Southern Illinois University*
Bill Seiler *University of Nebraska*
Paul Shaffer *Austin Peay State University*
Susan Thomas *University of Illinois*
Nancy Wendt *California State University, Sacramento*

No author or author team writes a book. We have used our knowledge and experience to prepare a manuscript, but the people at Wm. C. Brown Publishers must take the credit for making a book of it. Their professionalism is deeply appreciated. We especially want to thank Stan Stoga, Edgar Laube, Gloria Schiesl, Kay Dolby, Shirley Charley, and Vicki Krug. It has been a pleasure to work with these fine people.

Finally, we would like to thank our families, without whose support and willingness to excuse us from family activities, this book would not have been possible.

Speaking and Listening

1 *Introduction*

Outline

Objectives

After you have read this chapter you should be able to:

1. Compare and contrast a one-way and a process model of communication.
2. Identify, define, and explain the seven elements in the process model presented in this chapter, including:
   a. Source-encoder
   b. Channels
   c. Messages
   d. Decoder-receiver
   e. Context
   f. Feedback
   g. Noise
3. Compare and contrast public speaking and conversation.
4. List and explain four ethical responsibilities that accrue with increased public speaking ability.
5. Explain how public speaking skill can contribute to personal success.

PREVIEW

Effectiveness as a public speaker can contribute greatly to your personal and professional success. That effectiveness is based upon skill in developing and presenting ideas and upon self-confidence, notions that have existed at least since ancient Greece. The first step in building public speaking skills is to understand the communication process. Models help us achieve such an understanding. However, the models of communication do not indicate the aspects of public speaking that make it a unique part of the communication process. That is because public speaking is a relatively small part of the whole process. The models we use are designed to illustrate the whole process. Because public speaking is more structured and more formal than conversation, giving a speech sometimes makes people nervous. This anxiety is normal. It can be controlled, and learning to control it increases the speaker's self-confidence. Developing skills and self-confidence implies the need for ethical communication.

Congratulations! By enrolling in this public speaking course, you are making the first step toward an important contribution to your own future. By learning how to speak effectively, you will be able to communicate orally such important ideas as the concepts and skills you are learning in your other courses. Later this ability will help you communicate with and influence various people in your professional and public life. The knowledge you acquire in school, on the job, or during your leisure activities will be great, but unless you can communicate that knowledge—to individuals, as well as to large groups—few people will even know you have it. In any endeavor, those people who become successful usually have acquired certain knowledge and skills. They also have developed their ability to communicate: to share what they know, to convince others to believe what they do, or to get people to act in a certain way. Your ability to communicate who you are, what you know, and what you can do will greatly enhance your personal and professional success. Therefore, we congratulate you. We are convinced that the study of public speaking is a very important and beneficial endeavor.

No matter how much we reiterate the importance of this study, we as college speech instructors occasionally hear students remark that much of what is taught in the basic public speaking course is common sense. These students seem to feel that they already know much of what is taught in the course, and in a very general sense they may be right. They—and you— have listened to many speeches. You can usually tell a "good" speech from a "bad" one. While you may not have a checklist of good and bad speaking habits, you certainly know if a speaker successfully meets your own criteria for what constitutes a good speech.[1]

Why then have people for thousands of years studied rhetoric? Why do many colleges and universities across the United States require a course in public speaking? The answer is quite simple. There is a profound difference between being able to judge a speech when you are in the audience and being able to develop and deliver a speech that appeals to an audience.

Beyond the campus is a vast world of work and play and civic involvement. You will contribute to that world in many ways. Effectiveness in public address can only add to the quality of your contribution. This course and this text aim to help you learn to present yourself and your ideas in a public setting by teaching you various analytical and performance skills. We intend to do this by building on the commonsense knowledge of public speaking that you already possess.

It seems obvious that a clear relationship exists between your public speaking skills and your personal success. Think about it. There is a clear relationship between your skills and your success, and it is linked by your self-confidence. Your self-confidence provides the basis for the image you project. That image determines how people experience you and how much (and what) they invest in you. In return, what others think about you and invest in you directly affects your own sense of worth. We believe that by increasing your skill levels, you will increase your confidence in yourself and thus increase your personal success.

In this public speaking course, you will be asked to talk about yourself, about those things that matter to you and about objects, phenomena, and events in your world. These are the things you have talked about in conversation. In this course, you will need to adapt what you know to the public speaking situation. This text is designed to draw on your knowledge and experience. The illustrations and explanations, the presentation of materials, and the organization build upon what is already familiar to you. We often illustrate our presentation with anecdotes about our students. Although we have disguised some of the details in order to protect the privacy of people we care about, the stories are in fact true. You may have had experiences similar to these anecdotes; if so, you will be able to relate to them and learn from them. Our goal is to assist you in tapping your present knowledge about public speaking in order to build on it. Shortly, you will read a story about Terry Hall, which is a case in point. We want you to relate the story and its lesson to your own knowledge and experiences. In this way, this text will make you aware that effective public speaking is not some alien endeavor, but rather one that is firmly grounded in your own experience.

We have also provided examples that relate to the business and professional setting. Most of you will pursue full-time work within a few years after completing this course. By setting some of our examples in the work place, we hope to show you that what you learn in this course will have relevance to your future career. The skills you learn here can be applied in many significant ways to your future professional endeavors.

Your instructor will be a valuable resource for helping you integrate the information in this text with the resources that you yourself bring to the study of public speaking. He or she will develop exercises and assignments designed to augment your sense of organization and style, of what is sensible and correct. Your instructor is in a unique position to answer your questions and, more important, to provide comments and suggestions about your classroom presentations. We suggest that you make a point of consulting your instructor.

Your own history, this text, and your instructor are all important elements in your study of public speaking. However, the goal of successful speaking is elusive. The most important element in attaining it will be your own hard work. Remember, you are the one who chooses to prepare and practice, and to expose yourself to speaking opportunities. We are convinced that the extra effort you make will yield rewards far beyond this course that will contribute substantially to the quality of the rest of your life.

Public Speaking and Personal Success

You may be wondering what we really mean when we talk about the connection between public speaking and personal success. There are, we think, three areas in which you can attain personal success: (1) in your private life, (2) in your professional life, and (3) in your public life, beyond the world of work.

You may never have considered how enormously important public speaking skills can be in your private life. People need to like themselves—to view themselves as worthy and contributing members of society. Psychologist William Schutz believed that everyone has three interpersonal needs: (1) the need for inclusion, (2) the need for control, and (3) the need for affection.[2] These needs stem from what makes each of us feel good about ourselves—our self-concept. With practice and experience in public speaking, your confidence in your ability to express yourself will grow. As your confidence grows you will not only give better speeches, but you will be able to relate more effectively with those people in your personal life who matter to you—your family and your friends. The payoffs will have a rebound effect, because the success you experience in your personal life will enable you to pursue your more worldly endeavors with increased confidence and determination. As you give better speeches, and as people in your audience respond favorably to your speeches, you will gain still more self-confidence, not only as a speaker but as a person. In the long term, your ability as a speaker will continue to build your image in the eyes of others and your confidence in yourself.

Public speaking skills can make a strong contribution to your professional growth, too. Beyond the knowledge and skills you have acquired in your field of study, whether it be engineering or market research, your professional success will depend upon *how well you communicate* what you

George Gallup, Jr.

In *The Great American Success Story: Factors That Affect Achievement*, **George Gallup, Jr.**, together with his nephew Alec M. Gallup and William Proctor, distilled in-depth conversations with many of the most successful people in the United States about what contributed to their success. One of these factors was the ability to communicate well, which Gallup describes, along with an example of how one of his successful people learned to cope with speech anxiety.

Successful individuals need to communicate effectively—a call sounded over and over today. And true to form, the majority of our top achievers rated their oral skills at the top of the scale.

First of all, they're confident of their ability to speak in public, with 64 percent giving themselves an A grade. Also, 57 percent put themselves at the A level for their conversational ability. . . .

. . . Donald Seibert, former CEO of J. C. Penney, had a somewhat different experience with public speaking. He says he did well speaking extemporaneously before small groups when he first started to move up in his company. But when more than 8 or 10 sat before him, he felt his stomach get tied up in knots.

Although it took about 15 years and even a couple of visits to a physician to get some tips on handling stress, he finally worked things out. He discovered that when he felt himself tightening up, he could just take a deep breath and walk to the side of the podium—and that would usually cause him to relax. Apparently, there was some sort of physiological buildup of inner tension that was released when he moved about while speaking. . . .

Source: Gallup, George, Jr., and Alec M. Gallup with William Proctor, The Great American Success Story: Factors that Affect Achievement. *Copyright © 1986 Dow-Jones Irwin, Homewood, IL. All Rights Reserved.*

know. Your professional growth will depend partially upon how well you learn to manage the impressions you leave with others. They must see you as competent and credible.[3] If you cannot acquit yourself well, if you are not articulate and skillful in presenting your ideas, you will not make the right impression.

One of us attended a meeting in August 1986 that illustrates this point vividly. The group included about eight people—the members of a newly created Venture Capital Club. The club was formed so that people who have money to invest could meet to share ideas and to listen to presentations from entrepreneurs. Most of the entrepreneurs at that meeting were young—just a few years out of college. Three of the six presenters apologized for their lack of public speaking skills. Not one of these three found venture capital for his proposal. Of the three remaining speakers, two were virtually inarticulate; they were disorganized and unable to use visual materials, and they hesitated repeatedly during their presentations. Only one speaker was skillful in public address. That afternoon, he asked for venture capital of $128,000 to start up a small business. By the end of the reception that immediately followed the meeting, that speaker had four bids from the members of the Venture Capital Club. One of the bidders was asked why he decided to invest in that project. He responded, "Because that speaker knew what he was doing. He has his ducks all in a row, and his figures seem right. I think he's on to something that will make money. And, he was clear as a bell."

Public speaking skills are a valuable asset in your public life beyond the world of work. You will join groups in which you may have many opportunities to speak. Perhaps you will meet with the PTA in your community, join the Kiwanis Club, or attend the monthly meeting of the Women Executives Forum. Your church activities or community garden club activities will involve you in one-to-many settings. If your public speaking skills are polished, you will be in a strong position to make a meaningful contribution to others, and to yourself. Without such skills, you will be more likely to let opportunities pass.

Public Speaking, an Ancient Study

Although we speak of success in a modern context, much of the discussion in this text is rooted in the distant past. Rhetoric—the study of public speaking—has attracted the attention of some of the finest minds in humankind's intellectual history. The study of public speaking has an ancient and honorable history. Understanding even a small portion of that history will help you appreciate the study you are undertaking.

The oldest known manuscript, called *The Precepts of Kagemni*, is concerned with public speaking! This work dates from about 2900 B.C., in the fourth dynasty of ancient Egypt. While it is only a fragment including five paragraphs, two of those paragraphs are directly related to speech. Its message seems appropriate for our time: be gentle and persuasive, and avoid pushing.

Centuries later, about 450 B.C., a Greek philosopher named Protagoras became famous for teaching his students that there are two sides to every question, and that a good speaker should be knowledgeable enough about the subject to argue both sides. Protagoras was also concerned with grammar and diction, and he taught his students to develop and commit to memory short speeches on commonplace topics, so that they might be able to use them later in debate.

At approximately the same time that Protagoras lived, Prodicus began to call attention to the shades of meaning in words, and to stress the importance of using language correctly, and of defining terms. Prodicus is generally considered to have been the first teacher of linguistics.

Hippias, another teacher working at that time, considered training in memory to be essential to public speaking. Meanwhile, a sophist named Corax was teaching that speakers had to organize their ideas. He also stressed the importance of establishing and developing evidence to support the probability that an argument was true.

A teacher named Isocrates, who lived about a hundred years, from 436 to 338 B.C., was convinced that a good speaker had to be, first, a good person. He believed that words carry greater conviction when they are spoken by a person of good repute. His reasoning is still sound.

The great philosopher Plato lived from 428 to 348 B.C. He wrote two enormously important works about rhetoric, *The Gorgias* and *The Phaedrus*. In these works, Plato found fault with what the speech teachers of his day were teaching, and he set out what he thought they ought to be teaching, instead.

1. Speakers ought to know the truth of what they say.
2. Speakers ought to be logicians.
3. Speakers must have order and arrangement.
4. Speakers must know the nature of the human soul so that they can perform audience analysis.
5. Speakers ought to have a sense of style and delivery.
6. Speakers ought to have high moral purpose.

However, Plato wrote in a style called dialogue. His stories, while fun to read, lacked the directness of a text reference. Aristotle, one of Plato's students, began studying at Plato's academy when he was about seventeen years old and remained with Plato for approximately twenty years. It became one of Aristotle's goals to spread Plato's ideas. Using his genius, he expanded and systematized those ideas into a textual format. He wrote what has become the most profoundly influential book in the history of rhetorical thought, and titled it, simply, *Rhetoric*. Actually, there is not much in this book that Aristotle did not write about in his!

Over the thousands of years since Aristotle lived, other scholars from a variety of disciplines have studied public speaking and rhetoric and communication. Their writings would fill a vast library. The result of all that thinking and writing has been the evolution of a discipline that is often referred to as "speech," "communication," "rhetoric," and "oratory," or possibly something else. But no matter what it is called, the study of speaking and its effects has an ancient history and an honorable tradition.

The Process of Communication

The details and perspectives you will encounter as you read this book and participate in this public speaking course are derived from the history and tradition of rhetoric. We are concerned with the effectiveness of the communication event and are interested in the kinds of choices speakers make in an attempt to achieve their goals. While our focus on these concerns is

Lee Iacocca

One of America's most visible and respected business leaders, Lee Iacocca heads the Chrysler Corporation. Taken from his recent popular autobiography, this excerpt presents his ideas on the close bond between speaker and audience.

Of course, the more common way to communicate with your people is to talk to them as a group. Public speaking, which is the best way to motivate a large group, is entirely different from private conversation. For one thing, it requires a lot of preparation. There's just no way around it—you have to do your homework. A speaker may be very well informed, but if he hasn't thought out exactly what he wants to say, *today, to this audience,* he has no business taking up other people's valuable time.

It's important to talk to people in their own language. If you do it well, they'll say, "God, he said exactly what I was thinking." And when they begin to respect you, they'll follow you to the death. The reason they're following you is not because you're providing some mysterious leadership. It's because you're following them.

systematic and careful, we do not always approach these concerns from a single theoretical perspective. In our discussions we take freely from the research of many scholars from various disciplines, and from our own experiences as well.[4] The most important criterion that we have used in selecting what to include and what to omit is "utility." Is the piece of advice practical? Can the student use it? Whatever instruments we use to make the study, and whatever perspectives we take, do not lose sight that the focus is always on an important aspect of the communication process.

Public speaking is communicating in a one-to-many setting. It is characterized by the formal and structured presentation of a message. It is a communication event in which one person assumes primary responsibility as the speaker while the others constitute the audience and assume the role of listeners. Public speaking is only part of the larger process of communication—the process of message exchange through which people negotiate and share meanings.

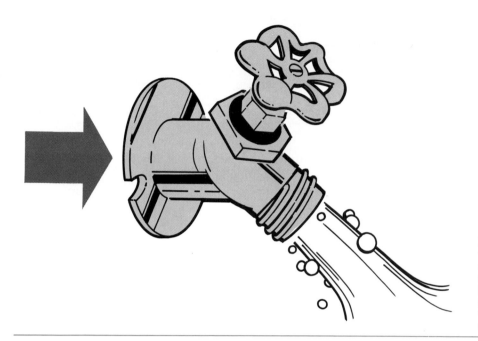

FIGURE 1.1 Some people think about communication as though it were water flowing through a pipe. Send it on its way, and if there are no obstructions, the message will reach its destination, essentially intact.

Models of the Communication Process

To explain the process of communication and to identify its elements, scholars and writers use models—sometimes in the form of drawings or three-dimensional forms—as well as written explanations to help focus their thinking. In this section we present some of those models to help you understand the communication process and how public speaking fits into that overall process.

A One-way Model

One of the main reasons people do not always communicate well, especially in public speaking situations, is that they have a mistaken idea of how communication works. They have a wrong model of communication in their heads. They seem to think that the communication process is like water flowing through a pipe. Once they send the water on its way (once they originate and send a message) they assume the water will get to its destination intact, assuming there are no kinks or blockages in the pipe.

This model, as shown in figure 1.1, is based on common sense and it has existed in one form or another for a very long time. It has been history's most influential and useful model of communication. Interestingly, variations of this model still appear in new textbooks, usually looking something like the one in figure 1.2. Even though this model is useful, it is also limiting. It shows some, but not all, of the components of the communication process. Scholars from Aristotle's time to our own have used models

FIGURE 1.2 A linear model of communication implies that communication is a one-way phenomenon.

to help them study communication. Each model lets the researcher focus attention on some relationship among special features of interest. For example, if you wanted to study the aerodynamic features of an automobile design, you might make a scale model of the car, place the model in a wind tunnel, and then blow smoke over it. If you did that, you would be using the model as a research tool in the same way that a scholar uses a communication model as a research tool.

People use different models for different types of study. If you wanted to know the optimum power-to-weight ratio for the same car, the wind-tunnel model would not serve your purposes. Instead, you would have to develop a mathematical model. Likewise, any model used to explain a process must be inclusive enough to incorporate the essential elements of that process.

The "water-pipe" model in figure 1.1 and the linear model in figure 1.2 are nearly identical. Both are one-way models. These models clearly imply that once the speaker has developed and presented the speech, his or her responsibility for the success of the speech ends. This mistaken notion has led an unestimable number of people to fail to have the impact they wanted on their audiences. Just because they said it does not mean that the audience heard it or understood it. Competent communication entails more than simply sending a message on its way. Obviously, this one-way model does not include all the essential elements of the communication process.

A Process Model

We want you to think of communication as a two-way phenomenon. In public speaking, the listeners have an impact on the communication event while the speaker is planning the speech, and while the speech is being delivered. It is critically important that you understand this point; without that understanding you are unlikely to achieve your speaking goals. Compare figure 1.2 to figure 1.3, a process model of communication. In the process model, communication flows in two directions and includes components not found in the one-way model.

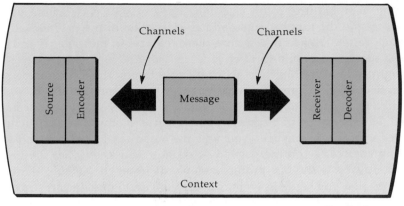

FIGURE 1.3 The process model makes clear that communication is a two-way phenomenon.

Source-Encoder

The *source* is the location of an idea. In the linear model, the equivalent for the source-encoder is the speaker. A source—say, yourself—gets an idea, and then translates that idea into codes that allow the idea to take form and shape, and to have substance (encoder). One such code, of course, is the English language. There are also nonverbal codes that can make an important difference in communication. You came to this class already knowing something about the verbal and nonverbal message systems. This text and this course will help you develop more fully your knowledge of these systems.

Channels

Once the source-encoder has developed an idea, it must be sent through *channels*, the pathways through which the message is sent. Notice that the term *channels* is plural. This is because we do not send our messages through only one channel. Suppose that you decide during class that you would like to have lunch with your friend. You approach her after class and invite her. You have used both verbal and nonverbal channels to send your messages of invitation. In public speaking, too, you will employ multiple channels. Your selection and use of channels will partially determine how listeners perceive you.

Messages

In even the most barren of all communication contexts, the print media, you cannot send only one message. This page you are reading provides a good example. You are receiving a message carried in the form of language. You are also receiving a message of type style, type size, and layout as well. There is also message value in both the color and the quality of the paper.

In public speaking, too, you send many messages at the same time. Your words, of course, are messages, and so are your clothes, your posture, your tone of voice, and your gestures. The artifacts that surround you, the lighting, temperature, color, size and shape of the space where you are speaking, and the number, ages, and attentiveness of the listeners all have message value.[5] You cannot ignore these features of messages if you want to be a successful public speaker.

Your personal credibility is also dependent upon the multiple messages that reflect who you are and what you think. For example, if you plan to submit a term paper to a professor, you will take care to type it or have it typed. The spelling will be precise, and the grammar will be as structurally correct as you can manage. You will use good quality paper and avoid spilling your coffee on the pages you submit. You know that the impression you leave with your professor depends upon the several nonverbal messages that you send, as well as upon the verbal one. In large measure, you know that these nonverbal cues tell the reader how to interpret what you have written!

Decoder-Receiver

The listener, a *decoder-receiver*, takes in messages and makes them meaningful. This decoding and receiving process is arbitrary and unique. Even native speakers of a language and their listeners do not have identical experiences with the same words of the language. If you want to be successful in public speaking, you must be mindful of this translating phenomenon, and skillful in making the translation. Both as a speaker and as a listener, your skills in this regard will bear directly on how well you communicate and how well you are perceived.

Context

The communication environment, or *context*, plays an important part in the communication event. You cannot limit yourself to a narrow understanding of this important feature of the communication process. Your personal and professional life will evolve in a large range of contexts. For example, as a speaker, you must not only think about such things as the temperature, lighting, and size of a place. You must also think about whether or not there is an adequate public address system, what precedes you on the program, and what follows. Otherwise, how will you be able to adapt to the conditions you find? If you do not concern yourself about these things, and adapt to them, you are not likely to make the impression you want.

Feedback

The concept of *feedback* is a relatively recent notion. Feedback refers to messages your listeners send you as you are sending them messages. Feedback lets encoders and decoders correct and control errors in the message exchange. Unless you learn to give and get feedback, you run the risk of errors that can be very damaging. To illustrate, let us assume that a member of your audience does not understand something you have said. If you are observing the audience while you speak, you might notice that this individual knits her brow and takes on a puzzled look. That expression, sometimes lasting only a fraction of a second, might influence you to repeat

An awareness of the effects of noise is the first step toward overcoming them.

yourself in different words. We would label that woman's expression as feedback in our model of the communication process. We would also label as feedback any comment that is directed at you from listeners. A simple "Beg your pardon?" or even a grunted "Ummmmmh" in a conversation serves as feedback. It turns the receiver into a source, and the encoder into a decoder. As a public speaker, you are always, and at the same moment, both a source and a receiver, and an encoder and a decoder.

The most important part of the communication process, from a learning point of view, is the concept of *noise*. Noise can be defined to include anything that interferes with the fidelity of the message exchange. It can be physical noise or it can be semantic noise. Physical noise is always noise in the channels. For example, if you are listening to a lecture in a classroom and someone begins to hammer on the wall outside the room, you would be distracted by that noise. Physical noise can be overwhelming. Semantic noise is any distortion that occurs when your use of language differs from that of another person. If your use of language causes you to bring a different meaning to an expression from the one meant by the speaker, semantic noise has interfered with the fidelity of the message exchange.

Noise

Terry Hall accidentally created semantic noise for his listeners one morning in speech class. Terry's speech topic was that college students use some language in private contexts that they do not use in public contexts, and that they should not live by what he called the double standard of language. He started his speech by uttering several powerful, four-letter words that he objected to. He did this for shock effect, but his plan backfired. By the time Terry had finished the first few words, the audience members were unable to listen to more. Even though his idea was to speak on behalf of a more moderate use of language, with less profanity, the audience went away from the classroom remembering only the overpowering introduction. He had made a serious error.

At the end of that class, one student asked the instructor his opinion of Terry's speech. Clearly, the student had found Terry's speech remarkable. Another student was overheard in the cafeteria that same day reporting Terry's shocking speech to others. A parent of still another of the students phoned the professor at his home that evening. The parent objected to the fact that her daughter had been subjected to such language in a university classroom. To say the least, what Terry did was mindless. As a serious student he should have known better than to create such noise. He should have known that his audience would not be able to tolerate such strong language. Terry Hall had created semantic noise. By his choice of language, Terry had created interference that got in the way of his ability to communicate with his listeners. In a different context, Terry's choices could have damaged his image in the eyes of his listeners. Fortunately, he was a student in a speech class—a place where people can make errors and learn from them without risking their personal credibility.

If you refer back to figure 1.2, you will see that noise does not appear in the linear model, and this is a critical omission. If the model of communication that you carry around inside your head does not include the concept of noise, you may well be ignoring this most important source of trouble. Noise fills up the communication process. While you cannot eliminate noise entirely, you can do a lot to compensate for its negative effects. One of the major goals of this text and this course is to help you learn how to compensate for the negative effects of noise.

Public Speaking as Communication

Up to this point we have discussed the general nature of communication. Let us move now from the whole process of communication to one of its components. Public speaking is, after all, one specific part of communication. Regardless of whether you are talking with one other person in some private setting or to a group of forty or fifty people, the process of communication remains unchanged. However, there are some important differences between one-to-one and one-to-many settings.

Both a conversation and a public speech require you to organize your ideas logically and state them clearly. For example, if you were telling a friend how to organize her resume, unless you organized your thoughts and chose your words carefully, you might say something like this:

> Make sure you mention your summer work. Your schooling probably should be listed in chronological order, but your work experience might look better in reverse chronological order. Skip the personal information unless you want to include it. Be honest about everything, but don't mention that you didn't attend a single meeting of the Management Club. And you could include a career objective.

Public Speaking and Conversation

Because you organized badly and perhaps because of your choice of language, your listener might well be confused.

Both a conversation and a public speech require you to analyze and to adapt to your listeners. To illustrate, suppose you want to borrow twenty dollars for a week. How might your request differ if you were asking each of the following people? Ignore the fact that you might never ask any one of these people to lend you money. Focus, instead, on how you regularly analyze and adapt what you say to your listeners.

Your brother
Your mother
Your best friend
A professor
Your employer

The point of this exercise is for you to realize that your conversational skills already include organization of ideas, and analysis of and adaptation to listeners. These skills are certainly important to you because you use them every day. They are common to both conversations and public speeches. The point is to apply these skills as you prepare for public address.

In addition, however, there are three important differences between conversations and public speeches: (1) their structure, (2) their level of formality, and (3) the degree of anxiety involved.

Structure

A public speech is highly structured. The parts of a good speech are carefully designed and carefully joined together so that they form a single entity having a clear purpose. The context, the messages, and the channels are all well structured.

Time, for example, imposes one kind of structure. Rarely will you give a speech in which you do not have some fairly clear idea of a time limit. An inviter might ask you to limit your remarks to about fifteen minutes. Another type of structure stems from the fact that the audience rarely becomes involved actively in the talk. Instead, listeners are expected to hold their thoughts to themselves. Perhaps there will be a question-and-answer session at the end of the speech, and perhaps not. If an individual member of an audience does interrupt with questions or comments, this is generally frowned upon by the speaker and by the listeners. These examples of the structural assumptions apply to a public speaking event, but they do not apply to a conversation.

This means, of course, that as a public speaker, you must organize your remarks far more carefully than you would in casual conversation. You must accomplish your goals during the speech, since you may not have an opportunity to express your point of view a second time. Therefore, you must think about the impact of your remarks on your listeners. At which points are they likely to raise questions or comments or opposing arguments? You must plan to respond at those points during the speech.

Formality

When you enter into a public speaking situation as a listener, you expect certain standards of behavior that would not necessarily hold true for casual conversations. For example, you expect the speaker to adhere to standards of grammar and usage that you do not always impose on conversations. How would you respond to the public speaker who said:

> It ain't right. It just ain't right. Them raisin' taxes and all. It's the gumment's fault that food prices is so high, what with their damn price supports and all. It just ain't right. It's gettin' so ya have to pay twice for whatcha get these days. 'Taint right.

While you might overlook such speech in conversation, you would be unlikely to overlook it in a public speech. Speech makers are supposed to be careful about matters of style and grammar. They are also supposed to pay attention to appropriate dress. The overall image that a speaker projects is important to the success of the speech.

Did you develop a mental image of the individual who spoke those lines? How do you imagine that person was dressed? To many students, this passage calls up a mental image of very informal attire, perhaps bib overalls and a plaid work shirt, high-top boots, and a straw hat. It certainly does not call up an image of, say, someone wearing a conservative business suit and tie, and highly polished wing-tip shoes. Most people in our society would expect a public speaker to take some care with his or her dress. The speaker, in turn, wants to dress appropriately in order to be taken seriously and not distract the listeners. You would undoubtedly select more formal clothing than blue jeans and a grubby tee shirt if you were going to give a speech to the local Rotary Club.

Public speeches are expected to carry more carefully drawn arguments and evidence than conversations, too. For example, you would not often cross-examine a friend who presents a claim without supporting evidence. We have all heard unsupported sentences like these without challenging the speaker.

> That movie was awful. It didn't have a plot that you could follow, and the acting was lifeless. And there must have been a hundred shots of the same background during the car scenes. Talk about low budget. . . .

A public speaker would be severely criticized for making such unsupported claims. You would rightly expect the speaker to show evidence for the assertion that the movie had no discernible plot. You would want the speaker to point to examples of lifeless acting. You would undoubtedly challenge the idea that there were a hundred shots of the same background, and you would want to know the actual budget figures for the film and a definition of *low budget* before you would accept the assertion that the film was a low budget production. To be effective, a public speech must be more formal than conversation in terms of language usage, delivery, and in the use of evidence and argument.

Perhaps it is the formality of the public speaking situation that creates the nervousness that so many people experience when they are supposed to give a formal presentation.[6] Regardless of the source of the anxiety, it seems clear to us that learning to manage any feelings of nervousness with confidence is very important to your professional growth and to your self-image.

Anxiety

Nervousness Is Normal. Most people tend to feel a bit intimidated about doing anything in public. Athletes know that the nervous feelings they experience before competition can make all the difference between winning and losing! Actors know that the stage fright they experience before the opening curtain gives them breath support and the extra energy necessary for them to do a fine job of acting. Feeling nervous is normal. But the difference between athletes and actors, on one hand, and the average person faced with giving a speech, on the other, is experience. The actor has learned how to turn those nervous feelings to an advantage. The athlete uses the physical experience of nervousness to "psych up," but the individual faced with giving a speech for the first time may not know how to use the extra energy constructively.

Gloria Steinem

People who often speak in public are not immune to the stress it causes, but they learn to control their apprehension. Here, one of the leading feminists describes her early reactions to large groups.

When magazines booked me on a radio or television show, I canceled out at the last minute so often that some shows banned me as a guest. Though I wasn't shy about bearding lions on a den-by-den basis, as journalists must do, the very idea of speaking to a group, much less before a big audience, was enough to make my heart pound and my mouth go dry. The few times I tried it, I became obsessed with getting to the end of every sentence without swallowing, and then obsessed for days afterward with what I should have said.

It was self-conscious. It was wasteful. I berated myself for this idiotic inability to talk on my own. When I once did show up on television to talk about the organizing efforts of migrant workers, host Bill Cosby tried to still my chattering teeth by explaining during a break that I had no *right* to be so nervous when I was speaking for a man as important as Cesar Chavez. That didn't help at all. After experiencing police riots at the 1968 Chicago Democratic National Convention, I got angry enough to try again, but only as a team with Jimmy Breslin, my colleague at *New York* magazine. That time, I got out about three sentences—but didn't have the confidence to resist false eyelashes that television makeup men then glued on female guests, thus making the medium contradict the message. . . .

. . . I say all this about speaking not only because it has been a major hurdle in my life, but also because it's a problem that seems to be common to many people who feel overdependent on the approval of others. . . .

. . . Nervousness never disappeared, but I learned three important lessons: (1) You don't die; (2) there's no right way to speak, only your way; and (3) it's worth it. . . .

Nervousness Can Be Controlled. Nervousness can be a healthy sign and a useful tool. Through understanding and practice you can learn how to control it. In chapter 2 you will study how to manage any nervousness you might experience as you approach a speaking situation. In the jargon of the field, nervousness about public speaking is called *communication anxiety.* We want to reiterate that communication anxiety is a common experience that you can learn to manage. For now, we simply summarize our best advice: practice, speak about topics that matter to you, prepare thoroughly, talk *with* your listeners rather than at or to them, and perhaps most important, think positively.

In the following story, Shelley Gold tells about how she managed communication anxiety in her first speech. Shelley had spent a lot of time helping her father, who owned and operated a dairy farm in Wisconsin. Her speech was about how milk is produced, graded, and packaged.

> I was terrified. Oh, I knew what I wanted to say, but my heart was beating so fast that I thought I was going to die. In fact, when you forced the issue that first time and told me that I had to give the speech, I thought about running out of the room. But after I got started I noticed that Joanie was pretty interested—or, I thought she was. And I looked around at the others. Bob was leaning forward and taking some notes, and Ellen was listening, too. After that, I sort of got into talking with them because it seemed like they wanted to know what I was saying. And then I was working with my visual aids and, for a while, I just forgot to be nervous. I could tell that I was reaching them. But I'm glad it's over.

Shelley's story is not unlike the stories of thousands of students who, at first, dreaded the prospect of giving a speech, but who learned to manage the nervous feeling that is so common. Your story will surely be like hers, if you are one of those who feel nervous before speaking.

Public Speaking and Ethical Responsibilities

You will have many opportunities to speak and thus to contribute to your personal success in life. We want to remind you, at this point, that the public speaking event confers on the speaker an opportunity to persuade and influence the audience. Persuasion and influence constitute a form of power. They imply certain ethical responsibilities that the speaker must accept. As a speaker, you have the responsibilities to be prepared, to be honest, to be careful, and to be realistic about your limitations.

Preparation

Because public speaking can influence others, and because public speaking always absorbs a listener's time and energy, you have an obligation to be prepared every time you speak. This means that you have a responsibility to know what you are talking about, to examine beforehand the evidence on which you are basing your conclusions, and to develop solid and sensible arguments. Imagine yourself making a presentation to a management group. Put the same premium on thorough preparation as you would on a presentation to that audience. Assume that your audience is listening just as critically to your evidence and arguments as would a group of managers who need to make an important business decision based on your remarks. Assume that your listeners are paying just as much attention to you as were those four venture capitalists who listened to one young entrepreneur and were willing to invest $128,000 into his project. Thorough preparation is the most reliable way to ensure success in public speaking.

Honesty

You should take care that what you choose to do as a speaker preserves the choices of other people. This notion needs some explanation. Suppose that you attempt to create a reality in your listener's head that you do not have in your own. The used car you want to sell a prospective buyer is about to throw a rod. You tell the woman that the noise is a normal part of that old car's personality, and is really nothing to worry about. Suppose, further, that you successfully convince her of that. Because you have been dishonest, your listener, now possessing an inaccurate image of reality, cannot make an intelligent choice.

As a speaker you will have opportunities to take advantage of listeners. However, you have an obligation to be honest. Surely you have heard of individuals who were taken in by evidence and arguments presented by speakers as true, only to find out later that the information was incorrect.

Accuracy

It is important to avoid overstatement of your position and to test evidence carefully. This responsibility may be one of the most difficult for people to accept, because we all have tendencies to exaggerate and to be careless about our uses of evidence. You can sometimes indulge yourself in exaggeration and carelessness among your family and friends. However, when you speak in public, your potential to influence others places you under a more rigorous set of constraints.

Personal Limitations

Our own feelings of self-esteem can lead us into problems that we could easily have avoided if we had accepted the responsibility to be realistic about our own limitations, but the ego is difficult to control.

Ellen Wilson, a senior student majoring in television production, volunteered to make a presentation to a large lecture class. The lecture class was a freshman-level survey course that described the broad field of communication studies. The professor was willing to provide Ellen the opportunity to speak, and was responsive to the idea of providing his students with a student speaker. But he was also concerned. The professor asked Ellen if she had ever made a speech to a large audience. He told her that the course had about 120 students that met in a large lecture hall with a brightly lighted speaking platform. Ellen said she was sure that she could handle it. The professor was still uncertain. He pointed out that it was not the same as working in a small classroom with fifteen or twenty students, and that the audience wouldn't interact with Ellen. Their expectations would be different, and the setting would be quite different, too. Ellen persisted. She was certain that she could handle it. "No problem," she said. "And I really want the experience."

As you may have already guessed, the actual event was a disaster. Ellen had overestimated her skills. When things did not go as she had planned, Ellen panicked, forgot her place, and dropped a handful of overhead transparencies. She was unable to regain her composure enough to salvage the class period. As a result, Ellen was embarrassed, and the class period was virtually wasted for those 120 students. All of that could have been avoided if Ellen had just been realistic about her limitations. She had an ethical responsibility that she did not accept.

We said earlier that this text will examine important features of the com-   ## This Text
munication process that apply to every communication situation, and identify those features that are important in the public speaking situation. The goal is not only to identify but to learn the skills that will make you an effective public speaker.

Here we present an overview of the rest of the text to show you how the text has been designed to help you acquire public speaking skills. Learning the skills of effective speaking in a speech class means giving speeches early and often, but that sets up a need for information about planning a speech and getting started. Chapter 2, "Planning the First Speech," is designed to give you important information and suggestions to prepare you for your first speaking experience. We recommend that you read this chapter right away. It is full of helpful suggestions and examples to get you started. In chapter 2 we make the assumption that your first speech will probably be a speech to inform. Of course, your instructor may have other ideas, and we certainly do not want to impose ourselves on that assignment. Even so, our suggestions will be helpful to you as you approach that first round of speeches.

In chapter 3 we take up the whole matter of listening. More and more people, such as those in business and managerial work, are coming to understand and appreciate the importance of effective listening. Understanding how people listen and some common problems people have while they are trying to listen will help you to be a better listener. That understanding will also help you make some important decisions about what to say and how to say it. Remember, public speakers serve as both sources and receivers of messages.

In studying the process of listening we also consider some reasons why people listen. What is it that causes people in audiences to pay attention? What do listeners perceive? How do they make decisions? What causes them to act? From the speaker's perspective, what should you do to anticipate your listeners? How do you adapt to the particular whims and tendencies of an audience? What channels and messages will be most helpful? What elements of noise must you avoid? Chapter 4, "Audience Analysis," answers these questions.

In chapter 5 we offer practical and helpful advice about selecting appropriate subject matter, and about focusing and narrowing that subject matter for speech making. Chapter 6 tells you how to organize that information for the best effect.

In chapter 7, "Beginning and Ending the Speech," we identify the purposes and functions of an introduction and a conclusion. Our experience—with literally thousands of undergraduate students and with hundreds of working adults who have asked us for help with their speaking—tells us that two of the biggest stumbling blocks happen in introductions and conclusions. Chapter 7 offers many suggestions, with illustrations, for avoiding these problems.

In chapter 8, "Delivery," we have included suggestions that you can respond to immediately. How to stand, how to gesture, how to use a visual aid, and other related topics of practical interest are included.

Chapters 9 and 10 explain in greater depth how to develop and support your ideas, and how to build your credibility with an audience. Of special concern is the language you use and how you use it, which we attend to in chapter 11.

Chapters 12, 13, and 14 describe the kinds of speeches that are most commonly delivered in our society. We offer specific advice about what you can do to make your informational, persuasive, and special occasion speeches effective.

Chapter 15 explains how to become an effective participant in group decision making and how to present the group's findings in a public setting.

Most students keep a few of their college textbooks for future reference. They begin building a library of works by choosing texts that seem to offer good advice that they can use later. We want you to keep this book for your library—to serve as a useful tool in the years to come. So we have included several informative sections at the end of this book.

Because we are committed to teaching by example, we have included a number of sample speeches. We have presented speeches by political and professional figures whose success has been based partly on their ability to speak effectively. In contrast, we have included some very excellent student work—three from people enrolled in a course just like this one, and two from *Winning Orations.* As you glance at those example speeches, you will notice that we have included marginal comments to point to the things we think make the samples noteworthy. You should find the sample speeches section to be extremely helpful as you plan for your own speaking assignments.

We have included a section on using the library, which includes some very practical advice about how to use a library for doing research, and about the most effective way to keep notes and records during your research. That advice is not limited to public speaking; you will be able to use it throughout your college career and, we think, for the rest of your life. The world's knowledge is yours for the taking if you know how to use the library.

The glossary of terms will be useful while you are reading, and while you are studying for exams and preparing for speeches during this course.

Later, the glossary will serve as a useful reminder of some of the most important concepts in public speaking.

In addition to the index of topics and authors, we have included an especially useful troubleshooting guide. If you have a problem or some question about how to prepare, plan, or deliver a speech, or how to understand or adapt to your listeners, or what makes persuasion more powerful, for example, you can turn to the troubleshooting guide. There you will find references to particular passages in the text that give time-tested and research-based advice.

Finally, we have tried to fill each page with helpful examples from a variety of classroom and job-related situations, and with study and remembering tools for your use. But however skillfully we have done that, we can never do as well as you can. So we hope that you will participate with us as you read this book. Consume it. Write your comments in the margins. Cross-reference its chapters. Make it your own, so that when you have completed this course, you will have a valuable record of your own insights and ideas, as well as a solid foundation in public speaking.

Over the years you will turn to this text often. People judge others as smart or stupid, competent or not competent, able or not able, on many grounds in addition to their personal fund of knowledge. You must be able to articulate what you know in a fashion that is clear, direct, and accessible. That makes the study and the struggle for increased analytical and performance skills in public speaking a very worthwhile endeavor.

Summary

Your lifetime will be full of opportunities to influence others, both in conversational settings and in public speaking situations. But even if you never give another speech in your life after this course, the study of public speaking is valuable to you. That is why this book is titled *Public Speaking for Personal Success*.

You already have some notion of what constitutes a good speech. But you will need help in expanding and structuring that knowledge. You can begin by looking at communication as a process, and at public speaking as part of that process. Elements in the process, such as noise, must be understood for public speaking to be effective. The public speaking situation includes features that are not evident in other communication contexts. Therefore, you need to understand both the similarities and the differences between public speaking events and more casual communication events. Public speaking is, generally, more intimidating than conversational speaking. Public speaking is more carefully structured and more formal than other settings—facts that appear to create nervousness in some people. Nervousness is normal and to be expected. It can be managed. By controlling the nervousness you might feel, you can turn the nervous feelings you experience to your advantage.

As you become more skillful in speech making, you gain power, which carries with it certain ethical responsibilities that you must accept. If you are prepared, honest, and accurate, if you build arguments on sound evidence, and if you are realistic about your own strengths and limitations, you can use that power to make contributions to the various environments in which you operate. Such contributions will make your own lifetime more rewarding. Those are lofty prospects, indeed, but they are within your grasp.

Key Terms

Channels   *Model*

Content   *Noise*

Decoder   *Process*

Encoder   *Receiver*

Feedback   *Source*

Messages

Discussion Questions

1. If you were going to develop an original model of the communication process, would you develop a linear model? Or, would you develop a process model? What elements would you include? Why?

   Suggestion: With a few of your classmates, try to develop a model of the communication process that represents the public speaking situation. You may wish, as a group, to present this model to your class.

2. List who you think are five of the greatest speakers of the twentieth century. What criteria are you using as you judge possible candidates for inclusion in this list? That is, what about the speaker makes him or her great? Would you include Adolph Hitler, Ronald Reagan, or Jesse Jackson? Why or why not?

   Suggestion: With two or three of your classmates develop a list of the century's greatest speakers. Display your list on the chalkboard, and compare it to the lists of other groups of students. Are the lists similar? Did each group use similar criteria?

3. Identify two people you believe are successful. What measures of success are you applying? Have you ever heard either of them give a speech to an audience?

   Suggestion: With a classmate, create a list of three or four successful people you know. Then ask those individuals about their experiences with speaking in public. Do they speak in public? How often? Do they find it useful? How so? Report the results of your study to the class.

1 For a very careful and systematic presentation of the theoretical assumptions that underpin this idea, *see* John O. Green, "A Cognitive Approach to Human Communication: An Action Assembly Theory," *Communication Monographs* 51 (December 1984): 289–306.

2 William C. Schutz, *The Interpersonal Underworld* (Reading, Mass.: Addison-Wesley Publishing Company, Inc., 1969).

3 Eric Gelman, et al., "Playing Office Politics," *Newsweek,* CVI:12 (September 16, 1985): 54–57.

4 Scholars have been studying communication behavior for more than twenty-five centuries. They have belonged to such broad-ranging disciplines as anthropology and art at one end of the alphabet, and zoology at the other end. We have tried to be eclectic in selecting and presenting ideas, so this book reflects a broad range of approaches.

5 For a thorough overview of the wonders of nonverbal message exchange, see Mark L. Hickson, III and Don W. Stacks, *Nonverbal Communication: Studies and Applications* (Dubuque, Ia.: Wm. C. Brown Publishers, 1985).

6 For an excellent review of the literature on communication apprehension (CA), *see* Thompson Biggers and John T. Masterson, "Communication Apprehension as a Personality Trait: An Emotional Defense of a Concept." *Communication Monographs* 51 (December 1984): 311–90.

Benson, Thomas W., ed. *Speech Communication in the 20th Century.* Carbondale, Ill.: Southern Illinois University Press, 1985.
    This excellent and very helpful collection of essays reviews the theory and research in communication produced during the twentieth century. Part II describes the organizational and conceptual issues involved in developing an academic discipline of communication. Five stars!

Larson, Charles U. *Persuasion: Reception and Responsibilities.* 4th ed. Belmont, Calif.: Wadsworth Publishing Company, 1986.
    This book approaches the whole matter of persuasion in today's world in a unique but highly useful and easy-to-understand manner. It prompts a quick and solid grasp of the main ideas in the extensive research literature on persuasion.

Littlejohn, Stephen W. *Theories of Human Communication.* 2d ed. Belmont, Calif.: Wadsworth Publishing Company, 1983.
    A rich source of facts and ideas, this book is a veritable annotated bibliography of important research and theory about meaning, information processing, language usage, conflict, and the like. It is copiously documented and very helpful as a reference work.

Thonssen, Lester, and Baird, A. Craig. *Speech Criticism: The Development of Standards for Rhetorical Appraisal.* New York: The Ronald Press Company, 1948.
    This is a classic work. Part II, "The Development of Rhetorical Theory," and Part V, "The Standards of Judgment," should be required reading for anyone who takes the study of public address seriously. A "five-star restaurant menu" of ideas.

2 *Planning the First Speech*

Outline

Objectives

After you have read this chapter you should be able to:

1. Define what is meant by self-disclosure.
2. Explain the main purposes of the first speech.
3. Cite the major problems in the first speaking assignment.
4. Begin a program of self-awareness to help you deal with your concerns about public speaking.
5. Identify the major physical and psychological characteristics of communication apprehension.

PREVIEW

A good beginning is important to success in any endeavor; it helps build confidence. Your first speech assignment provides you the opportunity to select and prepare a message, and successfully present it to an audience. We want this initial assignment to be a favorable experience for you. Therefore, in this chapter we will discuss the necessary steps you must take in preparing for your initial speaking assignment. We will emphasize the major matters of preparation and structure and attempt to satisfy your concerns about public communication and the apprehension you and other students feel as you approach this introductory performance assignment.

The opportunity to speak is one many of us approach with interest and apprehension. We feel ambivalent because this opportunity to share our ideas intrigues us, but we also have some reluctance about standing before our peers. In this chapter we will help you realize more of your potential as a public speaker. We want you to be successful. To achieve that aim, we will present some guidelines to help you organize your ideas and adjust more comfortably to public communication. Note the major headings and how they suggest important things you should know or do in preparing your first public speech.

Self-disclosure

Public speaking is an act of self-disclosure. It is a process in which you reveal psychologically meaningful information about yourself to others.[1] You share your ideas and feelings and tell others what makes you "tick." Your listeners have the opportunity to observe how you think, what interests or bothers you, and how you manage yourself and your challenges.

You may feel reluctant to tell others about yourself. Many people avoid public speaking because they want to avoid telling others how they feel, what they believe, and why. Some of us consider it a very great risk to show others who we are in that fashion. To explain this idea, most of us perceive other people on the basis of the way those people talk about their ideas. For example, when a person uses language such as *thoughtful, brash, soft-spoken,* or *forceful* to describe a public figure, we know that she is making a judgment of that public figure based on how the other person has represented himself in public. The thought of making ourselves the subject of such judgmental language may be more unpleasant than we know.

Your humanity is demonstrated when people hear you say that you like to go water skiing, live on a 350-acre farm, drive a turbo-charged car, once fell asleep in a math exam, enjoyed your trip to Minneapolis, hate the name "Buckeye," or had a second grade teacher who was the meanest person in the world. These personal disclosures allow other people a view of what is going on in your mind, and indicate to them your personal priorities and preferences. Self-disclosure is an important part of verbal sharing, a key human behavior.[2] It shows the humanity and the personality of each of us. Public dialogue reveals our viewpoints and why we feel as we do, and it may influence others to adopt similar viewpoints as a result of what we say and how we say it. It is easy to understand why some people feel reluctant and others are interested and willing to engage in public speaking, since it discloses the importance of events, people, and ideas in their lives.

We speak to express ourselves and to make our feelings and attitudes known. For example, you may have a strong personal view about what you believe is a worthwhile career and how to prepare for it. Or, perhaps you feel the most important issue facing people today is peace in a nuclear age. Your reasons for speaking may be to explain to others why you feel these matters are important and why they hold such a key place in your hierarchy of values. The process of speaking becomes an act of sharing ideas, experiences, and values.

Why We Speak

We speak to influence others in an attempt to alter their attitudes and subsequent actions. You may believe it is imperative that all smoking advertisements be banned from print media. Public communication provides you with an opportunity to share your thinking with a group of listeners and, ideally, persuade them to support your position. Or you may think that the cost of political campaigns has become excessive. Given the opportunity to speak publicly, you can identify the nature of the problem of campaign financing and potentially alter the way your listeners feel about spending in the race for public office.

In public speaking, the setting provides the economy of communication and the immediacy of reaction. For instance, if you attempted to share your ideas with fifty people individually, you would spend many hours repeating the same points over and over again. But if you spoke to all of them at once in public, you could convey the same information and have the opportunity to observe their reactions. In some cases, you could even choose to respond to their questions. There is an obvious economy in expressing the same idea to many people with roughly the same efficiency as if you spoke to them individually.

Audience-centered messages are critical to any information exchange. While planning your first speech, you must choose material that both you and your listeners will find interesting and easy to follow. Here are a few questions you might ask yourself as you think about audience-centered designs. Will the audience understand the words and ideas? Is the material developed at the proper level for college students? Is the message information they already possess? Chapter 4, "Audience Analysis," will help you answer these questions.

Choosing a Purpose

These are a few fundamental questions you must consider in designing your topic for the listeners in your audience. Speakers should seek audience reaction consistent with their goal. Remember, however, that no matter how interested the speaker becomes, *the speech is not successful if the audience fails to respond to your specific purpose.*

Inform

The purpose of the first speech you prepare will probably be to inform or to demonstrate. At least, our study of what goes on in first public speaking courses across the country suggests that this is the case. However, many excellent instructors prefer a different approach. You may begin by introducing yourself or a classmate or by talking about your pet peeve, for example, or you may be asked to persuade your classmates to some point of view.

We are going to assume that your first speech will be to inform or to demonstrate. Both of these objectives are similar in that they provide listeners with information. If your goal is to inform, your speech should add to the storehouse of information the audience already has about the subject. You might, for example, choose as your purpose a statement like this:

> *Specific purpose:* To inform the audience of the five specific steps
> followed in the manufacture of a Heinrich baseball bat. The
> audience should be able to list and explain those five steps from
> memory, using their own words.

This purpose identifies clearly for you and for your audience what you want to accomplish. It also suggests that you are going to take your listeners, step-by-step, through the preparation of a baseball bat from a piece of wood. This purpose includes *knowing your audience* and making certain assumptions about them and the knowledge they have. It is safe to assume that virtually every American knows what a baseball bat looks like and how it is used, but they are likely to be less familiar with the type of wood used and the processes involved in manufacturing and quality control. Knowing your audience in this case requires only common knowledge. Your purpose makes it clear to you, as speaker, what your aims and methods will be. By clarifying your purpose, you have simplified the process of preparing your first speech.

Demonstrate

The other common objective for the first speech is to demonstrate. In this type of speech, you not only inform but you rely primarily on a visual aid to clarify or explain a product, process, or procedure. Speeches of demonstration are, for example, very common in the business world. Here is an example of a purpose for a speech to demonstrate:

> *Specific purpose:* To demonstrate how Greyhound coordinates its
> major long-distance bus routes. The audience should be able to
> specify the sequence of events in the task and explain each step in
> the sequence.

This purpose could be fairly complex if you fail to limit your discussion. A caution to anyone who is preparing the initial speech is *do not try to accomplish too much.* This specific purpose would allow a speaker to use a map to show how buses traveling from New York to Los Angeles make connections with buses going from Miami to Detroit. The speech might explain how much time is allowed for a typical route, how carefully the schedules are prepared (including computer analysis of time, fuel, and possible highway conditions), and how reliable these schedules are when compared to actual connections made or not made by passengers. By using various visuals, such as drawings or listings of time schedules, the key points of the speech can be clearly shown.

As we have already mentioned, the speech to inform and the speech to demonstrate have similarities. There is overlap because demonstration always involves elements of information. A key to understanding the difference between informative and demonstrative speeches is that in most demonstration there is the element of "manipulation," the handling, movement or use of audio or visual supplements that help to explain or clarify the subject. In either type of speech, the explanation of a process can become very complicated, but the key to success is to keep it simple. *Keep your purpose simple, keep the development and main ideas simple, and keep the examples simple and easy to understand.*

Choosing a Topic

You began this course with an enormous amount of knowledge. Your life experience is a virtual "storehouse" of information. Even the most mundane topic offers a great deal to talk about if you just allow yourself to think about it for a few minutes. In a sense, the main problem in choosing a topic is deciding what *not* to talk about.

Beginning speakers often feel that even a three-minute speech is almost an eternity. If you have had that thought, then you do not realize how short three minutes can be. The normal speaking rate is 140 to 160 words per minute. If you speak at the upper limit of 160 words per minute, you would need about 500 words to fill three minutes. Some students write that many words on an essay exam just attempting to disguise their inability to answer a question. You certainly have enough ideas you can share on a topic to cover that period of time. Your challenge is to select one topic that will yield enough good material for you to use for this first speaking assignment.

Knowledge of Subject

Choose a topic you know well. You want to be confident of your information and of your ability to manage it. Do not plan to demonstrate how an automobile clutch operates if you know virtually nothing about clutches. That would invite disaster! Inventory your strengths and information to decide what you know that could interest others. If you are a "shade tree mechanic," then perhaps that topic would be a good choice. Ask yourself these types of questions.

What is my favorite recreational activity?
What has been my most interesting experience since I began college?
What kind of job do I have during the summer?
What is most important in my life?
What type of career am I pursuing?
What are the most unusual features of my neighborhood?

The answers to these questions suggest topics you understand very well. You understand them because you *live* them everyday. They are prime topics for a speech because no one but you knows much about them. Accept the challenge to explain to others a small piece about yourself and your life. You can certainly fill three minutes just developing answers to basic questions like these.

Pervis Washington, for example, began by saying he wanted to talk about his hometown, which was a center of the pocket billiard industry. In fact, the water tower for the town was painted like a giant eight ball. Pervis explained how the company had located there, how many people the company employed, and how the pool tables that were made there were shipped throughout the country. Pervis's small town had something unique about it, and his classmates learned something that otherwise they might never have known.

Another student decided to begin the course by discussing what "bugged" him. He went into some detail about how people who insisted on bringing young and crying babies to church services were a special peeve of his. But it did not stop there. When those people didn't take their infants to the "cry room" where the service could be seen and heard, the "bug" was even more bothersome. The speech was creative and well known to the speaker and it struck a responsive chord with the audience. *Choosing a topic you know well is an early step toward success.*

Audience Appeal

Select a topic that will relate to your listeners. Earlier we discussed the importance of knowing your audience. These people are central to your purpose—you intend to provide them with information, and you need their attention and interest. They will give it to you if you select a subject and develop it in such a way that it will have meaning and appeal. Audiences hear and enjoy the novel, the striking, the ideas that appeal to basic curiosities about people and things. Friendship needs and status needs are among the span of appeal that audiences hear and enjoy. For instance, a particular audience might be interested in what you suggest as proper combinations of clothing for a job interview. Should a woman definitely wear a skirt and blouse? Might a man wear a sport coat, or is a suit more appropriate?

All of us can relate to questions about topics like this because the topics bear on our lives. If you provide answers to the interests we have here, it is likely you will have the interest and attention of your listeners. But do not assume that just because you are standing in front of an audience, your listeners will be interested in the subject you have chosen. While this experience may be very exciting for you, your listeners, more likely, are merely listening to you talk to them about a subject they hope will be interesting to them.

Determining your purpose and selecting an appropriate topic are essential initial steps in preparing your speech. But once you have come that far, what should you do with the ideas and material you have pulled together? After all, an effective first speech does not just happen. It is the result of careful and thoughtful preparation. To help you understand what is involved in this preparation, we will concentrate on two aspects of organization: focus and structure. Focus refers to the narrowing and clarification of your ideas. Structure refers to the order in which you will present those ideas. Here are some brief guides to organization. We will refer to them later in the chapter, but they will be helpful here to get you off on the right foot.

Organizing the First Speech

Narrow your ideas to one or, at most, two major points. Apply what you know about outlining to help you make some key decisions. Keep a maximum of two ideas in the left margin and spend most of your time explaining them.

Try this example. Assume you have decided to demonstrate the proper stance and body position for an effective golf swing. Therefore, your two major points are (1) stance and (2) body position. Knowing those two points, you can begin to organize your thoughts. What will be the major ideas under each heading? Since this speech will be relatively brief, you cannot become very ambitious. But you must tell your audience your intended purpose so that the direction of your message is clear. You could talk briefly about how the feet should be positioned: the desired distance between them, how they should be pointed, and how the weight should be distributed. That will take about three minutes. Remember, however, these are the major supporting ideas that you may wish to clarify with example or physical demonstration. If you want to go further, you could talk briefly about shoulder position or head position. Do not try to conduct a coaching clinic. *Keep this speech simple and brief!*

After you have determined the major points and supporting ideas, you must structure them. A good speech has three parts: an introduction, the body (the discussion), and the conclusion. We will talk more about structure in chapter 6, but for now all you need is a basic understanding of these parts. In the introduction, you tell them what you want to tell them; in the body, you tell them; and in the conclusion, you tell them what you have already told them.

Communication and Apprehension

Important as it is to be well prepared for your first speech, the prospect of actually delivering the speech can be more daunting. As the time for the first speech approaches, it is prudent for you to work on yourself as well as the speech.

It is not unusual or strange to be concerned, or even fearful, of speaking in public. We call these kinds of concerns *communication apprehension.* You may be more familiar with the term *stage fright.* Both terms refer to the worried, fearful, anxious feeling you have when you speak to a group of people. Many speakers think something is wrong with them because they feel apprehensive, but the fact is, they are quite normal. The results of a study by Bruskin Associates reveals that 40 percent of the population is fearful of speaking in public.[3] Compare this to the 32 percent who are afraid of heights, the 18 percent who are afraid of sickness, and the 13 percent who are afraid of loneliness.

Society helps create our fears in the sense that speaking in public is an uncommon act. When you went through grade school and high school, how often were you required to stand in front of a group and speak formally to them? The book reports or the essay you read are burned into your memory very clearly because they were unusual events. Now, when you are required to perform this act regularly for a quarter or a semester, it is no wonder you feel apprehensive. You have had little if any experience. Being a self-confident person, in general, does not guarantee that you will feel confident in a public speaking situation. It is common to be apprehensive about this first speech. Those who say you have no reason to be nervous are either misinformed or they lack knowledge of human behavior![4]

Symptoms of Communication Apprehension

We all need to understand that it is normal to react with some concern to a situation we find unusual, or sharply different from what we do on a daily basis. By studying the characteristics of our reactions, we can understand better how to control our feelings.

Physical Reactions

Let us begin by assuming that you are nervous about public speaking. Some of your fears are manifested in physical ways. Your heart rate increases, your blood pressure increases, you perspire, your hands tremble, your knees feel weak, your face feels flushed, and you have an empty or sinking feeling in the pit of your stomach. These feelings are normal and are shared in varying degrees by the vast majority of people who speak in public. In a physically threatening situation, most of your responses would be similar to those you experience in a public speaking situation. They are common reactions to uncommon situations.

Other reactions to the speaking situation are also predictable. People tend to forget what they prepared so carefully. They avoid looking at the audience whenever possible; they gaze out the window, study the floor, or examine the ceiling. This is called *avoidance behavior,* and what it reveals most is lack of experience in talking to a group of people. Some people may not see any of the faces of the audience members, just a swimming mass, a group whose individual members do not exist. These psychological reactions are just as predictable and understandable as the physical responses to the speaking experience.

Psychological Reactions

You probably could count on the fingers of one hand the number of times you have been placed in a public speaking setting during your lifetime. So, it is no wonder if you also react in these ways. You would be showing the same physical and psychological responses that most people have when they are anxious.

Beginning speakers are a bit like Ponce de Leon, who searched for the nonexistent fountain of youth. They also are hunting for something that does not exist, a relatively easy solution to their fear of public speaking. But there are no "quick fixes." There is no small pill that will eliminate all the fears and anxieties from your system and help you become a totally relaxed speaker. Anyone who insists there is a quick and easy way to deal with your apprehensions either does not understand the problem or is misleading you. You can deal effectively with your concerns, but it will take time and considerable effort on your part. It is important to remember that competence builds confidence!

Dealing with Communication Apprehension

You can learn to exercise greater control over the symptoms of communication apprehension and turn those problems into personal assets. By learning methods of topic selection and audience analysis, techniques of preparation and practice for public speaking, and methods of organizing ideas for persuasive or informative messages, you can become a more confident and effective speaker.

Suppose someone approached you near the track before you tried to break your personal best time in the mile run and suggested you could break your own record with very little effort. You would be instantly suspicious. You would know that something as difficult as breaking your own record cannot be done easily. You might have to give up a few snacks, go on a diet, crawl out of bed early for training runs, and go to the gym for evening exercise sessions. It would be tough, but *it could be done.* It is hard work in public speaking, too, but *it can be done.* Here are a few guidelines that will help you with your first speech. We are not in a position to guarantee success, but careful attention to the following suggestions will greatly increase your chances of success in your first speech.

By All Means

Be Well Prepared. Plan ahead and prepare thoroughly. Do not wait until the day or hour before you are scheduled to speak to begin thinking about your subject or working it over.

Choose a Simple Subject That You Know Well, and Organize the Material Simply. So that both you and your listeners can follow it, use a format that is very easy to remember. For example, you could say, "I intend to explain how students register at Aaron Burr University. First, they read the schedule of courses. Second, they confer with their advisor about the courses available and what they need to meet graduation requirements. Finally, they prepare a schedule of times and courses and go to the Registration Office. Now, I'll explain each of these in more detail." Obviously, this is an oversimplified version of a basic speech, but it is plain and simple. If the ideas are easy for you and your listeners to follow, you will be more likely to feel good about yourself, and you will be much more likely to succeed.

Know How You Plan to Begin and End Your Speech. Prepare your opening sentences very thoroughly so you can feel more comfortable and more certain of yourself and your ideas. Getting off to a good start is very important, and you should have a clear plan for introducing your subject so that you will get the attention and interest of your audience.

It is also important that you have some plan for ending your speech. Many beginning speakers just stop and say, "That's all I have to say." You should relate your concluding remarks to what you have been discussing. For example, you could say, "So, you see, competent market research is one of the critically important factors in the success of any new business venture." Obviously, the speaker had been talking about the role market research plays in starting a new business. Another example might be, "What bothers me the most, though, is to hear the man who runs the boat rental dock say, 'You should have been here yesterday. They were really biting.' " In both cases, the conclusion serves as a unifying element, helping the audience realize the speech is over. It also makes it clear the speaker did not just run out of things to say but had a planned, intelligent way to complete the communication event.

Prepare a Brief Skeleton Outline. Most early speeches are what we call icebreakers; they are designed to get you on your feet and let you experience what it is like to speak in front of a class. Your instructor may have a different type of opening assignment. If you do make a speech of self-introduction or explain some basic facts or processes, it would be useful if you had a skeleton outline to help you remember all your major thoughts.

I. Cycling is my favorite sport.
   A. It provides exercise during most seasons of the year.
   B. It is relatively inexpensive.
     1. Bikes for recreation begin around $100.
     2. No specialized clothing is required.
   C. It does not require a high degree of skill.
II. Cycling is one of the fastest growing sports.
   A. It allows the participant time to "coast."
   B. It is very good for the cardiovascular system.
   C. Because it is an Olympic event, many Americans participate.

FIGURE 2.1 A skeleton outline serves to remind the speaker, but it does not substitute for thorough preparation.

Refer to the example of a skeleton outline in figure 2.1. Use the outline as a reminder in case you forget; it is your insurance policy against "going blank." But, do not allow yourself to spend much time looking at the outline instead of the audience.

Approach the Speaking Situation with Apparent Confidence. It may be that you are not highly confident, but there is no reason you should fall victim to a self-fulfilling prophecy. If you believe you can succeed, your chances for success increase greatly. If you act as though you are confident, you will become more confident.

Speaking is what we call a role-taking activity. You assume many roles in your daily life. You play one role as a student in the classroom, another role in your part-time job, and still another role when you are enjoying yourself with a group of friends. In public speaking, you will want to convey a sense of, "I have something important to say and I am confident about my ability to communicate that idea to you." Your role as a public speaker is to appear interested and well informed about your subject. People form impressions of us based on the ways we play our roles. Your challenge is to take the role of public speaker and play it well. A positive mental attitude toward speaking helps greatly to communicate to listeners a positive impression of your interest and ability.

Practice Aloud. It is very easy to run through a speech in your mind, but it is far different when you express your thoughts out loud. Try practicing aloud what you are planning to say. After your first attempt, you may decide that the way it "comes out" is not nearly as sensible or understandable as the way you had planned it in your mind. The fact is that we all crystallize our ideas when we commit them to speech or writing. So it is important that you practice aloud what you are planning to say.

Just as there are some things that you should make a point of doing, there are others that you should avoid.

By No Means

Because our ideas crystallize only when we actually verbalize them, it is important that we practice aloud.

Do Not Memorize Your Material. Many beginning speakers think the best insurance for a good speech is to memorize all of the words they plan to say. If you memorize your speech, you increase the likelihood of forgetting your material. Besides, you create more anxiety in yourself by worrying about whether or not you will remember all those words in the order you memorized them. Memorizing also leads to the increased use of written words, and a lack of apparent interest on the part of the speaker. Although chapter 8 points out the differences between oral and written style, one key difference is clear. If you remember what happens when a school child stands up and attempts to recite Lincoln's Gettysburg Address, you will see it immediately. We recognize the words as *not* belonging to the child, not just because we have heard or read the speech before, but because the language level is too abstract for the child. The child's voice usually has artificially high and low pitches. The child's natural cadence is overpowered by the language of the speech. We know instantly that the child has memorized something that he did not write. Unfortunately, when you write out a speech and memorize it, most of the same wrong behaviors occur.

You probably can recall going to a grade school play and seeing someone in the play forget their lines. The strain of performing in public helped cause that. Remember, as you approach this public event, you too can forget your lines if you decide to memorize them.

Do Not Write Out Your Speech. If you write out, word-for-word, what you plan to say, you will become committed to what you have written. Commitment to a word-for-word sequence of ideas eliminates the possibility of changing your remarks as you speak. By allowing your speech to become rigid, you will lose the ability to adapt to the shifting needs of your audience. In addition, by writing out your speech, you will begin to memorize it, and that will cause you to violate the rule about not memorizing your speech.

Written and oral language are very different. Oral language is more repetitive, and uses shorter and less complex words and sentences. As an example, determine which of the following is the oral and which is the written version of the same statement.

1. Professionally trained persons are inclined to verbalize their thoughts in more abstract ways, especially when speaking with their colleagues, than are persons not formally trained in one of the professions.
2. Lawyers, doctors, and dentists are more likely to talk to each other in jargon than are people outside these fields.

If you chose 2 as the example of oral language, you were correct. Your instructor probably can show you several examples of this problem. Because speech instructors listen to many student speeches, they can easily recognize speeches that are presented in written style. Generally, written speeches are less interesting, and the speaker appears to have very little involvement in developing or communicating the topic.

We caution you *not* to write out your speech. Rather, we encourage you to prepare thoroughly and speak directly to your audience in an interesting way.

Do Not Avoid Looking at Your Audience. The ceiling, the floor, your notes, or the window of the room will not react to what you are saying, but the audience will. That audience decides how interested you are partially by how much time you spend looking at them.

We make that same basic judgment in our daily conversation. We believe people are interested in us and our ideas if they look at us. You want the people in your audience to learn something from what you have said, or you want to affect their attitudes. To do that you must pay attention to them. You will find that they are not intimidating. Instead, they look interested and are sometimes amused at what you are saying. One of the rewards of public speaking is, after all, seeing the effect it has on people.

Having good eye contact with your audience will enable you to work with your audience. It is important that you adapt constantly to their changing needs. If they appear restless, you need to do something. If they look puzzled, you need to explain more fully. If they are straining to hear, you need to talk louder. If they do not understand you, you may need to slow down. You cannot adapt to your listeners unless you study them as you speak. Eye contact is the only way to do that.

Do Not Apologize for Yourself. Many beginning speakers start by saying, "I'm not very good at speaking in public, but let me try to. . . ." By apologizing, you prepare the listener to believe that you really are not very good, and those same listeners are going to listen for ideas and actions that verify your statement. Remember the notion of the self-fulfilling prophecy! Listeners often believe what you have suggested to them. If you are competent, you will act and become more confident.

Knowing Your Audience

The process of becoming better acquainted with your listeners is called "knowing your audience." Before you begin to prepare any message for an audience, you must understand what their interests and attitudes are likely to be. For instance, it would be impossible to drive to Harrisburg, Pennsylvania, without first knowing your present location. Similarly, it would be impossible to provide an audience with useful information unless you know how much they already know about the subject and how you can add to that information. Knowing your audience is the road map for the destination of successful speaking.

Chapter 4, "Audience Analysis," describes methods by which you can thoroughly analyze the target audience. But, without your figurative road map, your message could be completely misdirected, and you would finish without reaching your destination. Knowing your audience is absolutely critical if you want to have any impact with your message! Their present "location"—that is, their knowledge and attitudes about the topic—will help you decide what strategies you need to use to communicate successfully with them.

Common Concerns about the First Speech

Since you already know some of the major suggestions for dealing with preparation for this first speech, you might be interested in some of the most commonly expressed concerns about the first speech.

1. There is nothing for me to talk about that would interest others. (True or False?)

   False. Earlier in this chapter, we discussed possible topic choices. Regardless, some people think their interests will not be appealing to others. Like the pessimist who sees the water glass as half empty rather than half full, they underestimate themselves. The true challenge is *to relate the topic to others.*

Subjects as diverse as crocheting or engine repair can be made interesting. It depends upon how interested you are in the topic and how creative you want to be in developing the subject for the speech. Remember, *speak on a subject you know well, relate it to your audience, and let your enthusiasm help you make it interesting.*

2. I really doubt that I can succeed as a speaker. (True or False?)

   False. Thinking like this is self-fulfilling. Your listeners are anxious for you to succeed, but you must have confidence in yourself and in your preparation. First you must want to succeed, and then you must work to succeed. That is your part of the bargain. The audience, for their part, becomes a support group. They tell you the positive things you did and encourage you to "hang in there." Your listeners want you to succeed in speaking. If you approach the experience with a positive attitude, you will be prepared for the physical and psychological rigors of the situation.

3. I am afraid I will forget what I plan to say. (True or False?)

   False. You will not forget if you follow the suggestions we outlined earlier in this chapter. Select a subject you know and understand well, prepare thoroughly, prepare an outline but do not write out your speech, and practice it aloud until you are confident you know the ideas and the order of presentation. If you follow these suggestions, you are on the road to success in this assignment. Besides that, you can use notes; you can surround yourself with memory aids. In chapter 10 we will show you how to do this.

Summary

Your first speaking assignment is important to your success in future speaking assignments because it provides you with an impression of what public communication involves. Fear of speaking in public is a common apprehension. There are many ways to overcome both its physical and psychological forms. One of the most helpful guides to success in the first speech is to keep the speech simple. Among the other elements that are important to success is the selection of a topic that is appropriate and adequately narrowed for your audience. Understanding common concerns about the first speech and being aware of some guides to success will help you become more successful in your initial public speaking activity.

Beginning speakers should remember that thorough preparation, a positive attitude toward the speaking experience, and thorough practice before presenting a speech are some of the most important elements in achieving personal success. Ultimately, we think that an audience is very accepting. If the listeners think you are trying to make contact with them, they will overlook many of the things that you might call faults in your own speaking. The most important thing, then, is to remember that your listeners are people, too. They want you to succeed!

Key Terms

Communication
apprehension
Influence
Objective

Physiological reactions
Psychological reactions
Self-awareness
Self-disclosure

Discussion Questions

1. If people did not engage in public speaking, what effect would this have on society? Would it be a better or a worse place? How and why?

2. Can you recall listening to a speaker who did not know the audience? What effect did this have on the presentation and the audience? Remember how you felt as you listened. What changes could have been made if the speaker had understood the audience or situation better?

3. What kinds of reactions do you observe in people who say they are experienced in speaking and that it is an easy thing to do? How are they different from people with little or no experience? Make a list of the behaviors they demonstrate. Consider, especially, how they use the guides for success we outlined in this chapter. Be specific and be prepared to defend your list of experienced speaker behaviors in class.

Notes

1 Leonard D. Goodstein and Scott W. Russell, "Self Disclosure: A Comparative Study of Reports by Self and Others," *Journal of Counseling Psychology* 24 (July 1977): 365

2 Martin Buber, "Between Man and Man," in *The Human Dialogue: Perspectives on Communication*, ed. Floyd W. Matson and Ashley Montagu (New York: The Free Press, 1967), 115

3 R. H. Bruskin Associates, "Fears," *Spectra* 9 (December 1973): 4

4 Michael J. Beatty and Gregory S. Andriate, "Communication Apprehension and General Anxiety in the Prediction of Public Speaking Anxiety," *Communication Quarterly* 33 (Summer 1985): 175

Gibson, James W. *Speech Organization: A Programmed Approach.* San Francisco: Rinehart Press, 1971.

The beginning speaker will find this linear programmed text useful in deciding how to prepare for the first speaking experience.

Kibler, Robert J., and Barker, Larry L., eds. *Conceptual Frontiers in Speech-Communication.* New York: Speech Association of America, 1969.

This classic work outlines the directions for the study of speech communication. The recommendations and the discussion of fundamental concepts mark this as a landmark work in this field. Highly recommended for examination by the serious student of communication.

Ruben, Brent D. *Communication and Human Behavior.* New York: Collier Macmillan Publishers, 1984.

This is an excellent general introduction to the process of communication as an integral part of daily action. Its references will lead you to much of the major literature and significant findings in speech communication. Excellent for the student seeking an overview of all dimensions of the speech act.

Schiff, Roselyn L. *Communication Strategy: A Guide to Message Preparation.* Glenview, Ill.: Scott, Foresman and Company, 1981.

This book suggests a variety of ways for preparing for the initial speech and structuring messages so that they enhance speaker poise and are more understandable to listeners.

Yates, Jere E. *Managing Stress: A Businessperson's Guide.* New York: AMACOM, 1981.

A practical and fundamental discussion of stress and how to recognize signs of normal and excessive stress in daily actions. It is written in a highly readable yet well-documented style. The checklists permit a thorough self-evaluation.

Suggested
Readings

3 *Listening*

Outline

Objectives

After reading this chapter you should be able to:

1. Explain the significance of listening.
2. Define and explain the role of attention in listening.
3. Prepare a model of the listening process.
4. Cite the major problems in listening.
5. Identify methods for improving listening skills.
6. Begin a systematic program of listening self-improvement.

PREVIEW

More than half of our communication behavior is spent listening; it is the primary means by which we gain information and impressions from others. Most of us, however, are not effective or efficient listeners because of unfortunate behaviors we have learned. Problems in listening can be overcome if each of us understands the reasons why we listen inadequately.

Efficient listening is integral to successful communication, so any systematic study of the communication process must focus on the basic elements of listening. Part of that process involves learning specific techniques for improving listening behavior.

Within the last day or so, you probably had an experience like this. A friend, relative, or coworker asked you to do something while you were reading, watching TV, or calculating some figures. You may have replied, "Sure, just a minute." But when you got around to actually responding, you were not sure what it was that person wanted you to do.

Experiences like this are too commonplace for all of us. Our listening habits have deteriorated, or were never developed properly in the first place. Society has placed less emphasis upon the need for active and effective listening as we have increased our exposure to mass communication, especially television. We spend twenty-five hundred hours a year with media and twelve hundred of those hours are spent viewing television.[1] A large proportion of that time is spent in passive viewing, not in active participation and listening.

Listening is the fundamental language skill.[2] We spend more time engaging in listening activity than in any other single communication behavior. Since listening is a skill, it can be developed and improved through education, training, and practice. Some people say they could be good listeners if they wanted to, but they just haven't gotten around to "wanting to." Some do not even realize listening is a skill, or if they do, they do not believe it merits attention or cultivation. For still others, effective listening requires too much concentration and energy. These people do not recognize the critically important role of listening skills in our society.

Listening in Our Lives

Listening is our most common form of communication behavior. College students spend 52.5 percent of their verbal communication time listening, 17.3 percent reading, 16.3 percent speaking, and only 13.9 percent writing.[3] In the modern business world, one study found that people spend nearly 60 percent of their day listening.[4] These facts seemingly contradict our educational experiences; we spend years in school learning how to read and write.

Can you recall how much time you spent in a classroom being taught how to listen? Surely you can remember being scolded for not listening. Teachers expect you to do a good job of listening, and yet they have provided you with no formal training, or even much information about it. This point is driven home more thoroughly in research literature. Wolvin and Coakley point out that the schools too often believe that because students begin first grade with adequate communication skills, normal classroom teaching will give them sufficient skill to meet their listening needs.[5] But, as Nichols and Stevens found, the percentage of students who could tell what teachers were talking about when the teachers stopped in the middle of their lectures declined steadily as they advanced in school. Ninety percent of the first graders could respond correctly, 80 percent of the second graders, 43 percent of the junior high school students, but only 28 percent of the high school students could tell what the teacher had talked about.[6] Clearly, poor listening has an impact on performance in school, and without training, our listening skills deteriorate.

When communication fails, it is often because someone failed to pay attention. People often act as if they are listening, when in actuality they are thinking about something totally unrelated. If we are to listen more effectively, we must first concentrate on the quality of our attention.

Listening and Attention

Attention spans vary. Attention-drifts and our abililty to pay attention can have a great effect upon the quality and type of listening we do. Basically, listening involves the following:

1. Our decision to give attention, either voluntarily or involuntarily
2. Our decision to listen or not to listen
3. The difficulty of the mental task we face[7]

You would be giving *involuntary attention* if you responded to the "bang" of a car backfiring, a door slamming, or a professor tossing a book to the floor. *Involuntary attention* spans are very brief; they are the result, typically, of an abrupt intrusion into the immediate environment, such as a bright light, a loud noise, or a temporarily exciting moment.

Voluntary attention is the focusing of the mind on an event as the result of a conscious choice. During the period of voluntary attention the mind may drift momentarily. However, because you have chosen to listen, your attention returns to the event. Voluntary attention spans can be fairly long because they are the product of a choice. This issue of voluntary choice is closely related to voluntary attention. Our choice whether or not to concentrate is perhaps the most prevalent problem we face as listeners. We make this choice constantly.

Most of the college teaching we encounter is effective, but for a moment, consider the following example, which is discouraging to students and teachers alike: Professor Arthur began his presentation of the theory of conditioning in his customary monotone voice, failing to make eye contact with the students. Arthur had not finished his first sentence before Carlos' attention began to wander. Sitting in the last row, Carlos was soon fully absorbed in recalling the previous night's events when he and a friend had eaten pizza and listened to some tapes. This scene suggests that Carlos chose to do something besides listen. But his decision was a *voluntary* one, freely made from a variety of alternatives. Carlos could have chosen to listen and understand the lecture; he could have chosen to reflect on how much studying he needed to do to pass a test on the material being presented; or he could have chosen to concentrate on the graffiti carved in the desktop. Regardless, the decision to listen or not to listen is a voluntary one, and Carlos chose not to listen.

Each of us faces choices of this type dozens of times daily. Unfortunately, even when we give our voluntary attention, it is often for such a brief span that we get only part of the information presented. We may have good intentions and still not listen. Clearly, attention and listening have a strong interaction. We are free to make choices, and the result of these choices frequently is a loss in listening efficiency.

The level of difficulty that characterizes a message is also a problem but one of considerably less magnitude than the problem of voluntary attention. The use of many abstractions, vague terms, or unfamiliar vocabulary easily discourages anyone but the highly informed listener. Compound and complex sentences increase the likelihood that listeners will be "turned off." We are more likely to have effective, efficient listening if the statements that convey the message are simply and clearly stated. People shy away from ideas that are difficult to follow and understand. Effective listening is enhanced by easily understood statements.

Attention is also affected when we hear familiar ideas. We may pay attention, but often only as long as those familiar ideas are presented in a new way. Otherwise, we sometimes decide even subconsciously that we have heard it all before. Once that happens, it is very difficult to put ourselves back in a receptive frame of mind.

Causes of Listening Problems

Listeners carry a variety of mental baggage when they enter a listening situation. The more open-minded the listener, the greater the likelihood of productive and constructive listening. By the same token, the heavier the mental baggage, the less the likelihood of success. Following are some of the most common attitudes, or baggage, that can adversely affect our ability to listen efficiently and effectively.

Negative Attitude toward the Source

The impressions we make on others when we first meet them is extremely important. We implicitly acknowledge this by trying to act and look our best in situations where we hope to impress others favorably. Likewise, we, in turn, often make snap judgments of others based on superficial first impressions. If we view them negatively, we may turn off our attention and not hear what they have to say.

Our impressions are partially based on how credible we think the speaker is. Do you believe you would be interested in listening to a person tell you the importance of being honest if you know that person is cheating on his or her spouse? Or do you think you would listen to a salesperson who is "absolutely certain" what your budget will afford? How carefully would you listen to an expensively clad preacher who tells you to sacrifice all your worldly possessions for the cause he represents so others can be "saved"? You would probably not listen carefully to these people. These examples illustrate situations in which you are apt to view the speaker as having low credibility. When you have this negative attitude toward the source of a message, you typically choose not to listen to the message.

A negative attitude can also result from mannerisms such as an accent, a stutter, frequent or random hand or head movements, or such characteristics as dirty clothing or a lack of personal cleanliness. Or, you may choose not to listen because a person's facial or personal characteristics remind you of someone you do not like. By transferring a negative attitude of some behaviors or characteristics to the content of the message, you have generalized a negative attitude. The speaker *and the message* have taken on characteristics of low believability, and you will never know whether the message had some merit if you fall into this trap of generalizing a negative attitude. If you are honest with yourself, you can probably think of a person who creates a negative impression in your mind. How likely are you to listen to that person? Negative attitudes are usually generalized at the expense of effective listening. *Source credibility is a key element in developing negative attitudes toward a message and, therefore, in deciding to listen to a message.*

Disagreement with the Speaker

People are easily "turned off" by ideas that do not support what they believe. We rarely read newspapers that support the opposing political party (when we have a choice of which newspaper to purchase), and we avoid watching television programs that fail to present appealing ideas or situations. Do you think a nonsmoker would choose to listen to the pro-smoking arguments of a tobacco industry representative? Given a choice, would you listen to religious arguments that contradict your fundamental beliefs? The answer to both questions is probably *no*. We could learn much, even from those on the "other side of the fence," but because we disagree with them, we choose not to listen.

Jumping to Conclusions

When was the last time you began listening to a person speak, and before that person was very far along, you thought you knew the point he or she was going to make? An error of this sort is common, but most of us would say that we were just "anxious to speak up." Perhaps if we thought about this situation from the standpoint of the talker, we might not be so quick to judge. But notice that this pattern contributes to still another problem.

We start thinking about a dimension of the question when we ought to be listening! Nearly all of us have "jumped" or "leaped" to conclusions. We are somewhat impatient as thinkers and listeners because:

1. Our minds are working faster than the speaker's mouth. Available information shows that the optimum speaking rate for the comprehension of information is in the range of 275 to 300 words per minute, while the rate at which we think is about 500 words per minute.[8]
2. We are stimulated by the ideas and want to consider various alternatives.
3. Several thoughts about possible ideas may collide in our minds and we want to consider them before we forget them.

Most of us would plead guilty to one or more of these charges. Our impatience makes it appear that we believe we can read minds when actually we are thinking actively about the ideas being discussed. We are thinking about our reactions, we are impatient with the slowness of speech, and we begin to think about what we would do rather than about what the speaker is saying. Our challenge is to suspend judgment on what is being said. Take your time to listen to what is being said before you jump in with your version or with suggestions.

Some previous knowledge of the message being delivered can create problems that are similar to leaping to conclusions. If we understand part of what a person says, we often believe we can predict the rest of the message. How many times have you asked someone to let you say something, or simply interrupted, while they were talking? The people and the dialogue change but the principle remains the same. *Good listening involves hearing the other person out, not interrupting, keeping an open mind, and listening without preconceptions based on attitude, dress, appearance or manner of speech.*

A Listening Model

The initial step in preparing a model of any process is defining the process. For our purposes, we will use the definition of Wolvin and Coakley, which says that *listening* is "the process of receiving, attending to, and assigning meaning to aural stimuli."[9]

Consider listening as one part of the communication process. Let us view listening as analogous to a large water fountain that is fed by a reservoir of fresh ideas (fig. 3.1). In this case, the pump (source) shoots forth the water (message carrying the thoughts and words). The water falls and accumulates in a series of pools (listeners) around the fountain. This phase is the generation of ideas and reception of the message by listeners. *But the pump, fountain, and pool are separate parts of the process, just as the speaker, receiver, and message are separate elements in the communication process.*

Some of the water in the pools returns to the fountain through small overflow pipes. Before this feedback to the message returns to the speaker, it passes through a filter (the speaker screens the feedback) before some of

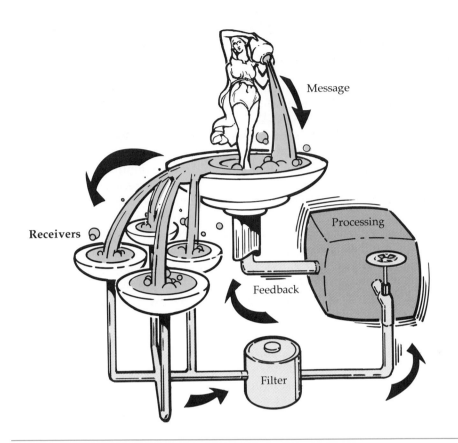

FIGURE 3.1 This process model makes clear that listening is part of a two-way process. The listener contributes effectively to the process by paying close attention.

it is repumped through the fountain. This is the phase in which the speaker makes use of visual and auditory feedback to modify the subsequent message. However, we must remember that the speaker does not rely primarily on the returned reactions but upon the well of water from which the ideas are extracted.

When we listen to messages, a similar situation occurs. We listen to the message coming from the speaker (the fountain). We receive the message (we are receptacles like the pools). As we listen to the language, we assign meanings based on our experiences with the words. We return some of our reactions to the speaker via visual and auditory media, but most of the message remains with us, just as the pumped water remains in the pool. The speaker continues to draw upon the wellspring of ideas, filters the reactions of the listeners, and pumps out many new and some recirculated ideas to the receivers.

Our model is essentially circular. While some of the information "pumped out" is lost through evaporation, a considerable amount of it is retained. The receiver's reactions (overflow) are used by the sender of the message. This model of listening illustrates listening as a dynamic process, involving constant movement and circulation of ideas and reactions. It assumes receivers will interpret and react to ideas in different ways depending upon their experiences.

The crucial components are present in this model. We have our source (the pump), the message (the water), the channel (the fountain), and we have the receiver (in this case, both the pool and the pump recirculate ideas).

We have said that listening is a difficult process because it requires attention by the receiver. This voluntary attention is essential or reception of the ideas is unlikely. Listeners must hold their fire if accurate reception of the message through the conduit is likely. Negative attitudes toward the source of the message may even cause the potential listener to stop receiving the message; at best it will result in some interferences in accurate reception. Jumping to conclusions has much the same effect. Now let us look at suggestions for dealing with these inefficient learning behaviors.

Improving Listening Behavior

By now it must be clear to you that each of us can be a better listener. We must approach listening in a positive manner because it is a complex and basic behavior. The rewards for effective listening are so great that it is difficult to imagine any reasons for postponing a program for improving our personal listening. Here are some things you can do.

Establish Common Ground for Understanding

The responsibility for a complete communication cycle does not lie exclusively with the speaker, or source, of the message. As a listener, you share the burden for understanding. If you do not attend, there is little chance you will receive the message, much less understand it. But, sometimes differences in the meaning of terms can cloud communication. Because we have different experiences with ideas and concepts, our perception of the words that describe those experiences may have various shades of meaning. Therefore, we must work very hard to establish a common ground with the other person in a communication exchange. *As speakers, we must try to understand the listeners—to adapt what we say to their level of language usage.* We will discuss this important idea further in chapter 4, "Audience Analysis," and in chapter 11, "Language." The following brief story will illustrate our point.

Students perceive expected course and test grades differently. After a midterm test in Chemistry, Soo-ling told her lab partner that she felt she probably had flunked the exam. She said she had no understanding of several of the questions on the test and that she was afraid of what would happen to her grade. Soo-ling's partner, Carla, was concerned too because she felt the test was very demanding. Several days later, when the tests were returned, Carla had failed the test, but Soo-ling had made the highest score in the class, missing only two of the forty items on the test. When Carla and Soo-ling discussed their grades, Carla found it difficult to believe that Soo-ling had thought she had failed the exam. Soo-ling explained she thought the test was difficult and *when she couldn't answer an item, she believed she had failed the test.* Soo-ling and Carla had different meanings for the word "failure." Carla listened and used the term *fail* in a way that she understood and which reflected her experience with the word. Obviously that meaning was different from Soo-ling's.

In cases like this, listeners have a responsibility to clear up confusions that arise from differing experiences. If we are confused, or the message is not clear, we have an obligation, as listeners, to say we do not understand or to ask for some clarification. Carl Rogers, one of the founders of humanistic psychology, believes that if we attempt to listen with understanding and try to see the idea from the other person's point of view, we will have a better frame of reference and more likelihood of understanding.[10] The following advice may help you:

1. Seek clarification of your understanding by asking questions as ideas develop.
2. Summarize what you think was said when you have an opportunity to verify the message of the other person.

Extend Your Voluntary Attention Span

As we discussed earlier, voluntary attention involves a choice that is made from a variety of available alternatives. Because it is a conscious, deliberate act, you can increase or modify it. Your level of motivation to give voluntary attention is the key to your success. The following suggestions may help.

Cultivate Your Attitude toward Listening

The question, "What does this have to offer me?" has the potential to increase both the length and intensity of your attention. If you enroll in a course believing that both the subject and the teacher will be interesting, chances are you will find much evidence to support your belief. The text book is likely to appear interesting, the lectures and discussions stimulating, and the teacher has a good chance of being perceived by you as effective. Remember our discussion of Professor Arthur and Carlos earlier in this chapter. If Carlos had forced himself to listen (if he had given that voluntary attention), the instructor might have been more positively perceived and Carlos would have gotten much more information from the course. In fact, the giving of attention and the resulting listening might have had a significant effect on the grade Carlos received.

The key to improved listening is, quite simply, a desire to improve.

Become an Active Participant

It is essential that we become more involved with the host of ideas we hear each day. We are bombarded with thoughts, proposals, objections, and positions. Only when we are actively involved with the ideas and their implications can we hope to become more effective listeners. We should be prepared to listen in every situation. That requires a considerable level of involvement. Certainly no one would expect you to be on the edge of your seat all the time, because there are some topics that lack interest or appeal for you. But being ready to listen is not just the absence of resistance. It means you have decided you are going to commit your mental and physical resources in an effort to gain as much information as possible from the listening process.

Take Notes

Committing ideas to paper makes you give more attention to what is being said. You certainly would not want to attempt this in everyday conversation, but in more formal communication situations, jotting down key words or phrases helps you stay on track and extends your attention span.

So often we hear an idea and we slip it into our memory bank with the intention of recalling it when we need it. For example, if we realize we need something from the drugstore, we make a mental note to pick it up the next time we stop there, only to forget the item when we arrive at the store. Because we tell ourselves that we can and will remember, we make no notes and have no one there to remind us. Without a written stimulus to help us recall ideas, we easily fall into costly listening mistakes.

If our pride, and habits, would permit a few notes of key ideas, *how much more likely we would be to increase our listening efficiency!* Instead of relying on our memory, we could refer to notes. How could you forget items, categories, names, or concepts that are written down? Some people live by lists that remind them of things they need to do each day. The process of listing important ideas as we hear them is no more expensive than the cost of a pencil and paper. *The payoffs are huge.* There are only large winners from this small investment.

A sudden desire to improve your listening activities will not change a lifetime of poor attention habits over night. You cannot just break a bad habit. You have to replace it with a better one, and that takes time and practice. For example, clergymen say that homiletic speaking (preaching) is among their most difficult communication challenges. In their sermons each week, which may last for only twenty or thirty minutes, they ask their congregation to alter their habitual behavior as a result of the message. They just cannot do it! Similarly, anyone who has tried to eat less, stop smoking, avoid speeding, or hold a temper, understands how difficult it is to extinguish undesirable behaviors and substitute a collection of alternative acts.

Be Patient

Likewise, improved attention span cannot be accomplished through preaching or merely by wishing. It is a *slow, adaptive process,* but you can succeed if you work at it by giving yourself an honest opportunity to do so.

In football, an act that prevents the receiver from making the catch is interference. The attention process is similar. The message is the "catch," and the noise constitutes interference. There always will be some noise that interferes with our ability to receive the message. Noise can be external or internal. External noise intrudes via our senses, such as sounds, sights, or even odors. For example, others talking, sirens, bright lights, loud colors, or the smell of something cooking all have the power to distract us. Internal noise occurs whenever our attention shifts to thoughts about a subject other than the one being discussed. It is obvious that all these elements cannot be removed, but we can work to reduce the interference.

Remove Interference

FIGURE 3.2 First Aid
Checklist for Listeners.
Responding to these
questions regularly will lead
to gradual improvement of
your listening power.

> Do I summarize material mentally as often as possible?
> Do I restate what I heard and ask for confirmation of my understanding?
> Do I identify emotionally loaded words?
> Do I create a physically favorable listening climate?
> Do I avoid interrupting?

There are ways you can reduce noise as interference. Concentrate on the source of the message. Work at reducing the impact of noise. Select an advantageous location for listening. Do not sit in the back of the room. Do not permit noise to come between you and the speaker. If the noise is self-generated, you need to work harder on your voluntary attention.

We have provided you with a variety of suggestions for improving your listening behavior. At this point you may be interested in a relatively quick way to determine if your listening behavior meets desirable standards. Look at the "First Aid Checklist for Listeners" in figure 3.2. If your answer to each of the questions in the checklist is *yes*, then you are on your way to improved listening. You have been able to distill our suggestions into a series of desirable listening behaviors. But it is a process that requires constant monitoring. It is easy to fall back into bad habits. Your best intentions have to be translated into the positive actions that are listed in figure 3.2.

Summary

Listening is our most common form of verbal communication behavior, but our inefficient use of this fundamental skill is costly. Some of our listening problems arise when we assume we know the ideas a speaker will convey. Sometimes we are unwilling to concentrate on extending our voluntary attention span. Sometimes the problem is a poor attitude toward either the person doing the talking or toward the subject matter itself. The process of listening involves the transmission of information through channels. The listening model illustrates the essential elements of the process.

Noise disrupts the reception process. Attitudes and experiences, plus our receptiveness to ideas, affect the amount and quality of information people choose to hear. Listening behavior is, largely, a learned activity. Everyone has the potential to substitute positive acts for interruptions. Jumping to conclusions, quick misinterpretation, and an unwillingness to place ourselves advantageously in physical settings so we can listen more easily all contribute to listening difficulty. Good listening can be learned by discarding the bad listening habits we have acquired over many years. Through a strong personal commitment and an understanding of what good listening involves, all of us can become much more effective in this basic skill that is so essential to the communication process.

Adaptive	*Involuntary*
Attention	*Noise*
Circular	*Summarize*
Interferences	*Voluntary*

Discussion Questions

1. How important is feedback to you when you speak? Do you actually modify what you say when you see how your listeners are reacting?
2. Is it possible for an active listener to become more "other" oriented? Does attention to ideas cause the listener's mind to wander, to think about alternative solutions to problems, and often to lose the speaker's train of thought?
3. How do you believe listening skill is related to the age and sex of a person? Are middle-aged adults better listeners than college students? If not, why not? Do you think that women are better listeners than men? Why do you feel that way?
4. Recall the last major speech that you heard. Did all the people you know leave that speech with the same understanding of the message? If not, why do you suppose various listeners interpreted the message differently? How similar is that to a conversation between two people who fail to agree on what has been said?
5. How often do you paraphrase what a person has said just to verify your own understanding of the message? How profitable do you believe that kind of self-monitoring would be?
6. Does difficult material make you want to listen less? If listening is "hard work" do you think most people become discouraged and stop trying?

Notes

1 Samuel L. Becker, *Discovering Mass Communication* (Glenview, Ill.: Scott, Foresman and Company, 1983), 405

2 Andrew Wolvin and Carolyn Gwynn Coakley, *Listening,* 2d ed. (Dubuque, Ia.: Wm. C. Brown Publishers, 1985), 18–19

3 Larry Barker et al., "An Investigation of Proportional Time Spent in Various Communication Activities by College Students," *Journal of Applied Communications Research* 8 (November 1980): 101–9

4 Leland Brown, *Communicating Facts and Ideas in Business* (Englewood Cliffs, N.J.: Prentice-Hall, Inc., 1982), 380

5 Wolvin and Coakley, 19

6 Ralph G. Nichols and Leonard A. Stevens, *Are You Listening?* (New York: McGraw-Hill Book Co., 1957), 12–13

7 Daniel Kahneman, *Attention and Effort* (Englewood Cliffs, N.J.: Prentice-Hall, Inc., 1973).

8 *See* David B. Orr, "Time Compressed Speech—A Perspective," *Journal of Communication* 10 (September 1968). 288–92; Wolvin and Coakley, 177

9 Wolvin and Coakley, 74

10 Carl L. Rogers and F. J. Roethlisberger, "Barriers and Gateways to Communication," *Harvard Business Review* 30 (July 1952):47

Suggested Readings

Floyd, James J. *Listening: A Practical Approach.* Glenview, Ill.: Scott, Foresman and Company, 1985.

This is an interesting handbook for the student in search of techniques for improving listening. Written in an extremely easy-to-read style, it provides sound basic information to persons exploring the complex field of listening.

Nichols, Ralph G., and Stevens, Leonard. *Are You Listening?* New York: McGraw-Hill Book Company, 1957.

The initial, classic work in the field of listening, this work is highly recommended for any serious student of listening or for anyone interested in the historical development of this area of communication behavior.

Steil, Lyman K., Barker, Larry L., and Watson, Kittie W. *Effective Listening.* New York: Random House, 1983.

This is a practical but scholarly work based on the principles of effective listening behavior, which provides application to daily situations. Written with a combination of practical field experience and academic background.

Wolvin, Andrew D., and Coakley, Carolyn Gwynn. *Listening.* Dubuque, Ia.: Wm. C. Brown Publishers, 1985.

This is the single most thorough work in the field of listening. Its wide-ranging discussion includes, among other topics, the role of listening, the types of listening, and the role of the recipient in the communication process. A must for anyone seriously interested in listening.

Planning the Speech: Getting Started

4 Audience Analysis

Outline

Objectives

After reading this chapter you should be able to:

1. Understand, explain, and perform an action continuum analysis.
2. Identify the important demographic variables related to your purpose.
3. Develop a demographic profile of the audience.
4. Infer the design requirements and constraints placed upon you by the audience's image of you as speaker, their image of themselves as listeners, and their image of the occasion.

PREVIEW

Your success as a public speaker is contingent upon how well you relate yourself and your ideas to the listeners you are addressing. Therefore, you must understand the listeners' needs and perceptions. Through demographic analysis, you can learn the characteristic features of your audiences, such as age, sex, socioeconomic status, and the like. These facts will enable you to group individual listeners together so that you can more accurately infer their needs and perceptions, and estimate how they will most likely respond to your speech. This analysis also tells you a lot about the kind of speech that will appeal to the audience with maximum effect, and it allows you to estimate what the audience already knows about your subject matter. This information will help you to design the particular features of a speech that adapt to a particular group of listeners.

David, a friend of ours, told us this story about how he learned the value of audience analysis. He had moved from Notre Dame to take a position as professor of English in a city in the Deep South. David, a self-styled "flaming liberal" and an expert on the Bible as literature, was working on a study of Ecclesiastes at that time. He had published several papers and had given several talks about his research, and it was natural for him to seek opportunities to continue these activities in his new position.

One day, about six months after he had taken up his new duties, David was invited to address a group called The Inquiry Society in a neighboring city. He quickly accepted the invitation and prepared his remarks in manuscript form.

On the evening of the speech, he went to the appointed place and discovered that about fifty individuals had arrived to hear his address. The evening began with a long prayer by the minister of one of the local churches. An aging gentleman was invited to lead the assembly in the Pledge of Allegiance to the Flag. The audience members spoke that pledge with passionate conviction. Then David was introduced.

> In essence, my message was to ignore the pessimism. Ecclesiastes is a wonderful, permission-giving statement. Live happily in the present. Do your own thing. Rejoice in your humanity. Experiment with your urges. Laugh. Love.

About halfway through the address David knew he was in trouble.

> I noticed that the audience was squirming. People were tense. They were coughing and passing anxious glances back and forth.
>
> What I hadn't realized in time was that these good people had a completely different set of basic assumptions from mine. Their view of the Bible was, and still is, that it is the literal word of God, and not to be tampered with. In their view, I was seventy miles off course!

> So my stories weren't well received, and some of the listeners openly disapproved. When it was over, I barely got a polite ripple of applause. My speech was a disaster, but I learned a lot from it.

David's problem was that he had little understanding of his listeners. If he had done a thorough job of audience analysis, he would have known how to anticipate their interests. He probably would have spent his time informing and educating them. Undoubtedly, that is what they expected him to do.

This chapter will show you a method by which you can make educated guesses about audiences in order to avoid the kind of error that David made. The central message in this chapter is that audiences are not monolithic; that is, audiences are not all alike, nor are the individual members of one audience the same. If you want to adapt your remarks to an audience, you must learn to identify an accurate set of stereotypes that will describe the important subgroups in the audience. You have to infer what these subgroups are likely to know or believe about you and your subject. You need to know what the subgroups are likely to care about, and what they are likely to accept as credible. The method for determining these aspects is called *demographic analysis.*

We will show you how to perform a demographic analysis and how to use the demographic profile of the audience to adapt to the audiences you address. However, there are no guarantees. Even the most carefully rendered analysis may overlook something that is crucial to the listeners' response. As every speaker, every politician, and every advertiser knows, some unanticipated factor may cause audience members to go in another direction from your speaking goal.[1]

The Audience as Individuals

Because the word *audience* is a collective term, we often tend to think it represents a single entity, a uniform mass. This is because we have many other collective terms in our vocabulary, including *herd, flock, covey, batch,* and *bunch,* that do infer a singular "monolithic" constitution. Notice that a batch is a number of things considered as one group, for example, a batch of cookies. A bunch, too, is a number of things considered as one, as in a bunch of grapes. A covey is a group of quail considered as one, and flock is a single group considered as one.

These terms imply that their referents are a single unit to be considered as one. While it is correct to say that a herd is in the south pasture, a flock is flying overhead, or the audience will assemble in the fieldhouse, it is not correct to consider an audience a single unit when planning a speech. An audience is a collection of individual human beings, each of whom is unique in many ways. Because of this, each of those individuals has feelings and needs, and can make choices from among some personal set of priorities, and each one will do so!

The Audience's Image of You as the Speaker

Perceived friendship
- Why am I interested in the lives of these listeners?
- Do they know it?

Perceived commonality
- What do I have in common with these listeners?
- Do they know it?

Perceived knowledge of the subject
- What qualifies me to make this speech?
- Do they know it?

Perceived motivation to speak
- Am I teaching or preaching?
- Am I grinding an ax?
- Do they know it?

Perceived trustworthiness
- Am I desperate?
- Have I been true to my word?
- Do I have a hidden agenda?
- Am I honest?
- Am I being honest?
- Is my good name intact?
- Do they know it?

The Audience's Image of Itself

Self-concept and self-esteem
- Do I respect the humanity of the listeners?
- Do they know it?

Open-mindedness
- To what extent are members of the audience open to ideas?
- Do they know it?

Shared values
- Do I care about the goals of this audience—about what they want—for their sakes?
- Do they know it?

FIGURE 4.1 A Checklist of Audience-related Factors that May Influence the Success of a Speech.

If you want to understand your listeners, you cannot treat them as though they are all alike. You must take into account their motives and their likely reactions. As a speaker you cannot talk separately with every individual listener. Therefore, the best you can do is identify a fairly refined set of subgroups within the audience and adapt your remarks to those individuals. By stereotyping the relevant subgroups, you will be able to anticipate their reactions.

What should you know about an audience, and how should you use the information once you know it? Regardless of your reasons for speaking—whether your purpose is to inform, to persuade, or to entertain; whether

Knowledge of the subject
- Do I understand and respect what the listeners know about this subject?
- Can I build on what they know?
- Is my view similar to theirs?
- Do they know it?

Prior related experiences
- Have these listeners had any direct or vicarious prior experience with any part of my subject?
- Do I value that experience?
- Do they know it?

Attitude/belief structure
- What attitudes and beliefs are the listeners likely to have about my subject matter?
- Do I respect those attitudes and beliefs, even if I do not share them?
- Do they know it?

Latitude of acceptance
- Are my subject and my purpose within the audience's range of acceptability?
- If not, do we have a shared premise?
- Do they know it?

The Audience's Image of the Occasion

Physical context
- Are features of space, lighting, temperature, and noise levels conducive to this speech and this purpose?
- Can I control them?

Social context
- Are there any particular expectations of the occasion that may influence how the listeners perceive me and my speech?
- Can I adapt to them?

you speak to honor a departing colleague, or to open a conference with a keynote address—the more you know about your listeners, the more likely you will be to adapt your remarks to their interests and needs.

Figure 4.1 displays some of the features of an audience that can affect your success or failure as a speaker. The strategic choices you make as you plan for your speech, including the matter of determining the specific goal you want to accomplish with the speech, will be largely influenced by these audience features.

You will want to infer the image your listeners have of you as a speaker, both prior to your speech and while you are speaking. Your credibility as a speaker will depend upon the image your listeners have of you. Unless they perceive you as friendly and interested in them, they may be unable to believe that you share a common ground with them. So, an accurate estimate of the listeners' image of you can tell you a lot about the communication choices you must make.[2]

Certainly you will want to know how the listeners perceive themselves, and what they expect from the occasion. How they perceive the occasion tells them how they should prepare to respond. Unless you know something of their expectations, you might be surprised by their responses. For instance, you know that listeners tend to develop standards of taste that they apply to various situations. You would not think of speaking at a dinner meeting of the Kiwanis Club held at the local Country Club without dressing up. If you are a man, you would undoubtedly choose a conservative suit and tie. If you are a woman, your choice would probably be a skirted suit and blouse, or a tasteful equivalent.[3] Beyond your physical attire, you will want to estimate how much the listeners know about your subject and where they are likely to stand regarding your point of view. You would be foolish and wrong to assume that an audience believes and thinks just as you do, or that the listeners know what you know.

Mark Williams, a computer engineer, was asked to speak at a meeting of the Executive Club, a group of upper-management people from various branches of the corporation for which he worked. He wanted to inform them of something he was excited about: a new generation of low-priced, high-tech computer printers that were being introduced to the market.

Mark elaborated about high-resolution images, liquid-crystal shutters, and photosensitive revolving drums. He explained how an electric charge was built up on the drum surface, then discharged by light striking against the surface of the drum. He compared this mechanism with laser printers, and concluded that either was superior to ribbon-loaded dot-matrix designs. It wasn't long before his audience was completely lost. What had seemed basic to Mark was entirely new to many of his listeners. He had wrongly assumed that their knowledge was comparable to his own.

Clearly, the only way to understand these things about an audience is to study its members and to make guesses about them. Systematic audience analysis is needed. Mark was highly valued as a computer engineer, but his failure to tailor his remarks to the audience left some of his listeners wondering about his awareness of *them.*

Performing an Audience Analysis

The question of greatest importance to our students when we arrive at this point is how to actually perform an audience analysis. The following steps set forth a systematic approach to the task.

When you know a group, you already know how to estimate the group's attitudes, beliefs, knowledge of the subject matter, and so on. This will be the case when you speak to fellow workers in your company or to people who work in the same industry, for example. But when you lack firsthand knowledge of the audience, you must plan your research.

There are at least three obvious ways to find out about audiences that you cannot access directly.

Step 1: Research

1. Ask the person who invited you to speak to describe the audience.
2. Ask individual members of the audience to help you estimate the probable demographic features of the rest of the audience members.
3. Ask individuals who have addressed the group before; they will be able to suggest something about the makeup of the audience.

The questions you ask these people are very important. Ask about every demographic feature you think might be relevant to your topic and purpose: the number of people in the audience, their sex, ages, race, educational level, and so forth.

If the person who invited you cannot give you a very clear picture of the audience, ask for the names of a few people who are influential with the group. Get their phone numbers and then call them. Do not hesitate to ask about relevant demographic features. No one will be offended by your curiosity, and the word will probably get out that you are really trying to become familiar with the group.

Occasionally you will not be able to identify anyone who is a member of the group you are to address. Even so, the inviting officer of the group might be able to identify other speakers who have talked with them. Get the names and if possible, the phone numbers of those speakers. Call them up and ask them to help you with your analysis.

On occasion, you may be unable to do any of these kinds of research. Suppose, for instance, that you are planning to address a student group at a rally, but you have no idea who will be in the audience, or how many people will be there. The only option you have is to make some educated guesses. However, you must be sure that they are based on as much factual information as you can obtain. To illustrate, one of our universities is an urban institution. The average age of the undergraduate student is twenty-six years. About 51 percent of the students are women; about 15 percent are black; and another 3 percent are international students. Almost all of the students are from southern states, primarily Alabama and the local community. Most of the students work part-time and attend school part-time. Fewer than 25 percent live on campus. All these data are available in the Office of Admissions and Records at any university.

Suppose that you are going to address about 350 of these students, which is the number estimated by the Dean of Students as having attended the last several student rallies on campus. Your idea for the speech is that all general education requirements should be abolished. On the basis of these data, you could infer that the student audience, being about twenty-six years of age, would exercise some maturity of judgment. They would probably be politically conservative and fairly religious (the predominating groups would be Southern Baptist and Roman Catholic, followed by a smattering of others). You can suppose that because they are fairly conservative in their views, they would resist changes, and would feel that the institution "knows" what is minimally required for a quality general education.

You could eliminate gender and ethnic identification as relevant variables, since neither of these would seem to bear on the subject or your position. Since most of the students do not live on campus, you have to assume that they are living in private residences within the community, and that some are living at home with their parents. Thus, a significant portion of the audience may discuss your ideas with other conservative and influential people in their lives.

This audience will probably distribute itself something like this:

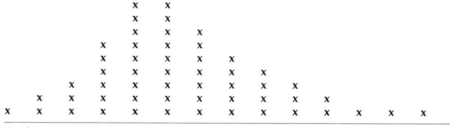

Because they are conservative, they will undoubtedly value the present system and be reluctant to change; and because many of them will compare their views with other conservatives, most of the audience will disagree with your proposal. In fact, some may actively oppose your position. A few will be neutral, and even fewer may actually agree with you.

As we have shown, it is possible to develop a stereotype and then prepare an analysis based on that stereotype. Keep in mind, however, that even when circumstances force you to develop a stereotype, you must view the audience members as individuals. Try to avoid thinking in terms of averages or of the typical listener.

Age
Sex
Race
Educational level
Political affiliation
Socioeconomic status
Religious affiliation
Occupations
Avocational interests
Organizational memberships
Geographic background
Information channels
Other_____
Other_____
Other_____

FIGURE 4.2 A Checklist of Some Important Demographic Features. No perfect or complete list of demographic features exists. In the spaces marked *other,* write additional demographic characteristics that may bear upon your subject or purpose.

Step 2: Demographic Profile

Review figure 4.1 again. It displays some audience factors that usually influence the outcomes of a speech. These are the factors you want to infer about listeners you do not already know. You can do that best by describing the audience in terms of a demographic profile. The question is, are there any demographic features that will make a particular difference to this speech?

Demographic data are facts about an audience (either one individual or a group) that categorize it by race, religion, sociological or economic class, and so on. This information has been considered essential to effective speaking for thousands of years, but in all that time scholars have not been able to come up with a single list of demographic features that can be usefully applied to every audience. Therefore, you will have to develop your own list of relevant features for each audience analysis you perform. Some of these features are displayed in figure 4.2.

We will use an example to illustrate how to identify relevant demographic features. Suppose you have selected the subject of law enforcement in your community as the topic for your speech. Suppose, further, that you have identified your objective: "After hearing this speech I want my audience to vote for legislation that will increase the freedom of law enforcement officers to investigate expected narcotics laws offenders."

The subject matter is drug-related law enforcement. The proposal is for increased freedom of police officers to investigate suspects. What are the possible areas for demographic analysis? You can use figure 4.2 as a workable checklist.

Is age a relevant feature? Possibly. If you assume that you will be addressing people of voting age, then the matter of voting age would not be relevant. However, if your intention is to work for support among men and women who are parents of teenaged youngsters, then age would certainly be a factor. An audience predominantly forty to fifty-five years of age would require a somewhat different approach from an audience that is predominantly twenty-one to thirty years of age.

Is the gender of the audience members a relevant factor? Probably not, although some evidence indicates that women are more easily persuaded than men and that they are susceptible to a different kind of persuasive appeal.

Would the social or economic status of the audience be a relevant issue? Almost certainly.

Would the educational level of the audience have anything to do with the likelihood of the members responding to your proposal? Of course it would. We know that people with more education tend to be more liberal than those with less education.

What other demographic variables can you identify from figure 4.2 that might affect a speech designed to persuade an audience to vote for greater investigative freedom of law enforcement officers when drug laws are at issue? Would ethnic identification be relevant? Geographical origins? How about political or religious affiliations? Would it matter if the audience members had all taken a course that presented the implications of investigative license upon individual freedom?

From this example, you can see that your subject matter and your purpose govern the relevant demographic variables you might choose to examine. Consider another example. Let us say that your topic is capital punishment, and you would like the audience to demonstrate opposition to any exercise of capital punishment anywhere in the United States. Your objective, or proposal, might be something like this:

> *Objective:* After hearing my speech, I want my audience to write to their congressional representatives asking for passage of a bill to abolish capital punishment anywhere in the United States.

Now using figure 4.2 as a checklist, you can see that many of those demographic variables can make a difference to you as you design your speech. For example, as people get older, they tend to become more conservative—to leave things as they are. Therefore, you would need to know the age range of your audience in order to develop the evidence and arguments that would be most persuasive. Sex probably would not make too much difference in this case. However, ethnic identification would probably be important to your success. How you develop your arguments and evidence will be influenced by the ethnic mix of your audience. Black and white people alike know that a disproportionately larger number of blacks than whites have received the death penalty. Whether this is a function of social class, economic status, or of an ignorance-poverty-crime cycle, the fact remains that blacks are more likely to receive the death penalty than whites.

The ethnic identification of your audience will certainly influence how you develop your arguments. And so it goes for each subject and for each audience. You must identify the demographic features that seem most relevant to your purpose.

After you have developed a demographic profile of your audience, you must try to arrange your listeners according to how you believe they will respond to your purpose. At best, you can only make educated guesses.

Step 3: Interpretation

In this section, we want to describe a method of analysis that will help you make those judgments. You can apply this method to every speech you ever make regardless of your general or specific purpose. It rests on the *theoretical* and sometimes confusing assumption that all communication is persuasion.[4] In other words, whenever you communicate with someone else, you are trying, in a sense, to change the way that other person thinks, feels, or acts. By that definition, then, even simple information-giving is persuasion. This is a somewhat confusing and controversial idea, but it has valuable potential for application. So, set your skepticism aside for the moment and imagine that every speech is persuasive. Every speech is aimed at working some change in the listeners. For example, when Bob Hope stands before an audience, he wants his listeners to laugh. The laughter represents a change in their behavior. When Lee Iaccoca stands before a group of investment analysts, his goal is to influence their thinking about the financial position of Chrysler Corporation. When you call your friend on the phone just because you were thinking about her, you brighten her day; you confirm her worthiness of herself as a friend and she feels better than she did before you called. The unstated, and perhaps unrealized, persuasive goal was a change in her feelings about herself.

Communication as Persuasion

The goal of information is to get your audience to think differently from how they think presently. The goal of persuasion is to get your listeners to do something that they are not presently doing. The goal of entertainment is to get your audience to respond in some different way, perhaps with a chuckle or a smile, or with relaxation where there was tension. In each of these situations, your goal is to elicit a change in your listeners.

Change, then, appears to be the central purpose of every speech. That goal gives rise to three questions:

1. What particular change do I seek from this audience?
2. What audience characteristics and features of the context presently motivate the audience to act as they do?
3. What audience characteristics and features of the context will motivate the listeners to change as I want?

The Action
Continuum

Since change is the central purpose of every speech, it is convenient to assume that regarding every imaginable subject, there is an action continuum at work in every individual. It includes acceptance or action on one side, and rejection or action on the other. Somewhere in the center represents neutrality. The action continuum might look something like this:

Rejection	Neutrality	Acceptance
Action against	Neutrality	Action in favor

In general, the aim of audience analysis and adaptation is to determine where your listeners are distributed along this continuum, then to design appropriate communication strategies to move them toward the right along the continuum. To understand how the action continuum works, imagine that you are one of four students who have announced their candidacy for the position of student senator. Everyone who supports the other candidates is acting against your campaign, and everyone who is supporting you is acting in favor of your campaign. The rest of the student population falls somewhere in between. So you might expect to find an audience distributed like this:

```
                            x   x
                        x   x   x
                    x   x   x   x   x
                    x   x   x   x   x
                x   x   x   x   x   x   x
            x   x   x   x   x   x   x   x
        x   x   x   x   x   x   x   x   x   x
    x   x   x   x   x   x   x   x   x   x   x
x   x   x   x   x   x   x   x   x   x   x   x   x
```

| Action against | Belief against | Neutrality | Belief for | Action for |

A different subject and goal would elicit a different distribution. During the early 1970s, for example, feelings ran strong about American involvement in Viet Nam. In the mid-1980s, the issue of legalized abortion erupted.

Suppose, for example, you wanted to give a speech on the abortion issue. You might imagine an audience distributed like this:

```
                x
                x   x                           x
                x   x                   x       x
            x   x   x                   x   x   x
            x   x   x   x           x    x   x   x
        x   x   x   x   x   x   x    x   x   x
   x    x   x   x   x   x   x   x    x   x   x   x
```

Action against	Belief against	Neutrality	Belief for	Action for

As you can see, a statistical average would not help you to design either a pro-abortion or anti-abortion speech that would have general appeal to such an audience. You would, instead, have to make some difficult choices about how you would proceed, and to what subgroup of the audience you would address your remarks. In order to do that, you would have to refine your thinking. Are you going to appeal to those people on the right side of the continuum? Will you prepare your remarks in an attempt to persuade those people just to the left of the center? What about the people at the extreme ends of the continuum? Can you ignore them? Or, do you think you should address them, too?

The General Purpose

The general purpose of a speech depends to a large extent upon your best estimate of how the listeners are distributed along the action continuum. More than one position will almost always apply, so you will want to estimate the rough percentages, or the *range of distribution*. This is important, as you will see, because it allows you to focus and refine your speaking goals.

Suppose that an audience is distributed along the continuum as shown here. What would you do?

5%	35%	40%	15%	5%
Action against	Belief against	Neutrality	Belief for	Action for

If your analysis is correct, the bulk of your audience is neutral or does not believe as you do. You will probably plan to focus your speech on getting that 75 percent to move toward the right on the continuum. This goal will require a speech that is quite different from one that would be required by a group that already supports you. You might want to design a speech to inform and educate, one that would include evidence and arguments designed to change belief and to convince.

FIGURE 4.3 Selecting the
General Purpose of a Speech.
Your understanding of how
the audience is distributed
along this continuum
determines the general
purpose you select.

Action Against	Belief	Neutral	Belief	Action For
Entertain	Inform	Change Belief	Convince	Stimulate to Action

Look at figure 4.3 to see why. By relating the action continuum to the general purposes of speech, you can choose among the five general purposes of speech: *entertain, inform* and *educate, change belief, convince,* and *stimulate to action.*

We are getting ahead of ourselves. In the next chapter we will detail how to select a topic and purpose for a speech. Here we are talking about audience analysis, and although these matters are intimately related, all you need to know for now is that the purpose you select depends on your analysis of how the target audience distributes across the action continuum. You can use the ideas in figure 4.3 to guide you as you approach this matter. In chapter 5 we will help focus and refine your understanding.

Once you determine the general purpose of the speech, your next step is to determine a specific goal statement. We believe that this is the single most important part of successfully adapting to a listening audience. A carefully worked out goal statement makes clear what a speaker must do in order to achieve the goal!

Adapting to an Audience — the Goal Statement

Teaching public speaking students the value of setting a single, clear goal seems to be one of the most difficult tasks. Yet, we feel that *setting a specific goal* in terms of *behavior that can be observed* may be the single most helpful way a beginning speaker can improve the quality of a speech. By setting a clear goal, one that can be observed, you accomplish two important things:

1. You impose a clear focus upon your thinking because the goal forces you to consider the audience members and their needs rather than your own.
2. You clarify the audience psychology, and thus understand better what will be required to accomplish your speaking goal.

Although some of our students have no trouble understanding the general purposes of speech, they have difficulty differentiating between observable and unobservable speaking goals. They also do not always focus clearly. So how do you do that?

To focus your speaking purpose clearly, you must first seek one well-identified, specific goal. Write down what you want to accomplish on a piece of paper, then search for connectors (conjunctions), such as *and, however, but* and the like. If you find any connectors in your goal statement, you probably are not focusing clearly on your objective. Consider these examples:

> *Wrong:* After giving my speech, I want the board of directors to approve my proposal for a new line of widgets and for the research staff to test them.
> *Better:* After giving my speech I want the board of directors to approve my proposal for a new line of widgets.
>
> *Wrong:* After hearing my speech, I want my listeners to believe that drug addiction is not exaggerated, and should be treated as an illness.
> *Better:* After hearing my speech I want my listeners to believe that drug addiction is not an exaggerated problem in our society.

These examples illustrate that in each "wrong" statement the speaker appears to have more to do than could be accomplished in a single speech. Success could be more readily achieved by focusing on a single goal, as shown in the "better" version of each example. Even so, a difficult problem remains to be solved.

Limited Goal

Suppose you have selected the broad topic of gambling as the subject matter for a speech you are planning to give. Where do you begin setting the specific, behavioral goal for the speech? You can begin by writing out one of these incomplete sentences:

1. After hearing my speech, I want my listeners to. . . .
2. After hearing my speech, my listeners will be able to . . .

Finish the sentence in terms of some behavior you could observe if you so desired. Tom Hanks completed it in this way, "After hearing my speech I want my audience to believe that gambling is evil." You might ask, "How will you be able to tell?" Chances are, you would get the answer, "I don't know." Tom's sentence refers to a goal that could create a change inside the heads of individual listeners. You would not be able to observe such behavior.

Tony DiSalvo's goal statement on the subject of gambling was better. "At the end of this speech I want my audience to be able to specify in writing the three evils that I see in gambling." In this case, Tony was thinking about observable behavior. *Specify* is an action word, and it fits the idea of an action continuum.

Observable Goal

Let us look at still another example. Ellen Vargas wrote, "At the end of this speech I want my audience to be able to explain in their own words why gambling is potentially damaging." Here, again, a specific action word points to observable behavior.

In order to turn a statement into a description of observable behavior, imagine a single member from the audience actually doing what you ask— acting on your goal. Figure 4.4 provides a number of words that elicit observable actions, and a number of words that do not. You can use this table to complete the sentence about what you want.

Learning how to identify a single observable behavior will tell you a lot about what you need to learn from an audience analysis, and how you should proceed with your strategic planning once you learn it. Here are some additional examples of student and professional work that turns general purpose statements into action goals. These examples are not perfect, but each one successfully focuses the speaker's planning and practice.

> *General purpose:* To inform the audience about how trust evolves in a
> relationship.
> *Action goal:* After hearing my speech, I want my listeners to be able
> to describe and explain the significance of Frank Dance's spiraling
> helix model of the trust-self-disclosure relationship.
>
> *General purpose:* To entertain the sales representatives in order to
> reduce their hostility about my proposal to reduce their mileage
> allowances.
> *Action goal:* After hearing my speech, I want the sales representatives
> to be able to name at least four company policies that we agree on,
> and I want them to laugh with me at least once.
>
> *General purpose:* To change the general audience belief that our
> government is right in Nicaragua.
> *Action goal:* After my speech, I want my audience to be able to list
> three reasons why U.S. policy in Nicaragua is wrong.
>
> *General purpose:* To convince the audience that the semester system is
> better than the quarter system.
> *Action goal:* After this speech, I want my audience to be able to
> specify at least four ways that the semester system is superior to
> the quarter system.
>
> *General purpose:* To stimulate the audience to action on the question
> of illegal aliens working in this country.
> *Action goal:* I want my audience to write a letter to either Senator
> Denton or Senator Heflin asking for introduction of tough new
> legislation that would make it more difficult for illegal aliens to
> find jobs in the United States.

Words that point to observable behaviors	Words that point to behaviors that cannot be observed
define	believe
distinguish	recognize
acquire	feel
repeat	think
identify	interpret
describe	interpolate
translate	conclude
rephrase	know
arrange	determine
draw	imagine
demonstrate	enjoy
choose	judge
classify	evaluate
write	conceptualize
tell	experience
propose	plan

FIGURE 4.4 A Partial List of Action Words. The use of action words will help you focus your planning and practice.

Looking at each of these examples carefully, you will notice that they share in common a general purpose statement that focuses attention on the subject matter and an action goal that focuses attention on the listeners. Notice also that each action goal makes clear that the speaker will have to design a speech that makes it easy and desirable for the listeners to achieve the desired action.

Your Class as an Audience

We want to mention something that may make an important difference to you in this course. It is easy for students to lose sight of the fact that their classmates are an audience. Many view the speaking situation in a classroom as entirely artificial, and to some extent it is. This is partially because the students in a classroom audience are captive, that is if class attendance is mandatory. In addition, with every speaking assignment, each student is expected to give a speech. So the listening task for class members is very difficult and arbitrary; at best, it borders on the impossible if the speeches are not carefully prepared and delivered in a lively manner. Such conditions would rarely if ever occur in a speaking situation outside the classroom. On the other hand, your classmates are truly an audience. Each individual in the classroom is a human being with feelings and wants and points of view. Each mind, each soul, in that classroom is significant, and each individual's time is valuable.

Respect for the Classroom Audience

We have found that the best classroom speeches are produced by students who approach the classroom audience with respect, who identify with and analyze their classmates as an audience. Successful student speakers think in terms of adapting themselves to the needs of their listeners—to making the speaker-audience relationship a real, present-tense phenomenon. In short, they take the classroom audience seriously.

Sandy Williams took her audience seriously. It was the beginning of her junior year. She had just been appointed editor of the student paper and she needed help. For her second speech of the term she decided to try to persuade members of the class to join the newspaper staff. Here is how she concluded that speech:

> There's something in it for the school and for the paper, of course. The paper gets out on time if enough people help to get it out. But there is something more important than that in it for you.
>
> You'll earn a little money. It won't be much, the budget is limited. Even so, it will be enough to help you get by. But that's not the most important thing.
>
> You'll learn to write better than you ever thought you could, with the help of two of the best writing coaches anywhere.
>
> You'll learn to discipline yourself—to meet deadlines, to organize your time, to think things through with a rigor of thought that will surprise you now and serve you well in the future.
>
> And in your senior year you'll have something that very few students can claim. You will have directly related working experience when you begin making applications for a job.
>
> And there is one last thing. I really do need your help.

There were twenty-five students in that class. Partly with that speech and partly by the force of her personality, Sandy persuaded three of those students to join the newspaper staff. Sandy respected her audience and took them seriously. Her attitude, in turn, encouraged them to take her seriously.

Analysis of the Classroom Audience

While you can learn a lot about your classmates by close observation and by talking with them, you will probably want to study their backgrounds and their attitudes about your speech topic in a more systematic manner. You may even be required by your speech instructor to complete a formal analysis for one or more of your speeches. How should you proceed?

One way of getting information is to interview members of the class. But that takes time and energy. Suppose you have twenty classmates! To make an appointment of twenty minutes with each of them every time you are preparing a speech would be highly impractical. A better method is to develop a questionnaire. You do not have to be an expert to do this. However, you need to ask a few simple, direct questions.

Three specific kinds of questions will be particularly useful for your purposes. One type of question is called a *forced-choice* question. It requires the respondent to pick an answer from two or more alternatives. You have lots of experience with forced-choice questions because you have answered multiple-choice and true-false questions most of your academic life. Here are two examples of forced-choice questions that were developed by a public speaking student.

Do you know what "random-access memory" (RAM) means?

_____ Yes

_____ No

_____ Uncertain

Do you know the difference between RAM and ROM?

_____ Yes

_____ No

_____ Uncertain

These questions limit the choice of responses that are available, so they generate a picture that leaves little doubt about the audience's responses. For example, you might discover that eighteen out of twenty-five members of the audience cannot tell RAM from ROM. But the forced-choice type of question doesn't give you very much detail.

A type of question that allows respondents a greater range for their responses is called a *scale item*. The scale item allows you to gather a better understanding of audience attitude, and it gives you much greater flexibility to discover what the audience knows or believes about a subject. Here are some examples:

To what extent, if any, do you worry about contacting AIDS?

Very worried |_____|_____|_____|_____|_____|_____|_____| **Not worried**

To what extent do you agree with these statements?

Capital punishment is legalized murder.

Strongly agree |_____|_____|_____|_____|_____|_____| **Strongly disagree**

Capital punishment should be abolished.

Strongly agree |_____|_____|_____|_____|_____|_____| **Strongly disagree**

Capital punishment is a deterrent to crime.

Strongly agree |_____|_____|_____|_____|_____|_____| **Strongly disagree**

Questions like these are especially helpful in learning the depth of commitment or conviction that an audience experiences. The difficulty with writing scale items is that you must be sure to balance them so that you do

---

1. Do you know the most important reasons why children run away from home?
    _____ Yes   _____ No   _____ Uncertain

2. Do you know about how many children run away from home each year?
    _____ Yes   _____ No   _____ Uncertain

3. Do you know how many states directly allocate money to support runaway children?
    _____ Yes   _____ No   _____ Uncertain

4. How serious is the runaway problem in the United States?
    Extremely   Not
    Serious |_____|_____|_____|_____|_____|_____| Serious

5. In your opinion, how difficult would it be to solve the runaway children problem?
    Extremely   Not
    Difficult |_____|_____|_____|_____|_____|_____| Difficult

6. What do you think should be done about the runaway children in this area?
    _____
    _____
    _____
    _____

        Thank you very much for your help!

FIGURE 4.5 A Questionnaire about Runaway Children.

---

not bias the respondent. For example, the second and third questions on the previous page may introduce a bias in the respondent against capital punishment. The fourth item may tend to balance them out.

In some instances, you might find that neither the scale item nor the forced-choice item tells you what you want to know. In that case you might ask a third kind of question, called an *open-response item*. Open-response items provide the respondent maximum opportunity to express an opinion, and to give detail, but they also invite irrelevant responses. Some examples of open response items are:

> Do you have an opinion concerning capital punishment? If so, what is it?

> How do you respond to all the publicity recently given to Acquired Immune Deficiency Syndrome (AIDS)?

The strengths and limitations of each of these kinds of questions tend to argue for a combination of question types in questionnaires you distribute to a classroom audience. Figure 4.5 shows a questionnaire that Marcy Vasalopolis used in preparing her speech about children who run away from home.

Since nineteen of Marcy's respondents did not know why children run away from home and another five were uncertain, Marcy spent some time reviewing the numbers. She was confident that she was really giving her listeners some important information. She also relayed the number of children involved—more than a million in the United States in August 1986, primarily from middle- and upper-class families—which seemed a staggering number to her classmates.

Most of the listeners already believed the problem was serious, so Marcy did not have to persuade them to that position. She could let the numbers speak for themselves. She could infer that her audience would welcome a proposal that seemed to offer some hope, since most of her listeners probably had no idea what was already being done or what they could do about the problem.

Reinforced with these inferences, Marcy argued that the Federal Government should pay for a program that developed shelters for runaways, and that the funding should be regular and massive. She pointed out that Congress would be holding hearings in the coming month on the matter of allocations for programs to help runaway children, and she asked her audience to sign a petition that called for greatly increased funding. Twenty-five signatures besides Marcy's were on that petition, which Marcy copied and sent to each congressman and senator from Alabama. Every student in the class, plus the instructor, had signed that petition.

Marcy's questionnaire worked very well for her. It was carefully thought out in advance; it was clearly stated; and because it was brief, the students were able to complete it quickly. If you keep these criteria in mind, you, too, will be able to develop a similarly useful questionnaire for your own use.

Summary

The purpose of this chapter has been to provide you a convenient method for doing audience analysis, and to tell you what to do with the information you gather. An audience is a collection of individuals who make choices based upon their needs and wants, and upon their perceptions and expectations. The task of the speaker is to anticipate, and then adapt to those choices in order to bring the listeners to the desired response. But the speaker cannot address remarks to each individual. A method of grouping them together into homogenous subgroups is needed.

When you can access an audience directly, such as a classroom audience, it is convenient to develop a questionnaire for gathering information about the audience. When, as happens more frequently, you cannot access an audience directly, you can use demographic data to draw inferences about what relevant subgroups of audience members know about your subject, and how they are likely to respond to your speech.

Action continuum analysis will help you to set the general purpose of the speech intelligently. The final step is to write a specific goal statement in terms of the listeners' behaviors. Such action goals help you to discover the communication strategies that are most likely to be effective.

Key Terms

Action continuum   *Demographic analysis*
Audience   *Demographic profile*
Audience analysis   *General purpose*

Discussion Questions

1. Using the demographic analysis checklist in figure 4.2 as a guideline and your class as an audience to analyze, identify how you think the class members would distribute along the action continuum concerning each of the following propositions. Work with one or two classmates, and be sure to justify your responses.

   a. Terrorism should be met with a military response.
   b. A Democrat should be elected President of the United States in the next election.
   c. The United States should return Guantanamo Bay to the Cubans.
   d. Women are an oppressed majority.
   e. Extensive racism is a thing of the past in the United States of America.

   Suggestion: As a group, select one of these topics, then perform an analysis of the classroom audience by developing and using a questionnaire. How did your original estimates compare to your findings when you actually surveyed the classroom audience?

2. Select a topic suggested by one of the five propositions above. Based on your analysis of the classroom audience, what would be the general purpose of a six-minute speech? Why? Specific purpose? Why? Can you justify your response by pointing to anything in this chapter?

3. In your opinion what are the three most important demographic variables influencing the classroom audience's probable position on the subject you have been working with? Why?

4. Given your group's responses to the above questions, can you outline a speech, including a statement of what evidence you would need in order to get the observable response you set?

1 For a recent report on this phenomenon, *see* Mary John Smith, "Contingency Rules Theory, Context, and Compliance Behaviors." *Human Communication Research* 10(Summer 1984):489–512.

2 This idea is not a simple one. *See,* for example, Martin J. Medhurst, "Resistance, Conservatism, and Theory Building: A Cautionary Note," *The Western Journal of Speech Communication* 49(Spring 1985):103–15. This interesting essay focuses on just one area of resistance: political conservatism.

3 *See* J. T. Molloy, *Dress for Success* (New York: Warner Books, 1975), and J. T. Molloy, *The Woman's Dress for Success Book* (New York: Warner Books, 1978).

4 This idea is not a new one, nor is it universally accepted, but it is very convenient for our purposes. For a careful analysis of the strengths and weaknesses of the idea (sometimes called "Information-Processing Theory of Persuasion"), *see* Stephen W. Littlejohn, *Theories of Human Communication, 2d ed.* (Belmont, Calif.: Wadsworth Publishing Company, 1983), 141–46.

Berelson, Bernard, and Steiner, Gary A. *Human Behavior: An Inventory of Scientific Findings.* New York: Harcourt, Brace and World, 1964.
This well-organized and easy-to-use classic work summarizes the literature on human behavior up to about 1962.

Clevenger, Theodore, Jr. *Audience Analysis.* Indianapolis, Indiana: Bobbs-Merrill Company, Inc., 1966.
This is one of the most influential textbooks ever written about audience analysis. Clevenger wrote it during a period when opinion research, statistical analysis, thought and belief systems, and the effects of electronic mass media were frightening and relatively new concerns. It is not too difficult, and very worthwhile.

Gibson, James W., and Hanna, Michael S. *Audience Analysis: A Programmed Approach to Receiver Behavior.* Englewood Cliffs, N.J.: Prentice Hall, Inc., 1976.
This is a good how-to-do-it book that you can read at your own leisure and at your own pace. We could not resist mentioning it here.

5 Selecting and Narrowing Your Ideas

Outline

Objectives

After reading this chapter you should be able to:

1. Set the general purpose of a speech that is adapted to a particular audience.
2. Identify the relationship between topic selection and audience analysis.
3. Utilize the major techniques of brainstorming in developing topics for possible messages.
4. Explain how a speaker utilizes the suspension of judgment to foster the generation of ideas for speeches.
5. Define what the terms *appropriateness* and *flexibility* mean in the combination of ideas for speeches.
6. Identify the major steps in the process of narrowing the topic for the audience and the situation.

PREVIEW

Successful public speaking depends partially upon the development of innovative ideas that are appropriate to the audience and the purpose of the message and the setting. An effective speaker recognizes that the likelihood of success depends upon the quality of ideas that are presented to listeners as the body of the message. Quality messages are, however, the result of generating many apparently divergent approaches. This variety of potential topics is subsequently evaluated for appropriateness to the classroom audience. Similarly, the topic must be tested to determine if it can be developed with sufficient clarity within the allotted time.

"There's nothing for me to talk about that would interest anyone else." "I just can't think of a topic that would fit this assignment!" Nearly every speech teacher has heard these comments from students, and even experienced speakers have these feelings as they begin preparing for a speech activity. These statements are usually made at the start of the preparation period. The speaker is saying, "Help me find a topic that is interesting to me and others." "Help me with my preparation; how can I choose a topic that will 'work' with this audience?"

There are no formulas for subject selection, but there are guides that will help you select topics that will interest both you and your listeners. In this chapter, we look at several guidelines and techniques that will help you choose either conventional or innovative ideas for your next speech. We emphasize the need to set a general purpose that matches your listeners, and then to narrow your subject adequately for the audience comprehension within the time frame of the speaking situation. Remember, however, that selecting what you consider the "right" purpose and the "right" topic does not mean your speech will be a success. This is only part of the series of steps you need to complete if your speech is to succeed.

The General Purpose

In chapter 4 we mentioned that it was important in audience analysis to select the general purpose of a speech with the audience in mind. We presented figure 4.3 on page 76 as a means of helping you know how to do that. Refer to figure 4.3 again. You will immediately recall that an audience is always distributed across an action continuum and that your wisest choice is to locate the place on the continuum where most of your listeners are likely to be found. Using figure 4.3, it is a simple matter to know what general purpose is likely to "fit" that audience and, therefore, to yield speaking success.

Here we want to take up each of those general purposes again but in much greater detail. Selecting the general purpose of a speech has clear implications for you as you bring your speaking ideas into focus. Let us look more closely at the general purposes of speech: entertain, inform and educate, change belief, convince, and stimulate to action.

Sometimes an audience is hostile. Its members are picketing, or shouting, or working in an opposing campaign. Rarely would you give a speech to such an audience, but it does happen occasionally. If you should ever find yourself in the presence of an audience that is acting against your position, you cannot do much except entertain them.

    Do not envision a stand-up comic routine. That might be very effective, but most people find it difficult to be funny. Besides, it is usually not necessary. By entertain, we mean speaking to ease the tensions of an audience, and to build rapport with them. In this sense, the term *entertain* means much the same that it does when you entertain guests in your home. You make the people feel welcome. You put on your best face. You are solicitous of their feelings, and you do all that you can to make them feel comfortable, with each other and with you. That is precisely what is meant by entertain in this context, too. You can read more about entertaining and special occasion speeches in chapter 14.

Entertain

When it is clear that a large portion of your listeners have beliefs that are different from yours, and assuming that yours are right, the general purpose of the speech must be to inform and educate. That is an enormous assumption, of course; but if you know the truth, and they don't, then it stands to reason that people who do not believe the truth need information. This reasoning can create problems, however, because people who disagree with one another usually think they know what they are talking about. Work carefully, then, as you develop information to teach an audience about another point of view. The next chapter develops this idea in greater detail, and so does chapter 12.

Inform and Educate

It often happens that a large segment of the audience hovers somewhere near the center of the action continuum. Although they have the information, they do not seem to be able to shift toward the right. There must be some reason, for instance, why individuals continue to smoke cigarettes, even though available scientific evidence demonstrates that smoking is clearly linked to cancer and heart disease and emphysema and high blood pressure and low-birth weights. There must be a belief structure that needs changing. An audience that knows the truth and still does not believe it requires a different kind of speech. You can read more about persuasive speaking in chapter 13.[1]

Change Belief

Convince

Once someone has moved through neutrality to your side of the action continuum, you cannot assume that person will stay there. You would be wise to secure that change by assuring the individual that the choice was a correct one. For example, an astute car salesperson will not let more than a week pass after you have decided to purchase a car before calling or writing to tell you what a wise decision you made. He or she knows that you must be helped over the after-the-decision doubts you may have about whether you made the right choice.[2]

This process is called convincing, and it has the effect of cementing belief. Convincing is important in social movement persuasion, to encourage people to continue on a path that they have already begun. For example, when the space shuttle *Challenger* exploded on live TV late in January 1986, the American space program was seriously threatened. The drama and tragedy of the event temporarily overshadowed confidence in the manned space program for most Americans, but not for the president. He knew that postponement or elimination of future flights would hurt many large corporations that had already made enormous investments in the space program. Some were involved in the actual production of space shuttle equipment, building rockets and component parts. Others were involved in developing satellites and related space equipment. He also knew that any civilian or military uses of space depended upon continuance of the shuttle program. The explosion had seriously shaken the confidence of corporate and military experts in the shuttle program.

President Reagan believed that the American people had to be convinced that they should continue tax support of the NASA space research and exploration program. Notice how skillfully he included an element of this goal in his eulogy for the *Challenger* astronauts at the Johnson Space Center in Houston, Texas:

> The sacrifice of your loved ones has stirred the soul of our nation
> and, through the pain, our hearts have been opened to a profound
> truth: the future is not free, the story of all human progress is one of
> a struggle against all odds. We learned again that this America,
> which Abraham Lincoln called the last best hope of man on earth,
> was built on heroism and noble sacrifice. . . .

Stimulate to Action

When an audience supports your belief, but is not acting as you would like, or you want them to undertake a difficult or dangerous task, the most appropriate general purpose for a speech is to stimulate them to action. People can agree, intellectually, that something ought to be done, but still not do anything about the matter. They need to feel a problem—to experience it emotionally—before they will act.

Under other circumstances, emotional involvement is a necessary condition to great effort. For example, we expect our leaders to address us as we embark on a new venture. The coach speaks to the team before the big

For the speaker who already enjoys the support and agreement of the listeners, the goal is to rouse them to action.

game. The general addresses his officers before a great battle. The chief executive officer opens the annual sales meeting with a rousing welcome. Almost always, these speeches are designed to stimulate emotional involvement.

Think of it as trying to develop a sense of ownership. The audience members must "own" a problem before they will act on it. That is, the listeners must have a sense that they are emotionally involved and affected by a problem before they are willing to act on the problem. At the most mundane level, you might remember how you responded to your father's request to mow the grass when you were younger. You knew that the grass needed cutting. You even took some pride in your work when someone said how nice the lawn looked. But you probably did not leap out of bed on the weekend saying, "Goody! Today I get to spend two whole hours behind the lawn mower." That is because you did not have a sense of ownership in the project.

As an adult, of course, you may still prefer not to mow the grass over other activities that could fill a weekend morning, but you probably don't think too much, one way or the other, about the task. Believe it or not, some people do leap out of bed looking forward to mowing the lawn.

Mary Jane Killgore gave the following remarks to stimulate students in her class to participate in the on-campus blood-bank drive. Notice how carefully she worked to build emotional involvement and a sense of ownership and pride in the audience.

> I thought you might like to meet a friend of mine this morning. He can't be with us here in the classroom, although I am sure he would rather be here than in his hospital room. Tommy is nine. He's a bright kid who is interested, more than anything else, in becoming an astronaut. And he has a good chance, too—even though he has something called "preleukemia." He has intelligence, curiosity, wit, and charm, and an amazing self-possession for a nine year old.
>
> Tommy has enormous brown eyes that seem to look beyond you. He smiles quickly and often. He seems at ease with people of every age. He is full of fun, and he is full of hope. What he doesn't have, and what he needs most, is your help. He needs blood, lots of it. And that can only come from people. And not only Tommy. There are many people who need blood in this community every day, and there is only one place where they can get it.
>
> Today, in the University Center, they're having a blood drive. They've come here, to our campus, because they know that a college campus is the best place to find a large number of healthy adults who have more blood than they need, and more caring and concern for their fellow man than anywhere else.
>
> They've come here knowing that all they have to do to get some help for Tommy is to ask you. They know that you've been helpful in the past. In fact, last year at this time you gave about half the blood that they collected, city-wide, in their whole campaign! In doing that, you gave back the lives, for a while, at least, to over a hundred patients who needed your help.
>
> And now they're asking for your help again. I am asking for your help, too, for my friend Tommy. He needs you. He really, really needs you, and he knows you'll help. Will you walk with me, right now, over to the University Center—for Tommy, and for yourself?

Mary Jane's audience was responsive to her call for participation in the on-campus blood-bank drive because she created emotional involvement in her listeners. They had a sense of ownership in the project.

Suppose that you are the speaker. Your idea is that the Rotary Club should provide the money for a local high school student to spend a year abroad. Suppose further that, based on your analysis, you believe that the Rotarians are distributed according to this next figure:

10%	55%	20%	15%
Action against	Belief against	Neutrality	Belief for	Action for

Considering what you have just read about the general purposes of speech, what would you be most likely to do with this audience? What general purpose would you select? Ninety percent of your audience ranges between neutral and belief in favor of your point of view. What will you attempt to accomplish with your speech?

You cannot afford to ignore the Rotarians who oppose your position, but you cannot afford to spend much time with them, either. If you are wise, the general purpose of your speech will be to stimulate emotional involvement and ownership. But what about the specific action you want? The next thing you must do is develop a specific goal statement. Let us now take a closer look at topic selection.

Notice again that setting goals carefully is a critical activity in audience analysis and in narrowing and focusing your ideas. These things work together so closely that it was a struggle for us to know where to put the information!

Significance of Topic Selection

Selecting a topic for your speech is one of the most significant choices you face as a speaker. How others evaluate you as a speaker is based, to a large extent, on the type of topic you choose as the focus of your ideas. Your major effort should be concentrated upon selecting a topic that both you and your listeners can view as *worthwhile, important,* and *interesting.* You must attend to these three concerns when selecting a topic because people choose to listen or not to listen based on these three criteria. This is your first major challenge in any speaking assignment: *select a topic that interests you and your audience.*

Topic Selection and Purpose

One of the major problems of beginning speakers is that they become confused about their purpose and do not achieve the purpose they initially selected. As you launch forth on your search for a topic, keep in mind that your topic *must be related to your purpose.* That will help you clarify how to approach subject selection and make choices.

For example, if your general purpose is to inform, then you are concerned primarily with the transmission of ideas and information. The following informative topics are a few examples:

Cats as famous pets
Laser disks
Careers in counseling
Grandfather clocks
Voting patterns of young adults
Optical illusions
Fine jewelry
Radial tires

These topics can all be discussed objectively, and can contribute clearly and specifically to your informative purpose without ranging into the area of persuasion. In a persuasive speech your objective would be to affect the beliefs, attitudes, opinions and actions of your listeners.

Let us use radial tires as an example. If your decision is to inform your listeners about radial tires, then your goal is not to persuade the audience that radial tires are a more economical purchase in the long run. Rather, you want to provide them with information and ideas about the subject. Most of your listeners probably do not know much about the technical construction of a radial tire. If you provide them with key pieces of information that will enable them to leave the room with an understanding of how a radial tire is constructed or why it is called *radial,* then your purpose and topic have merged nicely.

The same principles can be applied to a speech on the topic of optical illusions (What are they, how do they occur?), or the topic of cats as famous pets (What famous persons had cats? What kinds of cats have a place in history?). Purpose and topic selection interact strongly, and purpose "drives" much of the topic-choosing activity.

Let us see how your goal can be satisfied while considering the object of the message, the audience.

Topic Selection and Audience Interest

Chapter 4, "Audience Analysis," stresses that you must determine the knowledge, interests, and attitudes of your potential listeners. In selecting a topic, you must keep this key set of criteria in mind. The major question, then, is how do I find a topic that is interesting and appealing to listeners?

Will Rogers is quoted often as saying "I never met a man I didn't like." By this he probably meant that there is some aspect of each person that is likable or has interest. This special quality may not be readily discernible, but by keeping an open mind, you can find value in each person you meet. The same can be said of ideas: I never met an idea I didn't like. Every idea has value and aspects of interest. Whether the audience agrees or disagrees with your initial position does not really affect the value of your subject choice. It does matter, however, if they are interested and you make them want to listen. *There are no dull subjects, just dull ways of developing them.*

One major standard in choosing your topic is "Can I make it interesting?" The answer in virtually every case is "Yes." Whether or not the topic has an attractive title is a poor guide. Look at these examples of topics that may seem uninteresting.

Electromagnetic fields in your house
The forces in running
The downlink in satellite communication

These speech topics appear to be very technical and, perhaps, boring, but they were developed in unusually interesting and appealing ways. Successful communication often consists of making the ordinary into the unique. It means that you should give each topic a novel "twist." You can do this if you select a topic you can identify with and expand. Next we will look at the kind of thinking process that helps you select topics that have the potential for being interesting or different.

Psychologists tell us that one characteristic of creative thinkers is that they have many ideas. Of course that does not mean that all their ideas are good. In fact, many of their ideas are poor, but they develop many ideas. They develop these ideas by *brainstorming*, or considering anything that leaps into their minds.[3] They do not initially judge whether the idea is good or bad. That comes later. So begin thinking, and record all those ideas on paper; later they will be evaluated. In brainstorming, the key word is *quantity*, not *quality*. This is not the time to consider whether or not the idea is good. Try to keep in mind that you are attempting to generate many ideas, and that some of these ideas may be good points of departure for a speech topic.[4]

We will now look at a way to generate ideas for speeches using a system that works well for nearly every speaking situation. Sit down with a blank piece of paper in front of you. Invent some categories for your thinking. Call them "Who, what, when, where, why, and how." Arrange them in columns and begin to write down whatever enters your mind about the category. This is called the *idea incubation period*.[5]

Developing Ideas — Quantity

Who	*What*
A minister	Firecrackers
Tenants	Airplane
Military people	accidents
Our friends	Stereos
Sloppy dressers	Income tax
	Air conditioners

When	*Where*
Exam time	At home
Spring	New York City
2A.M. parties	Japan
Birthdays	The Superdome
Back-to-school	The office

Why	*How*
Wars	Submarines
Discrimination	surface
High tuitions	Wine is aged
Formal dress	Experience affects
White sneakers	behavior
	Rumors are
	spread
	Exams are failed

As you look at the list of potential topics, they seem terribly unrelated. Some of them may not appear useful to you or the audience, while others may suggest true potential. Do not jump to conclusions. It is easy to say that no one in your audience would be interested in *tenants,* or that *tenants* do not interest you and are not good topics for a speech. If you jump to those conclusions, then you have not been able to *suspend judgment.* Suspending judgment means you do not toss out ideas just because they seem unattractive at first. Instead of discarding ideas, collect as many as possible before you apply your critical standards. Those subjects listed under "Who, what, when, where, why, and how" are possibilities for a speech. You have let your mind roam and listed, without evaluating, many possible topics for a speech.

It is true that some of the topics might not work. For instance, you could have listed *white sneakers* or *the Superdome* and decided later when you applied your standards that they would not work. However, that is not your present concern. Careful attention to selecting ideas is a major step toward developing a successful speech.

Selecting Ideas — Quality

Now that you have developed a *quantity of ideas,* the next step is to select quality ideas from that list. This is another phase in the brainstorming process. It is also a basic characteristic of people who are creative thinkers. Remember that the best way to ensure high quality ideas is to have a large quantity from which to choose.

Combinations

Suppose you thought *Japan* was an interesting possibility in the "where" category, but you found it terribly broad, and it only reminded you of things like cars and electronics. Keep brainstorming, and try putting a pair of categories together. In this case, let us combine "where" with "who." By combining *Japan* with *military people,* we get the Japanese military. Does that sound strange? Perhaps you do not realize that Japan is now the eighth largest defense spender. Did you know that Japan has a "no war" constitution? The traditional army, navy, and air force arrangement is prohibited by their constitution. However, they are permitted "self-defense forces" that have ground, air, and maritime divisions. In 1985 their defense spending was $13 billion. Here is a nation that cannot have military forces as we know them, yet it is just behind France in defense spending. Is this topic beginning to arouse your interest? It may have great potential!

What are some of the other possibilities? Do the Japanese have a history of military domination? How is the military regarded in Japan? Why would they have a constitution that prohibits them from having military forces like all other countries in the world? See how the brainstorming process can lead to many possibilities with topics.

Another possibility would be to combine other topics we developed in the brainstorming process. If we combined *exam time* from the "when" category, and *rumors are spread* from the "how" category, we have the potential for another interesting topic. Can you recall the rumors that were spread among members of a class as they were anticipating Professor Johnson's first history exam of the semester? Because exams are a stressful time, students thrive on listening to and speculating about possible problems or tactics. A topic combination of this sort is fruitful for developing an idea about how exams are a prime opportunity for spreading rumors.

We have taken you through these exercises because most speakers do not permit themselves to make these kinds of associations. Look again at the list of terms under each of the six categories. Take any topic in one category and pair it with a topic in another category. Interesting or possible topic? Maybe. But with six categories and five topics in each, there are many potential topics for speeches. And this is just the beginning of brainstorming.

Allow yourself to make other combinations. For instance, under "why," what associations does the word *discrimination* create? Racial discrimination? Age discrimination? Job discrimination? Sexual discrimination? Regional discrimination? Name discrimination? This approach also has many possibilities. You can go in many directions with your ideas. You can even invent categories, so develop more topics or categories of your own.

An effective speaker is one who has creative ideas. That speaker also allows the mind to roam over a variety of possibilities. Do you suppose that in the near future we will be able to talk into machines that will print a typewritten manuscript of what we have said? Examples of possible ideas are legion. Why should we use motion picture cameras with film when videotaping gives us an instant image and allows us greater editing ease? Will laser beams that can read the contour of the human eye replace keys for locks, since no two humans have the same eye contours? Certainly there may be operational problems, but we must stretch our horizons. The speaker does not see just the mousetrap. There is a vision of a better mousetrap or a belief that something can be changed or improved. That creative person is a restless thinker, one who would like to make some changes in the world.[6] Are you that kind of person?

Flexibility

A flexible thinker is much like a musical composer. No new musical notes have been invented, but successful music writers have used that original collection of notes to create innumerable musical compositions. Willie Nelson and Beethoven, for example, both composed from the same musical scale, yet their creations are about as different as you could imagine.

Flexibility in thinking comes from your willingness to think in different ways about what appear to be very conventional subjects.[7] Such is the essence of creativity, which is a highly prized characteristic in modern, competitive society. A speaker's mind is not closed to possible subjects. For example, a speaker might be as interested in talking about why leaves change color in the fall, as why shopping malls are killing downtown areas in many cities.

Flexible thinking allows you to view a situation from several angles. Here is a suggestion. You talk with your friends daily about a variety of subjects and problems. Why not take one of those topics and use it for the topic of a speech? Let us assume you have strong feelings about the funding for athletics on campus. How seriously does that funding affect the kind of academic program you can choose? What if *all* intercollegiate athletic programs were required to be self-supporting? Would that ruin the intercollegiate program? Would that be a serious loss? Would the advantages outweigh the disadvantages? What are the alternatives to the current situation?

The flexible thinker looks for common topics with uncommon treatments. The flexible and creative speaker gives freedom to thought and is willing to take a few risks in originating ideas. *As a speaker, your first concern should not be whether the idea is right.* Instead, you should be certain that you have many ideas, and then you can begin deciding if they are right for you and your audience.

Appropriateness

Let us begin by defining the term *appropriateness* as it relates to the public-speaking situation. It refers to talking about ideas that are geared to the level of intelligence and sophistication of the audience. How much do they know, what kind of information do they have, and how did they acquire that information? The setting is also an important consideration. A topic that is suitable for a fraternity meeting may not necessarily be appropriate for a class setting. Finally, appropriateness is related to how well the speaker understands the topic and can get excited about it—an important point we covered in our discussion of audience analysis.

For a classroom audience, all the topics listed under the six headings we looked at earlier in the chapter appear to be possibilities. Apply the appropriateness standard to all the topics you have generated to see if you can develop and organize each topic so that it is interesting to both you and your listeners.

Appropriateness is based on considerations of the audience, the setting, and the interests of the speaker.

Tenants was a possibility we mentioned. Students living off campus are tenants in housing, and many of them are extremely interested in parts of that topic. Parts such as standards of cleanliness, adequate plumbing, sufficient heat, and noise control may be high on their lists of interests. Even those who are not tenants have heard about these problems. They may want to hear more, especially if you make it relevant to them.

Look again at our list of possible topics on pages 95 and 96. All of these topics could be appropriate for a classroom audience, but do they interest you? Do they all interest you equally? Probably not! *Income tax* may not be high on your list of preferred topics. Or, *white sneakers* may seem like something you just could not develop usefully.

Appropriateness has several dimensions. Remember, also, that your comments must be acceptable to both the female and male members of a college class. That may rule out such juvenile matters as "Why Keggers Are Fun," or "Skinny Dipping is a Worthwhile Sport in the Summertime." It rules in such subjects as "Music as Therapy," "Passenger Trains Are a Vanishing Breed," or "Flu Shots Make a Difference." These examples are intended to provide you with a notion of the topics that you and your peers can select for speeches. It also helps you erect some standards about the types of topics that are not desirable for a co-ed college classroom. Some students might argue that *back-to-school* and *2A.M. parties* could be combined as a good subject for the college classoom. It is true that *back-to-school* can be a topic with many dimensions. So too can *2A.M. parties.* However, unless the topic is developed in a substantive, researchable way, there can be problems. Responsible, adult communication involves more than a discussion of student drinking or unusual behavior. In this instance, appropriateness relates to the level of intellectual significance. Is your topic worth listening to as a serious, thoughtful examination of an idea? Or is it a thinly disguised effort to dress up a rationale for heavy drinking as a conditioner for getting ready for the weekend or going back to classes at the beginning of the semester? That is another dimension of appropriateness evaluation.

After you have developed your ideas, the next phase is to apply standards to determine if the topic will work for you and your target audience. The generation of ideas has supplied you with a quantity of material. The most desirable method for determining the good ideas as opposed to those that lack effective potential as topics is to apply what we will call "stock" questions to each of the topics.

1. Is the subject interesting or potentially interesting to this audience? Does it have those elements of appeal that are widespread with humans? Does it attract interest because it relates to your audience interests in personal success, curiosity, survival, or affection? Appeals like these appear frequently in topics that audiences find attractive. That is why subjects such as "How to Make a Million Dollars in Real Estate," "A Sixtieth of a Second Is a Long Time for a Camera," or "Love Helps Heal Physical Wounds," are appealing and effective ideas for listeners and speakers alike.

Consider the ideas you generated and apply this test to determine if it is appealing to others besides yourself. Remember, the listener must be interested if your speech is to have true success. If your answer is "yes," then you have the potential for an interesting and appealing topic.

2. Will the ideas or information you present be perceived as valuable by this audience? Value in this sense means "worth listening to." Is it likely your listeners will leave this communication experience with the feeling they have been exposed to some ideas that make them better-informed people, more critical or insightful listeners, more humane or sympathetic persons, or sophisticated consumers?

If your potential topic meets these early tests, you are ready to begin reducing the subject to manageable size. There are time limits imposed on all of us as communicators, so you must consider if the scope you intend can be managed in the available time frame.

Narrowing the Topic

You have discovered that topic selection is interesting and challenging, but you have also learned that topic choice by itself is not the answer. The narrowing process may be even more demanding because of the multiple choices within a single topic. Your decisions about what should be kept,

Audience interest may well be the most important factor in determining the success of a speech.

added, or discarded will do much to predict the success of the later organization and development of the speech. One of the most common complaints about presentations is that they are too long.[8] That should be a clear indicator that you need to evaluate carefully how much you have narrowed your topic.

You could say many things, but could you say them all within the time confines of your assignment? Naturally, you can not talk about all the features of tires, such as inflation, tire wear, safety, puncture resistance, and so forth, in only five minutes or so. Nor could you discuss the basic characteristics of leather shoes in a brief speech. While you could say much more, time restrictions force you to work with only one or two areas of the subject. Selectivity is part of the challenge of topic narrowing. You generate many different areas of a single topic, but then your responsibility is to choose only a few portions or one part of the topic for your speech.

What Could You Say?

What Should You Say?

You should say those things that are critical elements in the development of an understandable topic. If you are talking about a particular kind of tire, you might include a definitional phase (What is a radial tire?), and an explanatory phase (How does it work?). While the tire fits easily under these two headings, other topics may take more time and be more complicated to develop in this way. Similarly, if your objective is to explain the value of leather shoes as a long-term investment, you would also compare them to shoes constructed from man-made materials and explain why leather shoes may be superior. Your aims are *audience understanding* and *thorough subject coverage.* That is much more likely if you have narrowed your subject sufficiently.

Conservative Topic Choice

It is safer to select a conservative topic, one that has a good likelihood of appealing to your listeners—particularly the class you are addressing. Discussing circuses and their disappearance is a lower risk topic (and is thus more conservative) than a controversial subject like the "pro-life" movement. Another low risk topic is the pass-fail grading system on campuses, while the gay rights movement is a greater risk-taking venture in public communication. Risk taking can be very exciting and worthwhile, and it does have application in public communication, but if you wish to ensure a reasonable degree of success for your efforts, concentrate on subjects that have more potential for success. Conservative topic selection reduces the possibility of problems and increases your chances for accomplishing your purpose.

Determining Goals and Time

After selecting an interesting and useful topic, you are faced with the equally challenging issue of narrowing the topic so it fits the audience and the available time. There are multiple choices within any single topic, and the decisions you make about what should be kept or eliminated are critical.

Fred Kantor experienced difficulty in narrowing his topic. His assignment was to prepare a five-minute informative speech; he chose his topic and proceeded to develop it. On the day he was to give his speech, the class entered the room and saw that Fred had filled the chalkboard along one side and the front of the room with drawings and formulas. He began his speech by talking about the importance of the jet engine in modern society. At the end of twenty minutes, the instructor stopped him. He was approximately one-third of the way through the speech. He had hoped to explain the theoretical and practical applications of the jet engine to modern society, the mechanical operation and maintenance, and the opportunities the engine had for both commercial and military applications during the next fifteen years. If there ever was a case in which a speaker did a miserable job of narrowing a topic, this was it! Fred had not considered that his aim was too ambitious or that his topic was too broad.

A speech of approximately five minutes can explain adequately two or three main ideas at most. Clearly, you must narrow the subject so it can be covered adequately in the time available. As you narrow your topic, ask yourself these questions.

1. Have I stated, restated, explained, and supported each of my ideas?
2. Will listeners who have never heard about this subject understand me?
3. Are all my ideas clear and stated simply?
4. Thirty minutes after I finish, will my listeners be able to remember all of my main ideas and most of my examples?

Using these questions as a guide, refer to the list of categories for potential topics on pages 95 and 96. Let us assume you have decided to talk about "How Wine Is Aged in California Wineries." Obviously, this is a topic you could discuss for several days. Therefore, you have decided to use a specific winery as an example, in particular, the Robert Mondavi Winery in the Napa Valley. Does your audience know, geographically, where the Napa Valley is located? Or, do they even need to know that to understand the aging of wine? How much do you think you must tell them about how wine is made and about the composition of wine so they can understand the aging process? That is a crucial early decision you have to make because focusing on one part of the process may not leave you enough time to talk about the other adequately.

In fact, you might decide to change the focus of your speech. You might decide to speak about the gathering of grapes and their preparation for the aging process. Or, after analyzing your audience, you may believe it is safe to assume some basic audience knowledge about grape harvesting and handling. Here, as in all subjects, you have enormous possibilities. Your brainstorming and associations suggest many combinations.

Remember, as we pointed out in chapter 4, "Audience Analysis," that your audience listens to you with certain expectations. Are you fulfilling their expectations and adjusting to their predispositions as you narrow the topic? Things are getting complex! You are making many crucial decisions. You may have rearranged your topic or changed the general focus of your speech. Narrowing the topic can lead you in many different directions, but you should always have one idea clearly in mind: Is the topic narrow enough and adapted well enough to the audience for me to use it in my speech?

Narrowing the topic is like driving along a road and arriving at a fork in the highway. You must make a decision whether to choose the right or left. A bit farther along, you come to another fork and are faced with the same decision again. By asking questions about appropriateness, breadth, information, and attitudes, you can determine the proper direction in the topic narrowing phase.

Summary

Topic selection involves the generation of a large number of ideas through brainstorming, flexibility, and suspension of judgment. The effective speaker willingly considers ideas and examines all possible associated topics before tentatively settling upon one topic. Once a general topic has been identified, the narrowing process begins. Speakers must reduce the ideas to manageable size. Time, the breadth of the topic, plus the knowledge of the audience are significant factors. Audience analysis is a central element for successfully choosing and narrowing topics for public communication.

Key Terms

Appropriateness   *Innovative*
Brainstorming   *Jumping to conclusions*
Combinations   *Risk taking*
Conservative   *Suspension of*
Flexibility   *judgment*
Goals

Discussion Questions

1. Each of the following topics has at least one potential flaw that prevents it from being an appropriate or narrow enough topic for classroom use. Can you identify the flaw(s) in each?

   a. How money supply affects general public welfare.
   b. Examinations do not reliably indicate student knowledge of a topic.
   c. Driving while intoxicated should be punished by revoking the offender's license for life.
   d. Electrical engineers solve major problems in modern society.

2. Think of a topic that you might use for your next speech. What major strengths and weaknesses do you see in that choice? How could you narrow the subject so it could be more completely developed when you present it? Have you made it too narrow to appeal to your listeners, or is it *just right?*

3. Prepare a list of speeches you have heard by prominent people in the public arena. Which of those speeches seemed to ramble or included more material than the audience should have been exposed to at that time? How would you have narrowed the topic(s) to make them more appropriate for the situation? Be prepared to defend your choice in class.

1 The research on persuasion has generated enormous literature. The study of persuasion goes back more than twenty-three centuries. You probably could not read everything that was published in this broad field within this century, even if you studied nothing else for the remainder of your lifetime! Certainly, our discussion in chapter 13 only begins to scratch the surface.

2 For an interesting analysis of sequential messages as a persuasive strategy, *see* James P. Dillard, John E. Hunter, and Michael Burgoon, "Sequential-Request Persuasive Strategies: Meta-Analysis of Foot-in-the-Door and Door-in-the-Face," *Human Communication Research* 10(Summer 1984): 461–88.

3 Fredric M. Jablin, "Cultivating Imagination: Factors That Enhance and Inhibit Creativity in Brainstorming Groups," *Human Communication Research* 7 (Spring 1981): 245

4 Carl B. Holmberg, "The Pedagogy of Invention as the Architectonic Production of Communication and of Humanness," *Communication Education* 30 (July 1981): 233

5 Charles W. Kneupper, "A Modern Theory of Invention," *Communication Education* 32 (January 1983): 39–50

6 Adapted from Andrew D. Wolvin and Carolyn Gwynn Coakley, *Listening,* 2d ed. (Dubuque, Ia.: Wm. C. Brown Publishers, 1985), 102

7 Cal M. Logue, "An Exercise in Inventive Analysis," *Communication Education* 31 (April 1982): 149

8 H. Lloyd Goodall, Jr., and Christopher L. Waagen, *The Persuasive Presentation: A Practical Guide to Professional Communication in Organizations* (New York: Harper & Row Publishers, Inc., 1986), 15

Bormann, Ernest G., and Bormann, Nancy C. *Speech Communication: A Basic Approach,* 4th ed. New York: Harper & Row Publishers, Inc., 1986.
   This work is especially helpful in the development of innovative and effective topics for beginning speakers. The authors develop an effective relationship between the origination and developmental phases of the public message.
Buerkel-Rothfuss, Nancy. *Communication Competencies and Contexts.* New York: Random House, 1985.
   This work focuses on the interactional nature of communication variables. Its primary emphasis is on individual competence, and it stresses adaptive rather than *appropriate* communication.
Matson, Floyd W., and Montagu, Ashley, eds. *The Human Dialogue.* New York: The Free Press, 1967.
   This is the classic work on the study of human communication and oral interaction among humans. Its discussion ranges from the various roles of human speech in modern society to a philosophical examination of communication as dialogue. Any serious student of communication should have a copy of this book on his or her shelf.
Thomas, Stafford H. *Personal Skills in Public Speech.* Englewood Cliffs, N.J.: Prentice-Hall, Inc., 1985.
   This useful guidebook to major processes in the preparation and presentation of public messages is extremely specific and is written at an easy-to-understand level.

6 Organizing and Outlining a Speech

Outline

Objectives

After reading this chapter you should be able to:

1. Identify, explain, and use the following seven common patterns for organizing ideas for a speech:
   a. Time
   b. Space
   c. Problem to solution
   d. Cause to effect
   e. The natural divisions
   f. Induction and deduction
   g. The motivated sequence
2. Develop a planning outline using any of the above organizational patterns.
3. Develop a speaking outline from any planning outline.

PREVIEW

People usually organize ideas by time or space, by movement from problem to solution or from cause to effect, by resorting to the obvious branches of an idea that are suggested by the topic, by induction and deduction, and by a pattern called the motivated sequence. These organizational patterns have been shown to be very helpful and valuable in speech preparation.

You cannot realistically begin organizing your ideas until you have a fairly clear idea of your purpose and of the complexity of the ideas you want to organize. A planning outline will help you understand the relationships of the various parts of a speech, and a speaking outline will help you remember what you want to say, and also cue you to such things as when to refer to visual supporting materials.

"Wow! Dr. Feldman's lecture was fantastic this morning! He's really interesting and funny, too. Trouble is, later, I'm never quite sure how to round out my notes. Once I'm out of the lecture, the whole thing seems a blur. Just look at these notes. They're a jumble, and nothing seems to connect."

"Yea, I know," said her friend. "I tried to take notes for a while, but I finally gave up. I just couldn't follow that guy. I always had to spend a lot of time figuring out what his point was. How did you like the movie last night?"

The ability to organize ideas and the ability to evaluate the organization of others are two principal objectives of education. Unfortunately, we often do not or cannot manage it. As Dr. Feldman's two students implied that day, unless a speaker can organize ideas clearly and simply so listeners can follow, the members of the audience will give up trying.

The purpose of this chapter is to help you organize your ideas for speeches by presenting in a step-by-step fashion some of the best-known and most frequently used organizational strategies. In addition, we will suggest how you can outline a speech as a reliable planning technique and as a brief and useful speaking guide.

Methods of Organizing Ideas

The ability to organize ideas and the ability to evaluate the organizational patterns of others are critical skills in public speaking situations. These two abilities, if you actively cultivate them now, will serve you well for the rest of your life. How we go about organizing ideas appears to be an outgrowth of the way we understand reality and our relationships with each other. Conversely, the way we understand reality and our relationships with each other appears to be a function of how we organize ideas![1] In any case, careful and thoughtful organization of ideas is an essential part of the communication process, and it is especially important to individuals who speak to groups of other individuals.

The most commonly used organizational patterns for public speaking include: (1) time, (2) space, (3) problem to solution, (4) cause to effect, (5) the natural divisions of topics, (6) induction and deduction, and (7) the motivated sequence.

We usually think of time as a number of ticks that occur in a regular sequence. There are 60 seconds in a minute, 60 minutes in an hour, 24 hours in a day and so on. In fact, some people in our society are unable to think about time in any other way. They are accustomed to thinking about things as a history or time line of events. This chronological way of thinking about human events is one of our most common ways of organizing ideas because it provides a set of organization strategies that people can relate to easily and comfortably. For example, an individual may ask something like, "How do you do that?" The answer will probably be, "Well, first you. . ."

Time

Ask a little girl to tell you how she spent her day and she may say something like this:

> First I got up, then I went to the bathroom and took a shower and brushed my teeth. Then I combed my hair, got dressed, and went to school. I had to wait for the bus a long time, but it finally came. Then I went to my first class and the teacher talked about space. Then I went to recess. . . .

This little girl has organized events in a sequence from farthest to nearest in time. That is, she positioned herself in the present, then selected the most distant event that she determined was relevant to the request for information about her day. Chances are that this organizational pattern was helpful to her as well as to you in following through the important ideas.

This little girl could have used a time line in a variety of alternative ways for organizing her story about her day. She could have worked from present to future, or from the furthest future period that she felt was relevant backwards through time. She could have done so because she has a time line in her mind for use as a reference. For instance, she could have said something like this:

> Well, I just got home. But before that I had lunch with Billy. He had been quiet all day in school. At recess this afternoon he asked if he could carry my books. But during fifth period, he dunked my pigtail into his orange juice. This morning, right after we got to school, Billy was so quiet that he said almost nothing. That's it, except that I got up this morning and got ready. Boring.

In our society, the basic model of time strings events out in a line, or a series of clicks. Most of us feel we are bound to follow along the line, although as the girl did in this second example, we sometimes rearrange the sequence. Using the first example, the little girl could have worked up some other conceptualizations, too.

> *The Advent of Television*
>
> **DISCUSSION**
>
>   I. Television is older than you may think.
>   A. The first commercial television program was aired in 1939.
>   B. The first television coverage of a presidential election was in 1940.
>   1. Democratic national convention was televised.
>   2. Republican national convention was televised.
>   3. First telecast of election returns.
>   C. By 1948 there were 1 million TV sets in American homes.
>   II. Television boomed in the 1950s.
>   A. The first transcontinental TV broadcast was in 1951.
>   B. In 1955, President Eisenhower allowed TV into a presidential news conference for the first time.
>   C. By 1959 there were 36 million TV sets in American homes.
>   III. Television is here to stay.
>   A. In 1969 we had "live" coverage of the first man on the moon.
>   B. In 1980 TV helped Ronald Reagan establish a youthful and vigorous image.
>   C. In 1986 we had computer-assisted, laser-disk, interactive television-based educational systems.

FIGURE 6.1 Example from a Student Speech to Inform, Organized by Time.

I'm going to have a lovely day today. First I'll. . . .

The possibilities also include comparisons and contrasts among the past, present, and future. For instance, the little girl could have said:

> Today was wonderful, but yesterday was awful (and then proceeded to illustrate the differences by contrasting). Today it was sunny and warm, but yesterday it rained all day. Today I went to the park with my daddy, but yesterday I had to sit home and do homework.

Time is a very powerful tool in organizing many subjects; it provides a natural organizational pattern. Figure 6.1 displays a student outline for a speech about advances in communication technology. The outline clearly illustrates the use of time as an organizational pattern.

Space and Spatial Metaphor

Not only do people arrange their thinking according to time; they also arrange it according to spatial relationships.[2] The geographical, or spatial, mode of organization is ordering in terms of some physical or proximal relationship, such as from left to right or from near to far. To illustrate, suppose you asked the gas station attendant for directions. He might say:

> Drive south on Davis to Beech Street, then turn east and get on the Cross-town Expressway. Take the Expressway north for three miles. It's on the right-hand side. You can't miss it.

In this case, the organizational pattern is sequenced across space. It is based on some physical or proximal relationship assumption. Any spatial pattern can serve as the basis for geographical sequencing. You can move from side to side, from top to bottom, from outside to inside, from far to near, and so on.

Although there is a rich set of spatial relationships for every physical structure, we often overlook the potential for using metaphor of a physical structure as a means of arranging abstract ideas spatially.[3] To illustrate how the use of metaphor can help you organize a speech about the value of disciplined study habits, imagine an organizational pattern based on the metaphor of a house. The exterior would show how well the place is kept and the care with which the surrounding gardens are designed to provide the best possible "curb appeal." Compare these features to the external evidence of disciplined study habits: better grades, more free time to schedule other activities, and apparent self-confidence at testing time that comes from knowing the material.

Some of the rooms inside the house have specialized functions, while others serve more than one purpose. Could you find a way to equate the different room functions with the various ways of studying? For instance, the kitchen is a room for experimentation—for trial and error. The family room is a place where lively interaction takes place. The bedroom is a haven for rest, or for more intimate analysis and disclosure.

Allan Nakashima developed a spatial metaphor of a tool chest to describe his study of the general education requirement.

> The general education requirement is a lot like a tool chest. Each of the general areas—fine and performing arts, humanities, social sciences, physical sciences, and so forth—is like one drawer in that tool chest. If you pull open a drawer, you will find it to be divided into smaller spaces, and each space will include several useful tools. Of course, you may use some of the tools more than others, but if you want to be a competent person, you need them all.
>
> To get an idea of what you will find in the tool chest, pull open one of the drawers, the one marked Social Sciences. Here you will find anthropology, economics, geography, history, political science, psychology, and sociology.

Allan then developed the argument that each of these studies, like tools in the chest, is potentially useful for everyone, and that no matter how often the tool is used, the collection is incomplete without it.

Sometimes spatial arrangements and time arrangements overlap. For example, imagine trying to describe the trip suggested by the following map:

```
Cleveland                    Patterson                      New York
  X ----------------- X------------------ X ------------------ X ------------------ X
            Youngstown                          Jersey City
```

Supposing that you have driven from Cleveland to New York, name the towns in the order you passed through them. Clearly your list is both time ordered and space ordered. Sometimes these traditional modes of organization overlap, but not always.

A junior student provided another example of how space and time overlap. He wanted to explain to the class how to insulate a concrete slab floor—information he had acquired while working for his dad during summer recess. Notice that his organization of the sequence of steps is both spatial and temporal. Check his remarks against figure 6.2.

> In order to insulate a concrete slab floor, you have to figure out a way to lay down two layers of rigid foam insulation. The first step is to nail furring strips to the concrete. These should be ¾-by-2-inch wood strips, spaced on 16-inch centers, and they should follow the longest measurement of the room. (Here he displayed his first visual aid.)
>
> The second step is to cut and lay ¾-inch foam insulation with moisture-barrier side up between the furring strips (fig. 6.3). (Here he displayed and discussed a mechanical drawing as his second visual aid.)
>
> The third step is to install the second layer of insulation, and then a layer of ½-inch plywood as subflooring. Screw the subflooring into the furring strip (fig. 6.4).
>
> The last step is to top off the subflooring with any floor covering. You can lay either vinyl or carpet merely by spreading glue onto the plywood and laying down the material you have chosen. (Here he displayed a third drawing as a visual aid.)

In summary, space provides an easy-to-follow set of organizational patterns and strategies. When those patterns are displayed in two- or three-dimensional form, they create a sense of realism. They have value because they make it easy for a listener to relate to abstractions and to follow complex ideas.

Problem to Solution

There may be times when you will want to persuade an audience to adopt a proposal for change. That presents a very common speaking problem called persuasion, which is discussed in greater detail in chapters 9 and 13. Persuasion calls for a very powerful organizational pattern. Four such patterns have been used for hundreds of years because they are so effective. Notice that you do not have to use these patterns in their pure forms. In fact, you might find it appropriate to use them in a variety of combinations in your own speaking situations. Still, it is convenient and useful to describe these patterns as simply as possible. Remember that each is based on a relationship between problems and solutions.[4] Keep in mind, also, that the variations of this organizational pattern all assume that the speaker is making a proposal for some change (the solution) that is justified on the basis of some very serious harm that is inherent in the way things are done presently (the problem).

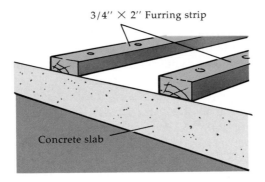

3/4″ × 2″ Furring strip

Concrete slab

FIGURE 6.2 The First Step in Insulating a Concrete Floor.

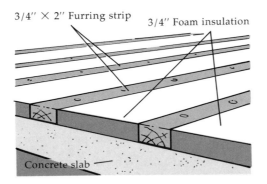

3/4″ × 2″ Furring strip   3/4″ Foam insulation

Concrete slab

FIGURE 6.3 The Second Step in Insulating a Concrete Floor.

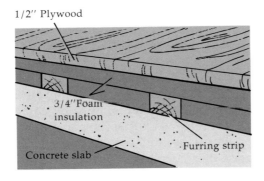

1/2″ Plywood

3/4″ Foam insulation

Furring strip

Concrete slab

FIGURE 6.4 The Third Step in Insulating a Concrete Floor.

1. *Need-plan.* You first develop a need in the minds of your listeners for the change you wish to propose, and then you describe the plan, showing how the plan meets the need.
2. *Plan-need.* In this case, you describe the proposal in detail, then show why the plan you have described is needed.
3. *Need-plan-advantages.* This problem-solution sequence adds a description of the advantages that will accrue to an audience if they accept the proposal.
4. *Comparative advantages.* While it is a variation of the problem-solution pattern, no particular problem is assumed. In this sequence you describe the proposal, then you explain that, while nothing is particularly wrong with what is happening presently, the proposal would bring certain advantages that cannot be obtained under the current situation, and that any one of those advantages would be enough to warrant the proposed change.

Let's examine each of these patterns of organization in greater detail.

Need-Plan

The need-plan pattern begins with the reasons why your audience should adopt your proposal.

> *Step 1.* Describe the problem in terms that the audience can relate to. Show the two or three most important parts of the problem.

To illustrate, refer to figure 6.5, which is a student-developed outline that follows the need-plan model. This outline shows that two important problems face the company because of the way the auto pool is being operated. First, record keeping is a burden to both the salespeople who use the cars, and to the staff members who run the auto pool. Second, the auto pool is losing money for the company because of inefficient and ineffective scheduling.

> *Step 2.* Show that the problem is serious.

The student argues that the problems create a truly large cash deficit. In addition, they cause poor morale among the salespeople. Finally, the problems damage customer relations: the salespeople find it difficult to make and keep their appointments and they cannot respond to short-notice service requests because they must first schedule the use of a company car.

> *Step 3.* Show that the problem is inherent in the present system.

Examine the student outline again. The argument is presented that the auto-pool system is to blame. An auto-pool system assumes that fewer cars used continuously will cost less than a greater number used infrequently. That assumption is the basis for operating the auto pool. But it does not take into account the realities of a salesperson's working life.

I. Our way of managing the auto pool is causing us problems. (*for*)
  A. The record-keeping system creates a burden. (*for*)
    1. Salespeople must remember to record every mile and destination. (*and*)
    2. They do not always do that. (*and*)
    3. Office staff must transpose the salespeople's records into the company record system. (*and*)
    4. This requirement creates an unnecessary duplication of effort. (*and*)
  B. The auto pool is losing money. (*for*)
    1. It is inefficient. (*for*)
      a. Errors are common. (*and*)
      b. Some cars sit idle. (*and*)
    2. It is ineffective. (*for*)
      a. Some salespeople can't always get a car. (*and*)
      b. Some cars sit idle. (*and*)
  C. The auto pool lowers morale among the salespeople. (*for*)
    1. Inefficiency creates unhappiness. (*and*)
    2. Ineffectiveness creates unhappiness. (*and*)
  D. The auto-pool system damages the company image with customers. (*for*)
    1. Salespeople find it difficult to maintain scheduled appointments. (*and*)
    2. Salespeople cannot respond to customer service requests on short notice. (*and*)
II. The auto-pool system is inherently to blame for these problems. (*for*)
  A. The system is based on an inappropriate assumption. (*for*)
    1. The assumption is that fewer cars, used continually, will be more cost effective than more cars used less frequently. (*and*)
    2. That assumption does not take into account the salesperson's needs. (*and*)
  B. The system was designed when the company was one-third its present size. (*therefore*)
III. The auto-pool system should be replaced with a better system. (*for*)
  A. Each existing car should be assigned to a salesperson. (*and*)
  B. Two new cars should be purchased and assigned. (*for*)
    1. This proposal would solve the problems described. (*and*)
    2. This proposal would be more cost effective than the auto-pool system.

FIGURE 6.5 Student Outline, Need-Plan Pattern.

Step 4. Describe the solution so that each part of the solution matches some part of the problem.

At this stage in the speech, the student proposed a one-to-one ratio of company cars to salespeople and attempted to show how such a proposal would solve the problems identified.

Step 5. Ask the audience to adopt your proposal.

In this step you make a simple request. For example: "There is truly a problem with the way we assign cars to our salesforce. The car-pool idea doesn't work. It damages morale. It damages our relationships with our customers. It inhibits our ability to provide service. And most important, it is creating a growing cash deficit because of lost sales and inefficient use of salespeople. What it saves in auto costs is insignificant compared to the costs. Won't you consider assigning a car to each salesperson?"

Plan-Need

The plan-need pattern merely reverses the order of the need-plan presentation. That is, you begin the speech by describing the solution you want the audience to accept, and then develop the need case—the set of problems that seem to warrant the proposals you are making. The burden of proof does not change for the speaker, but the organizational strategy may change the nature of audience perception of the ideas and arguments. You might wonder why anyone would want to describe a solution to a problem before the problem is developed. If your plan is simple but the need is complex, it is probably better to pull the plan to the first part of the speech. On the other hand, if the problem is simple and obvious and the plan is complex, or if the problem and the plan are about equally complex, it is probably more advantageous to develop the need first and follow with the plan.

Need-Plan-Advantages

An organizational pattern that includes need, plan, and advantages will be essentially similar to a need-plan pattern, with an added statement of advantages that will accrue from adopting the proposal. In this case you would probably want to follow the first four steps described under our discussion of need-plan, and then tack on the following three items in the order given.

Step 5. Claim that adoption of the proposal will generate certain significant benefits that are not currently available, and that any one of the advantages would justify adoption of the proposal.
Step 6. Develop and prove each advantage.
Step 7. Ask the audience to adopt the proposal.

Comparative Advantages

The comparative advantages sequence is a special organizational variation of the problem-solution pattern. In this pattern you describe your proposal, then argue that the proposal will generate certain advantages that are not available under the present situation, and that these advantages justify the proposed change.

IV. Adoption of this plan will accrue in advantages that we cannot realize from the present system. (*for*)
   A. Morale will increase. (*for*)
      1. Salespeople will have instant access to needed transportation. (*and*)
      2. Sales will increase. (*for*)
         a. reason or evidence (*and*)
         b. reason or evidence (*and*)
   B. Increased morale, by itself, would justify the proposed changes. (*for*)
      1. Happier salespeople are more likely to be successful salespeople. (*for*)
         a. reason or evidence (*and*)
         b. reason or evidence (*and*)
      2. Turnover would decrease sharply.

FIGURE 6.6 Outline of Advantages Portion of a Need-Plan-Advantages Organizational Pattern.

In a speech to faculty members involved in a "writing across the curriculum" conference, one participant used the comparative advantage format to argue that students should be required to pass a writing proficiency test before entering the upper division (junior and senior standing). He had a simple proposal and a clearly described set of advantages. The following is a very close approximation of the professor's remarks. It provides a clear example of the comparative advantages organizational pattern.

> If our goal is to assure that every graduate be a competent writer, then it seems to me that we cannot leave the job to our colleagues from the English department. They do a fine job, but they cannot do it alone. They need our help.
>
> But I have heard, and so have you, the arguments of faculty from many disciplines that they don't have time to teach writing; they barely have enough time to teach their own disciplines.
>
> I think we may not understand what really makes a difference in getting students to write better. Right now they don't think it's important. We all tell them that writing is important, but only a very few of the faculty outside the English department make effective writing a condition for getting grades. So the students don't believe it is important.
>
> Don't get me wrong. I think the English department is doing a fine job. But the job is larger than they can handle. To change all this, I offer a simple proposal. I propose that every student be required to pass a writing proficiency examination as a condition of entry into the junior year. The members of the English department have agreed to develop such a test, and to score it.

The advantages of this proposal are these. First, every student would know that he or she must learn to write in order to graduate. Thus, effective writing would seem important. Second, every member of the faculty would suddenly take a new interest in writing. This would result in a much clearer statement to students that writing is important. Indeed, you might say that every member of the faculty would become a writing teacher, since it would be in their own interests to become so. Without upper-division students, there can be no upper-division classes.

Cause to Effect

Sometimes neither time, space, nor problem-solution patterns seem applicable approaches for what you want to present. A very common way of thinking in our culture, and therefore an excellent organizational method, is to follow the cause-to-effect pattern. In this pattern you trace a link between antecedent conditions and their consequences. Thus, the cause-effect pattern is particularly effective when you want an audience to see that one set of conditions is responsible for another set of conditions.

In most uses of causal sequences, the speaker's specific purpose is to urge elimination of conditions that cause some undesirable effect(s). So, cause-to-effect ordering can be very useful when the persuasive problem is to convince the audience that perhaps:

1. The effects are really undesirable.
2. The causes are really responsible for those effects.
3. Elimination of causal conditions will not produce other equally undesirable effects.

Now let us look at a few statements that are based on cause-to-effect reasoning. Suppose you hear someone say: "I see you are still smoking. You better be careful. That habit is dangerous to your health." This is a clear example of cause-effect. You might hear this sentence. "If alcoholics are sick, let's help them. But first, let's get them off the roads." This argument clearly implies a cause-to-effect relationship. The cause is drinking, and the undesirable effects are drunk driving and the ramifications of drunk driving. Try a third one. You might hear a company advertisement on television admonishing you to "Live better, electrically." If you examine the statement, you will see a cause-effect pattern. The cause is electrical appliances, and the conveniences of electric power. The effect is better living. The quality of life portrayed in the commercial is related to the presence and function of electrical appliances—light bulbs, television sets, microwave ovens, computers.

Cause-effect arguments may be arranged in a variety of different ways. Figure 6.7 indicates some of the possibilities.

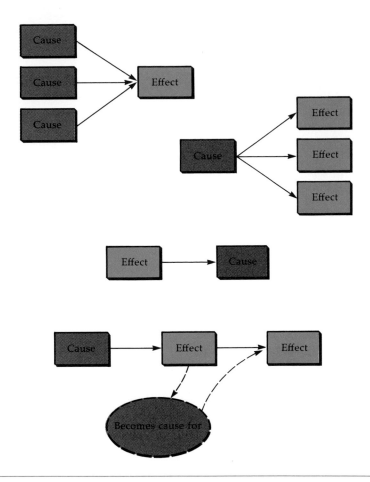

FIGURE 6.7 Four Variations of the Cause-Effect Pattern.

Natural Divisions

Sometimes the natural features of a subject suggest a method for dividing it into manageable units. This approach is sometimes called *the method of topics.* You may be more comfortable with this approach than with any other organizational pattern.

If you consider how people put their worlds together, you will soon see the value of the natural divisions of topics as an organizational strategy. People tend to think of things in terms of how the parts are related. This is especially true of physical things and of conceptualizations that have no referent in the concrete world. For example, we think in terms of the component parts of a person. She has arms and legs, bones and muscles, and a nervous system. These are tangible, physical, features. She also has a personality; she has wit, intelligence, and style. We think of these intangible features as parts, even though they do not refer to physical components of the person. While there is, in fact, a physical object called an arm, there is no physical object called intelligence.

Similarly, it is sensible to organize a large corporation into components. Those components, like the components of the person, sometimes refer to physical aspects, and sometimes to conceptual phenomena. You can arrange the operations component and separate it, in your mind, from the marketing component. You can also arrange the components of a corporation according to buildings and equipment and personnel.

The point we are making is that we categorize things according to natural divisions or topics, so it is useful to organize our ideas according to those same natural divisions or topics. To illustrate, human beings can be subdivided into men, women, boys, and girls, and into a multitude of other subgroupings. Sometimes your subject matter can easily be divided based upon your concerns and worries—for example, the good news and the bad news.

When subject matter seems to suggest logical and convenient lines of division, they constitute a very easy-to-use organizational pattern. Perhaps that is why you find the natural divisions so often used as an organizational method. For example, suppose you wanted to talk about the effects running a marathon has on the body. It would make sense to divide the analysis into the effects on the various bodily systems—cardiovascular, respiratory, musculoskeletal, digestive, and the like. Of course you would have more to say about effects on the cardiovascular system than on the digestive system, but the major divisions of the speech would be suggested by the widely-accepted division of the body into its major systems.

Induction and Deduction

The logical patterns of induction and deduction, which are two common ways that we think, provide still another method for organizing ideas for a public speech. *Induction* can be defined as a pattern of thinking that moves from specific details to a general conclusion. *Deduction* works the other way; it begins with a general conclusion and then draws specific instances from that general conclusion.

About the easiest way we can illustrate the difference between induction and deduction is to ask you to imagine an old-fashioned wagon wheel (fig. 6.8). Let the hub of the wheel represent the generalization, and the spokes represent the specific instances. Thus, when you work from the outside in toward the hub, you are working through the specific instances toward the generalization; you are working inductively. That provides a neat mnemonic device: Induction—from specific instances *IN* toward the generalization.

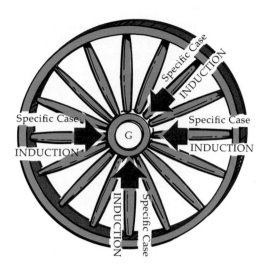

FIGURE 6.8 Induction and Deduction. *IN*duction works from the specific cases *IN*. Deduction works from the generalization (G) to the specific cases.

One student decided to use the inductive pattern of organization in a speech designed to get the audience to contribute to a food drive for the needy at Thanksgiving.

> Today I would like you to meet some people who live not far from here. Mrs. Johnston, a forty-three-year-old single parent, is trying to support her kids on what she can earn as a janitor. She has no education to speak of; and although she wants very much to remain independent of the welfare program, she is right on the borderline. So she has recently taken on a second job—a second building to clean. She does that after hours, when she might otherwise be home with her children.

The student developed this specific case and then moved to a second and a third:

> Tommy Willson is sixteen. He has had a job since he was nine, attending a paper stand on the corner of Davis and Government Streets. Of course, there is nothing very unusual about a kid with a paper route, except in this case, Tommy was earning about one-fourth of the family income! He dropped out of school as soon as he could, so that he could get a better job and make more money than he could as a part-time worker while he was going to school.

These individual cases led directly to the conclusion that a number of local families needed help in order to have an adequate Thanksgiving dinner. As a result of that speech, the student raised about seventy dollars.

Deductive thinking works the other way around. Here you begin with the general conclusion, and then point to specific instances that illustrate or prove the general conclusion. For example, one student began her speech to stimulate action with the question, "How long must we wait before the CIA involvement in Latin America gets us into another war? That certainly will happen if CIA activities are not curtailed." Then she developed three separate instances of CIA involvement that she believed were war-threatening.

Induction and deduction can be very powerful organizational patterns if they are used wisely.[5] The primary question then is, under what circumstances should you use them? Use induction when you want to build up suspense, or when the details are the primary issues you want to discuss. If your analysis shows that your listeners have the big picture already, you can use induction to ask them to work with you toward a conclusion. There are instances also when the reasoning process requires the use of induction, particularly when the conclusion you want to draw has the potential for controversy. In that case, motivate the listeners with a specific instance added to another specific instance as you lead them, inductively, to the conclusion.

Use deduction as an organizational strategy when your listeners do not know much about the subject matter and would, therefore, be unable to tie the supporting details together on their own. To illustrate, a student used the deductive pattern in a speech to inform. She was saying that she was skeptical of progress; that while many benefits had accrued, nevertheless, we were paying too high a price.

> Progress may not be our most important product. Oh yes, we have many wonderful advantages that our parents, and their parents, did not have—advances in health, and advances in transportation and communication. We have advantages in food storage and preparation that earlier generations never dreamed were possible. And, thanks to the industrial revolution of the last century and to the evolution of technology during this century, we can go to the store and buy almost anything we ever imagined wanting.
>
> But even so, we are paying an awful price, and most people don't even think about it. Progress is not our most important product. Pollution is.

At this point the student developed the idea that pollution is a growing problem, and she illustrated the problem with facts and figures about Mobile Bay, about national use of Alabama clay pits to dump hazardous wastes, and about a growing inability to dispose of potentially disasterous toxic materials at the national and international levels.

Induction, working from specific to general, and deduction, working from general to specific, are common thinking patterns. They provide a useful way to approach organizing ideas.

Shirley MacLaine

As the star of numerous films and stage performances, Shirley MacLaine easily communicated her feelings to large audiences. When asked to perform as a public speaker, however, her reactions were initially quite different. In her book, DANCING IN THE LIGHT, she describes how she successfully coped with the situation.

There were many times, over the course of my life, when I was asked to be a public speaker. Either to accept an award or to be a keynote speaker at a political rally. Public speaking terrified me. I always felt the need to have a prepared text to refer to. Either I would write the speech or a professional speech writer would do it for me. I couldn't feel comfortable doing it spontaneously. This discomfort began to ebb away too. I began to work only with an outlined idea in my head. If I carried notes with me, I found that little by little I didn't bother referring to them. I realized that it was what I was feeling that communicated to the audience more than the words anyway. The words, frankly, got in the way if I was in sync with my feelings. A pause or a decision-making moment was infinitely more effective than the studied intellectual twist of a well-planned phrase. Again, I was learning to trust in the moment and with my affirmation. My higher self was my guide.

Source: MacLaine, Shirley, Dancing in the Light. Copyright © 1985 Bantam Books, Inc., New York, NY. All Rights Reserved.

During the mid-1930s, Alan H. Monroe developed a pattern for organizing persuasive speeches that has been very influential over the years.[6] Most of the people who are now teaching college-level speech courses had to commit the motivated sequence to memory. It is a method that works because, like the others, it follows a predictable pattern of thinking that is common in our society. The motivated sequence has five steps.

Step 1. Attention Step

This step is designed to gain the interest of the listeners. The response you want from your listeners at this point is something like: "I really want to listen to this person." Suppose, for example, that you and other business leaders have been called to talk to a town meeting about the need to maintain adequate rail transportation. You think rail transportation is vitally important, but you are scheduled to speak last. Suppose further that the speakers have been addressing the audience from behind a lectern in order to use the microphone for about thirty-five minutes, and the audience is getting restless. Your greatest challenge may be to get their attention.

The Motivated Sequence

Victor Kiam

The president of Remington Products has been seen recently on television as a pitchman for his company's brand of electric shavers. As a successful entrepreneur, Kiam has had to communicate to a variety of people in a variety of situations. His advice for effective public speaking boils down to a few do's and don'ts.

I don't use notes and I don't try to memorize speeches word for word. I *do* draw up and commit to memory a specific outline for my speech and refer to it whenever I feel I'm starting to stray from the subject. I approach the speech as I would a conversation. If you use this approach, you'll also give the impression of having a hands-on knowledge of the subject you're addressing. Furthermore, once you've cast off the shackles of the neatly typed speech, you'll find your natural enthusiasm for the subject at hand is given free rein and will lend an energy to your words that might otherwise be lost.

Source: Kiam, Victor, Going for It! How to Succeed as an Entrepreneur. *Copyright © 1986 William Morrow & Co., Inc., New York, NY. All Rights Reserved.*

The point is that the first step in the motivated sequence is to get the attention of the listeners. There are numerous ways that you can do that. Factors such as movement, potency, contrast, and so forth can all contribute to listener attention. In chapter 7, some factors of attention will be discussed in detail.

Step 2. Need Step

The need step is used for developing or describing some problem, or for demonstrating that the audience has a need for the speech you are about to give. The attempt is to move the audience to the position that they have a reason to listen to you. "I need this information." "Something needs to be done." "More people need to feel this way."

You can develop a need in your listeners by tying the subject matter to something that matters to them. For instance, students sometimes complain about the difficulty of an examination. If the strategy is merely to complain, or is perceived by the instructor as merely a complaint, change is unlikely. But if the students can cause the instructor to identify with the problem, change is more likely to occur. For example, if the instructor comes to believe that the test is unfair or that it reflects badly on the instructor or that it damages the student-instructor relationship, and if such an issue matters to the instructor, then he or she might reevaluate the test.

One sales representative, working on her speaking skills in a continuing education seminar, presented a highly detailed and jargon-filled speech about the ink-taking capabilities of a certain grade of paper. The people in that audience were sales representatives for a large paper company. Even though the speech was not well developed and was full of jargon, this speaker had hooked into the interests of the audience. They needed her information, because they realized that the information could help them to sell paper. They knew instantly that the speech mattered, and so the speech was a booming success. It did not matter that the speech was badly delivered; that the speaker was nervous, note-bound, and somewhat negative; that she forgot her place; and that she spoke in an almost monotone voice. Those sales representatives asked questions, got involved in the speech, took notes, asked for repetitions, and elicited further explanation.

The need step, then, must tie the speech to the interests and attitude/ belief structures of the listeners. If the speech does that, the listeners are ready for the next step. If it fails at this step, the listeners will probably tune out the speaker.

Step 3. The Satisfaction Step

The third step in the motivated sequence is designed to present a solution to some problem. In other words, the purpose is to show how the problems identified in the need step may be solved. The goal of the satisfaction step is to get the audience members to think: "This is what I believe!" "This is what should be done." "This information is useful to me personally, so I had better listen."

Step 4. The Visualization Step

The purpose of the visualization step is to develop within your listeners an image of the consequences of their choices. If you want them to adopt some policy, for example, you would develop an image of the future that would evolve from adoption of the policy. You could also develop an image of the future if the policy were not adopted.

In the following speech excerpt, Tyrone Adams calls for a return to more traditional sex roles for men and women. He claims that the breakdown of the American family system is due to a blurring of traditional sex roles. Whatever your thoughts about his position, you will agree that Tyrone's speech provides a vivid example of the visualization step!

> If we don't return to more appropriate sex roles for men and women in America, things will only get worse. Imagine, if you can, a whole city of homes full of children whose mothers aren't waiting for them when they come home from school because they're working on their careers. These children will be on their own, supervised, if at all, by hired men who are paying more attention to the sports network on

In persuasive speaking, the motivated sequence is a powerful and effective organizational tool, provided each step is satisfactorily completed before proceeding to the next step.

TV than to what the children are doing. The houses won't get cleaned up, the kids won't study, and the family will eat its TV dinners every night from the microwave. In one generation, or two, we will have lost the benefits of hundreds of years of civilization.

Step 5. The Action Step

The action step of the motivated sequence aims at getting the audience to accept a proposal or to approve the speaker. The goal is to get the listeners to say: "I will do as you ask." "I believe you." "I feel very strongly about this." It need not be a long section; often, just a few words will do. For example, a woman at a rally promoting stricter drunk-driving laws said, simply:

> I have shown you the problem and what you can do about it. But, ladies and gentlemen, the problem will not solve itself. The Senate will not know your views if you don't tell them. You must act, and act now. Won't you please just sign these letters (handing out copies of a letter to the Senators from her state) and send them today? All it will cost you is two signatures and two stamps. Thank you.

In summary, then, we have said that people in our society tend to think and to organize their ideas in certain predictable ways. These natural ways of thinking provide the means by which you can best organize a speech. We described seven of these common thinking patterns and suggested particular strategies for using them.

Outlining the Speech

Once you have chosen an organizational pattern that makes sense, you are ready to develop an outline. There are many ways to outline ideas, of course. For example, some people prefer full-sentence outlines, others prefer topic outlines, and still others prefer to make no outline at all.[7] Some speakers have reported that they plan and prepare their ideas and work out the details of organization before they prepare an outline. They then use the outline as a means of checking the organizational structure for weaknesses or omissions. As you gain experience, you will evolve a system that works best for you. For now, let us consider two kinds of outlines: the planning outline and the speaking outline.

The Planning Outline

A planning outline serves to help you organize your ideas and plan how the various parts of your speech—the main ideas, the supporting arguments, the evidence, and so forth—will fit together. In almost every case of speech making, your planning outline will be structured the same. It will have an introduction, a body, and a conclusion. Each of these segments of your outline will contribute its own special functions. Together, they will constitute the structure of what you will say, and the principal tool for viewing that structure and making corrections when they seem warranted.

Of course, we all have our own individual preferences. Your instructor, too, will have preferences about what should be included in a planning outline, and you should check to make sure you are following those preferences, especially those regarding format.

At this point you should be ready to put it all together. To help you do this, we offer several suggestions that have been helpful for many years.[8]

1. *Write the specific purpose.* Write out the sentence we suggested in chapter 4: "After hearing this speech, I want my audience to. . . ." Complete the sentence in terms of some behavior that you will be able to observe, and then check to make certain that the sentence does not include a connecting term, such as *and* or *but*, or some other conjunction that tends to create problems with focus. You should have a single, specific purpose—not two or more. This strategy also provides you a way of checking how well your speech moves toward that purpose.

	A True Christmas Gift INTRODUCTION
Grabber:	As I drove here today, I was struck by the evidence of wealth that surrounds us just before Christmas. People were rushing about doing their last-minute shopping, arms filled with packages. We are told by the Downtown Merchant's Association that this is going to be a record-breaking year in retail sales. But not everyone in this county is so lucky.
Thesis (central idea):	Today, within just a few miles of where we sit, there are people who desperately need our help if they are going to have any Christmas at all.
Preview:	I am going to ask you to make a Christmas gift before you leave this room—a gift of caring that will do more good than all of those presents you will place under your own Christmas tree.
Transition:	But first, I would like to tell you a true story.

FIGURE 6.9 A Sample Introduction Showing the Parts.

2. *Label the parts.* Identify the introduction, the discussion, and the conclusion. Each of these labels should appear prominently in your outline. Some instructors prefer that they appear centered on the page, while others prefer that they be aligned on the left-hand margin. Be consistent, whatever you do. We will have more to say about introductions and conclusions in chapter 7, "Beginning and Ending a Speech," but for now, we want to focus your attention on how to outline them. Refer to figure 6.9 as we proceed.

Under the centered label *INTRODUCTION*, you might include the following subtitles. The *grabber* is designed to draw the audience's attention quickly, such as a startling statement of opinion, or a reference to some common experience of the audience. The *thesis statement* is a sentence that you make to the audience. It tells the audience what you want from them or what you plan to discuss.

Sometimes you will include a *preview*, a brief description of your analysis, or the main ideas. It is included to provide a quick overview for your listeners. They might need this help, especially for complex or controversial speeches, in order to follow you. A *transition* is a sentence or two designed to move the listeners smoothly from the introduction to the discussion. It might be something as simple as: "So, let's consider the first part of the problem we are facing. We don't have enough space to do what we are supposed to do." In this little example, the first sentence is the transition, and the second sentence is the first main idea in the discussion!

CONCLUSION

Summary: So what have we seen?
  I. A serious unemployment problem exists in this city.
  II. The problem is due to restrictive hiring practices and to contractors who bring in their own workers from out of state.
  III. Proposal: A labor protection ordinance should be passed by the City Council.
  IV. We need your support to pressure the Council.

Kicker: Twelve percent of the able-bodied workers in this town—representing over a thousand families—need your help, and they need it now.

Thank you.

FIGURE 6.10 A Sample Conclusion Showing the Parts.

Refer to figure 6.10 as we proceed. Under the centered label *CONCLUSION,* you might include the following subtitles. The *summary* is a brief recapitulation of the main ideas that you developed in the speech. The *kicker* is a statement designed to focus the thinking and the feelings of your listeners on what you have said, or on what you want them to do. You can read more about how to prepare these parts in chapter 7.

3. *Use a standard outline format.* Separate the body from the introduction by centering the word *DISCUSSION* on the page in all caps. Typically, you will identify superior and subordinate relationships among your ideas with a standard set of symbols. Identify the main points of your speech with Roman numerals, and the subpoints with capital letters or Arabic numerals. Of course, indent each level consistently to prevent confusion as you flesh out your ideas. There is no theoretical limit to how many levels of subpoints you should have, but common sense tells you not to go much further than four indentations. Figure 6.11 illustrates one standard set of symbols and a consistent indention pattern. You can see, immediately, how the parts fit together—which ones are equal in weight and which are subordinate.

4. *Use complete sentences.* If you compare the two sample outlines shown in figure 6.12, you will quickly see the advantages of committing yourself to complete sentences in your planning outline. Too often our students merely write topics and phrases. While this might be suitable for speaking notes, it does not force you to be crystal clear about your ideas and how they are related. In planning, clarity may be the most important factor governing your success.

```
                    DISCUSSION
       I. Main Idea
          A. First subpoint
             1. First sub-subpoint
                a. Supporting detail
                b. Supporting detail
             2. Second sub-subpoint
          B. Second subpoint
       Transition:
       II. Main Idea
          A. First subpoint
             1. First sub-subpoint
                a. Supporting detail
                b. Supporting detail
             2. Second sub-subpoint
          B. Second subpoint
```

FIGURE 6.11 A Standard Outline Symbol and Indention Pattern.

DISCUSSION	DISCUSSION
I. White light contains three primary colors. (*for*)	Three primary colors
A. Blue is a primary color.	blue
B. Green is a primary color.	green
C. Red is a primary color.	red
II. The human eye contains three receptors, each sensitive to one of the primary colors.	Receptors
A. sentence.	name of receptor
B. sentence.	name of receptor
C. sentence.	name of receptor
III. White light reflected from a screen stimulates the appropriate receptors, which send impulses to the brain.	Sequence light—reflector— receptor—impulse
A. development	Brain recreates
B. development	
IV. Brain recreates the scene from transmitted impulses.	

FIGURE 6.12 A Planning Outline and A Speaking Outline Compared.

5. *Write out transitions.* Moving from one segment to the next in a speech, and from one major idea to another, often presents a problem to even the most experienced speakers. Writing out transitional materials and identifying them clearly, as a planning technique, will help you focus your attention on how the various parts fit together.

Transitional materials are not usually part of the standard outline style you are using. Instead, go to the left-hand margin and write the word *transition.* Here is a sample transition from a student outline. Notice that this student used an internal summary to make the transition:

Transition: So now you have seen how the operations division works. It includes a production section with three departments, and a finance section with two departments. Now, let's look at the marketing division.

6. *Include bibliographical materials.* Most instructors will want you to follow a certain format for submitting bibliographical information, so be sure to check this out with your instructor. In any case, your bibliography will include the resource materials to which you referred when you prepared your speech. This would include, also, any interviews you might have conducted as part of your research. We suggest that you learn a standard form, or style sheet, and get into the habit of using it every time. You can look at "Using the Library" at the end of this book for more information on conducting and recording research.

7. *Develop a title.* Some speeches may not require a title—for example, remarks to a decision-making group to which you belong. At other times, and especially when you are invited to give a speech as part of a formal program, you will want to have a title. In these cases, develop a title that meets the following criteria:
   a. Does the title point to the main ideas of the speech?
   b. Does the title attract attention and interest?
   c. Is the title brief?

We have said that an organizational pattern may not be clear unless it is supported by a planning outline. Professor Feldman, whose lecture the students talked about at the beginning of this chapter, may have had a clear idea of the organization of his ideas, but he failed to structure those ideas in a manner that was obvious to his students. Close attention to a planning outline will help you to structure your speeches so that the organization will be clear to the audience. The time and energy you invest in early planning will earn rich dividends as you present your speech.

The Speaking Outline

A speaking outline is much briefer than a planning outline. Its purpose is to provide you with notes you can refer to as you speak. A speaking outline should be a very brief outline of the topics you will discuss. These topics should not be developed in any way. Here are some pointers that might help you write a speaking outline.

Senator John C. Danforth

The senior senator from Missouri provides a few insights into his methods for delivering clear and succinct speeches. His thoughts are taken from a personal letter to one of the authors.

The vast majority of my speeches are extemporaneous. I have found that the quality of my extemporaneous speeches is in inverse proportion to the length of my notes. When my notes are too elaborate, I tend to rely too much on deciphering what I have jotted down, and too little on putting my message across to the audience. Therefore, the best approach for me is to write out three to six Roman numeraled points, each with maybe three subpoints. The more I rely on thinking on my feet, the more power is in the message. . . .

To me, simplicity and clarity are far more important than poetic eloquence. One reason I like giving extemporaneous speeches is that, in looking at the audience, I can judge whether my remarks are understood, and restate ideas which, I feel, are not clear.

Source: John C. Danforth, United States Senator from Missouri.

1. *Follow the planning outline.* Use the same standard set of symbols and the same indention pattern that you used in your planning outline. If you alter the pattern, you run some risk of confusing yourself. That could have adverse consequences while you are giving the speech.
2. *Be brief.* Since the purpose of the speaking outline is to jog your memory, you should not need more than a few words. If your outline is too detailed, you may spend too much time looking at the outline and not enough time looking at the audience. So make your speaking outline as brief as possible.
3. *Make the speaking outline a working tool.* The speaking outline is a good place for you to make marginal notes about things you want to remember (fig. 6.13). Perhaps you have just met a member of the audience and you want to call her name during the speech. Do not leave her name to memory alone. You can print it in the margin of the speaking outline at the appropriate place. Similarly, suppose you have several visual aids that you want to show. A marginal note, or sketch, at the appropriate place in the outline will help you remember when to use the visual aids.

The value of carefully developed outlines can hardly be overemphasized. The stronger you make the internal structure of the speech, the stronger the speech will be. The more clearly your ideas are related to each

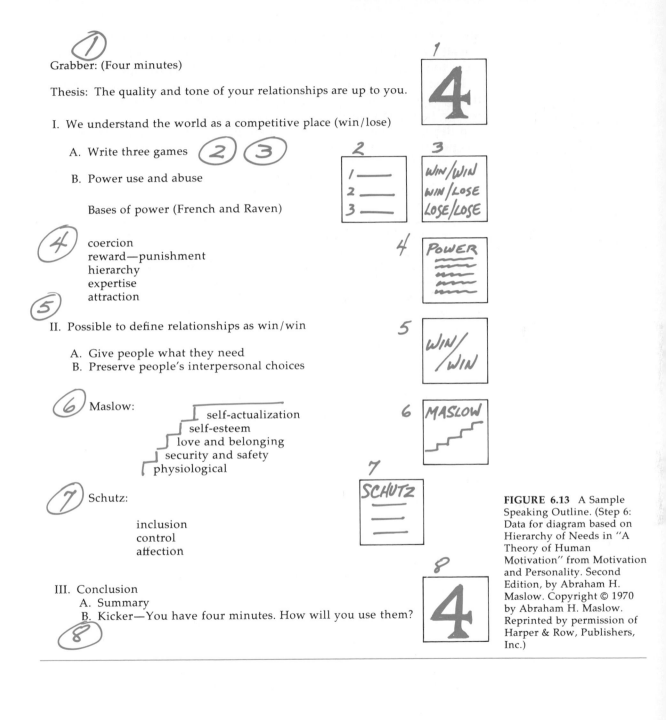

Grabber: (Four minutes)

Thesis: The quality and tone of your relationships are up to you.

I. We understand the world as a competitive place (win/lose)

　A. Write three games

　B. Power use and abuse

　　Bases of power (French and Raven)

　　coercion
　　reward—punishment
　　hierarchy
　　expertise
　　attraction

II. Possible to define relationships as win/win

　A. Give people what they need
　B. Preserve people's interpersonal choices

Maslow:　self-actualization
　　　　　self-esteem
　　　　　love and belonging
　　　　　security and safety
　　　　　physiological

Schutz:

　　inclusion
　　control
　　affection

III. Conclusion
　A. Summary
　B. Kicker—You have four minutes. How will you use them?

FIGURE 6.13 A Sample Speaking Outline. (Step 6: Data for diagram based on Hierarchy of Needs in "A Theory of Human Motivation" from Motivation and Personality. Second Edition, by Abraham H. Maslow. Copyright © 1970 by Abraham H. Maslow. Reprinted by permission of Harper & Row, Publishers, Inc.)

other, the more easily your audience will follow them. When your purpose is well focused, and when your ideas drive toward the purpose, you are far more likely to experience success when you deliver the speech.

In some sense, your outline is like a road map. You would not think of trying to drive cross-country to a place you have never been without referring to a road map. To a large extent, the ease and convenience of that trip depends upon the clarity and simplicity of the road map. You can imagine that you might very well get lost if you had no map at all.

Summary

The ability to organize ideas is a principal objective of education. That objective includes the ability to design appropriate organizational patterns and to identify the organizational patterns someone else uses. The best-known and most frequently used organizational strategies include time patterns, spatial patterns, problem-to-solution patterns, cause-to-effect patterns, the natural divisions of topics, induction and deduction, and the motivated sequence. These patterns work because each one follows a common way of thinking among fluent speakers of English.

Outlines are useful tools in planning and delivering a speech. A planning outline helps in determining the organizational sequence that makes the most sense for presenting a particular topic to a given audience. It is more detailed than the speaking outline, since it not only labels the main parts, but it also describes subpoints and shows relationships between major ideas. A speaking outline assists the speaker while delivering the speech. It is much briefer than a planning outline because its purpose is only to provide cues that will help the speaker stay on track during the speech.

Key Terms

Cause-effect	*Method of topics*	*Space*
Deduction	*Motivated sequence*	*Speaking outline*
Induction	*Planning outline*	*Time*

Discussion Questions

1. Describe to a group of your classmates how to get from your present location to your home. What organizational pattern did you use? Did you use it successfully? Ask your group to share with you their feelings about your success or lack of success. How might you have made the directions easier?

2. With a group, or the class, identify a course and a professor that you particularly enjoy. Can you find elements of how the professor has organized the course materials? What can you learn from this exercise that you can include in your own speaking?

3. Do you outline before you write? How do your classmates approach this problem? Often, people pattern their ideas in their heads, write the essay, and then make the outline. What are the advantages and disadvantages of this approach?

1 The literature is full of concern about what organizational and analytical skills are essential classroom subject matter. Jean Piaget, and his students, published well over five-hundred studies, about two-hundred of which have been translated into English. For a bibliography, *see* John L. Phillips, Jr., *The Origins of Intellect: Piaget's Theory* (San Francisco: W. H. Freeman and Company, 1969), 133–44. Over thirty years ago, Piaget wrote that organization is a central phenomenon in human cognitive behavior. *See* Jean Piaget, *The Origins of Intelligence in Children* (New York: International Universities Press, Inc., 1952), 7–8. Or, *see SCA Guidelines for Minimal Competencies in Speaking and Listening for High School Graduates* (Falls Church, Virginia,: Speech Communication Association, n.d.), a brochure that was provided to every state Department of Public Instruction by the Speech Communication Association.

2 Norman Geschwind, "Specializations of the Human Brain" *The Brain* (San Francisco: W. H. Freeman and Company, 1979), 108–17.

3 For an excellent development of this idea, *see* Philip Wheelwright, *Metaphor and Reality*. (Bloomington, Indiana: Indiana University Press, 1964). Chapter 2 is especially relevant.

4 We participated in academic debating as undergraduates and then coached academic debating at the college level. Our suggestions for this section on problem-solution patterns are drawn from that experience.

5 Some interesting research has recently been conducted to test the relative potency of inductively and deductively derived lists of compliance-gaining strategies. The results appear inconclusive. *See* Franklin J. Boster, James B. Stiff, and Rodney A. Reynolds, "Do Persons Respond Differently to Inductively-Derived and Deductively-Derived Lists of Compliance-Gaining Message Strategies? A Reply to Wiseman and Schenck-Hamlin." *The Western Journal of Speech Communication* 49 (Summer 1985): 177–87.

6 Alan H. Monroe. *Principles and Types of Speech* (Chicago: Scott, Foresman and Company, 1935).

7 While many people claim they do not outline, they probably do so, in effect, in spite of what they claim. They organize the materials into some sensible pattern in their heads and carry the pattern with them as they speak or write. This method is not recommended for beginning public speakers!

8 These suggestions are not original with us. You will find them in one form or another in nearly every textbook on public speaking.

Bruner, Jerome. S., Joodnow, Jacqueline J., and Austin, George A. *A Study of Thinking*. New York: John Wiley and Sons, Inc., 1956.
   The authors of this classic work in learning theory argue that organizational skill is one of the most basic and most general forms of cognition, and is fundamental to the thinking process.
Crescimanno, Russell. *Culture, Consciousness, and Beyond: An Introduction*. Washington, D.C.: University Press of America, Inc., 1982.
   This book concentrates primarily on how language structures the mind—how the reality of everyday life is largely a social creation. It considers the more intuitive, holistic way of knowing the world that is a function of the right side of the brain. We have included this reference here to provide perspective to the idea that, ultimately, organizing ideas for a speech works best when it relates to the perceptual and intellectual needs of the listeners.

Planning and Presenting
the Speech

7 Beginning and Ending a Speech

Outline

Objectives

After reading this chapter you should be able to:

1. Name and explain the functions of an introduction.
2. Name and explain the functions of a conclusion.
3. Identify eight methods for getting attention at the beginning of a speech, and develop an introduction using each of these.
4. Identify four methods for providing a final impetus to a speech, and develop a conclusion using each of these.

PREVIEW

A speech introduction should get attention and interest, establish rapport between speaker and listeners, orient the audience to what is coming, and set the tone for the speech. Quotations, illustrations, stories, overviews of the ideas to be developed, and simple greetings work well at the beginning of a speech. Some commonly used approaches, such as rhetorical questions and humor, are more difficult for inexperienced speakers.

A conclusion should review the main ideas and focus the thinking and feelings of the listeners on what has been said. It should include a summary of the main ideas and something upbeat that lends a sense of completeness or finality to the speech, and it should provide a motivating impetus to the listeners. Quotations, references to the introduction, and calls to action often work well to clarify for the listeners what is wanted from them.

Angel Rodriguez expressed the concern that many of our students have reported. "I have a good idea what I want to say, but how do I get started?" He had every right to be concerned about this important matter. Beginning a speech is not the same as beginning a friendly conversation. The first few moments of a speech can make all the difference in the effectiveness of that speech.

Lynetta Thomson had a different but related problem. She did not know how to end her speech. "Do I just say 'Thank you' and sit down?" she asked one afternoon.

"Why not? Does it feel awkward to you?"

"Yes," she said. "And besides, it seems like something is missing. I sure don't want to keep on talking, but I don't know how to quit."

Perhaps you have heard speakers who just do not know how to quit. They come to a logical finishing place, but they keep right on talking about some unrelated tangent idea. In the process they destroy the impact of their speech and their own credibility as well.

The purpose of this chapter is to describe what a speech introduction and a speech conclusion should do. Then based on these goals, we will make some suggestions about techniques that seem to help speakers begin and end their speeches effectively.

The Introduction

Purposes of an Introduction

In general, an introduction should call attention to your subject matter and establish the relationship between you, your listeners, and your speech. In particular, its purposes are to gain attention and interest, to establish rapport with the audience, to orient the audience members to what they are about to hear, and to set the tone for the speech. Your own common sense and experience, in addition to what you have read in previous chapters, suggest that these goals are extremely important to a speaker's success.

You will probably want to begin your speech with a "grabber." That is, you will want to devise some way to grab your listeners' attention. So, how do you begin?

Developing an Introduction

You can start with some especially relevant quotation. Here is how one student began:

> George Washington once said, "The very idea of the power and the right of the people to establish a government presupposes the duty of every individual to obey the established government."
>
> He meant pretty much what I want to say today. If we're going to have a government of laws, then we must obey the laws, or change them. If we're going to have elected officials, then we must live with what they decide, or boot them out of office. But we must not take the law into our own hands, and that is what we've been doing for the past two weeks.

Quotations

Most of us associate the use of quotations with famous statements made by prominent public figures. There is good reason for beginning a speech in this way. Some behavioral science research argues in favor of this approach. For example, Hovland and Weiss,[1] and then Kelman and Hovland,[2] identified what they called a *sleeper effect*. This effect is the tendency of listeners to separate the speaker from what he or she says. The finding implies the importance of using a truly credible source. Even after a listener has forgotten what the individual has said, she remembers her attitudes about the individual. To illustrate, if you were to quote Abraham Lincoln in support of your idea, a listener might forget the words from the quotation but he would probably remember that Abraham Lincoln had supported your idea.

Similarly, a notion called *the halo effect* suggests that if a listener is attracted to or invests credibility in a speaker, then that attraction and credibility will extend to what the speaker says. To illustrate, suppose a listener has high regard for a movie actor, thinking him to be attractive, dignified, prestigious, and honorable. That listener is likely to extend these feelings about the actor to what he says about a camera, for instance. The halo effect is assumed to work when famous athletes endorse products on TV.

Jim Davis applied the sleeper effect and the halo effect when he quoted Franklin D. Roosevelt to set the tone for his speech. Although his speech was somewhat technical, and based on the false assumption that his classroom audience would be concerned about the number of recent bank failures, his introduction was a fine example of direct quote as a "grabber."

> "We have nothing to fear but fear itself." These words of Franklin Delano Roosevelt were extremely appropriate during the days of the Great Depression. But the same statement has enormous implications for us today as we see banks and financial institutions again collapsing around us. We must remain confident in the integrity of our banks and savings organizations.

You do not always have to quote famous people, but the people you quote should be perceived as credible. To illustrate, Stephanie Chan wanted to support the idea that values should be taught in the home, and not as a part of the high school curriculum. She opened her speech with this quotation:

> My mother told me three things that have had the greatest influence on my life. She said, "Work hard, love your family, and be honest with everyone."
>
> Those words of guidance have helped me shape my actions and they have governed how I react to people and situations in my life. They can be a guide for you, too, in dealing with life and the people you encounter.

A *hypothetical quotation* is another type of quotation that you can use. You create a quote and then attribute it to a general category of individuals. We should sound a note of caution here. Some people may challenge the idea of a hypothetical quotation as unethical because a quotation, strictly speaking, is an exact record of something a person said or wrote. We think the issue of ethics rests on the speaker's intent, and most importantly, on whether or not the speaker makes it clear to the listeners that the quotation is hypothetical. Of course you have an ethical responsibility to your listeners, but that does not alter the fact that hypothetical quotations are used, and that they are effective.

Sometimes such a hypothetical quotation can be drawn from the pool of common knowledge and wisdom that you acquired during your growing-up years. Jane Birdwhistle did that when she gave this introduction:

> A favorite saying of the Indian is, "Man never walks in the same water twice." What they're saying is that you and I never touch each other, affect each other, or have the identical experience in precisely the same way.

Jane's hypothetical quotation worked very well to capture attention and to develop interest in her audience.

Startling Statement of Fact or Opinion

You can introduce your speech with a startling statement of fact or opinion; just be sure that your attempt to startle is both appropriate and to the point. The statement should be related to the listeners' interests, and in keeping with their expectations. Remember Terry Hall's unhappy experience that we described in chapter 1, and learn from his mistake.

Here is an example of a startling fact used as a "grabber."

> Ladies and gentlemen, one person in four in the United States will have cancer at some point in their life. One person in four! Think about it. In fact, reach out and touch your neighbor on each side of you. Now, look at the person in front of you. One of you will get cancer.

> Today I want to ask you to make a contribution to the American
> Cancer Society—a contribution that will support their vital research
> effort. . . .

Jodi Gilchrist used this statement to introduce a speech against drunk
driving.

> Death is not far away. Maybe only the length of your arm. If you are
> a drinker, death may be only as far away as the bending of your
> elbow, if you drive your car after you drink. Think about that the
> next time you reach for your favorite alcoholic drink.

Dan Catlin wanted to get his audience to register to vote. Here is how
he used a startling statement to begin his speech:

> People in the United States don't care who is elected president. They
> don't seem to care who represents them in Congress or in the state
> legislature. At the county and city levels, the picture seems the same.
> People just don't care.
>   The percentage of eligible voters in this country who actually vote
> has been decreasing over recent years. Now, fewer than half the
> eligible voters in this country are deciding who will determine their
> future. Frightening, isn't it, that people don't care enough to vote!

The object in each of these cases, was to arouse the audience—to startle
them to pay attention—by a statement or observation that riveted their
attention on the topic. These examples worked because each one is related
to the interests of the audience, and is direct and to the point.

You can verbally illustrate the problem you plan to discuss. Using an il-   **Illustration**
lustration in an introduction works best when you want to involve the
listeners emotionally in some problem. The illustration should be rich in
detail.

> There is a group of tumble-down shacks just outside Rochelle,
> Illinois, that might astound you. Just half a mile from the city limits,
> seventeen families of migrant farm workers are living in abject
> poverty. Up to six men, women, and children sleep together in the
> same hot room. There is a single cold-water pipe that those families
> share, but there is no bathroom. Instead, these people use an old-
> fashioned outhouse on the property.
>   These families are from Mexico, brought here by American
> businessmen to harvest melons and asparagus. And, although their
> conditions in that Illinois community are better than what they had
> in Mexico's slums, they are awful. . . ."

The key ingredient in developing an illustration of this kind is that
something in the illustration gives the listeners a way of identifying with
and relating to the situation. You want the listeners to be emotionally involved in and stimulated by the illustration.

Story

Most people like a good story, and especially one that is amusing or provocative. Select a story that you know well, and that applies to the subject you intend to discuss. The story should be full of relevant details so that the listener can imagine being personally involved in it. Mark Hinkle used this story as a very effective introduction:

> I was sitting in the doctor's office last week and I was thumbing through a magazine before my appointment. In an article in *Today's Health*, I read about how rushed each one of us is, but how precious our moments with our children should be. And that article reminded me of the song, "The Cat's in the Cradle." If you remember, Harry Chapin sang about how the father never could find those spare minutes to talk or visit with his child because there was another job that just had to be done, or another meeting that he just had to attend.
>
> After the child grew up and left home, his father talked with him on the phone many times. His dad said, "Son, could you stop by and see us next week?" and the son replied, "Dad, one of the kids has the flu and we're backed up with work at the office. But I'll be there soon, Dad. I'll be there soon."
>
> Dad asked the same question of the son several times, and on each occasion, the son's work, his family, or some problem made it impossible for them to get together. And it was then that the father realized that the son had grown up to be just like his father.

A story like this is designed to set the mood for the message. It need not be one that arouses the emotions quite so powerfully as this story does, but it should focus attention on the major theme of the speech.

In the following brief story, Mario Cuomo illustrates how you can incorporate the theme and some humor in a story for an introduction:

> A young Italian immigrant, at the close of the last century, wrote to his family: "Before I came here, they told me the streets were paved with gold. When I came here, I learned three things. First, the streets were *not* paved with gold. Second, the streets were not paved at all. Third, they expected me to pave them."[3]

A story of this kind requires a light touch; therefore, as you will see, it is not a strategy for everyone. Here it worked well because it pokes fun at the speaker himself.

One of the most effective and easiest strategies you can use is an overview of the ideas you plan to develop. An overview works well because it shows the listeners how what you are planning to say relates to them, and it allows them an opportunity to get the broad picture you have in mind. Here is a clear example from a student speech:

Yesterday you heard a speech about personal liberty and so-called open relationships. Today I would like to present the other side of the issue on sexual license. I want to caution you that to insist upon a freewheeling life-style with many partners is to invite more trouble than you can handle. You can gamble with herpes. You can gamble with syphilis. But you can't gamble with AIDS. . . .

A statement of purpose worked very well for John Joseph Wallace. Notice how clearly and effectively this introduction previews the direction and the major thrust John Joseph was about to develop:

There are many life insurance products on the market today, and you are faced with conflicting claims about what is best for you. I'd like to explain to you how a new type of life insurance policy called "universal life" has revolutionized the way people guarantee security for their families. And, I'll also show you how your life is insured while you accumulate high, tax-free interest on the money in your account!

As you can see, an overview prepares the listeners for what is coming by relating the main ideas to their interests and needs. This approach also makes it very easy for the listeners to follow the ideas while the speech is being developed.

You can start with a simple greeting, saying something like:

Good evening, ladies and gentlemen. My name is James Pavlovich, and I am especially pleased to be with you this evening. The problem I would like to discuss is. . . .

One of us was working with a group of top executives from a large corporation. One man in that group was very concerned about how he should introduce an important speech he was planning to give to an audience that would include the United States Secretary of the Interior. "How do I get started?" he asked. We recommended that he use a simple greeting. The greeting he used was no longer or no more elaborate than the one James Pavlovich used, but it worked well because it was short and businesslike.

Overview of Main Ideas

Simple Greeting

Humor

A touch of humor might establish goodwill and rapport with your audience. If you are clever and have a good sense of timing, and if the occasion and your speech justify it, you might try the light touch. We want to caution you, however, that humor is sometimes very difficult for inexperienced speakers, so be careful. We have seen people make the mistake of telling a joke that was not quite right. They ran quite a risk that they did not have to take. The joke tended to imply that the speaker was not serious about the subject matter. Be as sure as you can that your approach to humor is appropriate. If there is the slightest doubt, do not use it.

Rhetorical Question

A rhetorical question can be an effective way to begin a speech because it involves the listeners in psychological interaction with the speaker. A rhetorical question is asked to create an effect, and the question usually implies its own answer.

Asking rhetorical questions can be difficult, however, especially for inexperienced speakers. Sometimes the questions sound trite and studied, which can destroy the benefits of the strategy and damage the speech. For example, you may have heard a rhetorical question like the one Matt Foss used to introduce his speech supporting mandatory seat-belt laws.

> Did you ever think that you might be saving your own life when you put on your seat belt?

This question did not work very well because it is trite. Matt's second version worked much better because it was fresh and was directly related to the interests of his classroom audience.

> Think of a person you really care about—your girlfriend, your mother, or someone else you really love. Would you be willing to give just one minute to save that person from a lifetime of great pain?

Another good reason why you should be careful when you use a rhetorical question as a "grabber" is that, unless you construct it well, you may get the wrong answer. If that happens, you could appear foolish, or your introduction could lose the punch it was supposed to provide.

A student asked this question to introduce her speech to change belief. She was talking to students in a state where the drinking age was twenty-one. How do you suppose it was received by her classroom audience?

> Don't you agree that drinking ought to be a matter of choice for everyone who has reached the age of eighteen?

Some of her listeners were about eighteen, but some were much older. One woman was in her late fifties. A few of the audience members were opposed to drinking alcoholic beverages as a tenet of religious belief. One woman was an active member of M.A.D.D. (Mothers Against Drunk

A major purpose of both an introduction and a conclusion is to focus audience attention on the content of the speech.

Drivers). You can imagine, then, that the attitude reflected in the question was not universally shared by this class, so the rhetorical question did not help the speaker.

In summary, an introduction seeks to get attention, to establish a relationship between the speaker and the listeners, to state the purpose of the speech, and sometimes to preview what is coming. Research in behavioral sciences lends suggestions about how a speaker can design an introduction to help accomplish these purposes. An introduction will not be very lengthy, but even so, it is much too important to consider lightly. A good introduction can make all the difference between the success or failure of a speech.

The Conclusion

Purposes of a Conclusion

A conclusion should focus the audience's attention on what you have said, to signal to the listeners that you are finished, and to lend some final, motivated impetus—sometimes called a *kicker*—to the speech. A kicker is the last element of a speech conclusion; it is the last thing you say. Its purpose is to put your listeners in a conducive mood to do as you have asked or to make them think about your central idea.

Developing a Conclusion

When you keep the goals of a conclusion in mind, it is fairly easy to figure out how to end a speech. Undoubtedly you will want to summarize the main points and then find a way to focus the listeners' thinking. Since you are trying to end the speech, the strategy you use must provide closure— a kicker. Here, then, are the parts of a speech conclusion.

Summary

We recommend that you summarize your main ideas briefly. For example, Tim McDonald finished a speech against the capital punishment laws in this way:

> So, what have I said to you this morning? I've proved to you that capital punishment is not an effective deterrent to crime. I have argued that deliberately taking a person's life in order to punish the person is nothing more than legalized murder. And I have shown you an alternative that is more humane than capital punishment. At best, imprisonment without possibility of parole, coupled with intelligent use of the prisoner's lifetime, can make a positive contribution to society.
>
> But the law won't be changed unless you act. It is up to you, and to every right-thinking American. It's up to you.

Here is how Adrienne Hudson restated the major ideas of her speech as a way of reminding her listeners—all the PTA members at the middle school where her own daughter was enrolled—that more money was needed to support the schools.

> A good school system, then, consists of books, a sound and well-maintained physical facility, dedicated staff and maintenance people, and above all a qualified and highly motivated group of teachers.
> All these things take money. . . .

A summary, however brief, seems to us a necessary part of any conclusion. It helps the listeners remember the main ideas, and it serves as a means of justifying any final appeal you make.

Quotation

You can use a quotation to focus audience attention. Sometimes you may want to reuse a quotation that you incorporated in your introduction. At other times, you may wish to use something different. In any case, concentrate on reinforcing the basic theme of your speech as you select the quotation you will use.

One student urged his classroom audience to become more involved in government and politics. He used this quotation for his conclusion:

> So, in the words of John F. Kennedy, "Ask not what your country can do for you; ask what you can do for your country." Stop leaving the job of leadership and involvement to others. Take the initiative, show leadership, and encourage others to assume their roles as citizens in this society.

Another student in the same round of speeches used this conclusion:

> I believe George Bernard Shaw saw the ultimate problem man has with his own vanity when he wrote, "Titles distinguish the mediocre, embarrass the superior, and are disgraced by the inferior."

A theme that you have explored in the introduction can be reused in the conclusion with very powerful effect. After Mark Hinkle introduced his speech with the story of "The Cat's in the Cradle," he developed a speech that focused on parent concern and involvement in the affairs of their children. Then he closed with this reference to his introduction:

Reference to the Introduction

> I hope you won't be like the father in the song, "The Cat's in the Cradle." Will you be able to say you found the time for your children? Will you be happy to say that they grew up *just like you?*

This was an effective conclusion because it rounded out the central idea of the speech and focused the listeners' thinking and feelings on their relationships with their own children. Each of us has sometimes made poor choices among our priorities, and been "too busy" for our loved ones. Mark's speech forced the listeners to center on that idea.

You will often have a goal of asking the listeners to do something. The actions you seek may range from giving blood at the local Red Cross to reading a popular novel. When you do have such a goal, it is often the best strategy just to make a straightforward call for action.

Call for Action

Julie Hertzberger wanted her coworkers to contribute to the local United Way campaign. Her call for action was simple and direct:

> You know that the work of the United Way supports important programs and services that touch every sector of our society. You also know that you can afford to make a contribution. You can skip that movie you really weren't too interested in seeing. You can skip that can of beer. You can give up that pack of cigarettes. You can give your fair share to those who need your help.
>
> I'm going to hand out these pledge cards. I want you to fill them out, and I will pick them up from you before you leave work today. Please be as generous with others as you would want others to be generous with you.

It is important to remember that *what you ask for must be clear and easy to give.* If the listeners do not understand the exact action you want, or if it appears to them that what you want is difficult or confusing, your call has little chance of success. As you plan a call for action, you may want to ask yourself these questions:

1. Am I asking for something that I can hope to get?
2. Will the listeners know what I am asking for?
3. Am I making it easy for the listeners to act?

An important point you must remember about the conclusion is that it should serve, one way or another, to unify the message you have presented. The conclusion is the final impression you leave with your listeners. What do you want your listeners to take away from the speech?

Any request for action must be clear and relatively easy for listeners to respond to.

Decide clearly what the feeling, attitude, action, or information should be. Then craft your conclusion around that thought using the techniques we have outlined here. Listeners want "closure." They want to feel as if things are being brought to an orderly end. Moreover, that end should be consistent with what you have been saying in your speech. So develop your conclusion with those thoughts in mind and you will find that the likelihood of achieving your objective has increased as a result of developing an effective close.

Combinations

By now you may have realized that it is possible to combine several methods in a single conclusion. Many speech teachers recommend that speakers combine approaches for the strongest possible conclusion. Your closing words may be the ones most clearly remembered by your audience. Make them memorable.

Professor Nathaniel Parker combined approaches when concluding a speech in favor of variable work loads for university faculty. He delivered these remarks to the faculty senate, and provided a clear example of the power of combined approaches.

<table>
<tr><td></td><td>*Conclusion*</td></tr>
<tr><td></td><td>So what have we seen about the work load of our faculty? Whether we like it or not, work load differs according to a person's area of expertise and it differs according to that person's talents and</td></tr>
<tr><td>*Brief summary*</td><td>energies. Our work load policy ought to reflect those differences.</td></tr>
<tr><td>*Restatement of thesis*</td><td>And we are, ultimately, the ones who must act to change the work-load policy. Each of us in this</td></tr>
<tr><td>*How the thesis affects the listeners*</td><td>room is affected. Beyond that, the quality of our university, and the quality of the educational services we render to our students are at risk.</td></tr>
<tr><td>*Call for action*</td><td>Ladies and gentlemen, we must act now. Pass this resolution in favor of variable work loads for faculty. What is the alternative?</td></tr>
<tr><td>*Reference to introduction, restatement of theme combined with a powerful "kicker" that restates speaker position and focuses listener attention*</td><td>Like that old truck I mentioned earlier, if we don't take time for maintenance—if we do not insist upon time for our own research—we will surely begin to rust and to deteriorate. What will happen to the load we carry if that happens?</td></tr>
</table>

Summary

The functions of a speech introduction are to grab the attention and interest of the listener, to establish rapport between speaker and listener, to orient the listeners to what they are about to hear, and to set the tone for the speech. A conclusion should focus the thinking and feelings of the listeners on what they heard in the speech, and provide a sense of completeness and a final motivating "kicker" to the speech.

We suggested some communication strategies that will help to accomplish these functions. Introductions can begin with some relevant quotation, an illustration that points to the problem, a story that makes the point, an overview of the ideas to be developed, or even a simple greeting. Some approaches are more difficult. It is difficult to use humor well, for instance. Similarly, a rhetorical question is a more difficult opening strategy to use than some of the others.

A conclusion should always summarize the main ideas of the speech. Beyond that, the conclusion should provide some final, motivated impetus to the speech—some upbeat ending that lends a sense of completeness and finality to the speech. A quotation may be a useful strategy toward this end. A reference to the introduction sometimes works well. A call for action is often effective. Whatever you decide, the key is to make clear to your listeners the response you want from them.

Key Terms

Conclusion   *"Kicker"*
"Grabber"   *Thesis*
Introduction

Discussion Questions

1. Consider the following speech introductions. In your opinion, are these introductions good ones? If not, how would you change them?

   It used to be that a television camera weighed 200 pounds, and you had to have a tripod with wheels to roll it around from one place to another. At the same time, a videotape recorder was nearly as big as an automatic clothes dryer. But now you can get a camera that isn't much bigger than a coffee mug, and a VCR that's about the same size as an algebra textbook.
   The costs of these pieces of equipment have dropped at about the same rate that their sizes have dropped. So there is no longer any reason why the university shouldn't have a television production facility. I think we ought to have a major in television on this campus.

   Do you think we're about to have a new wave of small, inexpensive cars? In the last few years the Federal government has imposed upon foreign automobile makers such restrictive import requirements that the Japanese have virtually abandoned the low-cost field, but the Koreans and the Spanish are about to take up the slack.

   The explosion of the Challenger space shuttle makes it clear that the government ought to quit spending so much money on the American space-exploration program. It is too dangerous, and much too expensive.

2. In a small group, decide how you might develop a "grabber" and "kicker" to relate each of these topics to a classroom audience:

   Automobile repair
   Mountain climbing
   Money management
   Defense spending
   Capital punishment
   Chocolate mousse

Notes

1 Carl I. Hovland and Walter Weiss, "The Influence of Source Credibility on Communication Effectiveness," *Public Opinion Quarterly* 15 (1951): 635–50.

2 H. C. Kelman and Carl I. Hovland, " 'Restatement' of the Communicator in Delayed Measurement of Opinion Change," *Journal of Abnormal and Social Psychology* 48 (1953): 327–35.

3 Mario M. Cuomo, *Diaries of Mario M. Cuomo: The Campaign for Governor* (New York: Random House, 1984), 432.

Suggested Readings

We recommend that you visit the library and examine the introductions and conclusions you find in *Vital Speeches of the Day*.

There are many bound collections of speeches that you could study to see how famous speakers began and ended their speeches. An old one, but one of the best, is by Lewis Copeland, ed. *The World's Great Speeches* (New York: Dover Publications, Inc., 1958). *See also* the wonderful, 10-volume set by David J. Brewer, ed. *The World's Best Orations* (St. Louis: Ferd. P. Kaiser, 1899).

We suggest the following references for additional reading. You will find them very helpful in developing introductions and conclusions.

Eadie, William F. and Paulson, Jon W. "Communicator Attitudes, Communicator Style, and Communication Competence." *Western Journal of Speech Communication* 48 (Fall 1984): 390–407.

Gruner, Charles R. "Advice to the Beginning Speaker on Using Humor—What the Research Tells Us." *Communication Education* 34 (April 1985): 142–47.

McCroskey, James C. and Young, Thomas J. "Ethos, Credibility: The Construct and Its Measurement After Three Decades." *Central States Speech Journal* 32 (Spring 1981): 24–34.

Toppen, Christopher J. S. "Dimensions of Speaker Credibility: An Oblique Solution." *Communication Monographs* 41 (1974): 253–60.

8 *Delivery*

Outline

Objectives

After you have read this chapter you should be able to:

1. Compare and contrast several styles of delivery, and make appropriate selections from among them for a particular speaking situation.
2. Specify and explain how to rehearse a speech for greatest effect.
3. Explain the characteristics of effective verbal and nonverbal delivery.

PREVIEW

This chapter concentrates on the verbal and nonverbal elements of delivery. Delivery is the vehicle used to transmit ideas to listeners. The difference that often determines your success, the difference between an effective and an ineffective speech, is centered on the speaker's method or characteristics of delivery. For most public speaking situations, we recommend extemporaneous speaking, a style of delivery that requires careful preparation but does not involve memorization or reading. We show how to develop and use notes, how to rehearse, how to get yourself ready for the surprises and "glitches" that sometimes occur in even the most carefully planned speaking events, and what to do while you are actually delivering a speech.

Delivery, or the presentation of our ideas and ourselves, is for many speakers the most challenging and interesting portion of the speaking act. The delivery process is the moment of truth, and we are often judged as much on how well we present our ideas as on what we have to say. One of your public speaking concerns may be how you will feel and appear as you talk about your ideas.

Differences between Oral and Written Style

One of the major impressions we try to convey in a speech is that the speech appear *extemporaneous* (as if it were unrehearsed). We are going to discuss application of this notion to all types of delivery in the next few pages, but first we want to identify an important difference in the characteristics of written and oral communication.

Oral Style

Oral communication is characterized by (1) short words, (2) a moderate to high level of repetition, (3) concrete terms, and (4) the use of contractions. These four characteristics can be seen in the following brief passage.

> My major idea is that we all know money is important but we don't like to pay more than necessary for a product. In fact, we spend a lot of time and burn gallons of gasoline trying to find a bargain. We forget, when we do find that bargain, that we used up all our savings from the product in time and gas.

See how brief the words are and how the contractions are used. Notice how the major idea is repeated in several ways. *This is the way we talk*, and thus the reason we refer to it as "oral style." It is important in public speaking that much of the message appears in the oral style. It should sound as if you are talking in a conversational way with other people.

Written Style

Books, manuscripts, and printed material in general make use of the written style. If you look at the pages of this or any other book, you will notice that the written words differ from the way people talk. The statements are longer and more complicated, and because we can go back and reread them, there is less repetition.

When people speak as if they are reading from books or prepared papers, they appear to lack spontaneity or real enthusiasm. Consequently, we often do not feel compelled to listen. For this reason alone, it is important for you to appear to be speaking spontaneously. One of the best ways to do this is by using the oral style. Keep your language simple and do not be afraid to repeat ideas and use contractions instead of the more formal *do not* or *should not* type of construction. Try to note the importance of this approach as we talk about styles of delivery.

Selecting a Style of Delivery

One of the most important considerations that you must make before you actually present a speech is the style of delivery you will use. Should you memorize your speech and deliver it from memory? Should you recite from a manuscript? Should you try an "off-the-cuff" impromptu style? Should you speak extemporaneously? What kind of notes, if any, should you use?

The guiding principle in this chapter is that good speaking should appear invisible. The choices you make about delivery should not call attention to themselves. In other words, your listeners should not notice the choices you have made; they should be thinking about your ideas.

Producing a seemingly invisible style requires careful planning and depends upon your personal skills and talents, and your expectations of the norms implied by the speaking context. For example, the president of the United States almost always follows a word-for-word preplanned manuscript. To the extent that he is a skillful presenter, his remarks appear spontaneous, although they rarely are. There is good reason for this. A president's choice of words can have enormous international impact—they can threaten a nuclear war or damage the relationship between the United States and one of her neighbors or cause the stock exchange to register a dramatic decline.

An academic debater may have committed her first affirmative speech to memory. Her ability to "can" all the information and all the arguments, combined with the strict time limitations imposed by the rules of academic debating, make that possible and even desirable. If she is delivering it well, the memorized speech will sound spontaneous.

An account executive making a presentation to a management group from a client organization will probably deliver his well-prepared remarks extemporaneously, using a few notes and visual aids as guideposts from one idea to another. If he is doing it correctly, his speaking will seem spontaneous—his ideas will seem to be occurring to him for the first time.

A group member may be asked for her views about the solution that the group is considering. "Maria," says one of the members, "you've been working on this idea for a long time. Will you tell us what you think about this proposal?" Such a situation calls for an impromptu speech—an off-the-cuff speech delivered without the benefit of advance planning.

Indeed there are good reasons for choosing different styles of delivery. You must consider the advantages and disadvantages of each choice and make some practical speaking applications.

Memorization

The advantages of memorization lie in advance planning. If you elect to memorize a speech, you have the ability to choose the perfect sequence of ideas, the precise language, the perfect metaphor, and the subtle implication. You have the advantage of timing the speech and adjusting the precise time limits. You are able to cue others who may be helping you—for example, a lighting technician or a television director. And you have the advantage of knowing that you will have said exactly what you wanted to say.

Although you have all of these advantages, the disadvantages are greater. Unless your speaking situation requires a memorized address, you should probably avoid this style of delivery. What happens if your memory fails? What could be more agonizing for a speaker and more discomforting for an audience than the shocking silence where a forgotten line should have been? Nearly as worrisome is the misleading or disappointing experience of a half-remembered argument. What could be more confusing than the incomplete jigsaw puzzle that remains after a memory lapse?

A second disadvantage that argues against memorizing a speech is that it will *sound* memorized. Unless you are a very skillful speaker, the memorized speech will have either the monotone quality of a clearly memorized message or the sing-song rhythm of ideas that were committed to memory. It will leave the impression that you are more involved in remembering your speech than you are in communicating with your audience.

Finally, the memorized speech does not afford you the opportunity for any audience feedback. When you have decided, in advance, exactly what you are going to say, you tend to disregard any reaction from the audience. If you consider the audience important, it is clear that this feature of memorization can be a major disadvantage.

Given the advantages and disadvantages of memorization, you will have to make a choice. The requirements of the occasion and your own talents should guide you, but remember that the objective is to make your speech appear invisible. Hence, unless you are skillful enough to deliver a memorized speech so that it does not sound memorized, we would advise you against this style.

Many of our students are tempted to write out their speeches and then read **Reading**
them from a manuscript. Manuscript speaking has most of the advantages
of memorization and it avoids many of the disadvantages. However, in determining whether or not to read from a manuscript, you should carefully
consider the disadvantages of this style.

Reading limits your opportunity to make contact with the audience, or
to take advantage of the fleeting opportunities that spontaneously present
themselves in a public speaking event. Unless you have practiced thoroughly, you may spend more time making eye contact with the manuscript
than with your audience. Again, this style of delivery creates problems of
adapting to the immediate audience. There is no flexibility in the manuscript for making changes based on the way the listeners are reacting.

Finally, unless you are skillful, oral reading tends to sound stilted. This
is partly due to the differences between written and spoken language, and
partly to the mechanical process involved.

Conditions that might suggest using a manuscript include:

1. When each nuance of language must be carefully weighed.
2. When complex material must be presented in a particular sequence.
3. When technical assistants must be cued (television, lighting, etc.).
4. When something very important rests on the exact use of language.

If you *do* decide to read from a manuscript, make sure you *read through
the speech aloud many times.* Check the pronunciation of each word and
phrase. Remember that you want the delivery to sound spontaneous. Try
to have at least one "dress rehearsal," using props, visual aids, microphone,
lighting, and so on. Flip every switch. Turn every page. Make it sound as
though the speech were occurring to you for the first time, every time. If
you encounter a problem, run through the speech again, as many times as
necessary.

Impromptu speaking is speaking without preparation, without advance **Impromptu**
planning. It is also known as "spur of the moment" speaking. You will **Speaking**
have many opportunities to speak impromptu, but often it is not wise to
do so. If you must, if there is no way out of it, then you can use some simple
techniques that may help you. *Do not under any circumstances speak about
something you do not know well.*

Assuming that you are sufficiently knowledgeable about the subject and
you have been asked to share your ideas off the cuff, we suggest that you:

1. *Take a moment to organize your thoughts.* Ask for the time and then
   take it. Say something like, "I'll be happy to address that subject, but
   I would like a moment to collect my thoughts." Then collect your
   thoughts. No one will be offended by the momentary delay, and
   your speech and your credibility will benefit.

2. *Make a few notes.* A word or two can stimulate a complete thought. Begin by identifying the point you want to make or the position you want to take. Then quickly sketch out the subpoints.
3. *Organize around a simple, redundant pattern.* You might wish to follow the sequence: "Tell 'em what you're going to tell 'em, tell 'em, then tell 'em what you told 'em."

When speaking off the cuff, your introduction should be direct and simple. You might say something like:

> I strongly support a delay on making any decision. I don't think it is wise to do anything just now, and for two reasons. First, we don't know what the market is going to do; it's a gray area. And second, we really would be stretching our resources if we invest anything at this time.

Your discussion would attend to each of the ideas you mention in your introduction. In this example, you would develop the argument that the market is unpredictable, and that resources would be strained beyond comfortable limits.

To conclude an impromptu speech, summarize what you have already said. Using the previous example, you might say something like:

> So, what I have told you is that I think we should delay action for a while—until we have more information on the market and until our resources will support our actions.

Remember to acknowledge the audience. Finish with something like:

> Thanks for the opportunity to talk about this matter. I am confident that you will make the right decision.

Much of the speaking we do outside a classroom environment is of an impromptu type. We often do not have much time to collect our thoughts or to prepare in advance. So the guides we have presented here may have frequent use in your everyday life. Take your time, think carefully before you speak, and use a simple organizational pattern in an effort to be clear and concise.

Extemporaneous Speaking

The word *extemporaneous* refers to a speech that has been carefully planned, but that is delivered with few if any notes. Your concern is presenting ideas and supporting proofs in a logical sequence. Your goal is not a word-for-word progression of ideas. Since you have prepared carefully using an outline, all you will typically need is a few notes to remind you of your key ideas, in the order in which you plan to present them.

Extemporaneous speaking has most of the advantages of memorized speaking and manuscript speaking, but none of the disadvantages. It is more direct and spontaneous than either memorization or recitation. The speaker

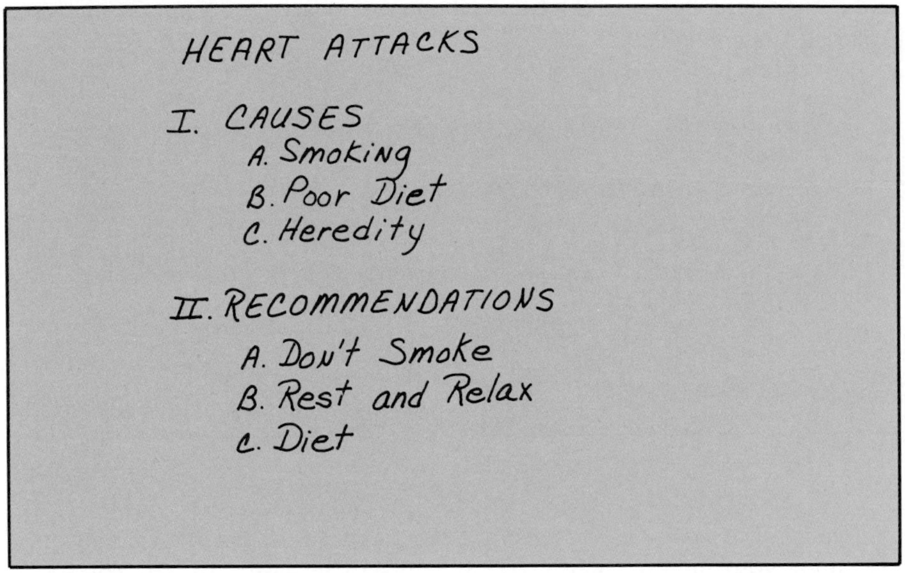

HEART ATTACKS

I. CAUSES
   A. Smoking
   B. Poor Diet
   C. Heredity

II. RECOMMENDATIONS
   A. Don't Smoke
   B. Rest and Relax
   C. Diet

FIGURE 8.1 An Example Note Card. A few hand-held notes will help you remember your main ideas and their sequence while not bogging you down and taking your attention away from the audience.

is free to interact with individual members of the audience, and the listeners are more likely to view the speaker and the speech as an interpersonal event that truly involves them as individuals.

Sometimes students have expressed the concern that the extemporaneous method does not afford them any help in remembering what they are going to say next. They worry that they will forget where they are going and where they have been. This is simply not the case, since the extemporaneous speaker has the benefit of notes.

The effective use of notes is one of the hallmarks of a successful speaker. Even though there is not a single "correct" procedure for using notes, there are some generalizations that will help you.

1. *Keep your notes to a minimum.* As a general rule, the fewer the notes you use, the better (fig. 8.1). If you include only a few words, you will not spend much time studying them. On the other hand, if your notes are extensive, you are more likely to immerse yourself in them. While there are exceptions to the rule, for the sake of practicality, try to limit yourself to a couple of words for each main idea. This general rule, of course, does not apply to direct quotes or to statistics that you want to convey accurately.

2. *Use cardboard or stiff paper.* Resist the temptation to type or write speaking notes on regular-weight writing paper. One or two notecards, or the inside of a manila folder in which you have placed overhead transparencies for the speaking situation, will work better for you.

II. King had prosperous family life   ← *Slide 6*
    A. Rev. King, Sr., was pastor.   ←
    B. Nice Atlanta house   ←———— *Slide 7*

              Slides 8, 9, 10
III. King was good student
    A. Atlanta U Lab. School   ←—— *Slide 11*
    B. Booker T. Wash. H. S. (grad. at 15)   ←— *Slide 12*
    C. Morehouse College (grad. at 19)
              Read: p. 43, as marked

FIGURE 8.2 Meta notes serve as reminders to attend to other aspects of the speech, such as when to display visual aids or read quotes.

3. *Design your notes for accessibility.* Your purpose for preparing notes is to jog your memory while you are presenting your speech. You should not try to develop a full-sentence outline or even a topic outline. Instead, confine yourself to a minimum amount of language, printed legibly so that you can see it easily from one or two feet away. One or two key words for each main idea should be enough to keep you moving in your intended direction.

4. *Make meta-notes.* Meta-notes are notes about the notes (fig. 8.2). Use them to remind yourself about such things as where and when to use visual materials, or preplanned movements. Use a meta-note if you plan to read directly from printed material in some other source. Write down the exact page and paragraph where that quote can be found. This will allow you to find the quotation easily.

5. *Use visual materials as notes.* The visual materials you offer your audience are readily accessible to you. If you have designed your visuals well, you can use them to refresh your memory at the same time the audience is viewing them. Remember, you want your speaking techniques to be invisible, and the moment to seem completely spontaneous. Dynamic, successful speaking depends on the impression of spontaneity.

We cannot overstress the importance of rehearsing a speech. Your success in delivery is directly related to how much control you take over the variables that can interfere with your presentation. For example, you can learn to pronounce any name with practice, and thus avoid stumbling over the pronunciation during the speech. You can discover the easiest and best way to make the transitions from one visual aid to another with practice. You can anticipate the problem of audiofeedback if you practice with a microphone and discover that its placement is causing audiofeedback. You can learn to follow your speaking outline easily with practice. You can work out any planned actions or gestures so that they seem spontaneous and natural, but only if you practice. Even though practice does not always make perfect, it certainly makes for a better speech.

Rehearsing Your Speech

Learning theorists have found that distributed practice is better than massed practice.[1] In other words, practice will have a more beneficial effect if it is done often in small meaningful segments than if it is done infrequently or in one large chunk. This thinking applies to nearly everything you try to learn.

Practicing for a Speech

Perhaps you learned to play a musical instrument as a child. If not, surely you can recall someone you knew who had to practice every day, if only for half an hour. Perhaps you, or a friend, took swimming lessons. Can you recall that requirement to practice daily? Even when you were learning to drive a car, you discovered that your skills improved with practice. The same is true with speech making. If you want to improve your skills, practice often. Do not mass all that practice into one session. Distribute your practice periods as broadly as your schedule will permit.

Even if you have planned a distributed practice schedule, the question becomes one of how to practice. Unfortunately, there is no single best method; that will depend upon your own needs, and you will have to discover the method that works best for you. Still, experience suggests these pieces of advice:

1. *Keep your practice sessions brief.* In the early stages, run through the speech two or three times each practice session if your schedule permits. Do not worry about the precise choice of language or about minor lapses in memory. In fact, do not concern yourself about any snags that may occur initially. Do not try to commit any part of the speech to memory. Do experiment with your use of notes and with the arrangement of ideas. (Should that first main idea really come first? What if you gave the whole speech backwards?) Try to relax and to get comfortable with the materials of the speech.

2. *Practice in different contexts.* Opportunities to practice occur throughout your day. You can run through the speech while you are taking a shower or while you are driving to work. You can practice while you are walking your dog, or while you are passing from one building to another between classes. You can also give the speech to your friends and loved ones, but of course you may not wish to impose on them too much.

3. *Practice with visual aids and mechanical equipment.* If you are planning to use visual materials, develop them in advance so that you can practice using them. Flip charts do not flip themselves. Photographic slides and overhead transparencies do not present themselves. The lights in a room do not turn themselves on and off. Pointers, pencils, and felt-tipped markers do not appear automatically. Microphones do not automatically adjust themselves to the right height. You are responsible for these things.

One of us delivered a speech to a local group of about fifty bank employees. They had paid for their dinner and the program, and there was a modest speaker's fee involved.

On the agreed-upon evening, the author appeared at the appointed place with a set of carefully prepared flip charts. In all, there were about fifteen visual aids, including drawings and some word-based charts that were arranged in sequence from the back to the front of a large pad of paper measuring about two feet wide by three feet high. The plan was to hang the flip-chart pad onto an easel that was designed to hold it.

"May I help you set this up?" asked the host. The author made a bad mistake, saying that he would be grateful for any help. Shortly, the trouble began. The author walked over to the flip charts and turned the first visual aid to the audience. The easel collapsed; its supporting structure had been badly damaged at some point in its history, and now it would barely support the weight of the flip charts. After some hustle and bustle, the easel and the pad were positioned again, and order was temporarily restored. Then, just as the speaker was moving toward the easel to display his second visual aid, the easel collapsed again. No longer would the easel stand on its own, so the host supported it while the speaker completed the speech. The evening was a disaster, but the experience provided a valuable lesson about practicing with visual aids and mechanical equipment.

Checking Equipment and Physical Space

Assume that you are ready to present your speech. You have practiced with various pieces of equipment, you know where each visual should appear, and you are ready with supplemental information in case someone asks you a question. You have rehearsed over and over again. You know the speech "cold."

Now is as good a time as any to offer you a piece of advice we have found useful to nearly all speakers: Murphy's Law will operate in nearly all settings, classroom or otherwise. Murphy's Law states "if anything can go wrong, it will." Experienced speakers will remind you that you should anticipate areas where problems can develop, especially if you plan to use any equipment during a speech. Develop a plan of attack that will enable you to continue even if your equipment or your use of it does not go according to plan. Have an alternative approach in mind in case the slide projector loses power, the easel collapses, or some other piece of equipment fails to function. Try to be prepared for something to go awry. Because you are under pressure, it is possible you may mishandle or misuse equipment or material that is crucial to your speech.

Your next concern is about physical space and equipment. Will the projectors and the projection screen be there? Will the screen be large enough? Will the microphone work? Will the audience be able to see and hear you? Will you be able to control the lighting? None of these questions can be safely ignored. You cannot assume that someone has double-checked for you. Go to the classroom or wherever you will speak and look it over.

If the room is long and narrow, you may need a public-address system. Is one available? If so, is it stationary? Is the seating arrangement the way you want it? Can it be changed? Does the change make sense? Is the lighting adequate?

When you arrive, locate the person who can make last-minute changes if you discover any problems. Tell that individual you are planning to do a walk-through and may want to make some minor changes. Find out where you can locate that person; or better, take that individual with you into the room where you will speak.

If you plan far enough in advance, and if you secure the help of someone in charge, you do not have to take the physical space you find as absolute. To illustrate, an industrial trainer in New York reported that he went to a meeting room in a hotel where he was planning to deliver a four-day seminar to management personnel in the paper industry. When he arrived, he found the room in a banquet arrangement as illustrated in figure 8.3. The seats were metal folding chairs without armrests. The lighting was dim because several fluorescent tubes had burned out, and one of the two duplex outlets in the room did not work. The banquet arrangement was not suitable for a teaching-learning experience. The participants would have had to walk past the trainer and in front of everyone in the seminar in order to go to the rest rooms. Had the trainer accepted these conditions, his seminar would have been badly damaged. But he got there in time to identify the problems and to make the necessary changes. Figure 8.3 shows the same room after the trainer had checked the physical space and the equipment.

Before

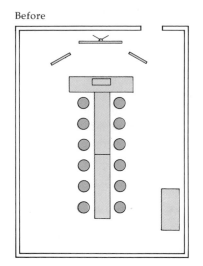

After

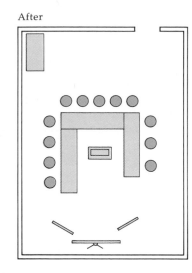

FIGURE 8.3 Seating Accommodations Before and After Rearrangement. The arrangement on the right clearly facilitates attention and interaction for the speaker and the audience.

Waiting Your Turn to Speak

In an earlier chapter you read that you "cannot not communicate." As soon as your audience sees you or hears you, you send signals that your audience receives and decodes. Your physical appearance and demeanor tell something about you. Keep that notion in mind as you are waiting your turn to speak. You are "on" just as soon as anyone in your audience notices you. Your task is to manage the impression you leave with the other people in that place. Your credibility and *your personal success as a speaker* may depend on how you present yourself during this time. We will deal further with this aspect of impression management shortly.

In the Classroom

Classroom speaking as an assigned activity has its own set of expectations. Some specific suggestions will help you manage yourself more effectively in this situation.

On the day you are scheduled to speak, arrive at the classroom five minutes or so before the class starts. Check out the room to be certain that the materials or equipment you will need are already there. If you are responsible for bringing a slide projector or other pieces of equipment, you should have them with you. Is there a lectern? Are the seats misarranged from an earlier class so it makes it more difficult for you to speak? *Know what you want for maximum personal success in this situation and be certain those items are there.* You should talk with your instructor the day before you are scheduled to speak to be reasonably sure the basic items will be present.

You should be sufficiently prepared so that if you are not the first speaker you will not need to concentrate all your attention and energy studying your notes or mentally rehearsing your speech. Look at the other speakers and try to listen to what they are saying. This is one way of reducing your own concern about your speech. In addition, a reference to one of those speeches can help you form a common bond with the audience.

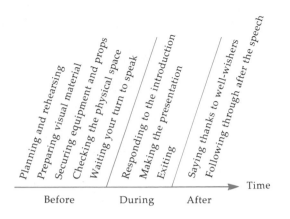

FIGURE 8.4 Time Line Showing the Divisions of a Presentation. The preparation work will absorb much of your time and energy, but do not forget to give some thought to your actions and general deportment when you are actually giving the speech or when it is over. (From Hanna, Michael S., and Gerald L. Wilson, *Communicating in Business and Professional Settings.* Copyright © 1984 Random House, Inc. Reprinted by permission.

When the time comes for you to speak, take a couple of deep breaths and walk *confidently* to the front of the room. Arrange your materials, including your notes, before you begin to speak. Pause and look directly at your audience for two or three seconds before you begin to talk. Then begin.

Outside the Classroom

After you have surveyed the room where you will speak and have satisfied your concerns, leave and stay away until about ten minutes before the event is to begin. If you are to speak after a dinner, arrive about ten minutes before the dinner is to begin. Remember, people begin forming opinions about you as soon as they notice you.

When you arrive at the location, find and speak to the host or hostess, or the person who invited you. Follow that person's lead. There may be some last-minute instructions or changes in plans that you should know, or some questions. If it is a dinner, you will probably be at the head table. Eat, but not heavily. Chat with the people near you. *Do not work on your speech;* you should already have the speech well in mind.

During the introductions and speeches, look at the speaker and listen. Participate as you would like your audience members to participate when you speak. Pay attention to what is going on before your speech. If something especially useful occurs—for example, an opportunity to set the momentum of your speech by playing off what another person has said—make a *brief* note. Remember that you cannot *not* communicate—you are "on" from the moment you arrive.

What to Do during the Speech

Figure 8.4 shows that a presentation has three parts: (1) responding to an introduction, or "getting on"; (2) delivering the speech; and (3) exiting, or "getting off." None of these parts is very complicated, but each presents special opportunities for you to gain acceptance for yourself and for your ideas.

Responding to the Introduction

"And now ladies and gentlemen, I am pleased to introduce. . . ." You hear your name and the applause of the audience. This is it; you are introduced.

Rise quietly but *confidently*. Walk to the lectern *confidently*. Stand quietly and *confidently* while the audience adjusts to your presence. Audience members need to feel that you are confident, that you have your act together, and that you know what you are talking about. You are in charge now, and they need to feel this, even if you don't.

Respond to the introduction quickly and politely. Resist the temptation to be cute or to elaborate on what the introducer has said. Say something simple like, "Thank you, Mr. Jones." If the introducer has been especially complimentary, you might wish to add something to the thanks. "Thank you, Mr. Jones, for that generous introduction." Pause for a moment, and then continue.

The purpose of not dwelling on the introduction is to move the audience's attention from the introducer to you. Do not waste their valuable time by being cute or bantering with the introducer. You have something more important to do.

Making the Presentation

That moment when a speaker becomes the center of attention—when all those eyes focus on you—seems to be an anxious moment for most people. Perhaps the most common question asked of speech instructors is "How do I actually give the speech?" The answer is not clear-cut because each individual speaker, including you, is unique. Advice that applies to one person may not fit someone else, so there is always some risk in developing a list of generic suggestions about what a speaker should do. Regardless, we will provide some suggestions that have proven, over time, to make a difference to most speakers. Each one is designed to help you establish a positive relationship with the audience, and to maintain that relationship while you are giving the speech. As you consider these pointers, keep in mind that there are always exceptions, and there are no absolute rules.

Verbal Concerns

The part of delivery involving the voice and the sound each of us generates when we speak is of major importance in the public setting.

Speak Up and Slow Down. Listeners depend on you for what they hear. If you are using a public-address system, the microphone will amplify your voice. If not, you must provide the necessary volume! This is difficult for most of us because we are unaccustomed to speaking at an increased level of loudness. Ask the members of the audience if they can hear you, and make whatever adjustments are necessary to assure that they can. A speech that is not heard cannot be effective.

Also, remember that the larger the audience is, the slower you will have to speak. Most of us get into a rhythm that is appropriate for talking to a small group and forget that floor noise, distance, poor lighting, and other distractions require a much slower delivery. Unlike the conversational setting, in public address your listeners cannot see you easily, hear each nuance of your voice and its inflection, pick up on micro-momentary changes in muscle tone, or read your lips. You must compensate for these disadvantages, so speak up and slow down.

Be Yourself. You are okay just the way you are. You don't have to be anyone but yourself. Indeed, you cannot be anyone but yourself. You don't have to be a great orator or a fine actor. You don't have to be especially articulate, and you don't have to have a beautifully trained voice to be an effective speaker. All you have to do is be yourself and let your concern for the subject matter and the audience show.

Keep the Microphone Out of Your Mouth. Since most of us are not accustomed to speaking into a microphone, we, typically, do not quite know what to do with a mike. You have surely witnessed a speaker who walked up to a microphone, adjusted it noisily, cleared his throat, and then leaned awkwardly to within a few inches of it and began to speak.

A good microphone is a sensitive acoustical instrument that will pick up your speech if you talk at a normal rate and with normal intensity. Go there early. Find out how to turn on the mike, and try to find out how far away from it you can go and still be within its range. Stay within that range and forget the microphone.

Nonverbal Elements

Much of what we convey in public communication is nonverbal. Your posture, the tone of your voice, your movement, your gestures, your eye contact with the audience, the clothing you wear, and the way you conduct yourself can make as great a positive or negative impression on your audience as can the things you say. Listeners don't operate unidimensionally. They "hear" with both their ears and their eyes. Therefore, you must attempt to manage the impression you create not just through what you have to say but in the ways you behave when you appear before others.[2]

Impression Formation. From the time that you first appear before your audience until you leave, you are forming impressions in the minds of your listeners. The confidence with which you approach the situation, the fact that you look directly at members of your audience, the determined but interested look on your face, and the ease with which you move all contribute to the feeling listeners have of your confidence and of your feeling about the speaking experience.

Listeners will pick up on a whole range of nonverbal cues— from style of dress to tone of voice—in interpreting your remarks.

You must remember to act as if you are vitally interested in your subject. *The way you behave is crucial* to the way that your audience will respond. The old saying that "actions speak louder than words" is very applicable. *What you do* in the communication situation often speaks louder than what you say.

Facial and Vocal Cues. Listeners can read emotions quite readily from a speaker's face. Pleasant and unpleasant emotions are signaled by the mouth and eyebrows; the unpleasant cues are more difficult to read accurately.[3] Observers can tell if you are troubled or at ease by looking at your eyebrows and forehead. If your lips are pursed or the corners of your mouth turn upward or downward, that also conveys your feelings with reasonable accuracy. The eyes and mouth in combination are the most reliable indicators of a speaker's emotional state.

The tone of your voice gives listeners an indication of your feelings. Studies show that listeners can accurately detect anger from the tone of your voice two-thirds of the time; more than half the time the sound of your voice can accurately communicate nervousness, and almost half of the time it accurately expresses sadness.[4] We introduce this information to show that a great deal can be communicated by the sound of your voice. When you practice your speech aloud, listen carefully to the tone and sound of your voice. Ask your roommate (if that is the person you choose to listen to you practice) if there is anything in the sound of your voice that is unusual. You also might ask if any of your physical behaviors (we'll get to those in just a few more lines) seem distracting. When you learn these things from an objective observer, then you have the basis for making some changes that probably will result in the creation of an improved impression when you speak.

It is important for you to remember that the way you look and the impression you create as you speak may be *critical elements* in your delivery. Let us look at some specific suggestions for some behaviors we think you should display and some we think you should try to avoid.

Body Movements

1. *Stand quietly or move for a reason.* In typical conversation, people move about naturally, gesture frequently, interrupt with questions or comments, and even turn their backs on each other. Using subtle signals in gesture or tone, partners in a conversation interact freely. However, in a public speaking context, much of this freedom is lost. It is true that many people continue to pace back and forth, and become so involved with what they are saying that they forget how they look, but remember that an audience does not forget. Plan your general movements. Stay within the confines that are presented by the context. For example, if you must use a microphone, then you have to stand next to it or carry it with you as you move.

   If you want to make a point by moving, do so. If your movement suggests a transition from one idea to the next, a point of greater intimacy with the audience, or some other special effect, then move. But have a reason for the movement, or stand still.

2. *Stand beside your visual aids, not in front of them.* You have undoubtedly seen a speaker turn his back to an audience to write on a chalkboard, and then position himself between the audience and what he has written. Do not create that problem for your audience. Prepare your visual materials in advance and practice using them. Stand beside the visuals as you refer to them, then put them away and move once again toward your audience.

3. *Don't fidget.* Avoid distracting audience attention away from the point you are trying to make by displaying random gestures and awkward postural cues. Try to avoid scratching, plucking at loose threads, adjusting your clothes, stroking yourself, or brushing dandruff from your shoulders. These behaviors are all right if you are in a casual setting, but they are most distracting to an audience.

Follow-through

Immediately after you have given your speech, unless good reasons prohibit it, thank the inviter or host, collect your materials, and move quietly from the lectern. Of course, if there are other speakers, you will probably be expected to sit through the remainder of the program.

Your exiting behavior should leave a favorable impression on the audience. You want them to think about the speech you have just made—about your key ideas. You do not want to dilute the effect of your own speech by the behaviors you choose.

In the long run, you may wish to follow through after the speech. For example, if your purpose was to influence key members of a subgroup in your audience, you knew that before giving the speech. You also knew which key members you wanted to reach. One or two weeks after the speech, you might call or write those people with a reminder, or to reinforce the content of your speech.

To illustrate, salespeople often make presentations to groups of potential buyers. Such presentations might be given by a representative of a commercial furniture wholesaler to a group of designers and salespeople who are employed by a restaurant supply and design house. Paper company representatives also give presentations to groups of printing company personnel.

As a marketing follow-through technique, salesmen for a large paper company often send a small gift to potential buyers they have addressed, as a reminder to purchase their company's product. One company that developed a new package for its high-quality writing paper in 1985 also created small note pads resembling the larger shipping carton. About a week or two after calling on a customer, its sales representatives sent one of these note pads to the person in the customer company who could make a decision to purchase their product.

It is clear that following through after the speech gives both you and your listeners an indication of whether or not your message had the desired effect. And that is tied closely to what you should do during the speech.

Our advice seems more like common sense than like expert opinion. Be yourself. Adjust to the listening needs and abilities inherent in the audience. Stand still, or move for a reason. Keep the microphone out of your mouth. Stand beside your visual materials. Resist fidgeting, and follow through after the speech.

Delivering a speech effectively requires planning, rehearsal, and attention to the details. In this chapter we followed a time line to organize suggestions about what you might do before, during, and after a speaking event to improve the effectiveness of your speaking.

Summary

Along the way we described several specific techniques for beginning and ending a speech. Getting started and getting finished are often difficult for even the most experienced speakers.

We cautioned you to keep in mind that each individual is unique, and that generally good advice may not apply in some particular instance. So it is up to you to select the communication strategies you will use, based on your own talents, on the purpose of your speech, and on the requirements of the occasion. Ultimately, our advice boils down to two things: be prepared, then be yourself.

		Key Terms
Extemporaneous	*Oral style*	
Facial cues	*Physical space*	
Impression formation	*Rehearsing*	
Impromptu	*Vocal cues*	
Memorizing	*Written style*	
Nonverbal		

Discussion Questions

1. Think of a speech you heard someone present recently. What speaker behaviors do you remember most clearly? Did they add to or detract from the message? Were those behaviors verbal or nonverbal? Which type seemed more important in that speech? Why?

2. Of all the prominent speakers you have heard, who do you think is the most effective? What is his or her method of delivery? Why do you believe that speaker has chosen that method? Be able to identify that person's strengths and weaknesses as a speaker, and to give suggestions for improvement.

3. What do you find is the best method to help remember your ideas? How widespread is the use of this method among other students in your class? What do you think are the advantages of this method for you or your fellow students? Are these advantages consistent with those outlined in this chapter? Why?

4. What are the most common nonverbal behaviors you see exhibited in the classroom? In what ways do they contribute to the effectiveness of presentations? Prepare a list of the nonverbal acts you see most commonly in classroom presentations. How do they contribute to or detract from speaker effectiveness?

Notes

1 Ernest R. Hilgard, *Theories of Learning* (New York: Appleton-Century Crofts, Inc. 1956), 350.

2 J. T. Tedeschi, B. R. Schlenker, and T. V. Bonoma, *Conflict, Power and Games* (Chicago: Aldine, 1973).

3 Judee K. Burgoon and Thomas Saine, *The Unspoken Dialogue* (Boston: Houghton Mifflin Company, 1978), 208.

4 J. R. Davitz and L. J. Davitz, "The Communication of Feelings by Content-Free Speech," *Journal of Communication* 9 (1959): 6–13.

Suggested Readings

Brigance, William Norwood. *Speech Composition.* New York: Appleton-Century Crofts, Inc., 1937 and 1953.
   This may be the very best book about developing and delivering a speech in the literature. Certainly it was one of the most influential. After more than forty-five years, this book is still used in some college courses, and is an excellent reference source.

Burgoon, Judee K., and Saine, Thomas. *The Unspoken Dialogue: An Introduction to Nonverbal Communication.* Boston: Houghton Mifflin Company, 1978.
   One of the most recent and comprehensive works exploring the research and implications of nonverbal communication in private and public settings. This is important reading for anyone interested in clearly and effectively explained work on the significance and application of nonverbal communication.

Hickson, Mark L., III, and Stacks, Don. *NVC—Nonverbal Communication: Studies and Applications.* Dubuque, Ia.: Wm. C. Brown Publishers, 1985.
   This text reviews and integrates the growing literature on nonverbal communication. It includes four highly practical chapters that explain how to apply the information in the home, on the job, and in social situations. The last chapter instructs the reader how to access the literature, and thus is a handy tool for anyone interested in nonverbal communication research.

Supporting Ideas with Evidence and Argument

Outline

Objectives

After reading this chapter you should be able to:

1. Define and then compare and contrast *beliefs and values,* and specify when supporting evidence is warranted.
2. Identify and explain the sources of evidence.
3. Describe five techniques for using statistics in public address.
4. Define and explain the use of testimony, definition and explanation, comparison and contrast, and illustration and example.

*P*REVIEW

The success of a speaking event depends heavily upon the credibility and the perceived importance of the ideas, which in turn depends upon the quality of supporting materials. Supporting materials must seem consistent with a listener's beliefs and values. Evidence comes from persons, documents, and things. Direct evidence does not usually contribute to persuasion in a speech. Persons and documents generate statistics and personal evidence. We offer five suggestions about the use of statistics: (1) use them sparingly; (2) round them off; (3) explain what they mean to the listeners; (4) be sure they are representative, sensibly generated, and reliable; and (5) use visual aids to help listeners understand them.

Personal evidence includes testimony, definition and explanation, comparison and contrast, and illustrations and examples. We offer suggestions for intelligent use of each of these forms.

The effectiveness of *any* speech depends on the mind-set of the listeners— on their beliefs and values. If you are going to be successful as a speaker, you must persuade your listeners that what you are saying is *credible;* that is, what you say must seem consistent with what they already believe. Your success as a speaker also depends upon your ability to persuade your listeners that what you are saying is *important* to them in some way. That your listeners agree with your analysis may not be significant unless they also think your analysis matters to them. Without that sense of importance, your listeners are not likely to be moved.

These two criteria—credibility and importance—identify the primary uses of supporting materials in public speaking. Put another way, audience members almost always have two questions in mind when they are listening to a speech: "How do you know?" "How does this matter to me?" You select and use supporting materials to answer these two questions, whether the speech is to inform or to persuade.

The purpose of this chapter is to show you how to identify, locate, and use information, evidence, and arguments that will support your ideas. Ultimately, you should be able to design speeches that will have appeal and seem important and reasonable to your listeners. To do this you must consider the beliefs and values of your listeners.

Beliefs and Values: First Considerations in Supporting Ideas

An individual's beliefs and values control what she accepts as true and important. To illustrate this fundamental notion, consider your own position on the "pro-life" and "pro-choice" controversy—the controversy over whether or not the government should permit and support abortions. Your position on this issue depends upon your values and beliefs. You will accept or reject what people tell you about this controversy according to what seems consistent or inconsistent with your values and beliefs.

Suppose you believe that life begins at the moment of conception. The moment the two cells combine, they constitute a living human being. Suppose, further, you feel that only self-defense or national defense justifies one human being taking the life of another human being.

If these suppositions are indicative of your beliefs and values, you will probably oppose any hint that the government should make abortion available to women on demand. But issues of this sort are rarely that simple. You may also hold other related opinions. You may feel that a baby is entitled to some chance of happiness, including parents who want the baby and can support it. You may view incest and rape as repugnant, and thus feel that a conception resulting from rape or incest would also be repugnant.

You can hold all of these opinions at the same time, and many people do! They are not necessarily inconsistent, and they do not seem inconsistent to people who hold them. You can see that they do confound the question of whether to support or oppose using federal funds to pay for an abortion.

Your position on the topic of abortion is not the question here. Rather, this example was used to show that a position on any issue depends on your beliefs and values. As a speaker wishing to learn how to present information to strengthen your arguments and to develop your personal credibility, you need to understand how beliefs and values work.

A belief statement is characterized by the use of the verb *to be*. This idea is not as simple as it first appears. Some statements that carry the word *is* (the present tense of the verb *to be*) are subjective in nature. That is, they appear to flow out of the judgment or imagination of the speaker. Others are objective in nature. That is, they appear to bear witness to an observable truth. Both kinds of statements, however, if characterized by a form of the verb *to be* are belief statements. Consider this example:

Beliefs

> This board *is* too heavy to pick up.

The "truth" of this statement is relative to the person making it. A five-year-old child might find the board too heavy to lift, even though you lifted it quite easily when you put it there. The child's statement is a belief statement, but it is highly subjective.

Consider another more difficult example—more difficult because it sounds more "objective." It makes reference to an observed truth, but again the truth is in the head of the speaker.

> That tree *is* a blue spruce.

This sentence seems factual. You might be able to verify the accuracy of the statement easily enough. You can look into any good fieldbook of natural history to make an identification. Or, perhaps you "know" the characteristic features of a blue spruce. If so, you can easily say "that tree is a blue spruce."

Nevertheless, the truth of the sentence is inside you; it is not inherent in the tree you are describing. You have made an observation and then sorted through your set of categories for trees in arriving at a name. The name comes to you because what you are observing seems consistent with a set of standards that mark a blue spruce from other conifer trees. Because all these things are true, the statement seems to be a statement of fact. You may accept it as a fact, but are you certain? How could you prove that the tree is a blue spruce? One way would be to ask an expert—someone whose opinion you trust. If you asked several experts and if they all verified your conclusion, you would say the statement is a fact. What is really at issue here is not the "truth" of the statement, but rather its credibility. Your statement, "That tree is a blue spruce," seems credible because the evidence presented supports your claim; the evidence verifies the statement and makes it believable.

A statement does not have to be verified or verifiable for someone to believe it. You may be so familiar with the characteristic features of trees that, once you name the tree a blue spruce, you do not bother to verify the accuracy of your statement. Even so, the statement requires some supporting evidence. Similarly, *any* belief that seems obvious warrants supporting evidence, and that is the problem. People do not typically attempt to verify the truth of a belief statement that seems obvious to them, which can create fairly severe problems. To illustrate, review these sentences:

> The Russian arms build-up is a threat to world peace.
>
> If given a chance, American farmers could feed the world.
>
> Computer error could not bring a nuclear war.
>
> Racism is the fundamental source of social problems in America's large cities.
>
> Poverty is the principal cause of international conflict.

These statements seemed obvious to the people who spoke them. Whether or not they seem obvious to you has implications for you as a speaker. It means that you will have to work very hard to present information and to develop evidence and arguments to support your ideas so that your listeners will focus attention on and attempt to verify their own beliefs. Suppose that you have decided to give a speech about cleaning up the waterways in your area. To be effective, you will have to present information and design appeals that seem consistent with the beliefs and values of your listeners. Remember that what they believe may seem so obvious to them that they have not bothered with verification.

Consider the belief statements you might use as the main ideas of your speech.

The stream *is* polluted.

The stream *was* polluted by the chemical plant upstream.

The managers of that chemical plant *are* responsible for the pollution.

You will see immediately that for someone else to accept these statements as true, you might have to develop some proof. You need to support your ideas. A listener would surely ask, "How do you know that the stream is polluted? How do you know that the chemical plant is the source of the pollution? How do you know that the managers of the chemical plant are responsible? Are they directly responsible? Indirectly responsible? How do you know that?"

One listener might be less accepting of your ideas than you would like—more accepting of the present situation—because that person's system of beliefs and values differs from yours. So, what seems important to her may be quite different from your own sense of importance. For example, she may think: "Well, perhaps there is some pollution, but because we need the jobs that the chemical plant brings, we should tolerate some pollution to keep the plant in operation." For you to be effective with this listener, you would have to present evidence and arguments with enough persuasive strength to prove your claim and to show the listener that it matters to her. You will have to overcome the effects that the listener's own belief system produces.

To review: When you make a claim that something *is,* you are making a belief statement. For someone else to accept that statement, you will probably have to supply supporting evidence. Remember the question, "How do you know?" Make a point of asking yourself how you know every argument in a speech. This will help you identify which of your ideas need support.

Values

A value is a statement characterized by the words *should* or *ought,* or by such judgmental terms as *good, beautiful, correct,* or *important.*

Consider the following value statements. A negative-sounding example will help us make the point more clearly.

Driving 70 MPH was a dumb thing to do. You ought to drive that car a lot slower. So much speed isn't safe. And besides, you ought to obey the law.

You're wrong, Henry. And besides that, you're ignorant. It may have been against the law, but it wasn't dumb. Besides, I had reasons.

Notice that each of these statements implies the existence of a set of rules that justify the claims *should* and *ought.* Also notice that the judgments involved in the statements are either directly stated or implied.

Look at a more positive, and therefore more subtle, example:

> That is a very interesting and informative course. And the
> information is so important! In fact, the course probably ought to be
> required.
>
> Yes, I agree. Maybe we should require it some time during the
> freshman or sophomore years.

Here both speakers are in agreement, so they are not as likely to recognize the judgments and rules that underpin their remarks. You can notice them, however, by being alert to *should* and *ought*, and to judgmental terms.

When you subscribe to some set of rules or standards that cause you to think *should* or *ought*, or to make judgments like *dumb* or *wrong* or *interesting* or *informative*, you are applying a value system.

Values are internal; they are inside you. According to the negative example above, the law says that people may not drive faster than 55 MPH. Regardless, there was controversy over the matter of driving speed. The laws of the land are external, and are not necessarily part of a person's value system. You may or may not agree with the law; you may choose to drive faster or slower, and you will make some kind of a choice every time you drive. If you stay within the legal speed limit, your choice rests on a value system inside you.

In the positive example, *interesting, informative,* and *important* are all internal notions. What seems interesting to one person may seem dull to another. To illustrate, rank the following subjects from 1 to 5, where 1 seems the most and 5 the least interesting subject to you. Then compare and contrast your rankings with your classmates. You will find that there are no uninteresting subjects, just disinterested people!

> _____ The all-time most valuable baseball team
> _____ Characteristics of a fine red wine
> _____ Similarities and differences between Reggae and new wave
> music
> _____ How to increase your knowledge of the stock market
> _____ Three approaches to organizing the files on a hard disk

The critical point we are trying to make is that when people think about what ought to be, they hinge their thinking on values that they hold. As a speaker, you may have to think of a way to adapt to, or even overcome resistance from, the listener's operating value systems. Clearly, the listener plays a central part in shaping evidence.

Let us look once more at the driving example to see how this works. Suppose that you have decided to make these arguments:

1. Most people are responsible.
2. Therefore, most people will act responsibly, given the choice.
3. In any case, people should be allowed freedom to choose the responsible option.
4. The law that limits speeds in the United States to 55 MPH does not permit individual drivers freedom to choose a responsible option.
5. Besides, a deliberate choice to exceed 55 MPH might be the most sensible choice for other reasons—for example, to move freight more quickly across the country, or because a particular automobile is designed to operate safely at high speeds.
6. Consequently, the law limiting speed to 55 MPH should be replaced with a more general law that gives people a choice about what is safe and reasonable.

You will see immediately that these claims are controversial. If the listener is going to accept them, you may have to develop evidence and arguments to support each one. Some of those arguments would have to appeal to the values of the listeners—the sets of standards inside their heads about what ought to be. Also, if you want your listeners to act on your proposal to replace the 55 MPH speed limit with something else, they must sense that your proposal matters to them. Thus, your listeners play an important role—perhaps the most important role—in developing evidence and argument.

Beliefs (*is*) and values (*ought, should, good*) work very closely together in the heads of listeners—to such a degree that people often cannot tell the difference. Therefore, as a speaker, your selection of evidence and arguments will have to appeal to both their beliefs and their values. A listener will ask you "How do you know?" Or a listener may respond, "Oh yeah? Show me." Sometimes a listener will respond, "So what?" If you cannot provide a satisfactory response, which seems consistent with what the listener already believes or values, the listener will probably reject your statements. You must have solid evidence to develop your arguments. Your success as a speaker is contingent on it.

Locating and Using Evidence

A definition of the term *evidence* that has been generally accepted for many years comes from one of the most respected textbooks about argumentation and debate ever written.[1] Evidence consists of ". . . informative statements which, *because they are believed by a listener or reader,* may be used as a means for gaining his assent."

Notice that evidence does not exist in isolation from statements. A fact without a statement about the fact is not useful in gaining a listener's agreement. As a speaker, you must do more than merely compile facts or figures. You must present them. How you do that may be as important as the evidence, itself.

You may wish to look at the matter of discovering and using evidence more carefully. What are the sources of evidence? What kinds of evidence are available? What pointers and suggestions about uses can be made that will enhance the power and credibility of evidence? How is evidence best presented?

The Sources of Evidence

There are three sources of evidence: (1) persons, (2) documents, and (3) things. In a court of law, things (real evidence) that you can see, hear, touch, taste, and smell can be very important. For example, the question of whether a person committed a murder might depend upon the real evidence of a handgun, or fingerprints on a drinking glass. To establish the guilt of a defendant, the prosecuting attorney might argue that the defendant's fingerprints were found at the scene, on both a drinking glass and on the murder weapon. It would follow that the defendant was at the scene of the crime, and had handled the weapon.

Most public speaking goals do not depend upon real evidence, but rather on information reported by human beings, either in testimony or in documentary form. By our definition, evidence consists of *informative statements* by people, which is called personal evidence. When a person says: "I know that I have this disease because my doctor told me so," the doctor's remark, because it was believed by the listener, constitutes personal evidence.

Our actions, as well as our beliefs, usually depend upon some form of personal evidence. The person might say: "Dr. Smith gave me a prescription for these pills. I've been taking them every day for the past week." Clearly, the decision to take the pills would depend upon the patient's faith in the doctor. The doctor's statements *must have seemed true*, and they *must have seemed important* to the patient. Personal evidence can take either written or oral form. In either form the credibility of the evidence is in the head of the receiver.

Questions about the quality of personal evidence include (1) whether or not the person giving the information is competent to give it, and (2) whether or not the source is objective enough to give it without bias. Other criteria include the (3) relevancy, (4) completeness, (5) accuracy, (6) recency, and (7) clarity of the evidence. Was the person giving the information in a position to know the truth? Was the person expert enough to give a correct interpretation of the information? Was the person biased? Does the person's information really bear on the question at hand? Does the information matter to the listener? Is the information current? Is the intended meaning clear?

Remember, a statement does not have to be verifiable for listeners to believe it. All that matters is that the statement seem consistent with the beliefs and values the listeners already have in their heads. The key is to relate the evidence to the listeners.

We will devote the remainder of this chapter to the most frequently used categories of supporting evidence. Keep in mind that the value and strength of the evidence you use depend upon your listeners. As a speaker, your task is to select evidence that will seem most credible and important to them.

The Nature and Kinds of Evidence

Facts and figures are among the most useful forms of supporting materials. Your ideas will be more vivid and interesting if you use real numbers and proper nouns. In chapter 11 we will touch upon this idea further in our discussion of the Ginger principle. The use of facts and figures makes it easier for a listener to decide that what is being said makes a difference to him or her.[2]

Specific Information

Look at the following two statements. The first statement is comparatively dull because it lacks detail. The second statement is filled with details that make the statement come alive. The facts and figures—the ginger—are the raw materials with which a listener can form an image. Again, you see that the listeners play an active role in making this form of evidence meaningful.

> Opportunities for making money are everywhere. All you have to do is keep an eye open to the possibilities, and have the courage to act.

> Your opportunities to make money are limited only by your imagination. A couple of years ago a real estate developer in Florida, John Stocks, heard that the junk left over from restoring the Statue of Liberty was going to be hauled out to sea and dumped. He wanted a piece of the original for himself, and he figured that other people would want a piece of the old statue, too. So, in February of 1984, Stocks founded a company to manufacture and sell medallions, plaques, sculptures, paperweights, and commemorative coins made out of pieces of the 200 tons of copper, steel, brass, and concrete that would have been dumped into the Atlantic. He bought the statue for $12 million and 15 percent of his gross sales for fourteen years. There is no telling how much money Stocks will make.[3]

Our point is that listeners find specific material to be more interesting and more convincing than generalizations. The more specific and vivid the information, the better.

Helen Roskowski was studying for a teaching career when she enrolled in her first public speaking course. She decided to give a speech on the importance of social climate in schooling, a topic of special interest to her, because she was planning to be a teacher. Her challenge was to show that the topic she selected also was potentially important to her classmates.

Notice how Helen used facts and figures as supporting material to relate the speech to her listeners.

> *Helen Roskowski's basic idea:* The social climate in the classroom depends on the quality of interpersonal relationships that exist there. Those relationships are crucial because they affect the amount and kind of subject matter that is learned, and they also set the pattern of learning behavior for the child's future as a learner.

> *What Helen Roskowski actually said:* Last week I had the opportunity to observe an arithmetic lesson in Mrs. Marty Leonard's third-grade class at Sumner School. I came away from that experience with a new respect for the importance of keeping order in a third-grade classroom. One little brown-eyed boy couldn't seem to sit still. So he did just the opposite. Billy—his name was Billy—was all over the place. He yanked a book out of Sarah's hands, and of course, Sarah went right after him to get it back. Another time he threw his book down and shouted "I hate this 'rithmetic junk."
> All the while, Mrs. Leonard just went right on—until, at one point, she had had enough. She shouted at Billy to be still and to sit down. Billy, for his part, decided to have a temper tantrum. And pretty soon the other kids were getting into the action, too. It took about ten minutes for Mrs. Leonard to restore calm. By then she had to go on with something else.
>   I thought to myself how important that incident might be to Billy and the other kids, not only this year, while they're trying to learn division, but all the way through their school years.

The detail in Helen's speech provided the listeners with the raw materials necessary for them to develop concrete images. In addition, the details suggested to the listeners that Helen knew what she was talking about. She had done the research; she had actually visited the classroom. Obviously she was telling the truth; therefore, her ideas must be right. As you can see from this example, factual material is more vivid and compelling than generalization. The use of specific information as supporting material helps your listeners find meaning in what you are saying.

Statistics

Statistics are not the same as the ordinary numbers you might use when applying the Ginger principle. Statistics are grouped facts—a shorthand method of summarizing a large number of cases. You use them as supporting material to suggest the extent of a problem, or to clarify or strengthen some point you want to make.

The world we live in is full of statistics. You are using statistics if you say "85 percent," or if you say "two-thirds," or if you say "millions of Americans can't be wrong." Most of us could not say precisely what these statistics mean, but that does not seem to decrease the effectiveness of statistics as supporting material. Keep in mind, though, that widespread use of unsubstantiated statistics does not change your ethical responsibility to be accurate and informed.

People seem to feel more comfortable when they have numbers to back up their suppositions. Because this is true, statistics can be very powerful supporting material in your speeches. But you have to be careful when you use them. Here is how Mary Jane Moore used statistics to develop her speech about holography (two dimensional images that appear three dimensional) as an important new technological advance. Her idea was that holography was already an important development, and becoming more so all the time.

> Holographs are cropping up everywhere, and in increasing numbers. By next year around 90 million people will have MasterCards that are embossed with holographs. They are cheap to produce and virtually impossible to change without destroying the credit card.

Frank Pepitone wanted to talk about the information age. He used statistics to back up his idea that information had become more important to our economy than material goods.

> Right now 70 percent of the labor force in the United States works with information instead of with physical things. Seventy-five percent of the American salary dollars go to managers and professionals. By far, the greatest part of the time spent in any office is spent listening, talking, finding facts, and dealing with mail.
> These statistics make one point very clear: we have got to learn to handle information more efficiently and more effectively. And the time for you and me to start is right now, while we're still in college.

Keep in mind that statistics can be powerful supporting material, but they can be very misleading. If you decide to use them, you need to be careful that you do not misrepresent the truth, and that you do not confuse your listeners.

Statistics can also be boring and confusing! Doyle Davis used too many statistics, and he did not explain them, in a speech about the importance of the mass media in our society. As a result, his listeners lost the thread of his ideas, and then their interest in his remarks. His speech would have been much better if he had used statistics more sparingly.

> There are about 300 million television sets in American homes. On average, those television sets are on about seven hours every day. By the time a child reaches the first grade, he will have watched ten thousand hours of television. Compare that with the ten thousand hours that a youngster spends through the first twelve years of grade school and high school.

About 75 percent of the television shows have violent themes, and it's an axiom among television producers that at least one so-called action scene appear within the first thirty seconds of a show. Of the four movies on cable last night, three were utterly violent and about 85 percent of the fourth one was violent. One hundred percent of the movies had violent themes, and about 80 percent of the scenes were also sex-loaded.

Here, then, are some suggestions—some dos and don'ts—that should help you and your listeners make the most of statistical data.

Don't use many statistics in a speech. We suggest that you use statistics as you would a spicy seasoning. Include just enough to prove your point, but don't use too many.

Do round off very complicated statistics. Say "eight million" rather than "seven million, nine hundred and sixty three thousand, four hundred and twenty-two." A listener needs your help in grasping and remembering statistics, so unless you have a very definite reason for using an exact figure, round it off.

Do explain what the statistics mean to the listeners. An explanation of what the statistics mean to the listeners is especially important when you are relaying very large numbers. For example, very few individuals can relate to the enormously large numbers involved in the federal budget. If you want an audience to understand those figures, you have to make them human in some way. This is exactly what David Lin did in his speech on the federal budget. Notice how effectively he made his statistics meaningful.

The federal government has estimated that in the fiscal year 1985–86, it will have receipts of 793 billion, 729 million dollars. Projected expenditures for the same year are 973 billion, 725 million dollars. The average man on the street can't even imagine how much money that is.

What these figures mean is that the government expects to take in about $3000 for every man, woman, and child in the United States, and to spend about $4000 for every man, woman, and child in the United States.

Do not use sloppy statistics. Use statistics only when you are sure that they are truly representative, that they have been generated sensibly, and that they come from reliable sources. To illustrate the problem of sloppy statistics, imagine that you have decided to take a survey on campus to discover whether or not students there would support the argument that the general education requirement at your institution should be abolished.

For a statistic to be representative of a larger group, you have to be very careful that the smaller sample is truly like the whole student body. For a statistic to be generated sensibly, the method used to collect it must be sensible. For a statistic to be reliable, the source must be knowledgeable and reliable.

This was exactly the problem Sam Baldwin faced when he determined to give the speech to abolish the general education requirement. He wanted to say that a large percentage of the students at the institution would favor his position, but he knew that he would have to support the claim with some statistics, and that he would have to answer the professor's question, "How do you know?"

Sam positioned himself outside the chemistry building. From 10:00 to 11:00 that morning, Sam approached students and asked them this question: "Would you favor the abolition of the general education core requirement?" In all, Sam interviewed twenty-three people; seventeen were men and six were women. Fourteen of the students said something like "Yeah" in response to Sam's question.

Just over 60 percent of the sampled respondents favored abolishing the general education core requirement. Do you believe that statistic truly represented the student body? Clearly it did not. Twenty-three students cannot reflect the overall viewpoint of a student body of fifteen thousand. The sample could not reflect the school's proportion of seniors, juniors, sophomores, and freshmen. Since 58 percent of the student population are women, Sam's respondents did not represent the gender mix at the institution. Because all of the students were interviewed as they were entering the chemistry building, it is reasonable to suppose that they had some purpose in going there, perhaps to attend a chemistry class. This suggests that the academic interests of the university may not have been represented in Sam's group. Were they all chemistry majors, or were all the major areas of study in the institution represented? We cannot know if the twenty-three students were full-time or part-time students. We cannot know their financial status or their academic background. We cannot know if the sample reflected the ethnic balance of the entire university.

Notice, also, that Sam's approach to collecting the statistics leaves much to be desired. Not only should he have selected a more representative sample, but he also should have asked his question differently.

In some colleges students are required to complete a certain number of hours in the humanities, in the sciences, and in the fine and performing arts. Within that broad general requirement, there often exists a core of courses—writing, algebra, and Texas history, for example—that every student in the institution must complete. Sam's question could be confusing. Had he been more skillful, he might have asked two questions—one about the general education requirement and one about the special and limited core of specified courses.

The Verbal Statements

Statistics show that airplane travel is much safer than car travel. But the safest way to go is by bus! Only 32 people died in buses last year—just .4 of one death per billion passenger miles travelled. Compare that with only 1 death per billion passenger miles travelled for scheduled airlines, 10.6 deaths per billion travelled for cars, and .8 of one death per billion for railroad passenger trains. The actual figures are: for passenger automobiles and taxis, 22,859 deaths and 2,154.4 billions of passenger miles; for scheduled airlines, 218 deaths and 213.6 billions of passenger miles; for buses, 32 deaths and 88.8 billions of passenger miles; for railroad passenger trains, 9 deaths and 10.9 billions of passenger miles.

Pie Chart "The Safest Way to Go"

Passenger automobiles and taxis: 10.6

Scheduled airlines: 1

Railroad passenger trains: .8

Buses: .4

Deaths per billion passenger miles

	Passenger deaths	Billions of passenger miles
Passenger automobiles and taxis	22,859	2,154.4
Scheduled airlines	218	218.6
Buses	32	88.8
Railroad passenger trains	9	10.9

FIGURE 9.1 Verbal and Visual Materials Presenting Statistics on Travel Safety. Both blocks present the same information, but the message is more vivid and more easily grasped by just a glance at the pie chart. (Chart by John Pack.)

You need to be sure that your statistics are representative, sensibly generated, and reliable. The same statistics have sometimes been used to support opposing sides in the same argument! Because statistics can be interpreted in many ways and because they can be used to accomplish so many different purposes, you should be particularly careful in selecting and using them.

Use visual aids to help the audience understand the statistics. Especially when you are trying to explain a statistical trend, such as the increasing federal deficit or the rise and fall of some stock market indicator, a string of sentences will not be nearly so effective as a visual aid.

In the next chapter you will study how to develop and use visual aids as supporting material. For now it is enough to say that you need to communicate through more than one channel, especially when you are using very complicated statistics. Your listeners need all the help you can provide them. To illustrate, look at the models in figure 9.1. Which model is easier for you to grasp: the verbal statements on the left or the visual aid on the right?

Statistics, then, are different from ordinary numbers. They provide powerful supporting material if they are used carefully. To reiterate, use them sparingly, round them off, and explain what they mean to the listeners. Be sure that they are truly representative and that they have been generated sensibly and responsibly. It is also a good idea to help your audience understand statistics with visual materials.

Personal evidence consists of informative statements. It can take many forms. Perhaps the most commonly used forms of personal evidence are (1) testimony, (2) definition and explanation, (3) comparison and contrast, and (4) illustrations and examples.

Personal Evidence

Testimony. Sometimes you will want to support your own opinion with the judgment of others. This strategy is sometimes called "argument from authority." It has particular value as a way to bolster an idea to give it persuasive strength and vividness. Testimony is any direct quotation, or a paraphrased version, of what someone else has said.

Suppose you wanted to give a speech about how to become an entrepreneur. As an undergraduate student, you may not have the personal experience to establish yourself as an expert in the minds of your listeners. Your argument that a person who wants to step out on his own in business ought to spend about seven years in a large organization working for someone else will have greater strength if you can support it with testimony. For example, you could directly quote Peter Drucker, the famous expert on management, or you could paraphrase his statement. Both would be testimony used as supporting material.

> *Quote:* Peter Drucker, the management expert, believes that a
> successful entrepreneur must first work in a large organization.
> Without that experience, ". . . he doesn't have the background.
> The most successful of the young entrepreneurs today are people
> who have spent five to eight years in a big organization. . . .
> [that's where] they learn how to do a cash-flow analysis and how

one trains people and how one delegates and how one builds a team. The ones without that background are the entrepreneurs who, no matter how great their success, are being pushed out."[4]

Paraphrase: Peter Drucker, the famous management expert, believes that a person cannot be successful as an entrepreneur unless he first spends about seven years in a big organization. He believes that what they learn there—such things as managing cash flow and training people and delegating authority and team building—are essential to entrepreneurial success.

If you want to use testimony well, keep in mind that *the source should be known and acceptable to the listeners,* or else *have some position or some achievement* that qualifies him as an expert. *The source ought to be an expert in the field.* Obviously, you strengthen the speech only if the source of your testimony has special training or experience that makes what he says valuable.

Usually, but not always, *the source ought to be free from bias.* If a source represents an interest group that would benefit from believing what he says, then the testimony is suspect. If that is the point you wish to prove, then the testimony could provide powerful evidence. But if you are attempting to persuade your listeners to your source's position, they must believe that the source is without bias.

Sometimes another person has said something so well that you can strengthen your own position just by quoting his or her language. So much is this the case that our society has collected and passed on the vivid thoughts of its notable thinkers for nearly thirty centuries. How could you improve on John F. Kennedy's tongue-in-cheek statement that "Washington, D.C., is a city of southern efficiency and northern charm"?

When should you quote directly and when should you paraphrase? No general rule governs this matter, but it is safe to say that a paraphrase is probably a good idea if the direct quotation is too complicated for the audience to understand it easily. Also, a paraphrase is probably better than a direct quotation if the quotation is more than a few sentences long.

John Naisbitt, author of Megatrends. *In using testimony, it is important that your audience accept the source as credible.*

Definition and Explanation. Definition and explanation can be very useful as supporting materials, especially for enhancing the clarity of abstract ideas. What do these words mean: *democracy, communism, fairness, loyalty?* Is a "freedom fighter" different from a "terrorist?" Or, does the difference depend upon whose side you are on? Clearly, these loose terms need clarification through definition and explanation.

If you want to be sure that your listeners are understanding what you are talking about, then you must define every important term in your speech. Two kinds of terms need definition. The first category includes very technical terms or jargonistic terms that only a specialist would be likely

The speaker must present information and evidence to support ideas that will cause the listener to verify his or her own beliefs.

to understand. The second category includes familiar terms that we use every day, but because of their various connotative meanings they convey different things to different people.

Jeanne Smolinski should have defined some terms in a speech she gave to her 2:00 P.M. class. She said, "The Pascagoula raw material upgrade for December showed a negative upgrade of $1.81 per barrel." No one in her audience knew that she meant they had lost about $1.80 per barrel in December!

An engineer from a paper mill was talking about his work during his night class in public speaking. He said, "Among the sensitivities we must deal with over and over are breakages in the Soft and Pretty line." No one knew that "sensitivities" were problems, or that the "Soft and Pretty line" was the production line on which toilet paper was made.

Comparison and Contrast. Comparison and contrast can provide very powerful evidence. When you compare things, you identify their similarities. When you contrast them, you identify their differences.

Comparison and contrast may be used for three rhetorical purposes: (1) to make things clear and vivid, (2) to substantiate or provide proof, and (3) to lend a sense of concreteness to such abstract terms as *goodness, justice,* or *equality.*

To make something clear and vivid, compare it to a thing that is well known to the listeners. For example:

> An 8-bit processor can only work half as fast as a 16-bit processor. Think of it as a machine that packs oranges, eight at a time. The belt brings eight oranges up to the box, dumps them, then brings another eight oranges to the box to pack. It can only pack eight oranges at a time.
>
> A 16-bit processor can pack 16 oranges every time the 8-bit processor packs eight oranges.

To use comparison and contrast as proof, compare or contrast the known with the unknown, then argue that what is true of the known is also true of the unknown. A good way to proceed is to follow this three-step sequence: (1) develop the comparison or contrast; (2) claim that the observations you have made are either consistent or inconsistent with what the audience members believe or value; and (3) conclude that since the things compared or contrasted are consistent or inconsistent in the ways you have said, they will be consistent or inconsistent in other ways, too.

It is important that you do not leave the formulation of these three steps to the audience. You must show the similarities and the differences. You must point out that what you observe relates in some way to the mind-set of the listeners. And you must not take for granted that the listeners will conclude what you wish them to conclude, all by themselves. You must draw the conclusions for them.

Here is how one speaker used comparison and contrast to argue against building an elevated interstate highway spur through downtown Mobile, Alabama.

> We have lots of evidence that putting an elevated interstate highway through a downtown area creates a slum in the area under the highway. This certainly has been the case in Kansas City, in Chicago, in Detroit, in Denver, in Los Angeles, and in New York. And it will be true of Mobile, as well.
>
> If you want to see what your support for the elevated highway will bring to Mobile, take a drive to New Orleans on Interstate 10; and when you get there, follow along the interstate, but underneath it. You will find empty buildings with broken windows. You will find abandoned cars. You will find winos sleeping in the doorways of abandoned businesses. But be sure to lock your car and close the windows, because you will also find a criminal element on that trip ready and willing to knock you on the head and steal your car and your money.
>
> I can't believe that anyone here wants that to happen in Mobile. But it most certainly will happen to Mobile if that highway is built. It has happened in every metropolitan downtown area where an elevated highway has been built. So the question is not whether we ought to have an interstate highway extension through the city. The question is whether we want to create a slum in our beautiful downtown area.

To use comparison and contrast to build a sense of concreteness, compare something that exists in the real world (something concrete) to the abstraction you wish to make seem more real. For example:

> Choosing to get married is something like choosing to take a trip on a bicycle built for two. You have to agree where you are going. You both have to work together to get there. In order to help make the trip pleasant, you will probably want to take turns at the handlebars. And, of course, preventive maintenance is a necessary part of success. If you don't give the bike a little oil now and then, and fix an occasional flat tire, you probably won't finish the trip.

Illustrations and Examples. The value of an example or illustration as supporting material for a speech can scarcely be exaggerated. You can verify from your own experience as a student how valuable illustrations and examples are to you, both as a listener and as a reader. This is especially true when an idea is very abstract, very complex, or very technical; illustrations and examples enhance your ability to understand and accept an idea. When you study, do you look for examples and illustrations to help you understand the more difficult materials?

The student speaker who made the following remarks about clinical evidence against smoking marijuana obviously appreciated the value of illustrations and examples as supporting materials. Notice that he used two pieces of illustrative material to question the value of the clinical research. His purpose was to create doubt in his listeners, and he was very successful in doing so, even though there are a good many gaps in his reasoning.

> This whole idea of smoking marijuana is filled with emotionalism. The idea of using marijuana is so emotionally loaded, in fact, that it is very difficult to get any objective research. But without objectivity in the research, you can't count on the findings. So we're left with the problem of not really knowing what to believe.
>
> To illustrate, the Food and Drug Administration says that men who smoke marijuana have been shown to have dramatically reduced sperm count. But what does this mean? Under closer scrutiny, the claim about reduced sperm count doesn't hold water because the research was so badly designed. All they did was ask the volunteers if they smoke pot. Oh, they found that the sample group had a lower sperm count, all right. But they never did show that it was marijuana-related. I suspect they wanted to, but they just didn't have the evidence.
>
> The FDA often draws conclusions without very much scientific reason to do so. In fact, they're now saying that marijuana smoking will cause cancer because massive doses of the by-products of marijuana smoking caused cancer in experimental animals. But the same kind of animals were injected with massive doses of B-complex vitamins—doses approximately equal to the doses of by-products produced by burning marijuana; and they, too, got cancer. That would not be grounds to ban B-complex vitamins, of course, since you can't live without the B-complex vitamins.
>
> I don't think it is enough reason to ban marijuana, either. Do you?

If you will glance back through this chapter (or any other chapter in this book) you will find numerous examples and illustrations. We have used them to help you understand and accept our ideas. We highly recommend that you, too, use this valuable form of supporting material.[5]

Summary

In this chapter we have said that your success as a speaker will depend on the mind-set of your listeners—on their beliefs and values. We also said that your success is contingent upon your listeners believing that what you have to say is credible, and that it matters to them. These two goals, credibility and importance, are the primary reasons for supporting your ideas with evidence.

A belief is a statement that may be characterized by the word *is*. A value is based on rules about how things "ought" or "should" be, or upon some judgment call, such as "good" or "beautiful" or "important." Any evidence you use must seem to the listeners consistent with their beliefs or values.

Evidence may be drawn from written and verbal testimony, and from things. Although a court of law may require concrete evidence of things to establish some truth, far more persuasion rests upon evidence that is generated by people, either in written or oral form. Testimony may be factual (verifiable) or it may be opinion. In the case of opinion, the value of the evidence lies in the credibility of the source.

We described and made suggestions for using facts and figures, statistics, testimony, definition and explanation, comparison and contrast, and illustrations and examples. These forms of support can be used to achieve a variety of specialized purposes, but the most important ones are to make the set of statements seem consistent to the listeners, and to make them important. In the final analysis, whether or not a listener is going to be moved by what you say depends almost entirely upon the quality of the supporting materials you use.

Key Words

Beliefs

Comparison and contrast

Credibility

Evidence
  direct evidence
  personal evidence

Example

Explanation

Illustration

Statistics

Supporting material

Testimony

Values

Discussion Questions

1. It is sometimes said that married people fight about three things: how to raise the children, how to spend the money, and sex. It is clear that people in our society have strong feelings about each of these topics, regardless of whether or not the statement is true. Compare and contrast your ideas on one of these topics with those of your classmates. How do you account for the similarities and differences?

2. Bring a magazine to class that you purchased—one that you had acquired before reading this textbook. With a group of your classmates, page through the magazine and study the advertisements. What supporting evidence and arguments do you find particularly effective? Why? Are these advertisements related to the interests, values, and beliefs of people your age, your sex, and your educational level? What do you make of your findings?

3. Pay particular attention to the kinds of personal evidence that you find in your day. Agree with your classmates to spend half a day making notes each time you hear or see some example of testimony, definition, explanation, comparison and contrast, or illustration or example. Bring your notes to class and compare them with your classmates' findings. Are there any similarities or differences? How do you account for these? Are you startled by the amount of personal evidence found?

Notes

1 Douglas Ehninger and Wayne Brockriede, *Decision by Debate,* (New York: Dodd, Mead & Company, 1963), 110. Emphasis ours.

2 Dale Hample, "Refinements on the Cognitive Model of Argument: Concreteness, Involvement and Group Scores," *Western Journal of Speech Communication* 49: (Fall 1985): 267–85.

3 Facts for this example were drawn from Carolyn B. Mandelker, "Buying a Piece of the Statue of Liberty," *Venture* (June 1985), 10–11.

4 Peter Drucker, in "The Entrepreneurial Mystique," *Inc.: The Magazine for Growing Companies* 7 (October 1985): 36.

5 Illustration continues to be an area of considerable research interest. For a recent essay, *see* William G. Kirkwood, "Parables as Metaphors and Examples," *Quarterly Journal of Speech* 71 (November 1985): 422–40.

Suggested Readings

Arnold, Carroll C., and Bowers, John Waite, eds. *Handbook of Rhetorical and Communication Theory.* Boston: Allyn and Bacon, 1984.
   This book provides content for the serious student. It has already become standard reading in upper-division undergraduate and in graduate-level classes. You really ought to examine this excellent work.

Ehninger, Douglas, and Brockriede, Wayne. *Decision by Debate.* New York: Dodd, Mead & Company, 1963.

Freeley, Austin J. *Argumentation and Debate: Rational Decision Making,* 6th ed. Belmont, Calif.: Wadsworth Publishing Company, Inc., 1980.
   These two books are "old chestnuts"—well known and well respected by speech and argumentation teachers. They are easy-to-read and thorough.

Toulmin, Stephen; Rieke, Richard; and Janik, Allan. *An Introduction to Reasoning.* New York: Macmillan Publishing Company, 1979.
   This is "must reading" if you seriously want to learn how to develop logical evidence and argument. It is well written, and a little deeper, but not as easygoing as the Ehninger and Brockriede text or the Freeley text.

10 *Supporting Ideas Visually*

Outline

Objectives

After reading this chapter you should be able to:

1. Specify, as part of your speech planning, what should be visualized.
2. Specify, as part of your speech planning, when and how to use visual materials.
3. Use convenience, cost, and communication power as criteria for selecting the best visual materials for particular applications in a speech.
4. Apply the criteria of simplicity and accessibility in judging the quality of visual supporting material.
5. Explain the rule of thirds, the influence of straight lines and curved lines, and the balance of triangles as design features for two-dimensional visual aids.
6. Relate the criteria of simplicity and accessibility to sketches and illustrations, and to the language and lettering of visual aids.
7. Explain how to use visual materials during a speech.

PREVIEW

This chapter is about choosing, making, and using two-dimensional visual supporting materials. Any visual material that lends support to a speech is called a visual aid. Use visual aids to simplify complexity, to help listeners organize your ideas, to control audience attention, to assist listeners in understanding and remembering, and to help yourself organize your thoughts or disguise your notes. Visually show problems, solutions, and benefits, and processes, procedures, and sequential steps.

The three criteria you must consider in choosing visual aids are convenience, cost, and communication power. Of those, simplicity and accessibility are the most important in designing visual materials.

The rule of thirds provides a basis for two-dimensional design. Use curved lines to suggest calm and delicacy. Use straight lines and angles to suggest vitality, energy, and action. Triangulate your design elements for balance, and control eye movement with blank space. If you must draw an illustration, keep it simple and resist using unnecessary labels. Language on a visual aid should be limited as much as possible.

When using visual aids, follow a simple sequence: introduce the visual, present the visual, explain the visual, and then put the visual away.

In the last chapter, you studied how to support your ideas logically and emotionally. We suggested that the critical challenge was for you to make what you say seem consistent with your listener's observations about the world and with his or her emotional ties to the world. One of the best ways to do that is by using visual supporting materials. In this chapter we will explain how to choose, make, and use two-dimensional visual aids.

A visual aid is any object, photograph, chart, graph, sketch, lettered poster, or the like that supports the speech or the speaker. Two-dimensional objects can be visual aids, of course, and so can three-dimensional objects, including the speaker's body! As a general rule, though, we think that two-dimensional visual material is superior in public address, because any three-dimensional object that is large enough to be seen is probably too large to handle.

The term *visual* implies something to look at and the term *aid* implies support. The visual material must contribute to the goals of the speech, or support the speaker in reaching his or her goals. Limits are implied in the language *visual aid*, because *if the visual does not lend support to the speech, if it does not help the audience follow or in some way assist the speaker or audience, then the visual material is not an aid.* Further, it is altogether possible that visual material may actually detract from the goal of the speaker.

There is no doubt that visually exciting material lends support and appeal to verbal messages. To illustrate, when Gannett Company offered consumers a free six-month subscription to the visually exciting newspaper *USA Today*, they expected to net about 15,000 new, but unpaid, subscribers. Instead, they got 450,000, and expected the promotion to have a negative effect on the company's profit margin.[1] There may have been other factors involved in this surprising success, of course, but the visual appeal of the paper played a very important part. The effective use of visual supporting materials will greatly increase your prospects for making any speech more successful. First, however, you need to know how to proceed.

In this chapter you will learn *when* to visualize, *what* to visualize, and *how* to develop the visual materials that will help you and your audience achieve your speaking goals. You will learn *how to choose* among a broad range of available visual aids, or *how to make* your own. You will learn *how to use* visual material to greatest effect.

When to Use Visual Aids

You use visuals for your own convenience and for the audience's convenience in your attempt to develop strategies that will move your speech toward its goals. In considering the needs of your audience first, you use visual aids for many reasons.

To Simplify Complexity

Although your ideas should be presented as simply as possible, there will be times when you must discuss complex material that your audience may have difficulty following. This happens commonly, for example, when technically trained professionals present technical materials to groups of managers or decision makers. These managers rarely are as well informed as the presenter in the technical area, which can create a design problem for the presenter.

To help the audience follow technical information, such as statistics, design features of equipment, projected cost-benefit ratios, and complex policies and procedures, a speaker needs to simplify the presentation with visual materials. Charts, graphs, tables, models, flowcharts, and the like are commonly used for simplifying complexity (fig. 10.1).

To Help the Audience Organize Your Ideas

Information can often be organized in more than one way, but the goals of the speaker demand that the information be presented in a carefully planned sequence. To illustrate, an academic debater may decide to discuss some compelling problem, and then lay out the overall design of a proposal for solving every aspect of the problem. To show how this proposal will generate benefits that cannot be obtained in any other way—benefits beyond merely solving the problem—the presenter must offer this information in a carefully planned sequence if the speech is to have persuasive appeal (fig. 10.2).

While you may never have the occasion to present so complex a speech, you may encounter a situation in which you must discuss two or three main ideas, each of which cannot be discussed intelligently unless it is broken down into two or three subpoints. Such a situation is more common than you might suppose, and it calls for visual supporting materials that will help the audience follow the complex organization of the speech.

To Control Audience Attention

Have you ever wondered how a tiny spot of light called a television can so consistently control the time and energy of so many Americans? Does it boggle your mind to realize that the average American household runs a television set more than seven hours every day? If you consider that a child entering first grade has probably spent more time in front of a television set than he or she will spend in front of a teacher through high school graduation,[2] you must realize that the network producers know something about managing audience attention.

Take a lesson from television. Although the TV set remains stationary, the image on television always moves, and in the process, it always asks the viewer to move. As a speaker, you can use visual materials with much the same effect. If you present an idea and then refer to a visual aid and then put the visual away, you move the audience's attention from yourself to the visual and then back to yourself again. If you present three or four visuals in this way, you move the audience from yourself to the visuals and back to yourself three or four times. If you also ask the audience members to focus their attention upon themselves as well—for example, by asking them to recall an experience or to notice something in their own need states—you increase the psychological movement by one-third.

To Help the Audience Understand Abstractions

Sometimes you will want to present information that is difficult for your audience to conceptualize. For example, if you want to show the physical relationships among organs in the abdominal cavity, you could use visual supporting materials to help your audience understand them.

This is exactly the problem that Ronald Reagan's surgeons faced when they went before the White House Press Club to describe the condition of the president's health in July 1985. During a routine surgical procedure to remove a small tumor from the president's intestine, the doctors found a larger, more threatening tumor on his colon, which they also removed.

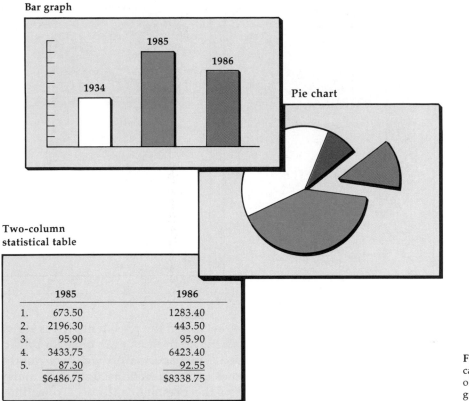

Bar graph

1934 1985 1986

Pie chart

Two-column statistical table

	1985	1986
1.	673.50	1283.40
2.	2196.30	443.50
3.	95.90	95.90
4.	3433.75	6423.40
5.	87.30	92.55
	$6486.75	$8338.75

FIGURE 10.1 Visual aids can take many forms, but often they serve a common goal—to simplify complexity.

NEED CASE

I The problem is *real*
  A
  B
  C
II The problem is *serious*
  A
  B
III The problem is *inherent*
  A
  B

PLAN

Action Plan
I Abolish the
  A
  B
II Repair the
  A
  B
  C
III Adopt the
  A
  B

ADVANTAGES

Advantages
I
II
III

FIGURE 10.2 Outline of First Affirmative Speech. When strict organization is critically important in a speech, a visual aid showing the organization can be useful.

Sketch 1

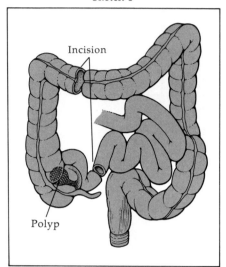

Sketch 2

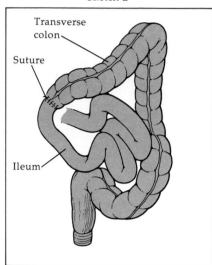

FIGURE 10.3 Without illustrations similar to these, it would have been very difficult for President Reagan's surgeons to explain the nature of the surgery.

The health of a president is news, because if the president's life is at risk, so is the nation's security. Consequently, no president can hope for privacy during a bout of illness. The president's physicians were well aware of this and knew that the reporters would ask many questions, until they understood fully the nature and extent of the president's illness. To facilitate their explanations, they used drawings and models to show where the tumor had been located and how they proceeded to remove it (fig. 10.3).

To Help the Audience Remember

When your speaking goal is not only to tell an audience, but also to help them remember what you have told them, visual aids are very useful. This is particularly true in speeches to inform.

A student representative told her audience of student court members that they needed to understand and remember the answers to three questions if they were going to come to a fair decision about her client. The student on trial was accused of damaging university property through malicious mischief. Apparently he had broken up with his steady girlfriend, drunk too much alcohol, and then smashed a lamp by throwing it across his room in the dormitory. The student court had the authority to expel the defendant from school if they thought he was guilty, and if the situation warranted such a response.

"You must remember these three questions," said the defendant's representative, and she displayed a poster, as shown in figure 10.4. "Did Tom Johnston do malicious mischief?" She pointed to the first question on the poster. "Were there any extenuating circumstances?" She pointed to the

FIGURE 10.4 The members of the student court were more likely to remember Tom Johnston's defense summary because his student lawyer provided a visual aid showing the main points of her speech.

second question on the poster. "Was what he did really serious enough to warrant expulsion from the university?" She pointed to the third question on the poster. Then she explained her position:

> Tom surely did break the lamp. He surely did throw it across the room. He surely did smash university property, and he has since bought a new one. But he did not do malicious mischief. Tom didn't just tear up the lamp in his room for the fun of it. He didn't do an act of common vandalism. He didn't set out, in advance, to trash his dorm room. He did not do malicious mischief, and that is what he is being tried for. So the answer to the first question is "no."
>
> And, clearly, there were extenuating circumstances. Tom's behavior can't be condoned, but it can be understood. Wouldn't you also feel like throwing something if you had just broken up with someone you loved?
>
> But suppose he had set out, in advance, to trash his room. And suppose, also, that Tom had not just broken up with Margaret. We deny these things, but suppose them anyway. You still have to consider the third question. Was what he did serious enough to merit throwing Tom out of college?
>
> Certainly not. A broken-up lamp is not worth a broken-up education. A smashed light fixture is not worth smashing a man's college program.
>
> So, as you consider what you will do about Tom Johnston, please keep these three questions in mind. They make all the difference in this case.

After concluding that speech, the woman walked to her chair, leaving the poster and its three questions on the easel in front of the student court. It was a dramatic use of visual material to help the listeners remember.

To Organize Your Thoughts Discreetly

Considering your own needs during the speech, you can use visual aids as a self-organizing presentational technique. Just as the debater, earlier in this chapter, used visual aids to assist the audience in following his thinking about the solutions to a problem and the advantages of those solutions, you can use visual aids to assist yourself in organizing your thoughts.

To illustrate, a frequent speaker in the South enjoys the reputation of being an excellent public speaker with a phenomenal memory. When he speaks, he appears to be speaking without notes, but the truth of the matter is that he surrounds himself with notes. They are four feet wide by six feet high! You guessed it; his visual aids are his notes. This man uses carefully sequenced overhead slides that provide his organizational motif and his notes. He moves through the speech, progressing from one slide to another—turning the projector on and off—as he develops his ideas. What the audience does not realize is that those slides serve the speaker as much as they serve the audience. The audience cannot see the notes he has printed on the paper frames of the slides, nor do they stop to think that the same visuals that help them to follow also help him in following his speaking pattern.

You can use visual materials when your own goals and needs or your audience's goals and needs seem to require them. Visual materials are supposed to aid you and your listeners in understanding and following your ideas, and to involve your listeners in what you are saying.

What to Support with Visual Materials

Perhaps you can remember an experience that you had in grade school. Your teacher asked you to bring something interesting from home to share with your classmates. If your experience was like most elementary school "show-and-tell" experiences, the little speech you made was limited to a brief statement or two and a demonstration of some physical object.

This is my dog. His name is Scruffy, and he can do tricks.

With this, the fourth grader turns to Scruffy and puts him through his repertoire.

Your own use of visual aids, however, must be much more than a mere show-and-tell experience, or you will not be successful. The key question is, what visual materials will help you and your audience reach the goal you have in mind; what should you visualize?

Often you will make presentations that ask listeners to understand and care about some problem. For example, you might present arguments and evidence to persuade a management committee to increase the equipment-maintenance budget for your section. This is the challenge that faced an engineer who works in the paper industry. A major problem in the paper-making process is corrosion, and the engineer wanted the management group to budget money for preventive maintenance. She also wanted authorization to shut down any machine briefly when she felt it was necessary to perform preventive maintenance.

Show Problems Visually

You must remember that people do not make decisions to solve problems if they cannot identify with the problems. If you want a management group to authorize shutdown of a paper machine (a decision that could be very expensive, indeed), then you must cause them to "own" the problem—to experience the problem as being directly related to them in some important way. They must understand that the problem is more compelling than the effects of a deliberate machine shutdown. Obviously, the engineer had a very challenging persuasion problem.

This is where visual supporting materials can play an effective role. Since the engineer could not bring the management group to the problem (corrosion is a slow, difficult-to-observe problem), she determined to bring the problem to them. A new motor housing had been installed in her section recently, which provided her the opportunity she needed. Every three days over a three-week period, she took close-up photographs of the new motor housing. Before taking each picture, she prepared a small sign indicating the date and time, which she then placed on the motor housing. Thus, she had a photographic record of the effects of corrosion on the new housing over a three-week period.

In addition, she photographed many examples of corrosion in other parts of the plant, and she calculated the costs of that corrosion and the cost of machine failure, accidental shutdown, and machine-part replacement. She put these figures on flip charts, along with cost estimates of preventive maintenance and planned shutdown. Then she presented her findings to the management group.

She was successful in persuading the management group to authorize what she wanted because she visualized the problem. In this way the managers came to understand clearly the nature of the problem and the need for a solution. People just will not try to solve problems they do not understand.

At some point in your life you will almost certainly want to give a speech in which you propose a particular solution to a commonly acknowledged problem. The purpose of the speech may well be to show that your proposal is the best of possible alternatives. Your chances for success will rise dramatically if your audience sees visual demonstrations of your main points.

Show Solutions and Benefits Visually

In the last chapter we mentioned that a group of city officials got the idea that there ought to be an elevated freeway connector running through downtown Mobile. They reasoned that such a connector would bring traffic through the downtown area, and that the result would be an improved downtown area economy. Obviously, there would be short-term advantages of many new jobs and greatly enhanced cash flow in the local economy.

Almost as soon as that idea became known, a second group of influential people in the community opposed it. They argued that a freeway connector would damage the appearance of the community, turn the area beneath the freeway into a slum, cut the city off from its water front, and create havoc with established traffic patterns in the city.

To persuade the local press corps, the city officials hired an architectural firm to develop drawings and a three-dimensional model of the part of Mobile that would be most directly affected. They wanted to show that the proposed freeway did not have to be ugly or harmful. Granted, it is difficult to trace persuasive effect to a single message, but nevertheless, it appears that as a result of the drawings and the model, several prominent newspeople in Mobile were persuaded to support the freeway extension.

If you want to involve your listeners emotionally in some proposal—to cause them to "own" the proposal—or if you want to show how a fairly complex plan of action holds together, use visual materials to enhance the persuasive power of your speech.

Show Processes, Procedures, and Steps in a Sequence Visually

Often in the world of work some process must be learned or a new procedure must be followed. Examples range from simple things, like filling in a time card, to very complex matters, such as making the transition for an entire trust department during a bank takeover. Whatever the case, when the purpose of a speech is to teach people to understand processes or to follow procedures, it is wise to use visual aids.

The personnel office of a large midwestern corporation decided to change its health-care benefit program from one insurance company to another. In making the transition, management determined that employees within five years of retirement should have the right to choose whether to remain with the old program or to enroll in the new. If they chose the new program, they would have to specify the coverages they preferred. This meant that each employee making the change would have to fill out a form, a procedure that could create confusion and some administrative problems if it were not followed correctly. So personnel decided to meet with those employees making the change to teach them the correct way to fill out the form. The speaker developed a series of overhead-projector slides to illustrate each step in completing the complicated insurance form.

In summary, then, use visual materials to support or illustrate problems, solutions, and benefits. Visually show processes, procedures, and steps in a sequence. These uses of visual material will help you and your listeners understand, organize, and follow your line of thought, and thus greatly increase the power of your speech.

How to Develop and Use Visual Materials

We have discussed what you should support visually, and when, but how you go about doing that is another matter. This section will help you by presenting answers in three categories: (1) how to choose the right medium for visual supporting material; (2) how to design and make your own visual materials when that seems advisable; and (3) how to use visual materials.

Choosing the Right Visual Medium

The choice of visual medium to support a speech is not a complex one, but it must not be left to chance. There are three criteria that you should consider: (1) convenience of use, (2) cost versus benefits, and (3) communication power.

Convenience

Convenience may be the least-valued criterion when students approach the matter of selecting a visual medium. But inconvenience can be a critical factor in your success as a speaker. For example, photographic slides come immediately to mind when people think about making a presentation. Developing a slide-supported presentation is time consuming and very costly, and the speaker who depends on photographic slides for visual support must manage the equipment, the lights in the room, some kind of reflecting screen, and the like. The first criterion to consider is whether or not the visual material is convenient to use.

Cost

Cost is another important consideration in choosing the right medium for visual supporting material. Table 10.1 presents a guide to making audiovisual equipment decisions. This table was first developed in 1979 by Robert Charles Reinhart, but we have updated it to reflect the comparative costs of these media as of 1986.[3] You will certainly be able to see that convenience and cost figure importantly in your choice of visual supporting material. In fact, some of the more costly alternatives, realistically, are open only to business and professional speakers. Nevertheless, we present the table to give you a notion of the range of possibilities.

Communication Power

The third criterion, *communication power*, may be the least understood of the three criteria. Table 10.1 indicates the size of the audience suitable for each medium. It also suggests how much creative talent is required for developing the materials and the approximate cost of that talent, (although these concerns may be more relevant to the kind of speaking you do later

TABLE 10.1   A guide to making audiovisual equipment decisions

EQUIPMENT[1]	REASONS FOR USING EQUIPMENT	EQUIPMENT COSTS (WEIGHT)[2]	PRESENTATION MATERIALS COSTS[3]
Flip Chart	Short lead time; little investment warranted	$63 (15 lb)	Per word cost: $25–40 for 1–5 words per page: $75–90 for charts, cartoons, etc.
Chalkboard	Informal in-house communications in boardrooms & offices	$13–134	None
Velcro Boards, Felt Boards, etc.	Informal but professional presentation to valued audience	$70–100 (21–33 lb for portables)	$4.50 per letter
Overhead Projector (3M)	Complex materials requiring extensive discussion	$230–490[4] (15–21 lb for portables)	$4–7 made in-house; $25–85 professional
Slides (1-Projector Presentation) (Kodak)	Important audience & message; professional tone wanted	$140–770 (10–15 lb)	Type only: $5–50; Art: $15–75+
Filmstrip with Sound, Pulse Advance (Singer)	Mechanically somewhat easier than slide & sound	$125–160 (20 lb +)	Same as slides
16 mm Sound Movies (Kodak)	Highly important audience; greatest impact; long life; simple, universal display	$735–1775 (35–40 lb)	$1500–6000 per minute of finished film
Videotape 1. Seen on monitor from prerecorded videocassette (Sony)	1 & 2: Important audience; credibility; cheaper, quicker production than film; quality not as critical as film	$299–600 for ½'' @ $1250 for ¾'' plus tape $8–15 (½'') $60 (¾'')	1 & 2: Very roughly, half the cost of film and less
2. Seen projected on screen (Sony)			

Source: "How to Select Your A/V Equipment," by Robert Charles Reinhart, Public Relations Journal, *May 1979. Figures updated to 1986 by the authors.*
[1]*Other specialty systems which may be of interest are: 3M's sound-on slide: multimedia using multiple slide projectors on slides with movies; Super 8 sound movies; sound tape presentations or sound with auxiliary materials; and opaque projectors, which are best for small conference situations.*
[2]*Figures are based on information available in 1986.*
[3]*Overtime for professional assistance or studio or lab time can add 50–100 percent to production costs.*
[4]*Software programs designed to generate overhead transparencies are now available and cost from about $100 to about $350. The computer equipment required can be about $4000, including the price of a laser printer.*

AUDIENCE SIZE	IMAGE AREA SIZE	PREPARING SCRIPTS	LEAD TIMES NEEDED		
---	---	---	PRODUCING MATERIALS	EQUIPMENT REHEARSAL AND FIRST SET-UP TIME	
10 or under	27" to 34" maximum	From hours to days	Up to 18 pages per day per worker	Minimal but needed
Approx. 16	18" × 24" to 48" × 96"	None	None	None
Up to 24	48" × 36" to 72" × 48"	From several days to weeks	Usually several days	3–4 hours or more
48 maximum	60" × 60"		Up to several days	Allow a few hours
Usually limited only by room size	6' or more	Plan on 2 or more weeks	Ideally, several weeks from storyboard to finished art	Several hours or longer for script-presented lines, less with programmed tape
Same as slides	Same as slides	Same as slides	Same as slides (Note: frame ratio is different from slides)	Same as slides
Usually limited only by room size	6' or more	Several weeks	1–5 min of usable footage per day's shooting	One hour or so
1. 1 person per 1" of monitor size; e.g., 25 for 25" monitor size	1. up to 25"	1 & 2 Days to Weeks	1 & 2 Instant	Instant
2. About 36	2. 40" × 30"			

in life). What it does not tell you is how powerful your choice of communication medium might be on the psychology of an individual listener. Clearly, a skillfully made color motion picture with sound and computer-generated graphics should have more holding power than an individual speaker who stands like a wood statue delivering a lecture from a manuscript. But there are no guarantees. The difference may be related to how the visual materials are made and how they are used.

Making a Two-Dimensional Visual Aid

Criteria

Two evaluative criteria can guide your thinking about two-dimensional design. They apply to every visual aid you will ever make. The visual material must be *simple* and it must be *accessible*. Simple means just that: plain, immediately obvious, easy to see from a distance, unmistakable even to a person who is not particularly intelligent. Accessible means that the visual material must relate to the experiences of the listeners. Mere numbers or lists of statistics, for example, will almost certainly confound an audience, even if the audience members are accustomed to working with figures. The figures must somehow be humanized—tied visually to the emotional status of the listeners.

Good visual materials result from your own consideration of the audience and what that tells you about layout and design. You do not have to be an artist to make intelligent choices, but you should not leave the selection and design of visual materials to chance, and you should not take them for granted.

Principles of Layout and Design

It would be impractical, if not impossible, to present a complete course in two-dimensional layout and design in a public speaking textbook. However, it is possible to present a few principles that will make it easier for you to develop your own visual supporting materials and to judge the quality of visual aids that others may develop for you.

The Rule of Thirds. The rule of thirds is based on the idea that a two-dimensional composition is most pleasing and interesting if its elements fall on or close to the intersections of imaginary lines that divide the plane into thirds, horizontally and vertically. Figure 10.5 shows how those imaginary lines have guided the composition of one speaker's visual aid. Her subject was the vocal mechanism, and she wanted her audience to be able to name and locate the primary resonating chambers for speech. Notice that the key elements in the visual "fit" the rule of thirds.

The Rule of Thirds

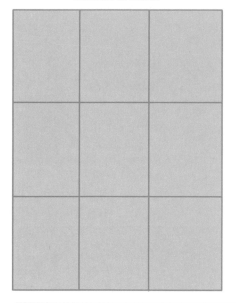

Visual Aid Showing
the Rule of Thirds

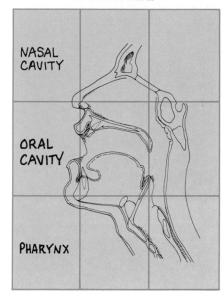

NASAL
CAVITY

ORAL
CAVITY

PHARYNX

FIGURE 10.5 Attention to
the rule of thirds will
improve the visual appeal
and effectiveness of your
visual aids.

FIGURE 10.6 Straight lines
and angles imply action and
purpose, while curved lines
suggest calm and delicacy.

Straight Lines and Curved Lines. Straight lines suggest strength and purpose while curved lines suggest calm and delicacy (fig. 10.6). If you want
to suggest vitality, energy, and action, then your visual aid should incorporate angles and straight lines. If you want to suggest tranquility or peace,
use curved lines in designing your visual materials.

FIGURE 10.7 *A:* Eye movement from right to left draws viewer into frame. *B:* Eye movement from left to right suggests movement toward viewer.

Lines can also suggest movement. If you draw the eye from right to left along a line, you forcefully pull the viewer into the image—probably because this direction contradicts our training to read from left to right. An image that draws the eye from left to right suggests movement toward the viewer (fig. 10.7).

The Balance of Triangles. Triangular compositions are virtually the aesthetic standard in Western painting and drawing. In a simple triangulated layout, the apex of the triangle locates the dominant element in the design.

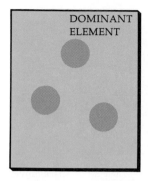

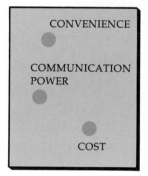

FIGURE 10.8 Three Examples of Triangulation. The viewer's eye is able to travel from left to right and up and down the page relatively easily when you incorporate a triangular composition in a visual aid.

You can experiment with triangles of different shapes to discover what is the most pleasing composition. Usually, the left-hand side of a two-dimensional plane is perceived as "lighter" than the right-hand side, so it can carry more material than the right-hand side without upsetting the psychological balance of the design (fig. 10.8).

Eye Movement and Blank Space. In two-dimensional design, blank space can be as important as, or more important than, the filled area. Graphic designers call blank space "negative space," and they use it to control eye movement. If you put too much material onto a two-dimensional plane, you eliminate the negative space, and you lose opportunities to control the eye movement and attention that negative space provides.

Figure 10.9 illustrates the power of negative space in controlling eye movement. Notice that the illustration on the left is so full of material that negative space is virtually nonexistent. Consequently, the eye does not know where to focus. But in viewing the illustration on the right, the eye immediately comes to rest on the most important feature of the visual aid.

Too full: No negative space.

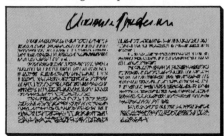

Negative space moves the eye.

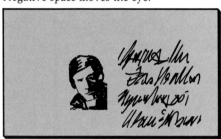

FIGURE 10.9 As with triangular composition, negative space facilitates and directs the movement of the viewer's eye.

Sketches and Illustrations. Carefully rendered drawings, paintings, or other art illustrations are usually more trouble than they are worth for visual supporting material. Still, it is sometimes necessary to develop a simplified sketch in order to illustrate your idea. A detailed technical illustration that has been copiously labeled is never a useful visual aid for a public speaker. As a general rule, keep a sketch or illustration as simple as possible. Often a freehand cartoon can be more effective than a carefully and meticulously rendered drawing.

Compare the three drawings in figure 10.10. Each drawing depicts the same technical problem. Which one do you think would be the most effective in helping a person who is not technically trained to understand the relationships of the component parts? Notice that the illustration on the far right in figure 10.10 is not as carefully labeled as the illustration on the far left. The lack of labeling, however, does not inhibit the ability of the visual aid to communicate what the speaker had in mind.

Sometimes our students are tempted to reproduce the kind of illustrative materials they find in their textbooks. We advise against that. The speaking situation does not present the same receiving problem for a listener that a reading situation presents to the reader. The reader has time to study and mull over the illustrations in a textbook. Indeed, textbook

Wiring Diagram

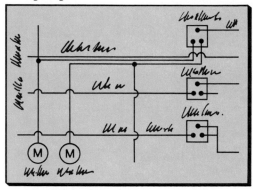

Simplified Wiring Diagram

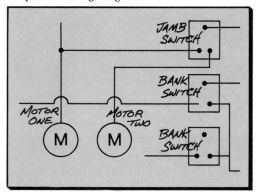

Diagram for a Visual Aid

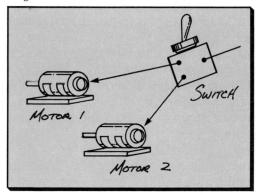

FIGURE 10.10 Most of us do not understand wiring diagrams—or any complicated system—at first glance, so we are attracted to a visual aid that shows only the important essentials.

FIGURE 10.11 An Example of What *Not* to Do with a Visual Aid. The drawing is not clear, and the overall effect is very confusing. Two drawings would have been better.

authors know that students often study the illustrative materials without reading the textual materials. So illustrations and tables in textbooks tend to be more technically rendered, and far more copiously labeled than the public speaking situation requires. The listener does not have time to study and mull over a visual aid. Instead, the listener must take what the speaker gives at the speaker's speed. Your goal as a speaker is to control the attention and interest of your listeners. Anything that inhibits your ability to do that, including extraneous language on a visual aid, should be avoided.

Figure 10.11 is a photographic reproduction of an actual visual aid that a student made to support a speech on rock climbing. She was an R.O.T.C. student who had just returned to campus from a two-week camping experience in the mountains. She wanted the class to know how climbers can hang from the surface of sheer rock, so she mentioned the devices that make this feat possible.

The label does not contribute anything special to this visual aid, except that without it, the remainder would be utterly incomprehensible. If you look carefully, you can almost see a figure, in silhouette, hanging from the face of the rock. Those two things to the right represent the anchoring devices. If this student's purpose was to show her audience how rock climbers anchor themselves to the surface of sheer rock, she should have developed a separate drawing for each of the anchoring devices (fig. 10.12).

Nut

Piton

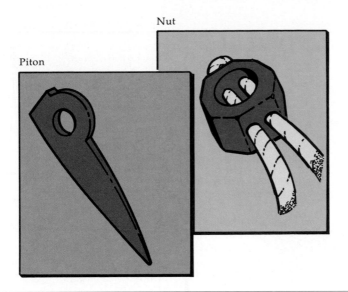

FIGURE 10.12 These sketches of a piton (left) and a nut (right) will give a listener a clearer idea of how a climber hangs from a sheer rock face than could the student's visual aid in figure 10.11.

Language and Lettering. Because a speaker can *announce* that a visual aid shows something, labels rarely contribute much to the visual presentation in a speech. A speaker can *point to* a particular component of a sketch and can *explain* what it represents. Since the visual materials will be removed from sight immediately after they are used, no extraneous language is needed on the visual. Compare the two drawings in figure 10.13. In the drawing on the right, all of the extraneous language has been removed. It is a cleaner, simpler, and easier-to-grasp visual aid than the drawing on the left.

Many, if not most, of the visual aids you will ever use in a speech will consist entirely of language. Outlines of major points, for example, are entirely verbal. They can be powerful supporting material in speech making, but they can be confusing. Again, the key is simplicity.

Lettering does not have to be a problem. Of course, most people are not lettering artists. When the nature of the speech requires quality lettering, and if you are not particularly adept at this skill, find someone who will do it right. In most situations, however, your own lettering will suffice if you remember a few pointers.

1. Print, don't write.
2. Print big.
3. Use block letters.
4. Use the simplest words you can.
5. Eliminate every word you can.

Too Much Language

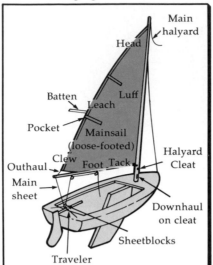

Language Removed

FIGURE 10.13 Keeping labels to a minimum is an important aspect of creating simple, easily understood visual aids.

Using Visual Materials: Matters of Delivery

The actual handling of and reference to visual aids while speaking is a simple matter if you think about the needs of the audience. But many speakers do not seem to know how to avoid the most obvious pitfalls. Figure 10.14 presents some pointers that you may wish to keep in mind.

Effective use of a visual aid in most public speeches will follow a predictable sequence.

Introduce the Visual

A simple introductory statement or two will suffice, but you must do something to prepare the members of the audience for a shift in the receiving task. You might say something simple like, "To illustrate this idea, I would like to show you a sketch that identifies the most important part of this problem. . . ." Such a statement tells the audience members that they are going to have to depend more on their eyes than on their ears—a shift in receiving skills that better speakers do not take for granted.

Present the Visual

Wise speakers present a visual smoothly and silently because they recognize that the listener must make that shift in perceptual mechanisms. After introducing the visual, as in the above example, put the visual on the easel or display it on the screen, and then step out of the way for a moment. You must give the audience members time to adjust, and time to satisfy their curiosity about the visual you have asked them to view.

> **Do** prepare your visual aids in advance.
> **Do** talk with your audience, not with your visual aid.
> **Do** introduce, present, explain, and then put away your visual aid.
> **Do** practice using the visual aid.
>
> **Don't** use the chalkboard if you can avoid it.
> **Don't** pass objects around for audience members to study while you talk.
> **Don't** stand between your visual aid and your audience.
> **Don't** stand with your back to your audience.

FIGURE 10.14 Some Dos and Don'ts When Using Visual Aids.

Explain the Visual

After a moment of silence, the audience will be ready for you to point to the visual aid, and to discuss it. Do not assume that the audience members have made all the connections that you want them to make. Take the time to explain the visual aid. Show its important points and explain its significance.

If you are using a flip chart or poster board, move back to the visual and stand beside it, and face your audience. Gestures such as pointing to some portion of the visual aid can be more readily accomplished from this position, and you will not have to turn your back on the audience.

If you are using an overhead projector, we suggest that you lay a sharpened pencil down on the slide so that the shadow of the pencil projected onto the screen becomes the pointer. Do not point to the slide with your finger. Do not fence with the slide by holding the pointer in your hand as you speak. The finger or pencil, moved only a couple of inches on the slide, will create a shadow that may move a foot or more on the screen. Such exaggerated movement will call attention to itself, sometimes with unfortunate consequences. One young man walked over to the projector and pointed to the slide with his middle finger. There, on the wall behind him, moving slowly up and down the wall was a finger gesture some five feet high. No audience member could resist the humor in the event.

Put the Visual Away

After you have used the visual material, get rid of it. Too often, speakers introduce and discuss a visual aid that is attractive and telling. It is designed to be visually exciting and attention getting. However, when the speakers move on to the next point, they risk losing the audience if they do not remove the visual materials after use. Keep in mind that audience members who are still thinking about your last visual aid cannot be thinking about what you are presently telling them. You are the only one who can prevent that distraction—that noise. Put the visual away when you are finished with it.

Summary

In this chapter we talked about when you should use visual aids and what you should visualize with those visual aids. Then we described how to go about choosing appropriate visual media and how to develop visual materials for a speech.

The best visual materials are simple and uncluttered, and they conform to certain principles of two-dimensional design, but you do not have to be an artist to select or develop visual supporting materials wisely. You cannot leave the selection and design of visual supporting materials to chance. Listeners must be able to relate to your ideas intellectually and emotionally. Visual aids are a principal means of helping them do that.

Key Terms

Accessibility   *Simplicity*

Communication power   *Visual aid*

Rule of thirds

Discussion Questions

1. Agree with a group of your classmates to spend some time watching television with the sound turned off. Count the number of times the picture changes during a two-minute period. Include every camera change, each time the angle of the camera changes by zooming, etc., and each time language is superimposed on the picture. Notice, especially, how camera angle and picture changes are used to focus viewer attention. Now turn the sound on and pay attention to the sounds. How do the sounds and the sights work together? Return to your group and compare notes. Are there any lessons to be drawn from this experience for you as a public speaker?

2. This chapter is filled with illustrative materials. Even so, it is not nearly so rich as any magazine. Bring a magazine to class. With a group of classmates, go through the magazine looking for examples of curved and straight lines, of triangulation, and of the use of blank space to control eye movement. Are they easy to find? What can you learn from this exercise about developing visual aids for a speech?

Notes

1 *See* "Gannett pays for success," *Advertising Age (16 December 1985),* 3–4.

2 The entire December 1985 issue of *Critical Studies in Mass Communication* is focused upon how much TV people watch—evidence of professional concern. Even in China there is a very high degree of penetration by the mass media. In Beijing, for example, 92 percent of 2430 randomly selected individuals view TV daily. A surprising proportion, since the Chinese have only been able to purchase TV receivers since 1976. *See* Everett M. Rogers et. al., "The Beijing Audience Study," *Communication Research* 12 (April 1985): 179–208.

3 Robert Charles Reinhart, "How to Select Your A/V Equipment," *Public Relations Journal,* May 1979.

Suggested Readings

An enormous amount of research and technology has evolved about the importance of visual materials to communication. *See,* for example, the 1 October 1985 issue of *PC: The Independent Guide to IBM Personal Computers* (4:20). The entire 250-page issue is devoted to visual aids generated by computers. *See* especially Stephanie Stallings, "Design Tools for the PC," beginning on p. 187.

11 Language: The Key to Successful Presentation

Outline

Objectives

After reading this chapter you should be able to:

1. Define *language*.
2. Explain the components of that definition.
3. Explain and provide examples of *abstraction* and *the triangle of meaning*.
4. Describe the relationship between language and influence.
5. Define and illustrate *signification*, *definition*, and *polarization*.
6. Discuss how self-concept emerges from and is reflected in language.
7. Specify and explain five suggestions for using language well, and incorporate them into your own speeches.

PREVIEW

Language is a system of signs and symbols that a speech community uses to share meaning. Language is thus a fundamental feature in each person's experiences and personal successes. Language is also an abstracting, generalizing, and categorizing system; it is the primary means by which people draw inferences about the world in which they live.

Four problems flow from the basic features of language: signification, definition, polarization, and map-territory confusion. In addition, language is directly related to the evolution of a self-concept and to the images that other people have of us. Thus, how we use language profoundly influences our lives.

A speaker may be perceived as assertive, aggressive, or shy. Whatever the perception, it bears directly upon the speaker's credibility. Beyond that, people tend to stereotype others—a tendency that creates problems for speakers.

To combat these problems of language and to help make your speeches more vivid and more potent, we offer five pieces of advice: (1) keep it simple, (2) be specific, (3) use action language, (4) use comparison and contrast, and (5) use illustrations.

Conversation at Wendy's   (Mobile, Alabama, June 25, 1986)

Woman at the counter:	What'll you have?
Professor Council:	I'll have the chicken breast sandwich.
Woman:	You want that with everything?
Council:	Yes.
Woman:	You want bacon on it?
Council:	Yes, I'll have everything.
Woman:	Everything doesn't include bacon.
Council:	It doesn't . . . ?
Woman:	It doesn't include bacon or cheese. They cost extra.
Council:	[pause]
Woman:	Do you want bacon and cheese on your sandwich?
Council:	No, I'll just have everything.

Actual Statements Taken from Insurance Company Accident-Report Forms

1. I thought my window was down, but found it was up when I put my hand through it.
2. I pulled away from the side of the road, glanced at my mother-in-law, and headed for the embankment.
3. To avoid hitting the bumper of the car in front, I struck the pedestrian.
4. The pedestrian had no idea which direction to run; so I ran over him.
5. I saw a slow-moving, sad-faced old gentlemen as he bounced off the hood of my car.
6. I had been driving for forty years, when I fell asleep at the wheel and had an accident.
7. In my attempt to hit a fly, I drove into a telephone pole.
8. That guy was all over the road. I had to swerve a number of times before I hit him.
9. The indirect cause of the accident was a little guy in a small car with a big mouth.
10. I told the police that I was not injured, but on removing my hat, I found that I had a fractured skull.

The images and impressions derived from each of these statements is a result of the sender's choices of language. If you found humor in the statements, the humor was in the unexpected and unconventional use of language. Any judgments you might make about the principals involved are based on language. Every good speaker knows that language choices are critical to success or failure as a speaker. The impressions that you leave as a speaker may make all the difference between being effective and successful or ineffective and unsuccessful.

In this chapter, we examine the nature of language and make suggestions about how you can improve your use of language. Our goal is to help you learn how to use language to relate yourself and what you say to your listeners as you deliver a speech. This chapter is more theoretical than the others. It has to be if we are to explain how language works in public speaking, so please be patient. In the end we will make some very concrete suggestions about the effective use of language in public address. Your choice of language, then, will depend on your understanding.

Language can be defined as a system of signs and symbols that is used by a speech community to share meaning and experience. Within this definition, there are at least five terms that need explanation. *System* means a dynamic phenomenon that includes all the components of language (words, grammatical rules, pronunciation, etc.) and all the relationships among those components. Every fluent speaker "knows" the system. Every fluent

The Nature of Language

Edwin Newman

Effective speakers have an appreciation for clear, direct, and forceful language. Edwin Newman, former television newscaster and commentator, describes the qualities of effective language, both written and spoken.

A civil tongue, on the other hand, means to me a language that is not bogged down in jargon, not puffed up with false dignity, not studded with trick phrases that have lost their meaning. It is not falsely exciting, is not patronizing, does not conceal the smallness and triteness of ideas by clothing them in language ever more grandiose, does not seek out increasingly complicated constructions, does not weigh us down with the gelatinous verbiage of Washington and the social sciences. It treats errors in spelling and usage with a decent tolerance but does not take them lightly. It does not consider "We're there because that's where it's at" the height of cleverness. It is not merely a stream of sound that disc jockeys produce, in which what is said does not matter so long as it is said without pause. It is direct, specific, concrete, vigorous, colorful, subtle, and imaginative when it should be, and as lucid and eloquent as we are able to make it. It is something to revel in and enjoy.

Source: Newman, Edwin, A Civil Tongue. *Copyright © 1975 The Bobbs-Merrill Co. Inc. Indianapolis, IN. All Rights Reserved.*

speaker "knows" the rules of how the pieces of language fit together, and every fluent speaker can create original, grammatically correct sentences. Thus far, you have been able to read the sentences in this chapter, but can you read this French one?

Je me sens quelque peu fatigue.

Because language is a system, we can communicate with each other. But if we do not know the system, we cannot extract meaning from it. If you do not know French, you probably cannot read the above sentence. Translated into English, it says, "I feel a little tired."

Sign is one of the two kinds of meaningful elements in language; the other is *symbol. Signs* announce the immediate presence of some object, phenomenon, or event. For example, you can grunt your acknowledgement of some other person's idea without uttering a word. You can signal how a sentence is to be interpreted by the sound of your voice and the way you use pauses, stress, and the like. You can signal your friend to "duck" by suddenly shouting the word. Each of these components is a sign, and a necessary part of language.

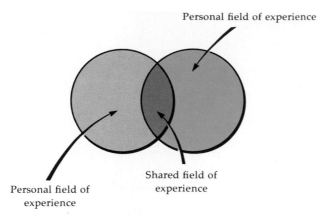

Personal field of experience

Personal field of
experience

Shared field of
experience

FIGURE 11.1 Your ability to communicate with your listeners partially depends on the extent to which you and they have shared experiences.

Symbols are agreed-upon units that stand for, or represent, something else. The printed page you are reading provides examples. Each word is a symbol that stands for some referent. Each sentence is a construction of words symbolizing some idea. Notice that people in a speech community incorporate a good many nonverbal symbols into their uses of language. The signs and symbols allow us to send and receive ideas. Without them we would not be able to do that.

A "speech community" includes all of those who use the same language system. People in a speech community understand each other's language, including their uses of jargon and colloquialisms. Individuals can exchange signs and symbols, expecting that others will understand what they mean. That is, they can share meaning and experience. If you say to your brother, "Let's go fishing," your brother will know what you want to do, and he will have some image of fishing that is essentially similar to your own. He may imagine a favorite place where the two of you have fished. He may recollect some happy time that the two of you shared. On the other hand, if you say, "I want a fair wage for the working man, and a fair deal for the unemployed," your listeners may have no way of relating to your ideas.

From these definitions you can see that how you use language can be the most important single component in your success—as a speaker and as a person. Indeed, it is so fundamental that some researchers have argued that language and culture are the most important part of all relationship development.[1] Perhaps we should take a closer look at the phenomenon.

Language and Experience

To the extent that your personal field of experience overlaps the field of experience that your listeners bring to a communication event, you will be able to share meaning and experience with them. Figure 11.1 illustrates this idea of a shared or common field of experience, and it makes plain how important "sharedness" really is to a speech community.

FIGURE 11.2
Understanding the
difference between direct
and mediated experience
will increase your awareness
of the need for careful and
precise language.

The circle on the left describes the entire range of one individual's experiences. The circle on the right describes another's entire range of personal experiences. The ranges illustrated include both direct and vicarious experiences—that with which the individual has come into direct contact and that which has been mediated, or indirectly experienced. You have direct experience with your own living quarters, for example; but, unless you have personally visited the Louvre, in Paris, your only experience with a painting called the Mona Lisa is vicarious. That is, you have some mediated experience—some indirect, edited association with the painting. The problem is that most of us, most of the time (including an audience full of people, and the speaker to whom they are listening) cannot or do not understand the difference. But the mediated experience is never quite correct!

To illustrate, the photograph of Leonardo's famous painting in figure 11.2 is not the actual painting. It is a representation of the painting. It is an edited version—a mediated version—of the painting. Your experience with this photographic reproduction of the painting contributes to and reinforces your vicarious experience with the painting. But did you notice

Geraldine Ferraro

Even though Geraldine Ferraro ran unsuccessfully for the Vice Presidency in 1984, she impressed voters with the close rapport she established with her audiences. As she describes in her autobiography, it didn't come naturally.

The campaign trail was never dull and often challenging. The first thing I had to learn was to get over my reluctance to do giant rallies. I'd always disliked them. I was far more comfortable giving speeches in more intimate settings, enjoying the give-and-take between the audience and myself, as in my town-hall meetings in my congressional district. Involving the audience in a dialogue, I've always thought, is far more instructive both for me and for them.

These rally audiences were different. The ten, twenty, or thirty thousand people who showed up usually weren't there to be enlightened, but to have an emotional experience. After waiting for two hours in the rain or jammed into a high school gymnasium, they didn't want to hear a long speech. They wanted to feel part of a political event, to be excited, to applaud and cheer. At a rally, the speaker is not supposed to talk at the people but with them, to interact with the crowd. I needed to have short, punchy lines and to know how to deliver them. At the beginning, I didn't have either.

that the size is different? You must take the photograph at face value, two dimensionally. Notice that subtle differences in color are rendered here in terms of dots of ink. If the quality of the printing process and the quality of the paper are good, the quality of the reproduction will be good. But these variables are beyond your control—they are part of the editing. You must *imagine* that the colors of ink used to render those ethereal blues are the same as the colors of paint Leonardo mixed and used. The moody brown-grays in the background, created by a photographic printing process called "color separation," may or may not accurately reflect the artist's original. Your experience is vicarious; it is not quite correct. Your experience with this painting is essentially similar to that of every other person who has never visited the Louvre, but who can name the painting anyway. Your shared experience of the painting lets you understand each other as you discuss it. Your shared experience with the painting lets *us*—you the reader and we the authors—communicate with each other as you read these sentences! Do notice, again, that we cannot quite know what is inside each others' heads, but we can still use language to communicate more or less well.

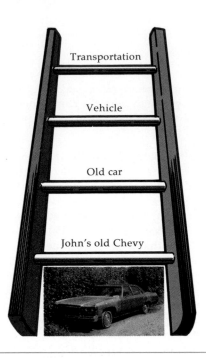

FIGURE 11.3 The Ladder of Abstraction. As your language becomes increasingly general and vague, the probability that listeners will form inaccurate images also increases.

To the extent that your personal field of experience overlaps the experiences of your audience members, you are able to share meaning with them. However, your experiences can never be exactly like theirs. As a speaker, you may be the medium through which they draw their vicarious reality, and that is a very serious responsibility. It implies that you must use language with precision—language that is carefully chosen. This idea will become more and more important to you as you attempt to relate yourself and your ideas to your listeners.

Abstraction

When you talk with an audience, you use language and nonverbal messages to convey meanings and experiences, but what do you actually communicate? Even within a single speech community, language is highly abstract; therefore, what you communicate to others is always an abstraction of objective reality or truth. This idea can be illustrated quite simply by pointing to the work of general semanticist S. I. Hayakawa, who developed an "abstraction ladder" to help his students understand this idea of abstraction.[2] Figure 11.3 displays his idea.

At the bottom of the ladder, below the first rung, you find reality—that which exists in the world outside your skin. Trees are real and so are flowers and sunshine, but you cannot "know" reality until you take it into your consciousness and process it. That processing of reality is abstraction.

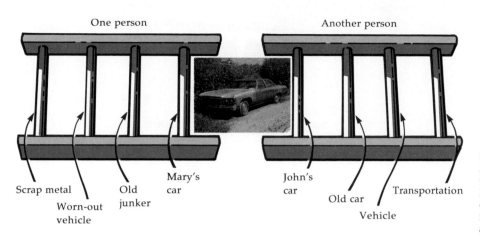

FIGURE 11.4 Double Abstraction Ladders. The fact that both speakers and listeners tend to abstract only serves to increase the importance of concreteness and clarity of language.

The first rung of the ladder is the least abstract of the rungs. In Hayakawa's metaphor, the higher you climb up the ladder, the broader your view of the world becomes, but the less detail you can see there. As you climb the abstraction ladder, the ability of your listeners to understand the reality at the base is similarly affected; their perceptions include more and more of the surrounding event. Consequently, they are able to perceive less and less of the detail.

Consider figure 11.3 again. At the base we have provided a photograph of an old Chevy. The first rung of the ladder is a fairly specific use of language. "John's old Chevy" points to a particular automobile that both you and John would be expected to recognize. At the second rung, the language "old car" could refer to any old car. What do you consider old? For one person, an old car might be any automobile built before 1985. For another, it might be any car with dents and rust and flaking paint, regardless of when it was built. To still another, a car would not be considered old unless it has survived the American roadways for twenty years or more. "Old car" is clearly an abstraction that would be visualized in different ways by your listeners. The third rung says "vehicle," which is more abstract than "old car." It embraces all vehicles—of any model, make, or age— regardless of whether or not they work! The fourth rung is the most abstract. "Transportation" can refer to any car, horse, bus, boat, bicycle, or pogo stick that could conceivably move goods or people from one place to another. Even your shoes could be included in this category.

Abstraction can create serious problems when people try to communicate with each other. Remember that as a public speaker, you increase the likelihood that each of your listeners will create a different image from yours when you climb the ladder of abstraction. In any case, both you and your listeners tend to use separate ladders of abstraction. Consider figure 11.4 to get an idea of how this can create a problem.

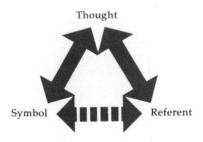

FIGURE 11.5 The Triangle of Meaning. Either the referent or the symbol can act as a stimulus for our thinking.

The process of abstraction is going on inside each listener. Each person lives in a world of words that he or she creates. Notice how far away from the shared reality each person is situated in figure 11.4, and notice the distance between them. Clearly, the process of abstraction makes it essential that you weigh your choices of language carefully. Your success as a speaker will be influenced by it in important ways, and so will your personal success.

The Triangle of Meaning

C. K. Ogden and I. A. Richards were concerned with this problem of abstraction when they tried to explain how language works in communication.[3] They conceived a "triangle of meaning" to show the relationships among the symbols—or words—people use, the referents symbolized, and the thought processes that go on inside the people using the words (fig. 11.5).

The referent angle of the triangle represents what people talk about. In a speech it could be the main lines of analysis, a problem, or some object or phenomenon you are trying to discuss. The symbol angle of the triangle represents the words people use to talk about referents. A symbol stands for something else; so each word is a symbol, and language is a symbol system.

The thought angle at the top of the triangle represents perception and interpretation of a referent or symbol. It is the intervening human process that makes it possible for us to communicate with each other. Thinking always takes place between the referent and the symbol. The dotted arrow that runs between the symbol and referent suggests that the relationship between these two is never direct. Rather, the referent or the symbol acts as a stimulus for human thinking. Figure 11.6 may help explain these relationships.

Notice that something happens to our thinking when we talk. If Ogden and Richards, and Hayakawa, are correct, then every time we speak we create the potential for communication error *by the very nature of the language we use.* These scholars clearly imply that people "see" different things in the old Chevy. One person might see a rusting junker; a second person

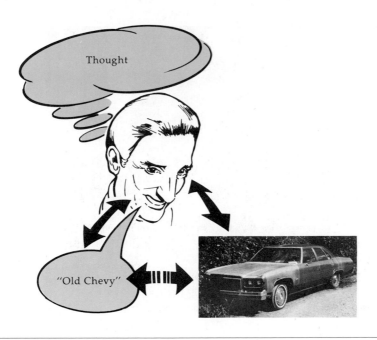

FIGURE 11.6 The fact that the referent or the symbol will stimulate a set of associations inside the observer means that distortion in language is virtually inevitable. Careful speakers recognize this problem and take steps to minimize its effects.

might "see" the absence of car payments; and a third might quickly impose an interpretation of low socioeconomic standing. The car or referent is rarely seen for itself; rather, it stimulates a set of associations inside the observer.

To summarize, what goes on inside your head as you speak is uniquely yours. It can never be the same as what goes on inside your listeners' heads. Your listeners have learned how to abstract, in part, as a function of their personal experiences and, in part, as a function of the influence of their various speech communities. You may be wondering, as our students often do, if what we have said thus far renders the matter hopeless. "Does this mean that there is no way a speaker can connect with the listeners in the audience?" No, it means that the speaker must be mindful of the problem, and use discretion in selecting and using words.

Language and Culture

Because of this obvious potential for a communication problem, you need to understand that a speech community includes everyone who uses the same language system. For example, everyone who uses English constitutes a speech community. The problem, however, is that a large number of subgroups exist within each speech community. Each sublanguage carries with it a special frame of reference and a special cultural viewpoint. In the words of Bruner, Goodnow, and Austin, "The speakers of a language are partners to an agreement to see and think of the world in a certain

The fact that we do not all see the world in the same way means that speakers must be careful not to assume attitudes on the part of listeners.

way. . . ."[4] They mean that a speech community agrees by its use of a common language to understand the reality outside themselves in essentially similar ways.

To illustrate, a speech community always evolves language to describe phenomena in the real world that are important to them. Fluent speakers of American English have hundreds of words that bear upon the general concept "car," because automobiles and auto transportation are so important to our society. Since we have so much language to talk about cars, the example of the abstraction ladder could take on special meaning. The abundance of language about the concept "car" allows us to perceive and understand subtle differences in meaning; we are able to share a very rich cultural experience.

On the other hand, our language for discussing camels is relatively sparse. Our idea of camels may be limited to one-hump and two-hump varieties, or to a brand of cigarettes. That is because camels are not very important to our way of life. In Arabic, however, about six thousand words refer to camels and the life-style that depends upon camels. Fluent speakers of Arabic have a far richer experience of camels than we do. As a speaker of English addressing an audience of people who speak English fluently, you can count on your listeners to share some part of your image of the world, but a listener's image will never be exactly like your own. This means that you must be careful to make your ideas clear and direct. You do that by choosing words carefully.[5]

When you speak, your listeners derive meaning from your sentences by inferring or guessing what you mean, based on what they perceive. The images they form and the messages they receive are a result of the inferences they draw. In a speech situation, listeners draw inferences largely from what the speaker says—from the picture he or she paints. Here we want to point out and explain four very peculiar language problems that speakers and listeners encounter: (1) signification, (2) definition, (3) polarization, and (4) map-territory confusion.

Language and Inferences

Using a word to point to some object or phenomenon is *signification.* You signify something when you say "that stereo." If you say "please bring my coat when you come," you have signified both an object (coat) and a phenomenon (bring). The problem is that people often use the same words to signify different things, and different words to signify the same things. A public speaker must be particularly careful to help listeners understand the true meaning of the words he or she uses.

Signification

Definition is a process of marking the boundaries of some named thing.[6] Definition, one of the most important aspects of language, serves in two critical ways: (1) it allows us to divide the things defined—to distinguish one thing from another and to mark the boundaries between them; and (2) it allows us to include and thus unify the things named—to hold like objects and events in similar regard.[7] The problem for public speakers is that we tend to assume our listeners will share our definitions, but they rarely do.

Definition

To illustrate this problem, consider how social movements are often named and defined with enormous impact. We cherish "democracy" and fear "communism." We celebrate "freedom fighters" and condemn "terrorists." We "preserve liberty" and they "seek world domination." Northerners fought the "war against slavery" while Southerners fought "the war of Northern aggression." You cannot assume that your listeners will define terms as you do. Rather, you must be sure to define the terms yourself, as part of your speech. Specify what you mean.

A third problem for speakers and listeners is called polarization. We polarize language when we think about the world as having only two values—good and bad, hot and cold, beautiful and ugly, and tall and short, for example. Just as the high-contrast photograph in figure 11.7 leaves out the gray tones and all of the colors, polarized language leaves out important intermediate information. The result is that the raw materials for accurate image building are just not there for the listener to use.

Polarization

At the height of the civil rights movement in the 1960s, people would say, "either you're part of the solution or you're part of the problem." In the 1980s, people who considered themselves part of "the moral majority"

FIGURE 11.7 Our polarized language leads us to think and talk about the world in a manner represented by this photograph. In reality, though, recognizing the many shades of grey between the extremes will increase the clarity and accuracy of our language.

opposed abortion laws and practices in a two-valued way. "You're either against abortion or you're for it." Moreover, those who were against abortion were "pro-life," with a clear implication that people holding more moderate views were "against life."

The English language has many pairs of words representing opposites but a poverty of language describing the range between the opposites. The opposite pairs tend to be extremes. Figure 11.8 provides a good way for you to center on the problem that this phenomenon presents to both a speaker and a listener. Take a few moments and try to place language in each blank space that suggests the range of positions along the continuua in figure 11.8. We have provided language between the extremes of *hot* and *cold* as an example of what you should do with the other polarized examples.

You will notice very quickly how limited your language is! You just cannot call up appropriate words to fill all the blanks. For this reason, you cannot think very clearly about the range of potential between those extremes! This is unfortunate, since the world is rarely at the extremes, but rather somewhere in the middle where our language fails us. Thus, we tend to perceive the world and relay our perceptions about the world to

Try to fill in the blank spaces between these paired opposites. We have filled in the first example to get you started:

Hot	*warm*	*tepid*	*cool*	Cold
Happy				Sad
Strong				Weak
Light				Heavy
Active				Passive
Sweet				Sour
Fast				Slow

How do you account for the difficulty in filling in the eighteen words?

FIGURE 11.8 Polarized Language. The polarized nature of our language may make this apparently simple task harder than you might think.

our listeners in extreme terms. They may notice this fallacy, of course, but more often they do not. You can imagine how this problem of polarization creates problems in a public speaking situation.

Osgood, Suci, and Tannenbaum were concerned about our tendency to polarize when they conducted the research that led to the enormously important book *The Measurement of Meaning*.[8] They discovered that the tendency to polarize existed in more than fifty of the world's languages that they studied. They concluded that the tendency is universal! It exists as a basic assumption in the language.

Consider the impact of polarization as you try to represent the world to an audience. Suppose, for example, that you are going to speak on the controversial subject of capital punishment. Your position is against capital punishment because you think that it does not deter crime, and that the risk for error in the judicial system is too great. Besides, you are morally opposed to anyone taking another person's life. The truth of the matter is that capital punishment may very well deter crime in some cases. Some individuals probably do stop to consider the consequences of a capital crime. While you are generally opposed to taking another person's life on moral grounds, you probably can imagine some circumstances in which that would be acceptable—as an act of self-defense, for example, or as an act of war.

The point is that the language we use to describe the world tends toward polarized extremes even though the real world is not purely good or bad, hot or cold, black or white, or completely ugly or perfectly beautiful. Yet, if we think in these polarized terms, we have an inaccurate image of the world. The guesses—the inferences—we make will be wrong, too. As a speaker, you are the one who must compensate for this tendency to polarize. If you want to be effective, accurate, and successful, you must be aware of the problem and then choose the language you use with great care.

Map-Territory Confusion

Words are symbols that stand for something—for their referents. People often tend to confuse the word with the referent, a problem that is sometimes called *map-territory confusion*. If you respond to a word as though the word were the real thing, then you are experiencing map-territory confusion. Sometimes this confusion creates real problems for people.

A listener may confuse the word you choose with its referent, reacting to the symbol directly and in the present tense, rather than to the thing it represents. To put this problem into a public speaking context, suppose you are engaged in a public debate with someone else for the purpose of informing the audience or persuading them to your point of view. This activity is common enough, especially when politicians are running for election to office. Let us say, further, that the subject is euthanasia. Your position is a moderate one. You feel that under certain circumstances euthanasia may be permissible. Your opponent in the debate is adamantly opposed to any such position and is using strong language. Imagine how the language might create map-territory confusion for the listeners, and how that, in turn, might create problems for you as a speaker.

> *A passage from your speech:* I want to be very clear. I think each of us has a right to die with dignity and to choose a painless death under certain circumstances. For example, I know a person who cannot recover from her cancer. She is going to die. She is beyond the help of our best doctors. She will die a horrible, painful death from a disease that has been eating away at her insides for months and months. She is in agony now, both physically and emotionally. She wants to die, but she cannot end her own life. Surely she has a right to a better way.

> *A passage from your opponent's speech:* My opponent wants to be clear, but I don't think that speech was very clear. In effect, what you heard was that soft words will persuade you to a position that is counter to all the basic laws of God and humankind. Let's look at those words. How clear are they? Does euthanasia mean putting someone to sleep? I think not. It means murdering a person— deliberately taking another's life. And what does it mean to say the words, *die with dignity?* That speaker told you it means the right to ask a physician to violate his Hippocratic oath, the right to violate the law of God that says, "Thou shalt not murder." We are to believe God did not know what he wanted! Do not give anyone a lethal injection in the name of human compassion. It is murder, plain and simple.

Can you see that map-territory confusion might create problems with the terms *murder, putting to sleep, killing babies and old people,* and *letting the terminally ill go to God?* Even if you can read these terms objectively, think of the many readers—and your listeners—who cannot. Some people will surely respond to such strong language symbols as though the symbols were the facts that they represent. That confusion of the symbol for the thing it represents is a common error.

All of this suggests to us that a speaker, knowing people tend to make this common error, must take care to control for the effects of the error. As you will see, that control comes from intelligent and careful choice of language.

Language and the Self

A final aspect of language usage seems especially relevant to students of public speaking. There is a clear relationship between the language people use and their selves. Language is self-reflexive; that is, the language one uses reveals a good deal about oneself.[9] To illustrate, suppose you are part of an audience listening to a speaker in the ballroom of your university student center. Your friend turns to you while you are waiting for the evening to begin and says, "I'm really excited about hearing Dr. Kissinger speak tonight. He is so knowledgeable and so important." Just then the lights dim and the president of the Student Government Association says, "Ladies and Gentlemen, good evening. I am very pleased to have this opportunity to introduce the president of this University, who will introduce Dr. Henry Kissinger. I admire President Whiddon because of his consistent and long-standing commitment to excellence—a commitment you can find reflected all over this campus, including this very evening's event. It is just excellent that we have an opportunity to hear our principal speaker tonight. . . ." Soon the president of the University takes the podium. "Ladies and Gentlemen, the man you are about to hear is one of the most outstanding public servants in the history of the United States of America. . . ."

As each of these speakers talks, his language reflects his concepts of himself and his world. The self-reflexive language contains clues about the speaker's view of himself and about how he would like the listeners to view him. Some of the clues are intentional (". . . I admire President Whiddon because. . ." ". . . one of the most outstanding public servants. . .") and some are unintentional (". . . I'm really excited about hearing Dr. Kissinger. . . ."). Whether they are intentional or unintentional, however, the speaker's choices of language say a lot about his view of things. The language is self-reflexive.

It seems to us to make sense when we say that you should consider very carefully how you express yourself. Whatever you say, whether accidentally or on purpose, will contribute to your audience's image of you and your credibility.

Two matters of language choice seem especially significant in what we reveal about ourselves: (1) the interactive style of a speaker, and (2) stereotyping.

Interactive Style

Some people are *aggressive,* some are *shy,* and some are *assertive* when they talk with others. These features of a person's interactive style can be described in terms of their language choices.

Aggressive behavior is evident when a speaker chooses language that is:

1. *Self-enhancing at the expense of others:* "I did it all; he didn't do his job."
2. *Expressive but depreciating of others:* "He's a jerk."
3. *Assuming, especially of control of other people's choices:* "You must do as I ask; you don't have a choice."
4. *Goal-achieving by hurting others:* "I'll get to the top, no matter who has to get hurt."

Shy behavior is characterized by language that is:

1. *Self-denying:* "I'm not a very good scholar. I wasn't well trained."
2. *Anxious or inhibited, and may even sound hurt:* "I'd really like to, but . . . . (sob!)."
3. *Encouraging or allowing of choices by others, often at the speaker's expense:* "Go ahead. Don't mind me. You take the last hamburger. I wasn't hungry anyway."
4. *Not goal-achieving:* "Oh, well, I guess it's really not important that I . . . .")

Clearly, in a speaker-audience situation, language chosen from either of these two categories can work to your disadvantage as a speaker—especially regarding your credibility. Somewhere between aggressiveness and shyness lies assertive behavior. Robert Alberti and Michael Emmons believe that assertiveness is the most desirable interactive style.[10] It is characterized by language that is:

1. *Self-enhancing:* "I'm okay. I know this material."
2. *Expressive, but in a positive way:* "So, ladies and gentlemen, this proposal will mean real growth for the economy, more jobs, more construction, and more money."
3. *Choosing, especially of choices by the self for the self:* "I'd prefer this approach, and I hope you will agree."
4. *Goal achieving:* "So let's build a graduate program, and let's begin now."

Our position is that learning to speak assertively can contribute positively to your credibility and, therefore, to the acceptance that your audience may give you and your ideas.

Stereotyping

You may have heard sentences like these:

> "What do you expect? She's a woman, isn't she?"
> "You guys are all alike."
> "Friends are friends, but business is business."

Mario Cuomo

As one of the most highly regarded orators on the American political scene, Mario Cuomo has several clear and definite ideas about the speechmaking process. Here are a few of them, taken from the *Diaries of Mario Cuomo*, with additional commentary by the authors.

Cuomo is one of the few politicians who prepares most of his own speeches. Of one speech, Cuomo attributed success to three factors: "It's an emotional speech; I wrote it myself and, therefore, was familiar with it; and it was typed on cards. There's no question that reading from cards makes the delivery better."

Although Cuomo has used assistance in writing speeches, Cuomo's own diary notes his dissatisfaction with finding a person who could perform the task adequately. What then are the qualities necessary for a Cuomo speechwriter? Someone who "is sensitive, gentle . . . who loves arranging words and singing songs in prose.

Important also in Cuomo's oratorical success is his speaking style. Although he spends many hours writing polished addresses, he has also been known to throw away the speech in favor of simple "talk." At the heart of his approach to speaking is an exchange of ideas with his audience. Referring to his 1983 inaugural address as governor of New York he notes: "I think the principle effectiveness was in the ideas— simple ideas that a lot of people feel good about. . . . I think people want to feel good about themselves and the world. We are often a cynical people, but we don't want to be. We'd prefer to believe, to hope, to love . . . if only for a little bit."

From Diaries of Mario M. Cuomo: The Campaign for Governor, *by Mario M. Cuomo. Copyright © 1984 by Mario M. Cuomo. Reprinted by permission of Random House, Inc.*

Each of these sentences implies that the speaker is viewing people and relationships stereotypically. Stereotyping can be defined as the process of applying a fixed and rigid set of judgments about a category to an individual representative of that category. Such behavior can make a negative contribution to the credibility of your ideas as a speaker. We want you to think carefully about stereotyping. Stereotyping behavior can be very subtle and difficult to discover in human interactions, especially when the operating stereotypes are our own. The major problem with a stereotype is that it is usually misleading.

At times, especially in the early stages of relationships with individuals or groups, our stereotypes are useful. For example, a teacher knows how to interact with a classroom full of students because of preconceived stereotypes of how students behave and relate to teachers. In return, students know how to act on the first day of classes because they, too, hold stereotypes. But it takes awhile for students and professors to warm up to each other. That is because their stereotypes do not take the individuality of human beings into account—something that must happen before the student-teacher relationship can be mutually rewarding.

What we say says a lot about us. If we speak and act on the basis of stereotypes, we are running the risk that our shallow stereotypes will not "fit." That, too, is self-reflexive. That, too, says a lot about us. How would you judge the credibility of a professor who never gets beyond the first-day-of-class stereotype of a student? We think you will prefer the professor who relates to you as a person. We think listeners prefer speakers who do that, too.

Suggestions for Using Language Well

We know that language can create problems, and we also know that language can be used to create many special effects of imagery, of mood, and so on. What, then, can you do to avoid the pitfalls and to use language more effectively as you speak? The problems we face as textbook writers and the advice we offer here are neither new nor original. You can turn to any good English composition textbook and find good advice about using language for special effects, but implementing this advice is quite another matter. The speaker usually does not have the advantages of time that a writer can draw upon, especially the extemporaneous speaker. Since most speech teachers ask their students to speak extemporaneously—that is, without manuscript and without memorization—the advice we offer must be easily adaptable to that style of speaking.

We assume that you will be generating original sentences as you deliver your speech. What can we tell you that will actually assist you? These pieces of advice come to mind because they lend vigor to your speaking style, because they can be developed on the spur of the moment, and because they address the problems we have discussed in this chapter. Learning to use these suggestions may require a good deal of practice, however, because they do not come naturally.

Keep It Simple

Although the individuals in an audience may be very well educated, we advise you to keep your language level as simple and plain as possible. Prefer the nickle words to the eighty-cent words. Do not use any twelve-dollar words at all! This suggestion will be particularly helpful in avoiding the pitfalls of a listener abstracting, or confusing the symbol with its referent.

This does not mean that you cannot be vivid in image and powerful in language choice. Rather, your choice of language should match the ability of the least skillful listener in your audience. The larger your audience, the more you need to be aware that their collective ability to listen to you goes down. Did you know that television broadcasters pitch their programming to an assumed audience of sixth graders?

Even the Navy argues that writing does not demand big words and fancy phrases. Someone in the Navy Department argues that the guts of English are in its small, often one-syllable, words. That individual recommends:

Instead of	Try
accompany	go with
accordingly	so
advantageous	helpful
attached here-with	here's
at the present time	now
close proximity	near
cognizant	aware
concur	agree
constitutes	is, forms, makes up
contains	has
discontinue	drop, stop
enumerate	count
fatuous numbskull	jerk
feasible	can be done
inasmuch as	since
inception	start
magnitude	size
necessitate	cause
parameters	limits
promulgate	announce, issue
pursuant to	by, following, under
recapitulate	sum up
remuneration	pay
subsequently	after, later, then
terminate	end
transmit	send

FIGURE 11.9 Simpler Words and Phrases. Your choice of language should be targeted at the least skillful listener in the audience. Simple language often has more communicative force than fancy language because simple language is understood by more people.

To illustrate this idea, we have included in figure 11.9 part of a three-page list of suggested language options that was distributed by someone in the Navy Department in an effort to improve official writing. The suggestions emphasize the point we are trying to make. Simpler is almost always better because it compensates for all those problems of distortion that we have described.

Be Specific

The listener must take whatever you present. If you want the listener to form an image, then you must provide the ingredients for that image. General statements and concepts just do not provide sufficient input. Daniel McDonald, a professor of English, uses what he calls the Ginger principle, to emphasize the importance of being specific by using proper names and real numbers wherever possible. He derived the name for this principle from the illustration he uses. Here is the original sentence before the Ginger principle is applied:

> His cousin drove me to a nearby wood, where we sat drinking beer
> and listening to music until very late.

The problem with this sentence is not that it is grammatically incorrect. The problem is that it does not provide specific information for the listener to use in forming the desired image. This often results in utterly wrong inferences. Now, let us put in some specific detail—some ginger:

> His cousin, Ginger, drove me to Johnston's Wood in her brand new
> cherry-red Mustang convertible. We drank a half-case of Stroh Light
> and listened to her George Benson tapes until 4:00 A.M.

Notice that this second version of the story, filled with specific detail, provides the raw materials for image building. You can imagine the scene more clearly because of the specificity.

The value of specificity becomes apparent when you listen to a really good storyteller. The next time you go to a party, test this idea for yourself. Notice which individuals get the attention of others at the party. Notice what they say. They are the people around whom groups of party-goers gather. They sprinkle their talk with real names and real numbers. They hold attention because they are specific.

Use Action Language

As you talk, use the active voice; let the subject of each of your sentences do what the verb says. The inferences that your listeners draw and the images they form will be more accurate.

Look at the two descriptions that follow. The first one is in the passive voice and the second is in the active voice. Keeping in mind that the listener has to take what you give, and that the images your listeners develop depend, largely, on the language you present, which statement do you believe would impact an audience most favorably?

> *Passive:* As time passed my excitement was increased. Every horse on
> the track was being passed by Johnson's horse. The big horse,
> Interloper, would be reached by Johnson's horse at the far turn.
> The stretch run would be a head to head race.
> *Active:* My excitement increased with each passing moment.
> Johnson's horse was flying, now, passing everything on the track.
> At the far turn he'd come head to head with the great horse,
> Interloper. They came thundering down the stretch together.

Action language also includes short sentences, time words, and interrupted rhythms. Compare these passages from a student speech. The first passage is from a tape recording of the original speech. The second is from a revised version that the student wrote after learning about short sentences, time words, and interrupted rhythms.

> *Tape Recording:* We are now, in 1985, in the midst of a new era—the communications age. But our American schools aren't preparing our students to cope with the new age. Technology is changing so very rapidly that yesterday's advances are obsolete. But the schools aren't changing, and perhaps they can't. They don't have the technology and they don't have the know-how to change. But clearly, something has to be done, and it must be done now.
>
> *Revised:* We are all affected. We can't escape the problems of the communications era. But we're not ready, and the schools are not ready. Technology has changed the educational calendar, but it hasn't changed the educational system. Each day is but a single tick of the giant clock of history. And the hands on the clock are moving us relentlessly toward a new day in history at a real-world speed that leaves us breathless. It's 17 minutes before midnight on that clock. We'd better do something, and do it now.

Learning to use action language is not difficult, but it takes practice and a little advance planning. The benefit that comes from learning is well worth the effort. Action language helps the listeners develop more vivid and more accurate images. Like "ginger," action language helps you *show* the audience what you mean.

Use Comparison and Contrast

Comparison and contrast (synonymous with *analogy and antithesis*) provide one of the most powerful ways of adding vividness and accuracy to speech. They place one concept against another to show similarities or differences.

The analogy of the clock, with its references to time, in the last paragraph of the previous speech segment gives the passage a sense of urgency and force that it would not have had otherwise. The power comes from comparing or contrasting something that is unknown with something that is known. An audience does not have any other way to relate to a new idea!

Be careful; you can overdo comparison and contrast, and you can create some really unusual associations by accident. Indeed, overused and mixed metaphors (using more than one metaphor in a single illustration) are the two most common problems when using figurative language. Here is an amusing example that came in an argument by the local coordinator of an organization called March Against Crime.

> The Youthful Offender Act is a sacred cow for trial lawyers and other special interests with clout in Montgomery. . . . The purported purpose of the act is to prevent the "stigma" of the crime from tainting the good name of the criminal. Said unworthy purpose is lost in the dust of the aforesaid cow. That's who's on first.[12]

Other examples of mixed metaphor will help clarify this problem. At one time or another, our students have been "snowed under by the sands of time," and "in deep water over the horns of a dilemma." One student told us that people in her religious denomination were "up tight about premarital sex," while her friends in a different denomination were more "laid back."

Comparison and contrast are very useful in overcoming problems with wrong definition and stereotyping. They raise interest levels and they provide listeners a way of understanding abstract ideas. But they must be used with care.

Use Illustrations

People think about concepts in a predictable way. First, they try to visualize a concrete image in their heads that makes sense to them. After that, they can deal with concepts more abstractly. Our advice thus far, including the advice to use illustrations, is designed to help you help your listeners form concrete images. The more you can do this in public speaking, the better. Consider your audience. It will usually be comprised of a broad range of people from different walks of life, and with differing abilities to receive and process your messages. Abstract ideas that may carry meaning for some of the members of that audience will have no meaning value for others. An illustration or an example will provide audience members with a common ground.

Consider your own experiences and you will see immediately that this is true. Do you sigh with relief when, in the midst of a fairly technical classroom lecture, the professor says "for example?" When you read abstract materials in a textbook, do you look for and study the illustrations and examples as a means of understanding what you are reading?

A long-time professor of speech communication is supposed to have said, "Illustration is the engine that drives a speech—provides it energy and movement and direction."[13] Use many illustrations and examples to clarify your ideas.

Summary

We began this chapter with the argument that the impressions you develop of other people, and the impressions you leave with them, depend largely upon the language choices you make. You can learn to make those choices more intelligently if you understand the nature of language. We defined language as a system of signs and symbols that is used by a speech community to share meaning and experience. Then we defined each of the key terms in the definition. We concluded that people live in a world of words, a world that is based on language. The more skillful the use of language, the greater the ability to exchange and share meanings.

Language, by its very nature, creates problems. One of these is abstraction. We presented Ogden and Richards' idea of the triangle of meaning to illustrate that symbols and referents do not relate one-to-one with each other. Rather, they must be filtered through the thinking processes of individuals. In addition, language and culture are so closely intertwined that it is impossible to know which comes first. Since each speech community uses language in its own unique way, members from different speech communities will have a limited ability to exchange meanings.

People think fluently in the language they use fluently. This idea allows us a closer look at the relationship between language and inference, and problems that flow from naming. These include problems with message reception and image formation that grow out of signification, definition, polarization, and map-territory confusion.

Language is closely related to the self-concept and to the images we send about our own credibility. We contrasted assertiveness, aggressiveness, and shyness, and we related these to stereotyping and the self-fulling prophesy. Given that these features of language apply to everyone, what could we tell you that would utilize these ideas and help you to use language more efficiently and effectively? What approaches to language use will, therefore, enhance your chances of personal success? We settled on these: keep it simple; be specific; use action language; use comparison and contrast; and use many illustrations and examples.

Key Terms

Abstracting	*Generalizing*	*Signification*
Aggressive	*Map-territory*	*Signs*
Assertive	*confusion*	*Speech community*
Categorizing	*Polarization*	*Symbols*
Definition	*Shared meaning*	
	Shy	

Discussion Questions

1. What is language? Ask five of your friends this question—people who have not studied public speaking or communication—and notice how their responses compare and contrast. How do you account for the similarities and differences?

2. Pay close attention to a televised commercial. If possible, videotape the commercial, then write out the exact language used—both spoken and written. Can you notice any relationship between the choices of language and the intended goal of the commercial? In terms of this chapter, what are those relationships?

3. Examine any radio or television commercial, and one or two print-medium advertisements for the same product (beer, cars, perfume, bank services, etc.). How does the language usage compare with the five suggestions we made for using language well? Given the intended audience and the purpose of the messages, do you think the language choices were wise ones? Why or why not?

Notes

1 Charles R. Berger and James J. Bradac, *Language and Social Knowledge: Uncertainty in Interpersonal Relationships* (London: Edward Arnold Publishers, Ltd., 1982).

2 S. I. Hayakawa, *Language in Thought and Action* (New York: Harcourt Brace Jovanovich, Inc., 1964).

3 C. K. Ogden and I. A. Richards, *The Meaning of Meaning,* 3d ed. rev. (New York: Harcourt Brace Jovanovich, Inc., 1959).

4 J. S. Bruner, J. J. Goodnow, and G. A. Austin, *A Study of Thinking* (New York: John Wiley and Sons, 1956).

5 Richard A. Cherwitz and James W. Hikins, *Communication and Knowledge: An Investigation in Rhetorical Epistemology* (Columbia, S.C.: University of South Carolina Press, 1986). These writers have argued cogently that although reality "out there" exists independent of the perceiver, nevertheless, it is the capacity of language to "embody" reality that allows the emergence of meaning.

6 Kenneth Burke, *A Grammar of Motives* (Englewood Cliffs, N.J.: Prentice-Hall, Inc., 1945).

7 Kenneth Burke, *A Rhetoric of Motives* (Englewood Cliffs, N.J.: Prentice-Hall, Inc., 1950).

8 Charles E. Osgood, G. J. Suci, and P. H. Tannenbaum, *The Measurement of Meaning* (Urbana, Ill.: University of Illinois Press, 1957).

9 For an interesting and informative discussion of this idea, *see* A. A. Athos and J. J. Gabarro, *Interpersonal Behavior* (Englewood Cliffs, N.J.: Prentice-Hall, Inc., 1978), chapter 3.

10 R. E. Alberti and M. L. Emmons, *Your Perfect Right: A Guide to Assertive Behavior* (San Luis Obispo, Calif.: Impact Publishers, 1974).

11 Daniel L. McDonald, professor of English, University of South Alabama, Mobile, Alabama.

12 Lillian R. Jackson, "Made My Day," quoted in *Mobile Register,* 25 April 1985, 4A.

13 Attributed to Dr. Ralph G. Nichols of the University of Minnesota at St. Paul by Charles U. Larson of Northern Illinois University.

Suggested Readings

Bandler, Richard, and Grinder, John. *The Structure of Magic: A Book about Language and Therapy.* Palo Alto, Calif.: Science and Behavior Books, Inc., 1975. Two volumes.

This is a fascinating and highly useful work. Volume I focuses on language and volume II focuses on nonverbal messages. In volume I, the authors have described the language usage skills of some of the most talented psychotherapists. Their insights are directly applicable to public address. Volume II is less directly applicable to the public speaking situation, but it provides clear insight into the nonverbal choices that people make, including some of the inferences those behaviors suggest to the receiver.

Casagrande, Jean, ed. *The Linguistic Connection.* Lanham, Md.: The University Press of America, 1983.

This book is a collection of lectures by famous and not-so-famous scholars on a broad range of language-related topics. It is easy to read and is highly informative.

Cherwitz, Richard A., and Hikins, James W. *Communication and Knowledge: An Investigation in Rhetorical Epistemology.* Columbia, S.C.: University of South Carolina Press, 1986.

This book may be the clearest presentation of the relationship between language and knowledge available. In our opinion, every serious student of communication should have read this book.

Ebersole, Frank B. *Language and Perception: Essays in the Philosophy of Language.* Washington, D.C.: University Press of America, Inc., 1979.

We highly recommend this book. It is not easygoing but it is very rewarding reading. The essays address such questions as: Does physical reality determine the form of our language and the kinds of words in our basic vocabulary? Does language determine what we perceive? Does language incorporate a certain view of human actions and a certain view of the future?

Common Types
of Speeches

12 *Informative Speaking*

Outline

Objectives

After reading this chapter you should be able to:

1. Explain the unique characteristics of a speech to inform.
2. Define what distinguishes an appropriate topic for an informative speech.
3. Identify techniques used in effective informative speaking.
4. Explain the major forms of exposition.
5. Identify the most common problems observed in informative speaking.

PREVIEW

In informative speaking, ideas are passed from a speaker to an audience. The message can be as simple as explaining how a pump pulls water from a well to a complex discussion of what is involved in testing intelligence. Informative speech considers the information the members of the audience already possess and then builds upon that base to increase their mental storehouse. This chapter discusses the major goals and techniques used in effective informative speaking, and it identifies common problems in preparing and presenting informative materials.

Informative speaking seeks to expose people to ideas or information they have not encountered previously. Because a great deal of business and professional speaking is informative, acquiring the skills of informative speaking will serve you well.

Goals of Informative Speaking

The essence of sharing information is transmitting an idea from one person's mind to another person's mind with essentially the same understanding. That sharing of ideas is the primary aim of informative speaking. Your exposure to formal education is part of a learning process in which the major function of the instructor is to convey information to students. Consequently, you have been exposed to various forms and styles of informative speaking.

Expand upon Known Information

We are not creatures living in a mental vacuum. We move from those things we know and have experienced to those things we do not know or have not experienced. In the process, we become informed and educated.

The first goal of an informative speaker is to expand on what the audience already knows. For example, an audience can easily understand an explanation of preparing for backpacking if you show how it resembles packing for a trip. You must decide what your important needs will be and then take along those items that will satisfy those needs. Since not everything can go you must make choices. In backpacking, weight is important. Heavy items will be put aside while lighter ones will be taken. This example takes listeners from something they have experienced (going on a trip) and shows similarities between that experience and an activity that some people do not understand (backpacking).

As we pointed out in the chapter on supporting ideas, explaining a new idea involves showing the relationship between what is known and what is unknown. The steps must be small and simple to understand so that listeners can follow them easily.[1] A second example may help clarify this point. All of us know that the penny is the smallest denomination coin issued by the United States, and we know it is copper colored. However, most of us are not well informed about how pennies are made. If you proceeded from the known to the unknown, you could develop a hypothetical trip through the Denver Mint, including a quick look at the raw materials, the machinery used to stamp the coins, the counting and security systems, and the industrial nature of the entire coinage process. From our meager knowledge of a simple coin, which we sometimes think is scarcely worth saving, we would learn interesting and intriguing aspects of its manufacture, and we would acquire information that we did not already possess.

You possess huge amounts of information, much of which you do not know you have. For example, as you drive down the street you see that the speedometer and odometer are moving. As you drive faster, the odometer registers the miles and tenths of miles more quickly. You know if you slow down so will the odometer and speedometer. An engineer could explain this process to you mathematically, but you understand the basic principles of time and motion from your personal experience.[2] It is information you have (through experience) but you are not aware that you possess it. An informative speech could clarify what you know, what it means, or how it could be expressed or explained by a mathematician. Thus, a second purpose of informational speaking is to clarify what an audience already knows.

Clarify What We Already Know

Consider this example. You know that a tight, thin string when plucked gives off a higher-pitched sound than when the string is held loosely. But you may not be aware that the same laws of physics apply to the vocal mechanism. When your vocal chords are tight, your voice yields higher-pitched sounds. People with thick chords generally have lower-pitched voices than those with thin chords. You know some of this information from plucking a guitar string or watching someone tune a piano, but you probably never thought of applying it to an understanding of the pitch of the human voice.

You may have basic information on both of these subjects. Learning that the speedometer/odometer is a complicated speed and distance equation or that the human voice follows basic rules of physics adds to the information you already have. That is a major objective of informative speaking.

One of our more perplexing experiences is making a decision about what material is appropriate for an informative speech. As you answer the following questions, you should be able to decide if your topic is satisfactory for your audience at the time you will speak.

The Selection of Informative Topics

"Does this audience know enough about the subject to follow what I plan to say?" Or, "Does my approach to this topic consider the background of my listeners?" Chapter 4, "Audience Analysis," will help you answer these questions and assist you in the choice of an audience-centered subject.

Topic Appropriateness for the Audience

You need to keep in mind that there is a great deal of difference between firsthand experience and information gained by reading or listening. Firsthand experience is more striking and, usually, more memorable. It is important that you be aware of whether the *kind of information the audience holds is firsthand or casual.* For example, if everyone in the audience has bowled, it would be easier for them to understand and easier for you to explain what a *strike* means. An audience familiar only with the use of the term *strike* as it applies in a baseball game would require a different approach. The nature and extent of audience experience and knowledge is a key factor in preparing an informative speech.

For many years, men assumed women did not understand the technicalities of a football game. When football public-relations staffs offered football fans instructional sessions, which assumed no deep technical background of the game, they were surprised to discover a huge demand by both men and women. Evidently, men were not especially well informed on the technicalities of the game either. No one had provided a climate in which intelligent and interested, but not highly informed, people could learn the basic facts without embarrassment. The audience members of both sexes shared interests and a lack of knowledge. This was a rich climate for informative dialogue and the result was very positive. The fans were better informed and became more interested and intelligent in their observation of the game. People became *fans,* athletic programs prospered, and the public-relations impact was extremely favorable. *The topic was developed in a way that was appropriate for the audience.*

Topic Appropriateness for You, the Speaker

As a speaker, you must talk competently about a subject you understand. Are you a well-informed person who is articulate? Have you selected a subject you know and can present well? An audience must see you as someone who has ideas or facts that they have not heard or would not understand thoroughly without your help. If the listeners perceive you as a well-informed, interesting communicator on a topic, then you can open their minds to your message. Unless they have that image of you, your speech will not succeed.

You can imagine the difficulty that Mike, a twenty-two-year-old college graduate, had when he went to work for an agency of the United States government. Because he was bright and articulate, he was soon assigned to do public relations speaking for agency programs. One day, Mike was sent to Madison, Wisconsin, to address a group on the psychological problems some people face when they retire. When he arrived at the meeting room and looked out over his audience, he discovered that no one in the room, except him, was younger than fifty-five.

Clearly, his speech topic, his own age, and the ages of his listeners combined to put Mike at a great disadvantage. Everyone in the audience had more firsthand knowledge about Mike's topic than Mike did. The topic was *not appropriate,* either for Mike or for his audience.

The criteria of *competency and appropriateness* are two characteristics each of us expects in an informational message. We do not want to listen to someone who does not appear well-informed about the speaking topic. We look for someone whose grasp of the subject is thorough and keyed to the information level of the listeners. The speaker should *know and understand* what he is discussing. The following dialogue is a good example of the kind of approach that will turn an audience off in a hurry:

> *Student Speaker:* I'm not too sure about some of the facts on this topic, but let me tell you what I read in the library.
> *Typical Audience Reaction:* If your information came just from the library, I guess maybe you don't know any more about this than I do, so we're just sharing ignorance. *Or,*
> I was beginning to get the idea that you weren't too sure of your subject. You just confirmed my suspicions by telling me you don't know much.

A listener must believe it would be advantageous to listen to a speaker. That is the type of informative speaker you should strive to be. If you choose a topic you know well and if you speak clearly to your listeners, you will be meeting the basic requirements of effective informative speaking. Consider the following as an example of a speaker who establishes competency and creates an acceptable climate for the message:

> Today I'd like to tell you how being captain of my high school soccer team helped make me a leader and a more sensitive person than I was before I had that obligation. Serving as captain helped me understand that I was a model of how the members of the team should play and act, even when things didn't go our way. And I had to provide them regularly with an example of how it is just as hard to win well as it is to be a graceful loser. And maybe that was the hardest part of being a leader.

Consider another example of a speaker who establishes competency and creates an acceptable climate for the message:

> Today I'd like to tell you why work in photography can be both financially rewarding and personally satisfying. In my personal experience, working as a photographer's assistant for the last two summers, I learned that there's really a great chance to meet different kinds of people, to find their best characteristics, and then try to freeze that impression on film. Sure, there's room for lots of creativity like getting a star image on a photo snapped at sunset, taking pictures at night and seeing that headlights create streaks across the film. Besides all that, a person who does a good job in photography can expect to make at least an average or above average salary for a college graduate. Let me tell you more about this interesting field.

This is a case of a student talking to other students at their level of understanding and experience. It is not necessary to have had elaborate life experiences; summer jobs can qualify each person to speak with a reasonable degree of expertise.

Common Types of Topics for Informative Speeches

A multitude of questions can be used as topics for informative speeches. Some of them may not occur to you immediately. They are easier to develop if you consider them as categories of topics. The types listed below should suggest possibilities and guidelines in your selection of questions for speeches.

Processes or Procedures

In chapter 2, "Planning the First Speech," the speech to demonstrate was introduced as an example of a process or procedure that used a visual aid. You should be aware, however, that visual aids are appropriate for virtually all types of informative speeches. Events, persons, processes, and procedures may, or may not, lend themselves to the use of visual aids as a means of explaining or clarifying an idea.[3]

An explanation of the water purification system in a major city provides an example of a process—actually a complicated procedure—that could be explained with or without the use of visual aids. The challenge you face when describing a process or a procedure is to explain, simply and clearly, the basic steps. Here is an example of the main ideas of such a speech:

Purpose statement: To inform the audience of the basic steps involved in purification of water for the City of Indianapolis.

    I. Purposes of Water Purification
   II. Steps in the Purification Process
       A. Initial Filtering of the Water
       B. Use of Sedimentation Beds and Filters
       C. Introduction of Purification Chemicals
       D. Testing of Product before Distribution
  III. Quality Control of Water in the City System

This speech focuses on the specific processes the chemists and workers follow in examining and treating the water supply. As a speaker, you might decide to use visual aids to show the types and quantities of chemicals needed to purify the water supply for a city of over 500,000 people, or you might elect to explain the process verbally through the use of comparison, contrast, or other techniques that enhance listener understanding.

If visuals will help and if they fit within the assignment, then you certainly should use those tools to help you reach your goal. Their use certainly is not restricted to speeches involving a *process* or *procedure*. They are applicable to all six common types of topics discussed in this chapter. For more information about visual supporting materials, turn to chapter 10.

Many student speakers comment that giving an effective informative speech is very similar to grade school show-and-tell experiences. However, there is much more to informative speaking than showing and telling. Informative speaking includes the transmission of information, the clarification of ideas, the explanation of concepts, or the identification of processes and procedures. None of this is expected of an elementary school child when she tells about her pet kitten. Showing something to an audience and then explaining it to them is central to much of our communication. The object helps, partially, to explain itself, but the rest of the job is up to you, the speaker, to fill in the blanks that make the material interesting and easy to follow and understand.

Processes and procedures can range from decision making in a large corporation to an explanation of how to change the oil and filter in an automobile. They can be as complex as the operation of a gyroscope or as basic as the reasons that highway right-of-ways are mowed only three times during the summer months. The key is to select information that is interesting and appealing to you and then place it in a framework that is intriguing to a group of listeners. Success is often a result of enthusiasm, of a positive attitude toward your topic. When listeners share that enthusiasm, prospects for success are enhanced even further.

Events

Our lives revolve around significant events. Few of us have difficulty remembering where we were or what we were doing when a major national event or a personal triumph or tragedy touched our lives. The topic you select for an informative speech does not need to have that kind of earth-shattering significance, but you must realize that people's lives are tied up with events. When preparing for a speech to inform, you have an opportunity to share an event you experienced with an audience and to indicate the interesting and significant features in ways that will touch their lives, too.

Recently, a midsize American city opened its first major shopping mall. While such an event would be of only passing interest in many communities, in this community the mayor and all the city luminaries appeared with bands, and hosted a week-long series of special events to celebrate the grand opening. This event was of major importance in the city that year. A report of the civic event might include an explanation of the significance of the center to the community and the importance its opening had for city residents and persons in outlying areas.

Important occurrences in history are also excellent choices for informative speeches. You might choose to talk about the repeal of prohibition and the problems associated with it, or you might explain the eruption at Mount St. Helens or its effect on the lives of people and/or the world. How about the stock market crash of 1929 and the drastic effect it had on the lives of many people in the United States and, ultimately, the world?

Diverse subjects? Yes, they certainly are, but no more diverse than the events that are going on every day in the world. You have the opportunity to choose from all of history to the present moment in developing an angle or view of an event in a way that enlarges audience understanding and interest. How much does your audience know about the eruption at Mount St. Helens? Do you think they really understand or know the issues of prohibition or the effects of the Vietnam War? Or, did they merely hear their grandparents talk about these events at a family gathering?

Persons

The lives or actions of people are excellent bases for informative speeches. Biography often provides information about a person's life that was previously unknown to listeners. For example, many people are not aware that Bill Bradley was an all-time state high school basketball scoring champion in Missouri. He then lead Princeton University to the NCAA finals, was a Rhodes Scholar, and had a successful professional basketball career with the New York Knicks before he became a United States senator.

Most of us know that many famous people and leaders have a fatal flaw. John Wilkes Booth was such a man. Although he was a famous actor, few today know much about his acting or his life, except that he was the assassin of Abraham Lincoln. Booth and the events of his life provide an interesting example of how we fail to remember the promising career of a prominent person, but rather how we focus on a single, momentous event in which that person became a key player. Here is interesting material from which attractive informative speeches can evolve. The use of a person as the subject for an informative speech assumes you will reveal information that is interesting or developed in a unique way for your audience. The person you choose to discuss need not be a national figure. Rather, you could discuss someone who has had an influence on your life or the lives of people who are unknown to your audience. *Reader's Digest* runs an essay every month about people. Few are famous. Some are unknown except to the author, but they all have made some important contribution to the lives of others, and that is what makes the essays so popular.

An effective informative speech about a person involves a type of selective biography. Speakers choose significant elements of a person's life and weave the fabric of a message around those central elements. It might be the person's character, humble origin, lack of self-confidence, or burning drive for success.

In selecting people as speech topics, you may find it easier to choose people of significant stature in the modern world. Mother Teresa, Enrico Fermi, or Dag Hammarskjold may not be familiar names to each of you, but these people have made major contributions to the world as you know

Subjects for informative speeches are beyond number. Remember, there are no uninteresting subjects, only disinterested people. You must find a way to relate your ideas to your listeners.

it today. Do you know which one of these persons was (1) Secretary General of the United Nations, (2) a recipient of the Nobel Peace Prize, (3) a major contributor to the development of the first atomic bomb? Some students might recognize some of the names but not associate them with the events, recognitions, or the offices. *Your contribution* would be to enlarge the scope of their knowledge.

Places

For many, geography or historical significance is only moderately important. Only in grade school did many of us study the magnificence of design exemplified by the capital city of Washington, D.C. Relatively few have stood on the steps of the Lincoln Memorial or gazed upon the Washington Monument, or seen the Capitol or the White House. Each of these is a topic of architectural and design importance, but they represent only a few samples of the many possibilities for informative speaking about places. In many cases, you may be a walking sourcebook on the location of significant places because of your personal experience.

The white sands of Gulf Shores, Alabama, the cool summer breezes blowing in the Straits of Mackinac, Michigan, and the historical flavor of the gold mines in Cripple Creek, Colorado, all are ammunition for telling listeners unique and interesting facts, features, or details. There are many places much closer to home. The garage out behind the house, with its exposed skeleton, may suggest a speech on antique building methods. The church you attend may have a lovely stained-glass window or a work of art to discuss. The small town courthouse may hold a story or two for your audience. Even the trunk in the attic may hold a wealth of speech ideas. From the magnificent to the obscure, all topics have possibilities. Once again, we want to say that your enthusiasm has the potential for making any topic interesting to your listeners.

Definitions

Explaining the meaning of words or phrases is another way you can develop ideas in an informative speech. A definition is a statement of the meaning of a word or words as used by a speaker.

Joan used definition in this way for an informative speech.

> When I was growing up in central Ohio, we said we were living in the Midwest. Of course, it was some distance to the East Coast and even farther to the Pacific Ocean, but since the bulk of people lived between the Atlantic Ocean and the Mississippi River, it seemed only natural for us to call ourselves midwesterners.
>
> When I was about twelve, we moved to Indiana, and the label Midwest moved with me to that state. A few years later we moved to Nebraska, and I concluded that I was now truly living in the Midwest.
>
> Suddenly, it occurred to me that Midwest was a matter of perception. Ohio was Midwest, and, as I moved across the country, the boundaries of the geographic definition moved with me. *It all became relative.* Now that I live in Missouri, I consider myself mostly "midwestern." I can justify it on the grounds that both geographically and in terms of the true center of population in the United States, I am very near the middle. How would you describe the geographical location of your birthplace or your present residence?

Your goal in informative speaking is to clarify and explain your ideas, not to confuse your listeners.

Definition can be a crucial instrument in helping you accomplish your task. What you should try to do in using the technique of definition is to follow a sequence called "Name It, Explain It, Clarify It, Conclude It."

1. State the term or situation you hope to explain.
2. Define or clarify it through example, illustration, or situation.
3. Explain its importance or value to the audience.

Here is a case in point: suppose you have decided to define the term *creativity* for your audience. Already, you have named it. Explaining it may involve saying "creativity is little more than putting together things we already know exist in a new and different way." Clarify it by saying, for instance, "most of the medicines that are developed in pharmaceutical labs today are not made from new elements, rather they are combinations of known ingredients mixed together in different proportions." You could use other examples. You might decide to show how bottlers of soft drinks do not add anything "new" to their products; they just combine already known ingredients in different proportions. You now have named, explained, and clarified that creativity is putting common matters together in unusual or different ways.

Your final challenge is to conclude your idea by wrapping up this informative presentation with a unifying theme, such as "There's really nothing new under the sun"; "Creative people may, in fact, be those who look for the uncommon in the common"; or "So creativity is not the gift of a few; it is available to us all."

The speech by Joan, earlier in this chapter, is another illustration of how these steps can be incorporated successfully in using definition as a technique for informative speaking.

Through definition, you can develop a topic in an interesting way for an audience. You define and explain a term in ways your audience can understand and appreciate.

Concepts

One definition of the word *concept* is "the understanding of an idea or event." We deal with concepts every day, but not all of us interpret concepts in the same way. For instance, each of us has a slightly different notion of the concept "the good life." If you were to ask other students what their concept of "the good life" is, they might say, "having a good job with a high salary," or "taking a vacation at a prestigious resort." Their concept of "the good life" may be different from yours, but that does not mean it is wrong.

You can use a concept as the topic for an informative speech. For example, the concept "flextime" in the industrial workplace is a potential topic. Flextime involves varying the starting hours of employees. Some begin as early as 7 A.M., while others begin as late as 10 A.M. Each employee works eight hours and takes regular work and meal breaks. Flextime allows employees the opportunity to adjust their full-time work schedules to their own needs while satisfying company requirements. In this example, we defined the concept first and then explained and clarified it. Good informative speeches state and then define the concept early.

What concepts intrigue you? How about "on-line scheduling of classes" for college courses? It involves registration for courses at computer terminals, and thus supposedly eliminates those "endless waiting lines." Could you get the courses you need? What happens if you need a course and it is already filled? The computer cannot listen to your complaint. How could you develop this topic to appeal to the interests and concerns of a college audience?

How about security systems that allow entrance to private areas only after verifying identification by scanning the "composition of your eyeball." Since each eye is different (like fingerprints), the concept seems foolproof as a security check. Do you think it is practical? Where would its use be most beneficial? How expensive would it be? It is a concept that is being applied frequently in industrial security situations today.

These examples of topics for informative speeches need development, and they may raise more questions than they answer. That is the challenge to the informative speaker: provide answers to questions!

Policies

National, state, local, and institutional policies are frequent subjects for informative speeches. The following list suggests the variety of policies that you could explain or clarify. Notice that each of these topics bears on every student listener. Each is important and thus has a good deal of interest value, so each is a good topic for an informative speech.

Policies

Deficit spending	Automation
Mandatory use of seat belts	General education requirements
Required auto insurance	Dress code
Capital punishment	Final exam policy
Corporal punishment	Prerequisites
Preventive maintenance	Late registration fees
Can deposit ordinance	Drop dates

A speech on a proposed or already operating policy has the advantage of providing the speaker with a ready-made organization for the talk. The description and discussion of the topic becomes the format for presentation.

To illustrate, if you choose to discuss a can deposit ordinance, you would first need to explain that, under the ordinance, a deposit would be collected by the merchant for each beverage container sold. When the empty can is returned, the deposit would then be refunded. The container could be glass, metal, or plastic, but a scale of charges based on the size of the bottle or can would be necessary. The objective of the ordinance is to reduce the littering of beverage containers tossed from cars or left lying in public park areas. Several midsize communities in the Midwest have passed such ordinances and found them effective in reducing the littering of beverage containers.

Techniques of Informative Speaking

In developing a successful informative presentation, the main objective is effective and accurate transmission of ideas from one person (the speaker) to a group of people (the audience). Three important techniques will help you accomplish that goal: (1) clarity, (2) simplicity, and (3) concreteness.

Clarity

Clarity means "easily understood." Dictionaries define the term in different ways, but their common reference point is that clarity refers to something that is easy to follow or comprehend.

How many times have you heard someone say, "I just don't understand what you're saying"? Part of the difficulty may be that you have not organized your ideas basically enough for listeners to understand them easily. For them to grasp the message in your informative presentation, it must be strikingly clear in structure and in the language that surrounds that structure.

Class lectures sometimes illustrate this problem. Let us use history as an example. A professor tries to explain the origins of United States involvement in World War II. But you become lost when he talks about the relationships between Russia, Germany, Italy, and Japan. He does not make it clear to you and others that the Russians and the Japanese dislike each other and that the Russians and Germans distrust each other. So you become confused because of a lack of clarity in his statements and organization. That lack of clarity *could* be the result of your lack of understanding the direction of his remarks or his failure to tell you what he was going to do in class on that day. The requirement that you face is to organize a set of ideas so they are easy for your listeners to follow while you express your thoughts clearly. You need to ask yourself if the ideas you have developed are clear to an uninformed listener.

Could your listener, who knows nothing about transistors, explain the basic features of a transistor after your informative speech on that subject? If your answer is "Yes," then you probably have developed ideas that are basically clear. If they are not clear, an uninformed listener would have no chance of understanding what a transistor does or how it does it.

Understanding the organization of ideas is central to clarity of structure and statement. Successful public speaking is contingent on clarity of organization, which will greatly assist you in presenting your ideas, and it is essential if your listeners are to absorb and remember what you have said.

A simple organizational structure is fundamental to the clarity of ideas. Briefly it involves (1) preview: tell them what you are going to tell them; (2) presentation: tell them; and (3) review: tell them what you have told them. This pattern may appear too simple, but it is a very good way to verify the soundness and clearness of your organization and the ease with which it can be followed. If you cue your listeners, there is a much better chance that they will follow what you are trying to tell them.[4]

Let us apply this pattern to public communication. The introduction in many speeches consists of *telling them what you are going to tell them.* It is more or less a preview of the important ideas in your speech. It may be a summary of your main points or a call to be interested in a topic or some interesting facets of the subject you are going to talk about. *Tell people what you are going to talk about.*

The second phase, *telling them,* is the body of the speech. It is the transfer of information and ideas, whether informational or persuasive, from your mind and mouth to their ears and minds.

The final phase, *telling them what you have told them,* is a summary of major thoughts. In some types of speeches it is not necessarily appropriate to do this, but we know that restating an idea several times (both internally and at the end of the speech) leads to greater understanding and retention.

Simplicity

Simplicity is an often-misunderstood term. Here it means fundamental and easy to follow. It does not mean "talking down to listeners," nor does it suggest that they are anything less than highly intelligent persons. The essence of simplicity in an informative speech is a structure that contains the following:

1. A clear thesis.
2. A few main ideas, clearly expressed.
3. Materials that support and explain those main ideas.

Based on what you have read in the previous chapters of this book, you recognize these as the ingredients of a well-organized speech. Informative speaking is intended to present ideas clearly in a way that is easy for listeners to follow. Simple ideas are easy for people to understand during a speech and easy to recall after the speech is over. Simple language means that your thoughts are expressed in words that are basic, clear, and understandable to all your listeners.

A prominent theatrical producer supposedly argued that if you could not write your idea on the back of his calling card, the idea was not clear enough to present!

Much of what you understand about communication with others centers on the principle of concreteness. *Concreteness is grounding a concept of principle in specific facts under actual circumstances and conditions.* In contrast, abstraction permits the listener to interpret ideas and words based primarily upon personal experience or feeling. Put another way, a concrete statement includes particular facts—proper nouns, real numbers, actual places, vivid descriptions of circumstance and condition, and simple words rather than very difficult words. We have called this idea the Ginger principle.

Concreteness

Let us look at a few examples of vagueness to help you understand why specific statements are easier to understand.

> I believe in the Constitutional rights of all people, but there must also be concomitant responsibilities.

> Instructions for the assembly of all parts is included inside.
> Appropriate for five- to twelve-year-olds.

These statements are vague; they do not give us specific direction. Because they are vague, they are subject to misinterpretation. Let us look at the same statements made in a more concrete way.

> The Constitutional right of free speech is one of our most valuable rights as a free people. Although we have the right to "speak our mind," we must remember that we're not free to say everything in public that we think. There are laws of libel. We cannot shout "fire" in a crowded theatre, and we need to recognize that there is always another side to every issue. Free speech is one of our most valued rights, but we must manage it with maturity and good sense.

> The instructions for the assembly of all parts are included on the packaging. To assemble this toy you will need a Phillips screwdriver, a crescent wrench, pliers, and six ⅝" stove bolts, 1¼" in length. Please be certain to *read all instructions before you begin to assemble any part of this toy. If the parts are not assembled in the proper order, the toy will be inoperable. BATTERIES ARE NOT INCLUDED.*

These more concrete statements build upon the vagueness of their earlier versions. They tell us more precisely what is meant or what we should do. That is the point we are trying to make. The more concrete your choice of language, the clearer and easier it is to understand.

As you contrast the vague statements below with the more concrete examples, you should gain a clear sense of the difference between them, and recognize the value of concrete statements in listener comprehension. Compare and contrast the following pairs of statements:

> *Concrete:* The temperature gauge tells you if the water temperature of your auto engine is in a safe range.
> *Abstract:* A gauge monitors engine temperature safety.

Concrete: You are fifteen minutes late for this job interview. If you
       are late for the interview, you may be late for work, too.
Abstract: Your time-related behavior cost you this job.

Concrete: During the last quarter, United States exports of corn and
       wheat to foreign countries fell for the first time in five years.
Abstract: The United States balance of trade in farm commodities is
       down.

Specific, concrete statements decrease the opportunities for misunderstanding and misinterpretation, and increase the prospects for success. The
mission in an informative speech is to be clear, interesting, and understandable. You will be more likely to reach that goal if you avoid abstractions and vagueness.

See if these examples help you understand the differences even better.

Moderately abstract statement: The basic principle of establishing
       premium payments of high scale for younger drivers is the
       concept of "risk exposure." Data indicate clearly that the accident
       occurrence of drivers under twenty-five years of age, especially
       male, warrants a higher premium charge.
More concrete statement: Drivers under twenty-five must pay more for
       auto insurance than older drivers because they have more
       accidents. If you are a male, you are more likely to have an
       accident that is charged against your insurance than if you were a
       female.
Very concrete statement: Your car insurance is going to cost you more
       until you are twenty-five, especially if you are a male. It could cost
       you twice as much at age twenty as it does at age twenty-five. The
       cost is higher because a twenty-year-old is more likely to have an
       accident than his parents or most people over twenty-five. You
       may be a very safe driver, but the accident statistics don't lie.
       Insurance companies base their rates on the number and cost of
       claims, and drivers under twenty-five—especially male drivers—
       have the greatest number of claims that cost the greatest amount
       of money.

These three statements reinforce the idea that the more basic, clear, and
illustrative a statement is, the easier it is to understand. The first example
sounds like it was prepared by an insurance executive for a conference.
The other two examples make the same point more concretely.

Concreteness, then, is a major challenge for you. Audiences understand
ideas more clearly when they are expressed in basic, simple terms. A word
such as *parsimonious* may describe the frugality with which a person man-
ages money, but you also could call that person a *tightwad* or a *miser*. Which
is more concrete? How about the difference between *nonperforming loans*
and *bad debts*?

The more basic, clear, and illustrative a statement is, the easier it is to understand. This speaker leaves no doubt concerning her viewpoint.

Stick with descriptions and statements that listeners understand and are unlikely to misinterpret. If you mean, "The idea is lousy, it won't work, and it will cost us ten dollars more than we make in a month," say that! Do not slip into the abstraction that, "The idea is unappealing and besides that it is not clearly affordable in our budget." This second statement lacks force and clarity, mainly because it is not specific and concrete. Getting ideas from your mind to the mind of the listeners is your mission. You can accomplish it best if you stick with simple, direct sentences made of simple words that specify real people and real numbers, and that provide the materials your listeners need to form concrete images.

Speeches call out for materials that clarify and explain the statements you make. There are many ways you can explain and support these ideas. Here we will remind you of a few of the more common ones. We described these earlier, in chapter 7.

Forms of Exposition

Quotations

You can use statements by sources of authority to establish and clarify an idea. We are all accustomed to hearing people quoted as we listen to television or radio. The use of quotation in informative speaking is mainly to clarify or prove an idea that has been introduced. Your purpose in using quotation might be to show that a "power figure" feels the subject is as important as you say it is.

Quotations should not be just tossed at an audience. *They need to be introduced, presented, and interpreted.* Use quotation to buttress your position. Remember to tell the audience of the expert qualifications of the person you are quoting. Similarly, it may be extremely useful to mention the background or professional interests of the person being cited to enhance further the believability of the quoted statements. Tell the listeners of (1) the qualifications/credentials of the person being quoted and the circumstances in which the statement was made; (2) the meaning of the statement (interpretation); and (3) a restatement of the quotation in your own words.

An example of a badly chosen quotation from a student speech shows how these principles should be applied. Della Robinson referred to the comic strip *L'il Abner* when she discussed the importance of computers in education. She wrongly supposed that everyone would know the fictional cartoon character Senator Claghorn, who always seemed to have an answer, no matter what the problem. This wrong assumption was a mistake. Here is what Della said:

> To support the idea that computer literacy is crucial for any college graduate, listen to what Senator Claghorn said recently when speaking to the National Academy of Sciences: "There is not a single area of American education that has more universal use than computer literacy. Our libraries, our financial institutions, our schools, our businesses, and our government all demand that the successful employee understand and be able to use the computer." We all know Senator Claghorn as a former president of How-About-U and chairman of the Senate Education Committee. His comments indicate the importance he and his colleagues in Congress attach to the understanding and use of computers. It is easy to see that he feels computers are one of the most important elements in future work success.

The quotation cannot be expected to stand on its own if the listener does not know the source. Once you have introduced and presented the statement, it is crucial that you provide the audience with an interpretation of the quotation. In this example, the interpretation phase tells us that Senator Claghorn has made a strong statement in support of the speaker's thesis and that his feelings on the topic are shared by other national figures.

However, the listeners in Della's audience were confused. She needed to be much more careful in introducing, presenting, and interpreting the quotation.

Here are two additional examples of quotations, both of which have been used much more wisely.

> Most of us are bothered greatly by the threats of bombings and the taking of hostages. But, how do world leaders react to terrorism? According to the president of the United States, "International terrorism cannot be tolerated by civilized people any longer." It's clear from this statement that the president is as outraged as the rest of us at these uncivilized acts and appears to be on the verge of engaging in some preventive action.

> Nonpartisan information, information coming to us from sources who do not have an "ax to grind," is more objective and causes us to consider it more seriously than would the same facts presented by someone with a vested interest. The Congressional Budget Office is that kind of nonpartisan, information-gathering group in Washington. Let's see what they have to say about our budget-balancing act. "The Congressional Budget Office stated last week that we need to reduce spending by at least 15 percent to have any chance of balancing the budget." It's clear from this statement that, according to impartial sources, spending reductions are the only way we can realize a balanced budget in the foreseeable future.

Each of these illustrations has an introduction, a qualification of the source, a presentation and an interpretation of the information, and a restatement of the major portion of the idea. Thus, the quotation becomes a believable and understandable item of support for the idea the speaker is presenting.

Examples

When you use a single instance to clarify or explain your ideas, you are using examples. A series of examples provides the basis for much of reasoning. You begin to build generalizations on the grounds that a large number of specific examples have led you to that conclusion. That notion was part of our discussion of inductive logic in chapter 7. The example, as a form of support, must be typical or representative. You can find unusual examples of nearly everything if you look far enough: "man bites dog," "woman zips self into designer jeans and is rescued by fire department." Because these are not typical, they should not be used to support an argument.

Much of our informative talking is based on the use of specific examples to clarify or establish the truth of our statements. The following are illustrative:

The Malaysian culture is an example of how both modern and traditional patterns of courtship are integrated at the time of marriage.

Smoking is one of the major causes of death in this country today. For example, as a result of extensive laboratory tests, the surgeon general of the United States has linked heart disease, cancer of the bladder, lung cancer, and high blood pressure to cigarette smoking.

Great force is exerted when a runner's foot strikes the ground. For example, a "heel strike" creates a force two to three times the weight of the runner's body when the foot meets the surface.

It is not true that professional golfers make most of their money from prizes or endorsements. Jack Nicklaus and Arnold Palmer are two examples of successful golfers who also have profitable incomes from their own businesses and whose names have become household words.

Statistics

The use of numbers or figures to explain relationships is a common way to explain or clarify. When you find numbers or data presented to support a position, you encounter what we call statistics. They can be confusing, and you should follow these guidelines when you use them in your speaking:

Round Off Figures

Two-hundred-and-ten-thousand people watched a soccer match in South America last year.

The national deficit this year is approaching $300 billion.

Auto deaths in the United States last year reached seventy-five thousand for the first time.

Interpret

Statistics alone can be confusing and/or meaningless. Clarify and interpret statistics so that your listeners can draw the appropriate conclusion. For example:

One million children a year are victims of abuse. That's equal to about the population of greater Kansas City, Missouri, who are victims of adult abuse each year.

The death of 2,500 people in the Bhopal, India, chemical disaster is as great as a crash of eight Boeing 747s with all persons on board killed.

These clarifications and interpretations help the listener to relate to the numbers emotionally and conceptually.

The general direction represented by statistical data can be most meaningful to an audience. Statistics alone may have little meaning, but, when
a clear pattern can be shown by citing several statistics, then the data have
relevance and make sense. For example:

> Airfares have been affected by "fare wars." A year ago round-trip
> flights from St. Louis to New Orleans cost between $350 and $400.
> Now the bargain rate is $98. Low fares abound. Last year it cost $320
> to fly from New York to San Francisco. Now you can make the trip
> for $99.
>   Interest rates have dropped steadily since 1979. At that time, the
> prevailing rate was 17 percent. We saw a decrease to 14 percent by
> 1981, a drop to 12 percent by 1983, and to 7.5 percent by 1985.

You can see the power these examples have. They show a trend, and
people are interested in trends.

Informative discourse involves providing information that will move listeners from the known to the unknown. Comparison and contrast show
similarities and differences between the known and the unknown. In short,
they tell you that an object, concept, or idea is "like" or "different from"
one you already know or understand.

Comparison and Contrast

   Here are examples of both comparison and contrast. Notice how effectively these examples help you to identify with the ideas.

> *Comparison:* You might feel as if you're in a swamp this year.
>   Compared to last year at this time, we have eleven more inches of
>   rain. Compared to the norm, we are a full foot over the average in
>   rainfall and it's only June!
> *Comparison:* You'd certainly be pleased with the new Cadillac this
>   year. Like the Mercedes, it has independent suspension, elegant
>   and sophisticated styling, a luxurious interior, a simple yet
>   functional control panel, and a computer-controlled fuel system.
> *Contrast:* The power hitters in baseball today are good, but they don't
>   compare to Babe Ruth. There were fewer games the year he set the
>   record. The fields, the equipment, and the traveling all made it
>   more difficult to play at peak efficiency. Yet, no one except Babe
>   Ruth has hit 60 home runs in 154 games.
> *Contrast:* The United States National Safety Council has shown
>   conclusively that the 55 MPH speed limit has reduced the number
>   of people killed in auto accidents on the highways. But officials in
>   Belgium, which has the third highest death rate per million on
>   highways in Europe, say "Nobody can prove that higher speeds
>   on highways mean more deaths."

It is easy to see how real and specific comparison and contrast become
when you use them to illustrate similarities and differences. They are concrete and human. They illustrate the use of emotional and logical support
already discussed. They are an important ingredient in successful public
speaking.

Summary

Informative speaking is a key test of your ability to pass information to listeners. The basic concern of the effective informative speaker is to state ideas clearly, and to express them with limited opportunities for misunderstanding. An effective speaker must select a few compelling ideas, and use techniques of clarification and support that will reinforce the major ideas and make them interesting. Informative speech is, essentially, a sharing experience with a primary goal of understanding. Simplicity of organization and clear expression of ideas by the speaker will make the accomplishment of that objective likely.

Key Terms

Appropriateness   *Statistics*

Clarity   *Examples*

Types of topics

Discussion Questions

1. What is the basic difference between an informative speech and a speech to demonstrate? Can you inform without demonstrating? Is a speech to demonstrate "show and tell?" If you take the "show" out of "show and tell," do you have a speech to inform?

2. In your experience as a listener, what kinds of topics have been most successful in the development of informative speeches? What characteristics did they have? How do those compare to the ones that are discussed in this chapter? Be prepared to explain.

3. Concreteness sounds like a desirable characteristic. Choose objects in the classroom and assign abstract (or more abstract) terms to them. What is the result of that assignment? Is information more easily communicated? Why or why not?

4. In effective speeches that you have heard recently, how did the speaker use the "name, explain, clarify, conclude" sequence? In what way did it contribute to the impact of the speech? Would the speech have been more effective without it?

Notes

1 For more suggestions on informational speaking, *see* Bruce E. Gronbeck, *The Articulate Person: A Guide to Everyday Public Speaking* (Glenview, Ill.: Scott, Foresman and Company, 1983), chapters 6 and 7.

2 For the position of a classical rhetorician, *see* Dennis Bormann, "Two Faculty Psychologists on the 'Ends' of Speaking: George Campbell and Johann Sulzer," *Central States Speech Journal* 33 (Spring 1982): 306.

3 Richard A. Katula and Celest A. Martin, "Teaching Critical Thinking in the Speech Communication Classroom," *Communication Education* 33 (April 1984): 164–65.

4 H. Lloyd Goodall, Jr., and Christopher L. Waagen, *The Persuasive Presentation* (New York: Harper & Row Publishers, 1985), 62–63.

Suggested Readings

Linkugel, Wil A.; Allen, R. R.; and Johannesen, Richard L. *Contemporary American Speeches*, 5th ed. Dubuque, Ia.: Kendall/Hunt Publishing Co., 1982.
An excellent sourcebook for models of effective informative discourse. Section 3 "Speeches that Impart Knowledge," is especially useful both as a guideline and for the specimen materials that are introduced.
Olbricht, Thomas H. *Informative Speaking*. Glenview, Ill.: Scott, Foresman, 1968.
A handy paperback concentrating solely on the concerns and structure of the informative presentation. Originally designed as a text, it has now become a better-than-average quick reference source for students interested in developing appeals for, designing, and supporting informative presentations.
Phillips, Gerald M., and Zolten, J. Jerome. *Structuring Speech*. Indianapolis: Bobbs-Merrill Co., 1976.
A recent version of how-to-do-it in organizing/developing ideas. This is an especially attractive piece of reading for the student interested in the organization and support of informative discourse.

13 *Persuasive Speaking*

Outline

Objectives

After reading this chapter you should be able to:

1. Identify the types of propositions used for persuasive speeches.
2. Explain the roles of logic and emotion in the persuasion process.
3. Understand the principles for success in persuasive communication.
4. Cite the major needs underlying the human bases for action.
5. Explain the techniques of speaker credibility.
6. Identify the techniques for the effective presentation of issues.

P*REVIEW*

Persuasive speaking is intended to affect the attitudes and beliefs of listeners. By understanding the motivations of listeners, speakers are able to evaluate and potentially change how each listener feels about facts, values, and policies. By combining logic and emotional appeals with a concern for the needs of listeners, speakers hope to move the attitude of the audience in the direction determined by the speaker.

Factors such as the credibility of the speaker and the ways in which messages are presented have a significant impact on the outcome of the persuasive setting. Through a knowledge of techniques of presentation and use of materials, speakers can be more certain that their messages will have long-term consequences on audience feelings and predispositions to act.

Nature of Persuasion

Speeches to persuade are aimed at urging people to change an attitude or belief, or to perform some act. Persuasive speaking is a common part of our everyday life. People speak to others in an effort to influence their thoughts, feelings, or actions. Some of the thoughts may involve statements like:

Hey, I've had enough studying for one night. Let's go get a pizza.

You know the concert tickets go on sale today, and the good seats will go fast. Do you want me to pick up a ticket for you when I get mine tonight?

Honey, I love you, but I've got to tell you that your shirt just doesn't go with those slacks. Maybe you ought to. . . .

Think of persuasion as a large balloon filled with positive and negative charges of various sizes (fig. 13.1). Each of those charges represents an experience with a person, place, or thing. In this case let a "typewriter" represent the experience you are considering. You can add experiences about "typewriters" to the balloon for the rest of your life because the balloon will not explode. As you add experiences, however, the "shape" of the balloon is changed by the mix of impressions and attitudes you acquire about typewriters. Each experience may make only a slight change but as the experiences accumulate, a substantial change may result.

You are not likely to change the overall shape of your feeling about a "typewriter" by adding a single plus or minus to this balloon, but over time the change can be substantial. Likewise, the influence of a single persuasive speech probably will not be enough to make you change your mind drastically about typewriters, or anything else for that matter. If you dislike typing, for instance, a single speech outlining the features and advantages of a new electronic typewriter probably would not convince you to like typing. You may, however, begin to be less certain of your previous feeling and thus begin to "lean" toward the speaker's position as a result of that speech.

FIGURE 13.1 A single persuasive speech ordinarily does not bring about a large change in listeners' opinions. Rather, it will become part of the mix of impressions that each listener maintains on that topic. Hence, the goal in persuasive speaking, realistically, is to cause a shift in audience opinion toward the desired direction.

In persuasive speaking your goal is to get people moving in the desired direction. Do not become overly optimistic and expect huge changes from a single message. If you remember that your speech is one event in a series of experiences for your listeners, you will have a more realistic view of what you can expect them to believe or reject.

Types of Differences

Persuasion is a matter of choice. On virtually every subject there are at least two points of view. Your position as speaker may differ from that of your listeners. Sometimes that difference may be one of degree while at other times the difference may be substantial.

You may feel that it is vital that we balance the federal budget. Your listeners may agree, but they may feel that it will take some time. Perhaps they think that low-interest loans to students for the cost of their education must be continued while you are convinced that loans should exist only for those whose family income falls below a certain dollar figure. These examples illustrate differences of degree, not of basic position.

There also are differences of basic position. When your audience analysis indicates the audience holds a much different view from yours, do not expect to work miracles through a single speech. You will not convert an atheist to a fundamentalist by a single speech. You will not convince an audience opposed to a state income tax that they should become ardent supporters as a result of your speech. Work for limited goals. Your likelihood of success will be much greater.

Types of Propositions for Persuasive Speeches

Before examining standards and techniques used in persuasion, we will look at the type of propositions used as the basis for persuasive messages.

When you decide what you plan to accomplish in a persuasive speech, you first develop a topic into a "proposition." A proposition is, briefly, a type of proposal. Propositions fit into three categories: (1) fact, (2) value, or (3) policy. How you put a proposition into a category is important because the category helps you define more clearly how to specify the purpose of the message. The category helps describe and define how the organization and appeals will be developed.

Propositions of Fact

A proposition of fact is a statement that something is true. Some examples of propositions are:

> Altitude sickness occurs in at least 20 percent of the population.
> Asphalt highways do not last as long as concrete highways.
> Most forest fires are caused by human carelessness or arson.

For each of these propositions, it is possible to establish the *truthfulness* of the statement. When you define a topic as a proposition of fact, you establish that your aim is to verify your position. Your mission, then, is to compile and present evidence and argument that will convince the audience of the accuracy of your position. For example, your listeners may suspect that forest fires are caused largely by humans. You assume the responsibility for introducing the information that will convince them that your statement is factually true.

A proposition of fact helps to define and to suggest what the persuasive speaker will do to persuade the audience.

A proposition of value attempts to establish that persons, places, or things are good, bad, valuable, worthless, right or wrong, and so on. Examples include:

> Manhattan real estate is the most valuable in the world.
> Swimming is the best all-around form of exercise.
> Stalin was a more dangerous world leader than Hitler.

As a persuasive speaker, you assume the responsibility of introducing the body of information, the appeals, the criteria, and the evidence that your listeners will apply in arriving at the same conclusion. The proposition of value, simply put, says that something is more valuable, more important, or truer than another. The persuasion occurs when you introduce evidence and argument that establishes your position as the correct and/or the most accurate one.

A proposition of policy argues that something should be done. We hear statements daily that can be categorized as propositions of policy. Here are a few statements that fit this category:

> You should try to pay for purchases by cash rather than charging them.
> Mail should be handled by private carriers.
> Tuition costs should be lowered next year.

Many situations require us to make "ought" decisions. "Should I cut this class?" "Which computer should I buy?" "Should I spend the rest of my money on a movie or a pizza?" You are familiar with the types of argument, both pro and con, that arise as you think about such propositions. Self-justification, hunger, variety, or relaxation are some of our rationalizations. Because we spend so much of our time thinking about courses of action and their advantages and disadvantages, it is easy to see why the *proposition of policy* is an important element of persuasive communication. Determining that a topic fits into this classification will help you establish the kinds of arguments and evidence necessary to achieve your speaking goal.

Knowing the classification of a proposition makes the job of persuasion easier. It helps you *define and structure* the speech. The structure and support become the key ingredients of an effective persuasive presentation.

We have stressed the importance of knowing and understanding the position of your listeners throughout this book and particularly in chapter 4, "Audience Analysis." Persuasive speaking demands that you tailor your message to the position your audience holds on the topic. For example, if your listeners strongly oppose federal aid to education, you cannot approach the topic as if they all support the idea. Your role is to move them from the position they hold or the attitudes they possess toward the direction stated by your specific purpose.

More than any other type of speech, persuasive speaking demands a high degree of adaptation. It requires that you understand the beliefs and feelings of your listeners as you attempt to modify their behavior. Change is usually not easy but it is the aim of persuasion. Unlike the goal of informative speeches to transfer information, persuasion requires changing your audience's feelings and attitudes about a topic. This type of oral communication requires you to determine where your audience stands on an issue and how far you can reasonably expect to move them with your message. Then you must develop a message that adjusts to their positions without compromising your own. Finally, you develop a speech that represents an adjustment between the two positions. Perhaps you can see why your arguments are more likely to be effective if they are moderately rather than extremely different from the position already held by your listeners.[1]

Consider how a student might prepare for a classroom speech advocating the ban of handgun sales. This is a controversial topic. Because our Founding Fathers built the "right to bear arms" into the Constitution of the United States, many people feel that no restrictions should be placed upon the right of citizens to have rifles, shotguns, or pistols in their possession. You must determine how your audience feels on this topic before you begin to develop the arguments and positions you intend to pursue. Do any members of the audience belong to the National Rifle Association? If so, they will be opposed to any form of gun control. As you study your listeners (as we discussed in chapter 4), you may discover that their age, socioeconomic status, and knowledge of the topic suggest that they are mildly in favor of the proposition. If that is the position you determine inferentially, then your task becomes simpler. You now will work to move a slightly favorable audience to a stronger gun-control position. You will accomplish this by organizing your arguments and evidence according to the information you have gained during audience analysis. Remember, your message calls for only a moderate attitude change. It reflects how far you can reasonably expect listeners to move during a relatively brief speech. Be realistic. Work for limited objectives! You cannot expect to move an audience very far with just one brief speech.

Techniques of Persuasive Speaking

Speakers inevitably search for formulas that will move an audience from point *A* to point *B*. If life were simple and people were highly predictable, you would always be able to craft messages that would cause the desired change in your listeners. That has not been possible in earlier generations and it will not be attainable in the 1990s. Although no magic formulas have been developed, some guidelines should help.

People like to think of themselves as rational human beings. Usually we see ourselves as logical people. You trade in the refrigerator when it is fifteen years old because logic tells you it should begin to fail by the end of that time. (We call that planned obsolescence.) When the physician prescribes medication for you to take four times a day, you take it as directed because you want to become healthy again. You are behaving logically and reasonably.

Humans are affected not only by logic but also by emotion. People are not exclusively logical when they make decisions. Knowing that, you will surely want to combine emotional and logical appeals as a means of changing or otherwise affecting listeners.

For several years the Surgeon General's Office and the American Cancer Society attempted to convince people to stop smoking but their efforts failed. Their public messages during the early stages were primarily logical. They went something like this:

> You know that smoking causes cancer in the lungs of laboratory
> animals. Scientists have shown us that if a product produces cancers
> in lab animals, it also will produce them in humans. It's clear from
> the evidence that people who smoke are much more likely to be
> victims of lung cancer. Please stop smoking so you won't become
> another statistic.

Those arguments are logical and objectively true, *but they did not stop* people from smoking. In fact, the number of female smokers under thirty-five actually increased, which suggests that something was wrong with the message and/or the appeals. Consequently, the Surgeon General's Office and the American Cancer Society modified their appeals:

> There's no reason you should die before your time. If you're a
> smoker, you're playing with a deadly weapon. Each day you're
> inhaling a mixture of poisonous gases as you *pay to die an early death.*
> Americans are dying at a record rate because they can't "shake the
> habit." How valuable is your life? Is it worth $20.00, $50.00, or
> $2,000,000? If a pack of cigarettes costs approximately $1.00 and if
> you smoke a pack a day, you're paying $365.00 per year to die a
> premature death. How do your family and friends feel about the
> prospects of your early death? How do you feel?

This is an extremely emotion-laden message, presented to the public both as media commercials and as part of public speeches. The sponsoring organizations discovered that their persuasive appeals to the American public had more effect when they combined emotional and rational elements. This discovery suggests that you should determine the basic logical foundations for your speaking appeals and combine those appeals with the appropriate

Logic and Emotion in Persuasion

emotional appeals. (See the discussion of Maslow's hierarchy later in this chapter.) Emotional and logical appeals combined with arguments and supporting evidence provide an effective starting point for your persuasive speech. Each audience must be considered separately because the outcome of predominately emotional or logical appeals cannot be predicted with high accuracy.[2] Your analysis of listeners will help you design a message that will make the appropriate combination of appeals work.

Guides to Successful Persuasive Speaking

The following suggestions will play a large role in your success as a persuasive speaker.[3] While they will not guarantee success, they will increase your chances of achieving your objective.

Be Informed. Know as much as you can about the subject you are planning to discuss. Your first task is to research the topic; you should be the expert. An effective speaker should know the issues, arguments, and evidence on both sides of a question.

Be Confident that You Will Be Effective. If you do not feel confident, at least *act* confident. We are talking about the concept called the self-fulfilling prophecy, which we discussed in an earlier chapter. If you believe you can be successful, you increase the odds that you will be. Self-confidence without preparation or knowledge is not the aim, however. When you have analyzed the purpose, the audience, and the material, you must believe that you are qualified and prepared to present and *persuade* the audience. Confidence, both apparent and real, suggests to listeners that you understand their needs and that you have solutions and ideas they should accept.

Speakers who appear to believe in themselves are more likely to gain the approval and the agreement of the audience. It is a matter of speaker credibility. You are engaged in a role of "selling yourself" to your listeners.[4]

Know Your Listeners. You need to be extremely sensitive to the kinds of people with whom you are interacting. Are they farmers, carpenters, insurance agents, salespeople, waitresses, bank executives, or barbers? How strongly do they and the community they represent feel about this question? Each audience is unique. Your knowledge of the various dimensions of your target group is absolutely crucial to your success. (Chapter 4 explored this matter in depth.)

Audiences have formed their reactions as a result of their experiences, and they search for information and ideas that reinforce what they already believe. Sensitivity to the reasons for audience belief helps you understand why they feel or believe as they do. For example, if you grew up on a family farm in the United States, you probably believe that a vital part of American life stems from the rural segment of our society. If your farm has been in your family for several generations, it is likely you will be receptive to arguments asserting that corporate farms and "agri-business" are leading to the downfall of the family farm and rural American life as we have known them. You are not likely to agree with a speaker's idea that more industrialization of farming will answer our problems. Even if the speaker introduces an appealing and valid line of argument about the efficiency of corporate farming, you may still reject it as irrelevant or in error. This is because we permit ourselves to be affected emotionally and rationally when we form an opinion. Your experience on the farm brings emotional thoughts and associations to the speech. Certainly the logic of the speaker alone will not convince you that your family was wrong for several generations.

The strategy you use in arranging your ideas for listeners has a strong impact on their acceptability. Here, we will provide you with a few guides that will help you decide how to "order" your ideas. We will also suggest some techniques that may provide you with an improved opportunity to accomplish your goal of affecting the attitudes of your listeners. In chapter 7 we described in some detail how to organize ideas for public address. The suggestions we include here supplement that chapter, but more specifically they will enhance the power of your persuasive message. How you organize your ideas can have a direct bearing on how persuasive those ideas will be.

Present Issues Carefully

Present One Viewpoint. If your audience is generally receptive, if you want to get immediate change, or if the audience is unaware of another side of an issue, show only your side of the argument.

Assume that you are trying to convince a college audience to buy a turbo-powered car when they make their next purchase. They might be generally receptive to this idea. Many consumers are unaware that automotive engineers agree the turbo is more prone to mechanical problems after 50,000 miles because of the stresses placed on the engine by the turbo-powering. You are looking for immediate change in audience attitude. Given this situation, your best strategy would be to present only the arguments supporting the purchase of a turbo-powered car. If you present the negative arguments (the other side of the issue), you are less likely to accomplish your goal because you have introduced information that is directly contrary to existing attitudes.

Present Two or More Viewpoints. When the audience is aware of the other side of the question or may encounter that other side, you should present both sides. If you assume your audience is already familiar with the strengths and advantages of a turbo-powered car or are likely to be exposed to information about some of the disadvantages of turbo, this calls for a change in persuasive strategy. It means you should give them information about the strengths and weaknesses of the turbocar. Otherwise they will do one of two things: (1) If they know the other side, they will assume you were not able to present stronger arguments in support of your position, or (2) if they hear the other side shortly after your speech, they will be vulnerable to the negative arguments and more likely to assume that the ideas you presented lacked strength because they never heard the counterarguments until that time.

When you introduce the other side of the question to your listeners, you alert them to the fact that there are two sides. That introduction should include the basic arguments against the other side. The audience will then know why they should buy a turbo-powered car and be equipped to challenge the arguments that turbocars are not a good investment.

Be Explicit. When talking to an unsophisticated audience, you are more likely to get opinion change in the desired direction if you specifically state what you want them to do or believe. For example, if you were speaking to an audience about the balance-of-trade deficit in the United States, and that audience was relatively uninformed about the meaning of balance-of-trade, then you would need to spell out exactly what you want them to believe. In this situation you might tell them that you want them to "buy only American-made products," or "insist on more import restrictions." Those are explicit statements. You probably would use those statements as part of a major portion of the speech when you discuss the problem and call for some audience action. In this situation, you would *state clearly for the audience what you want them to do or believe.*[5] When an audience is not knowledgeable about your subject matter, leaving the decision "up in the air" or not being specific may confuse them!

Imply Your Conclusion. With well-informed or intelligent audiences, you should imply the conclusion. To illustrate, if your audience is well informed on the matter of trade and deficits, it would be more useful to imply a conclusion than to state specifically what you want.

These two arguments provide examples:

> High unemployment in the shoe industry means we can't tolerate competition from low-priced imports.

> United States high-technology products are the reason you have digital watches, micro-computers, and Teflon cookware.

Here we have constructed two arguments for a case and implied the direction for belief/action, but we have left the conclusion and the action to the listeners, depending on their intelligence and understanding of the situation for action. Remember that well-informed, sophisticated listeners do not usually want a speaker to prescribe how they will or must behave.

You avoid giving an audience that feeling if you do not make precise suggestions about how they should behave. Let your arguments imply the conclusions about national trade policy you want your sophisticated listeners to draw. Do not insult their intelligence.

Avoid the Appearance of Manipulation. If an audience recognizes that you are trying to persuade them about some fact, value, or policy, they may resist the effort. For example,

> Today I'm going to persuade you that a Bolvo microwave oven is the best buy on the market. I intend to show you that its low cost and simple operation make it the ideal apartment or dormitory cooking appliance. Finally, I'm going to persuade you that the cost of the microwave is far outweighed by its timesaving and convenience features.

Clearly, this is an effort to sell a particular product. It would be best to avoid "waving a red flag" in the faces of listeners. Clues that tell the audience you are trying to persuade them increase their resistance to persuasion.

Most of us are aware that we are affected by others and what they say. We do not, however, like to be told *explicitly* what they intend to do and then observe them doing it. Persuasion scholars call this "statement of manipulative intent." Extensive research in persuasion shows that when you tell an audience how you are going to influence them you reduce the likelihood that you will accomplish that goal.[6] The bottom line is: *don't open your persuasive speech by making a statement of your purpose.* Instead, present your arguments and proofs carefully, according to the suggestions for strategy and structure we discussed earlier in this chapter. Avoid the "statement of manipulative intent." Steer the audience in the direction of feeling they have "bought" an idea instead of someone having "sold" them an idea or product they did not like or need.

Hierarchy of Needs

What motivates people to feel, believe, and act as they do? Abraham Maslow was one of the most influential theorists who studied human motivation.[7] He developed what he called a "hierarchy" of human needs, which will help you understand how people are likely to respond to your message. Figure 13.2 displays the hierarchy in much the same way that Maslow presented it.

Maslow believed that people are driven by "need states" to act as they do. He believed that we require the satisfaction of certain physical and psychological needs for our lives to be reasonably complete. He ordered these needs in a hierarchy. His idea was that these need states fluctuated continually and included, in some degree, one or more of the motivators in the hierarchy.

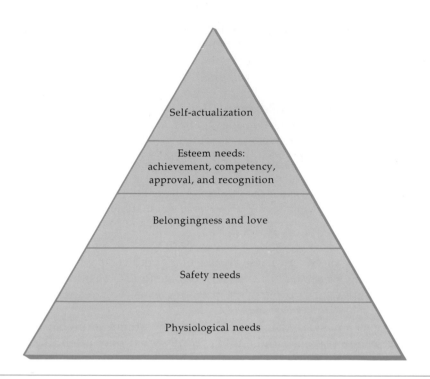

FIGURE 13.2 Maslow's Hierarchy of Needs. People are motivated to think and act on the basis of these needs, according to Maslow, and they will attempt to satisfy the needs in ascending order. Understanding this will help you craft your persuasive messages. (Data for diagram based on Hierarchy of Needs in "A Theory of Human Motivation" from *Motivation and Personality,* Second Edition, by Abraham H. Maslow. Copyright © 1970 by Abraham H. Maslow. Reprinted by permission of Harper & Row, Publishers, Inc.)

An important assumption in Maslow's thinking is that some needs are more significant than others. His idea was that the lower the need on the hierarchy, the more vital it is to an individual's life. People will strive to satisfy the more basic needs in the hierarchy before they shift to the higher order needs. For example, our need for food and water takes precedence over our love and belongingness needs. Social scientists, for instance, point to the need for satisfaction of basic states such as hunger as the foundation for changes and restructuring of governments around the world.

Need states vary in strength and we make choices in satisfying our needs. Some of our choices are more strongly inclined to societal pressures and others to personal drives. Let us look at the characteristics of each level of the hierarchy and see how an understanding of these characteristics can be employed by a speaker in appealing to the needs of an audience.

Physiological Needs

The physiological needs are the most basic needs in the hierarchy. They include the need for food, air, and water, for sexual release, for elimination of waste, and so forth. If these needs are left unsatisfied, they can become the most predominant motivating force in a person's life.

The need for physiological satisfaction provides powerful motivational appeal in persuasion. A speaker could use the physiological needs in an argument for environmental safety. We all need clear and pure water and air. A speech addressing the importance of uncontaminated water and air would, of course, incorporate features of the physiological needs. A persuasive speaker could build upon those needs (and rights) with statements supporting action to remove lead from gasoline, concern with "acid rain," and pollution controls imposed by the local, state, and federal authorities. Physiological needs are powerful building blocks in constructing persuasive messages that arouse our most basic concerns.

Safety and Security Needs

The safety and security needs include the need for security, freedom from harm and fear, protection by the law, and for order in life. These needs play an important role in the choices people make; therefore, they provide powerful motivational appeal in persuasion. We all want to feel safe when we drive our car in traffic or when we go to bed at night. We want to feel secure that we will have enough money to buy the items we need and want. Speeches about "law and order in society," or "no one likes the drunk driver," are based on our needs for safety and security. Here are some others:

Women Take Back the Night
Buckle Up for Safety
A Man's Home Is His Castle

If you were to select safety in the home as a speech topic, this would illustrate a safety and security need. All of us believe we should be secure in our living space. We spend enormous sums of money in purchasing locks, burglar alarms, and sonar devices because we feel inadequate in protecting our homes and ourselves against intruders. Why not speak to that need, either using satisfaction through greater care in going about your daily activities (locking doors, checking with neighbors) or perhaps through the acquisition of an additional safety device? In either case, do not ignore the personal need for safety and security as a strong motivating factor for listeners to public communication.

Love and Belongingness Needs

The need for love and belonging explains why people become attached to and dependent upon social groups, parents, and peers. This need includes the desire to be accepted by others, to receive attention and love from one's spouse, children, and relatives, and perhaps most importantly, the need for personal acceptance and approval. It also explains why becoming an "insider" rather than a "bystander" is an important part of social development. We seek affection and attention from others; we spend much money to have the latest style of clothing, haircut, or car; and we attend the "right" events—all because of our need for love and belonging.

You can apply this need as part of a persuasive effort, too. For example, the bandwagon appeal works. ("Everyone is doing it, don't be an outsider." "Join the crowd. Buy Zagnow Candies.") Indeed, the love and belonging needs may be the primary motivators in getting people to buy designer jeans or a sports car, or to attend a concert. You can use this knowledge of needs to convince people to contribute to a campus blood drive or to join a service-based campus group.

If you were to talk about how important love is to people universally, you might begin the speech with a discussion of the formative childhood years. You could point out how important bonding and the need for love and affection is to the infant. As we grow older we lose some of our dependency, but we still need affection and love from others. You might choose to talk about our search for companionship and affection from a member of the opposite sex as we reach adolescence. Obviously, this is merely a sample of how you can incorporate this need into your repertoire of need appeals in a persuasive speech.

People also are moved to change their attitudes based on love and belonging needs if they think that a spouse, child, or some respected acquaintance will improve their standing. As a speaker, you can select appeals that relate to the love and belonging needs of people, then craft those needs into the format of your message. Show people how changes in attitudes or behaviors will help them satisfy their need for love and belonging.

Self-Esteem

Your view of your personal competency, your reputation, or your status or prestige are all included in your self-esteem needs. People like to think of themselves as unique and valuable. As a speaker, you can use this powerful motivational appeal by identifying which parts of the esteem need apply directly to your speech, and then designing an appeal to the self-esteem needs of your audience. For example, advertisers tell us we can realize our self-esteem with these appeals: "Show your leadership potential." "The few, the proud, the Marines." "For people on their way to the top." "It doesn't get any better than this."

Take a cue from them. The next time you plan to speak, consider inquiring why some students study so hard. There are many ways you could build that into the heart of your message. Think about a speech that deals with why some students excel and others do not. Is it because they are slow learners, or is it because they do it to satisfy their own need for self-esteem? As a speaker, do you satisfy some of your own needs for self-esteem by demonstrating that you are capable of talking publicly before a group of your peers? Try to remember as you begin to design your persuasive message that the need for self-esteem is one of our basic needs. It is entirely possible to build a speech around the matter of self-esteem.

The human motive for self-actualization includes the need for self-fulfillment, for creativity, for imagination. It is the need for novelty, ingeniousness, and originality.[8] Maslow saw self-actualized people as spontaneous, uninhibited, expressive, and natural in their expression of ideas or feelings. The problem is that many people "shut off" much of what is within them and, as a result, do not experience self-actualization. This need fits at the top of Maslow's hierarchy because people can satisfy their physical and social needs and still not feel content or satisfied.

Many people are faced with the dilemma of what it will take to make them happy. They may have money, recognition, a good job, excellent health and a group of friends, yet they feel unsatisfied. If you ask them, often they will answer, "There's just something missing." That "missing" something may well be their need for self-actualization. It could range from writing poetry, canoeing down a white-water stream, or a feeling of inner peace about personal accomplishment. It may be that they want to paint a picture, write a shocking novel, build a house with some striking architectural features, or plan and plant a flower garden that is truly unique. Whatever it is, that need to become a "complete person" can be a powerful motivator. It hinges on a need for realization of one's highest potential. Your role as a speaker is to determine if the message you are tailoring for your audience can appeal to this dimension of human needs. If it can, how will you integrate it?

Do you intend to arouse your audience by saying, "Did you ever wish you could just toss your present job out the window and go to the Rockies? If you got there, what would you do? Would you paint, ski, take pictures, or backpack? Let me explore with you some possibilities and I think you will see a visit like this would not only be valuable but interesting to nearly everyone."

Certainly, this would arouse attention. You would appeal to that dimension of self-actualization, that untapped element in their lives. They would like to see what is over the next mountain. Use that type of motive appeal to encourage audience involvement and as the basis for presenting your persuasive message. You will find that within each of us is a need (although often latent) to achieve or create something that distinguishes us as a person. Tap that human need.

Self-Actualization

A synonym for *credibility* is *believability*. Whether or not listeners believe what you say is critical to your success in audience-centered speaking. You must be believable if you expect to have *personal success in public speaking* and move listeners in the desired direction.

The guides of successful speaking we have discussed also are basic elements of credibility. Credibility involves the perception of *goodwill* on the part of the speaker, and it also is part of the general activity of successful speaking. What we have discussed as guides to successful speaking also

Speaker Credibility

involves much of what we identify as components of credibility. Just as credibility involves the perception of goodwill on the part of the speaker, so too is it part of the broad matter of successful speaking. The effective speaker is the "good person who speaks well." That suggests speakers who are attractive in their intellectual and physical approach, who are believable in their ideas and their support, and who approach speaking as an ethical, responsible personal and public undertaking. You can increase your credibility by understanding how audiences judge the believability of speakers.

Subject Knowledge

Give the audience reasons to believe you are well informed about the subject. Show expertise and an understanding of what a listener knows as you develop a message. Clarify ideas for your listeners to produce maximum effects in your persuasive efforts. Credibility involves a perception that the speaker is well informed, interested in the listeners, aware of the various issues involved, confident of success, and capable of expert judgment on the subject.[9]

As part of establishing your credibility, take into account how much your audience knows about the subject. If you intend to talk about personal investments, just tossing terms at them like *no-load funds, put or call options, junk bonds,* and *zero coupon offerings* suggests that you have not bothered to determine how much the listeners know about the subject. If speaking is to be audience centered, doesn't it seem reasonable that a "believable speaker" would consider audience knowledge and then build the message on that knowledge? In this case, it would be useful to explain how a mutual fund operates as part of the process of creating a more positive impression of yourself and your ability to deal with a subject like personal investments. Otherwise, listeners may get the impression you are speaking just to hear the sound of your own voice.

Trustworthiness

The *perception* of trustworthiness is a significant factor in persuasion.[10] Are you someone who honestly presents the issues to your listeners? Can you be trusted? We all dislike deception, particularly from people who publicly mislead us. You have a special obligation to present arguments that are honest representations of the facts.

Trustworthiness is closely related to the matter of ethics in public communication. Honest representation of ideas is the "bedrock" for anyone who expects others to believe them and follow their suggestions. When you speak publicly you have a special responsibility to state the facts and the arguments clearly and honestly. Shading the truth or twisting a position has no place in ethical persuasive communication. Many police stations have a sign in their interrogation rooms stating, "If you tell the truth you don't have to worry about being consistent!" Speakers must be honest and truthful; this is the base of the ethical dimension of public speaking.

For example, trustworthiness would be damaged considerably if you argued that cigarette smoking studies have demonstrated no conclusive link between smoking and the various forms of cancer, heart disease, and lung disorders. Of course, you might introduce some evidence that shows the inconclusiveness of scientific studies, but there is overwhelming medical evidence proving that smoking seriously damages health. Few people doubt the causal link, so arguments that smoking is not a dangerous habit can have a serious negative impact on your credibility. Your desire to have a positive impact on listeners is tied closely to your perceived trustworthiness.

Your believability is affected by personal appearance. For example, if you are speaking about the importance of investing your money wisely, you should present yourself as a person who has achieved success in this activity. Your credibility would be increased if you discussed this topic while wearing a dress or suit rather than a tee shirt and cutoffs. You must adapt your appearance to the nature of the topic and the goal you hope to accomplish.

Personal Appearance

Be prepared to speak in a well-informed way about the possible investment options—stocks, bonds, certificates, mutual funds, money market funds, and savings accounts—that are available to a prospective investor, and explain simply and clearly those choices. Listeners tend to believe (and accept) the arguments of people who appear well informed about the topic and who offer external evidence (in this case their attire) of their knowledge.

Credibility is strongly linked to how much the audience agrees with the speaker's message. The degree of audience agreement is not an attribute the audience confers on the speaker. It results from the statements of the speaker and the reactions of the listeners. A message that is not consistent with what an audience believes will have a negative effect on the perception of the speaker. To illustrate, suppose the audience is a group of college students. If you take the position that a college education is not a worthwhile investment, it is easy to understand why the message would not receive acceptance. You would be telling these students that they are wasting their money and that their value judgments are poor.

Extent of Audience Agreement

In this situation, your credibility would suffer because your position is at odds with what the listeners already believe. Your position and that of the audience are in fundamental opposition; they are dissonant.[11] If the listeners can, they will find a way of resolving the difference between what you are saying and what they truly believe. One method is for the listeners to identify additional reasons for believing the way they do. In that case, the dissonance (disagreement) is reduced but the credibility of the speaker

Listeners view a speaker as highly credible—and are more likely to allow themselves to be persuaded or entertained—if the speaker's values and judgments are similar to their own.

suffers. Listeners do not place high believability in people whose values and judgments are distinctly different from their own because they seek consistency between their beliefs and their actions. They may passively tolerate a message that is contrary to their basic beliefs about educational values, but they are unlikely to change their attitudes about the value of higher education. They may decide that you are not well informed and that you have a peculiar sense of values.

You should not just "tell audiences what they want to hear." Certainly there are many situations where your position and that of the listeners generally coincide, but your efforts should not consist of merely reinforcing their existing position. An ethical communicator analyzes the audience. If the findings indicate that the position of the audience and the speaker vary, the speaker then determines the appropriate strategies for modifying the audience's position. The ethics of persuasion require that you present your convictions honestly. An example of dishonesty would be telling an audience that the national debt is really meaningless because we only "owe" ourselves. The audience might want to hear that, but a more ethical position would be to say that the debt is real and is important because it affects how much we pay for the money we borrow and the stability of our economy.

We have seen that credibility refers to the "believability" of the speaker. Does that person know something about this subject? Do you perceive that person as honest and trustworthy? Are you willing to accept what he or she says at face value? Is this speaker's position generally consistent with what you already believe? If your answer to these questions is "yes," then the speaker is someone who is credible to you.

Credibility and Persuasion

A major concern of any speaker is the need to be consistent in the arguments that are presented and in the materials that are used to support those arguments. It is easy to fall into traps of poor reasoning. We want to introduce several of the major fallacies to you so you can avoid using them in the construction and presentation of your messages.

Fallacies in Argument

These fallacies are errors in the reasoning process and are characterized by failures to examine carefully such matters as cause and effect, the preponderance of evidence, or the absence of supporting material.

Logical Fallacies

Sequential Fallacy. Known as *post hoc, ergo propter hoc,* sequential fallacy literally means that we ask listeners to believe something is true because it was preceded by something else. Translated, this Latin phrase means "after this, therefore because of this." An example of the "post hoc" fallacy might be saying that we should expect the stock market to rise because the NFL League Champions won the Super Bowl. In most years when the NFL Football Champs won the game, the stock market rose, but it did not rise because they won the game. There is no causal relationship between the two events, although one is coincidentally linked with the other.

Appeal to Popular Opinion. This fallacy makes extensive use of the "bandwagon approach." It may begin with the argument that "everyone knows" or "all the students at this school agree," but it lacks the evidentiary support that must first prove that "everyone knows there is life on Mars." Rarely does everyone agree on anything (a violation of the "allness" concept), so be wary of any appeal suggesting that you should respond in a particular fashion because most or all people feel or act that way.

Two-valued Logic. This fallacy assumes that there are only two sides to a proposition, idea, or argument. Essentially, it argues that matters are either "black or white" and that there are no intermediate shades of gray. In actuality, more matters fall into the gray area than at the extremes. In an everyday conversation, this fallacy might occur when a friend says, "If you're not for me on this issue, you oppose me." The fact is that you may support some of the person's ideas but not agree with others. Arguments (and life) usually are not either/or situations, and you should be leery of reasoning that calls on you to accept a two-sided logic in analysis.

Begging the Question. This fallacy involves restating the idea and then using it as the reason for itself. For example, a speaker might say, "Felipe is a careful driver because he hasn't had any accidents." The question has been begged because the claim (careful driver) is used to form the reasoning (he hasn't had any accidents). It is easy to fall into this trap, which is known as *petitio principii.*

Fallacies of Evidence

We have stated several times the importance of sustaining any argument—the speaker introduces ideas and uses evidence to support them. However, you must be wary of some fallacies in the use of evidence to support your ideas.

Hasty Generalization. When you draw conclusions on the basis of too little evidence, your conclusion is flawed and, perhaps, so is the heart of your message. Because two policemen were convicted of taking bribes does not mean the police force is corrupt. A hasty generalization based on that limited number of cases would certainly suggest the contrary. However, many of us are vulnerable to this type of fallacy.

False Dichotomy. An effort to divide a question into only two parts when, in fact, there may be several divisions illustrates this fallacy. An argument of this sort might be, "The only way we can reduce the national debt is to reduce spending or increase taxes." Actually, there are many ways to reduce the debt and they certainly are not limited *only* (a warning word) to the choices offered. When a speaker suggests that there are *only* these choices, you should listen carefully. The speaker is probably attempting to limit the options to the ones that can be most easily or conveniently discussed. Beware of someone who attempts to oversimplify; there probably are several other options.

Long-Term Effects of Persuasion

How long will the effects of a persuasive speech last? People are concerned whether or not changes endure. They are concerned also with what factors make it possible for persuaders to have a long-term influence on the attitudes and actions of listeners. Here are some principles that can have a powerful impact on the effect of a persuasive message.

Time

Over time, people become occupied with other matters, and as a result, the influence of a persuasive message diminishes. To illustrate, you can become very excited at the time you hear a political speech. You might even decide to work hard to support the speaker. But after a day, a week, or a month, the influence of that message diminishes because other more immediate matters take precedence in your life. You may still believe the candidate is the "best person," but the influence to support actively the candidate may be no more important to you than what you had for lunch yesterday. What this suggests to you as a speaker is that you will probably need to follow up on your persuasive appeals. For example, you may want to phone or write key people to review their commitment to your position just before they decide how to vote.

When people become physically or vocally involved in the communication process, they are more likely to be influenced by it. Look again at the example of the political speaker. You have listened to politicians speak at conventions and watched how they managed their audiences. Often they ask the audience questions such as "Can our opponents manage the government? Can they understand our national needs? Is their position sensible? Would you vote for a party that failed on all these questions?" Of course the answer to each of these questions is "no."

Listener Participation

The speaker is trying to involve the listeners in the communication process by having them answer questions or by making brief predictable statements in response to a question. By participating, the audience shows personal interest. If your listeners are interested, the chance of them being affected is greater. Active involvement increases the opportunity for persuasive impact over a period of time. You, as speaker, can increase the likelihood of persuasive outcome if you give the audience opportunities to participate in the communication event. That participation could involve raising their hands, repeating a statement made by the speaker, or coming forward to demonstrate acceptance of the message.

Repeating a message increases the length of its influence. The participation concept we just examined also applies directly to message repetition. Active participation increases the impact and prolongs the effect of a message while repetition of the key parts of a message helps us to "internalize" the message.

Message Repetition

Even as far back as World War II, we knew that recruits who presented messages (with which they did not necessarily agree) that asked others to reenlist were also more likely to reenlist themselves! The reenlistment effect was the result of repeating the message to others.

Advertisers today frequently apply this repetition principle. If they are trying to sell a soft drink, they attempt to get the prospective buyer to repeat the slogan or message as often as possible. When you hear "It's the real thing," or "Pepsi, the drink of a new generation" often enough, you begin to repeat the message to yourself. The connection between recalling the message and believing that the product *may* be the one you should purchase becomes stronger as a result of your repeating the message.

Modern business applies this principle daily to our lives in persuading us to buy products and services. You can apply it, too. As a persuader, you can increase the influence of your message by having the audience repeat the message, or restate the major part of the message several times in slightly different language. Combining these techniques increases your chances of achieving your goal.

If you are trying to convince students that grades are important to their success when they enter the work force, you may wish to merge that principle with income. You could say, for example, "Grades do make a difference in determining which companies will be interested in hiring you." Later you might refer to that comment by saying, "You'll remember that I mentioned grades are important when entering the work force. Grades are the academic way of measuring success. You'll also be graded when you are an employee, but the grade you receive will be indicated by your income and the raises you receive." Finally, you might repeat the argument a third time saying, "Making good grades now or at least working toward improving the grades you already have will help prepare you for that cumulative evaluation that occurs when you pursue full-time employment."

In this example, grades, employment, and money are tied together. The same general argument has been presented three times but each time using slightly different language. The speaker has used message repetition to increase audience retention and probable acceptance of the message.

Summary

Persuasive speaking involves careful analysis of audience attitudes and the use of that information in the construction of a message designed to alter the listener's attitudes and/or beliefs. Your use of a combination of logical and emotional appeals coupled with a knowledge of basic human needs is a second key element in charting progress in persuasion. Speaker credibility, an understanding of the techniques of persuasion, and your knowledge of the long-term effects of persuasion identify the major elements that predict your probable success as a persuader of people. Effective persuaders are concerned with demonstrating to audiences that they are well informed on the topic. These speakers also are conscious of the need to be seen as someone presenting information acceptable to their listeners while not appearing to manipulate the attitudes of their audience.

Key Terms

Propositions for
persuasion
Logic
Emotion
Hierarchy of needs

Speaker credibility
Fallacies
Long-term effects

1. When you listen to a public speech, how do you determine the credibility of the speaker? In the most recent speech you heard, how important was speaker credibility to your acceptance of the message?
2. Which of the levels of appeal in persuasive messages tends to be most effective in situations where you deal with your peers? Why? Is that level also the most effective for other speakers whom you know?
3. In designing a speech for the president of the United States, what major strategies do you believe the speech writers incorporate into the speech when they hope to affect the attitudes and/or the beliefs of the voting public? Provide an example for discussion.

Discussion Questions

Notes

1 *See* Edward L. Fink, Stan A. Kaplowitz, and Connie L. Bauer, "Positional Discrepancy, Psychological Discrepancy, and Attitude Change: Experimental Tests of Some Mathematical Models," *Communication Monographs* 50 (December 1983): 413–30.

2 *See* H. I. Abelson and M. Karlins, *Persuasion: How Opinions and Attitudes are Changed,* 2d rev. ed. (New York: Springer Publishing Co., 1970).

3 Adapted from Philip G. Zimbardo, Ebbe B. Ebbesen, and Christina Maslach, *Influencing Attitudes and Changing Behavior,* 2d ed. (Reading, Mass.: Addison-Wesley Publishing Co., 1977), 223–30.

4 James C. McCroskey and Thomas J. Young, "Ethos and Credibility: The Construct and Its Measurement after Three Decades," *Central States Speech Journal* 32 (Spring 1981): 24–34.

5 Phillip R. Biddle, "An Experimental Study of Ethos and Appeal for Overt Behavior in Persuasion," Unpublished doctoral dissertation, University of Illinois, 1966.

6 *See*, for example, Charles U. Larson, *Persuasion: Reception and Responsibility,* 4th ed. (Belmont, Calif.: Wadsworth Publishing Co., 1986); Wayne N. Thompson, *The Process of Persuasion,* (New York: Harper and Row, 1975); Wallace C. Fotheringham, *Perspectives on Persuasion,* (Boston: Allyn and Bacon, 1966).

7 Abraham H. Maslow, *Motivation and Personality* (New York: Harper and Row, 1954).

8 James L. Adams, *Conceptual Blockbusting* (San Francisco: San Francisco Book Co., 1976), 121.

9 McCroskey and Young, "Ethos and Credibility."

10 For a full discussion, *see* Zimbardo, Ebbesen, and Maslach, *Influencing Attitudes and Changing Behavior,* 98.

11 Ibid., 68.

**Suggested
Readings**

Cronkhite, Gary. *Persuasion: Speech and Behavioral Change.* Indianapolis: Bobbs-
    Merrill Publishing Company, 1978.
    Considered an introductory work in the field of persuasion by many, this
    book contains a host of useful scholarly references and a thorough
    background on persuasive theories and techniques. An excellent source book
    for speakers interested in the comparative effectiveness of various persuasive
    approaches.
Engel, S. Morris. *With Good Reason: An Introduction to Informal Fallacies,* 3d ed.
    New York: St. Martin's Press, 1986.
    A lively book in the field of reasoning replete with contemporary
    illustrations. For anyone interested in the application of reasoning and
    fallacies to contemporary situations, this book provides informative and
    entertaining reading.
Larson, Charles U. *Persuasion: Reception and Responsibility,* 4th ed. Belmont, Calif.:
    Wadsworth Publishing Co., 1986.
    This is a sweeping but thorough analysis of the roots and techniques of
    persuasion. It is especially strong in its analysis of the persuasive campaign
    and movement. Definite reading for student speakers who seek a strong
    contemporary understanding of persuasion theory applied to society.
Maslow, Abraham H. *Motivation and Personality.* New York: Harper and Row,
    1954.
    This is a well-written and highly regarded classic work in the field of
    motivation. Persons interested in the origins of motivation will place this on
    their *must* reading list. The basic discussion of gross human needs presented
    is used widely today as an explanation for human behavior and motivation.
Zimbardo, Philip G.; Ebbesen, Ebbe B.; and Maslach, Christina. *Influencing
    Attitudes and Changing Behavior.* Reading, Mass.: Addison-Wesley Publishing
    Company, 1977.
    This is one of the most popular books written in the area of attitude and
    belief construction and modification. It introduces the theory and
    applications of social control to the persuasive context in a highly readable
    but scholarly way. Highly recommended for students of persuasion and
    attitude change.

14 *Speeches for Special Occasions*

Outline

Objectives

After reading this chapter you should be able to:

1. Explain what is meant by a speech of special occasion.
2. Cite the primary characteristics of a speech of introduction.
3. Identify the major differences among the various types of speeches of praise.
4. Understand the particular role played by each of the speeches for special occasions.

PREVIEW

Speeches of special occasion bear characteristics that make them unique from other forms of public discourse. The audience expects a specific kind of speaker behavior and the situation demands that certain rituals be followed. Although most of us rarely are called upon to deliver one of these speeches, special occasion speeches significantly affect our self-concept and the perception others have of us.

Speeches of special occasion play a unique role in the ritual life of American society, business, and politics. Learning how to incorporate the special features of each of these types of speeches will enable you to become a more effective speaker as well as a more critical evaluator of those types of messages.

Most of your public speaking will be of the informative or persuasive variety, but on occasion you may find yourself preparing to speak in a ceremonial setting. For example, you might be asked to introduce Tim Arthur, whom you have known since high school, or you might be asked to present an award to Betty Simpson, who has worked with you for the last four years. In both cases, the ideas we have suggested for informative and persuasive speaking may seem somewhat inappropriate. You are not the center of attention; the audience is waiting to see and hear the person you are introducing or honoring. These special occasion speeches call for a different approach.

In this chapter we will explore the most common types of special occasion speeches and outline the major requirements for each. We will provide models that will meet the basic requirements of each type.

Special occasion speaking is a challenging role because the expectations for your success are perhaps greater than for a formal speech. Your time is usually more limited and so are the suggested procedures for preparing and presenting these speeches.

Speeches of Introduction

You may someday find yourself in a role where you are asked to introduce another speaker to an audience. That speaker might be a friend or it might be a political figure who has come to campus as part of "Arts and Science Week." Suppose you have been selected to introduce a speaker at the banquet. What do you do?

A speech of introduction should not distract the attention of the audience away from the featured speaker. Its purpose is much like an introduction to a speech. It should help get the attention of the audience members and prepare them for what is to follow. You would be wise to limit yourself to only two minutes or so when introducing a speaker. To accomplish your goal, you should secure some basic biographical information about the speaker.

1. What are the speaker's qualifications?
2. What credentials does the speaker have in the field of his or her speech?
3. What do the speaker and audience have in common?

This basic biographical and audience-centered information will help you secure the information that will make your effort successful. Table 14.1 presents the criteria for a speech of introduction. You will find criteria applicable to each type of special occasion speech presented in this chapter. Refer to the tables as a handy checklist to determine if you have completed the basic requirements.

TABLE 14.1 Criteria for a speech of introduction

1. Brief (about 2 minutes).

2. Qualifications of speaker.

3. Speaker credentials in the topic field.

4. Reasons for audience to listen.

5. Thorough knowledge of the speaker.

If you are not personally acquainted with the speaker, it will probably be wise for you to arrange an interview with him to get the vital information and a more complete picture of the *total* person. You can also interview a close friend or relative of the speaker. Just as you would research a topic before you gave an informative speech, this information gathering phase will provide you with the facts and background ideas that will help insure an effective introduction. Use table 14.2 to check if you collected the kind of information that will help make your introduction a success.

Here is a sample introduction of a speech given by Sam Traxer at a Rotary meeting. Look carefully at the use of information provided by Sam.

> It's an honor for me to introduce the mayor of Whoopup to you. His consistent knowledge of the problems of rural people in this state has made him an outspoken advocate of increased government aid to the farmer. In fact, last year he led a delegation to Washington. He personally presented the petition many of you signed for more liberal farm loan conditions to the Secretary of Agriculture.
>
> As a farmer himself, the mayor understands the needs of rural people. If ever there was a dynamic representative of farmers and their concerns, he's it. Join me in welcoming Ben Edelblute, a successful farmer and a hard and dedicated worker whose primary concern is the future of the American way of life. It's my pleasure to introduce a man some have called "Mr. Rural America." He's here tonight to talk to us about promises of the future for agriculture in America.

TABLE 14.2   Interviewing checklist

1. How well do you know this person?

2. How long and in what way have you been acquainted?

3. What do you think is this person's most outstanding characteristic?

4. Why do you think this person has been so successful?

5. How is this person different from the "average" person?

6. What four words do you think best describe this person?

7. How do this person's contemporaries regard him or her?

Notice that this introduction shows the results of some "homework." The credentials of the speaker are outlined and the introduction stresses the commonality of aspiration and accomplishment of speaker and audience. Obviously, the listening audience is a rural group and the speaker is someone who intends to speak to their needs and concerns.

You can be more personal as you tell about the speaker's strengths if you are personally acquainted with the speaker. Here is an example of that kind of situation in an introduction given by Paul Simpson.

> I have the opportunity today to introduce our speaker who has been a close friend nearly all my life. We graduated together from Hillcrest High School. If I were to tell you the year of our graduation, I'd be revealing both her age and mine. That would be an embarrassment to me since we've both had the same time since high school but her career has been on a very fast track.
>
> She attended the University of Illinois and majored in accounting. After four years, she graduated *summa cum laude* and accepted a position with Arthur Andersen as an accountant. After three successful years, she joined the General Accounting Office of the United States Government as an auditor. She moved up rapidly and, last year, was promoted to the rank of senior auditor in charge of cost analysis. One of her major areas of responsibility, she tells me, is in the examination of defense equipment maintenance costs.
>
> Clearly, Maria is unusually well qualified to provide all of us with an insider's perception of why the cost of national defense is the largest single item in the national budget. It's a pleasure for me to present my good friend, former classmate, and senior auditor from the General Accounting Office, Maria Close, who's going to explain why maintenance is the hidden enemy in defense costs.

Both of these introductions meet the criteria we outlined earlier. Refer to the checklist in table 14.1 to see if you have included all the appropriate materials. If you focus on chapter 4, "Audience Analysis," you will see that the major features of speeches of introduction include those audience oriented matters we stressed in that chapter.

Several types of speeches fit into the category of speeches of praise. Broadly speaking, the major features of these speeches are:

Speeches of Praise

1. Identification of the reasons for recognition.
2. Recognition of the outstanding features of the person or persons being recognized.
3. Description of some valued accomplishment.

In all such speeches of praise, it is a good idea to include statements stressing the unique features of the people or the occasion, and reasons why the audience should join the speaker in paying tribute. These criteria apply not only to the speeches of tribute but also to eulogies, which we discuss later in this chapter.

Tribute

It is common to give a speech of tribute when, for example, you recognize a coworker for a major promotion or you honor a community leader for exceeding a fund raising goal. In these or similar instances where you are praising personal accomplishments, you should remember the key elements shown in table 14.3.

To highlight the elements shown in table 14.3, you must do your homework. Basic biographical information on the person you are recognizing is first. If you are familiar with the individual's record of personal and professional accomplishments, it is possible you will be able to work with the information you already know. What is the nature of their accomplishment? Did they overcome some significant obstacles? Were there personal barriers that made their goal very difficult? Did competition make their achievement especially notable? In short, *what makes them worthy of recognition?* Details may be very important here. A collection of small achievements may result in a major goal being realized. Show how those "small steps" led to the achievement!

TABLE 14.3 Criteria for speeches of tribute

1. Reason for recognition.

2. Standards for success.

3. How a person or an organization meets those standards.

4. Additional reasons for recognition.

Fred Wortham used several of these techniques in recognizing Calvin Peete as a leading money winner in the Professional Golfer's Association standings.

> I'd like to tell you the story of a man who overcame adversity and became one of the leading professional golfers in America today. First, he was black. How many successful black golfers are there on the professional tour? You can count them on the fingers of one hand. Their environment doesn't provide blacks with access to country clubs and opportunities to spend money on golf lessons and days of practice on the course.
>
> But this man perfected his game on the public golf courses in spite of the handicap of his color. Oh, yes, he was a good golfer, but there are lots of them around. He could break par on his local course regularly, but he'd never make it in "the big time." Why?
>
> You see, Calvin Peete was too old. He was twenty-five years old and hoped to be a successful professional golfer. If you're not established in professional golf before twenty-five you don't have much of a chance. Besides, Calvin had a handicap. His left arm was crippled and he couldn't straighten it completely. Those of you who play golf know how important it is to have strong, straight arms to be a successful golfer.
>
> But Calvin always liked to battle the odds. He felt that his color, his age, and his physical handicap were reasons why he must succeed. With the complete cooperation and support of his wife, he earned his "card" and qualified to play on the Professional Golfer's circuit. Was he a success? If you'll just look at the PGA record for the last four years, you'll see that he's among the top five money winners, the golfer who drives the ball in the fairway from the tee most frequently, greens in regulation most frequently, and among the top five in the lowest number average strokes per 18-hole round of golf? Is he a success? Ask all those "rabbits" who chase the golf tour as it follows the sun. Ask those golfers who learned to play at expensive golf courses, took daily lessons, played college golf, and joined the tour in their early twenties.
>
> Look at Calvin Peete if you want to see a person who defied all the odds, overcame physical and racial handicaps to become one of the leading golfers on the circuit. Ask Calvin what it takes. He'll tell you, very quietly and humbly, that you just can't quit.

Clearly, here is a person who meets the standards for recognition (tribute). The speaker followed the formula to incorporate those features in his talk. Fred did not have the opportunity to talk with any of Calvin Peete's friends or with his spouse. He succeeded in paying tribute to him by collecting biographical information through extensive reading in sporting and golf magazines, and the information he presented was as objective as possible.

The key to a successful speech of tribute is a clear understanding of what makes a person worthy of recognition. Often this means that you must search for details to appreciate the obstacles that the person overcame, the effort expended, the risks taken, and the like.

Measure that brief excerpt against the criteria for a speech of tribute found in table 14.3. You will see that the basic biographical information is incorporated. Did Calvin Peete overcome barriers in accomplishing his goals? That is the central message of this speech of tribute. The barriers are specifically and clearly identified. They set up a context that focuses attention on accomplishments. Fred selected some of Calvin Peete's major accomplishments for recognition against that context.

A special type of speech of praise that we often hear is the eulogy. Its most common appearance is at a ceremony following a death. The expectations for an effective eulogy are quite similar to the general speech of tribute discussed earlier, but there are several criteria that you should observe, as shown in table 14.4, if you are the speaker at a funeral or a memorial service.

Eulogy

TABLE 14.4 Criteria for eulogy

1. Identify your knowledge of the person.

2. Recognize the "humanness" of the person.

3. Identify ways the person was concerned with others.

4. Restate the common character and concern of the person.

You should be familiar with the person who is the subject of the eulogy. If you do not know the person or if you are not familiar with the person's accomplishments or character, do not agree to speak. There is nothing more awkward than making empty generalizations. Be ready and able to point to those significant, human characteristics of the subject. Discuss what made the person unusual or outstanding. Was it because she was a good, decent, hard working mother? Was it because he was always willing to help others solve their problems in spite of his own difficulties? No assumption is necessary that the person was a world leader. Plain, simple people and their basic "goodness" are the basis for this society. Audiences expect a eulogy to focus on this human side of the person because it is the very fragile nature of life that is being recognized.

Speaking at the funeral of his own brother Robert, Ted Kennedy touched upon those very human characteristics in an eloquent way. He asked that people not glorify his brother beyond those simple virtues he thought were important. He then outlined how Robert Kennedy gave voice to and practiced those virtues in his life. It was a moving speech, brief, and one that serves as a powerful model of a eulogy.

1   In behalf of Mrs. Kennedy, her children, the parents and sisters of
2   Robert Kennedy, I want to express what we feel to those who mourn
3   with us today in this cathedral and around the world.
4   We loved him as a brother and as a father and as a son. From his
5   parents and from his older brother and sisters, Joe and Kathleen and
6   Jack, he received an inspiration which he passed on to all of us.
7   He gave us strength in time of trouble, wisdom in time of uncer-
8   tainty, and sharing in time of happiness. He will always be by our
9   side.
10   Love is not an easy feeling to put into words. Nor is loyalty or trust
11   or joy. But he was all of these. He loved life completely and he lived
12   it intensely.
13   A few years back Robert Kennedy wrote some words about his own
14   father which expresses the way we in his family felt about him. He
15   said of what his father meant to him and I quote:
16   "What it really all adds up to is love. Not love as it is described
17   with such facility in popular magazines, but the kind of love that is
18   affection and respect, order and encouragement and support.
19   Our awareness of this was an incalculable source of strength. And
20   because real love is something unselfish and involves sacrifice and
21   giving, we could not help but profit from it . . ."
22   Beneath it all he has tried to engender a social conscience. There
23   were wrongs which needed attention, there were people who were
24   poor and needed help, and we have a responsibility to them and this
25   country.

26   "Through no virtues and accomplishments of our own, we have
27 been fortunate enough to be born in the United States under the most
28 comfortable condition. We therefore have a responsibility to others
29 who are less well off. . . ."
30   A speech he made for the young people of South Africa on their
31 day of affirmation in 1966 sums it up the best. . . .
32   "The answer is to rely on youth, not a time of life but a state of
33 mind, a temper of the will, a quality of imagination, a predominance
34 of courage over timidity, of the appetite for adventure over the love
35 of ease. The cruelties and obstacles of this swiftly changing planet
36 will not yield to the obsolete dogmas and outworn slogans; they
37 cannot be moved by those who cling to a present that is already dying,
38 who prefer the illusion of security to the excitement and danger that
39 come with even the most peaceful progress. . . .
40   Each time a man stands for an ideal, or acts to improve the lot of
41 others, or strikes out against injustice, he sends forth a tiny ripple of
42 hope. . . .
43   And I believe that in this generation those with the courage to enter
44 the moral conflict will find themselves with companions in every
45 corner of the globe. . . ."
46   My brother need not be idealized or enlarged in death beyond what
47 he was in life. He should be remembered simply as a good and decent
48 man who saw wrong and tried to right it, saw suffering and tried to
49 heal it, saw war and tried to stop it.
50   Those of us who loved him and who take him to his rest today pray
51 that what he was to us and what he wished for others will some day
52 come to pass for all the world.
53   As he said many times in many parts of this nation to those he
54 touched and who sought to touch him:
55   "Some men see things as they are and say why. I dream things that
56 never were and say, why not."*

Considering the circumstances under which this speech was given, it is
easy to understand why many consider it to be extraordinarily moving, in
addition to serving as a very effective model of a eulogy. The speaker was
paying tribute to his own brother at his brother's funeral, attempting to
translate the goals, achievements, and words of Robert Kennedy into a
statement of thanks for the opportunity to have lived with him and been
exposed to his philosophy. The speech offers us an opportunity to observe
how ideas are generated, organized, and crafted into a message that incorporates the words of the object of the tribute, while still paying honor
in an objective fashion.

*This speech is reprinted by permission from *Vital Speeches of the Day,* July 1, 1968,
pp. 546–47.

Note how effectively Edward Kennedy uses family reference in the first two paragraphs as a means of "bonding" the subject to the grief of the family. Then, he utilizes direct quotation (lines 26–45) to highlight the philosophical sensitivity of Robert Kennedy and his concern for his fellow man. Note the call of Edward Kennedy (lines 46–49) for listeners to avoid making his brother larger in death than he was in life. He beckons his listeners to follow the call of Robert Kennedy to "dream things that never were" (lines 55–56). Edward Kennedy wisely follows the admonition to avoid overstating the merits of the person or activity to which tribute is being paid. The speech is an interesting model and one from which a variety of passages could be chosen to illustrate the mix of criteria for a eulogy.

Commencement Speech

Most of us think we know what a commencement speech should be like, but most of all we believe it should be relatively brief. Perhaps the most common failing of commencement presentations is that they are long-winded. While the audience wants to hear brief, glowing statements about their children, relatives, or friends, their primary concern is with the ritual. They want to see the presentation of the diplomas. Whatever precedes that presentation should be brief, complimentary, and perhaps slightly challenging. Table 14.5 lists the main points you should include in a commencement speech.

TABLE 14.5   Criteria for a commencement speech

1. Comment on the nature of the occasion.

2. Tribute to the contributions and the sacrifices of the graduates and the audience.

3. Provide challenge or define role of graduates and methods for success.

This commencement speech by University President Tim Laird illustrates the application of those guides.

> I want to be the first to applaud these graduates for their efforts and the sacrifices they made to be here today. I know the hours they've spent "cracking the books" when the sounds of spring called them outside to toss a frisbee or join their friends at the movies. I know how tempting it is to "put off" the reading or writing assignment that is due until that last minute because the personal calendar is full of events that are much more attractive—events like a stop at Taco Bell or a "cruise" down fraternity or sorority row.
>
> But I also want to recognize the parents today without whose sacrifices none of you would be here. It was your folks who placed your needs for education ahead of their own desire for some of the better things of life. They had to dig deeply to pay the tuition bills

and skip the dinners out they thought they would be able to afford once you had gotten beyond high school. They suffered along with you about your goals for your life and your job opportunities after graduation. They have wanted for you the chances they never had. They're the model parents. Yes, they may have a fault or two, but they want for you a life just a bit better than they have had. And isn't that what you will want for your children? So this is an occasion for recognizing both the accomplishments of the graduates as well as the sacrifices of the parents.

Today, I want to challenge each of you graduates to be a success. And becoming a success is not easy. But I think I may be able to give you three suggestions about how you can be a success, regardless of what kind of job you choose to take.

First, learn your field. Whether you are an electrical engineer or an electrician, *you must know your field*. And ideas are your best friends and resource. (Here Tim *briefly* discussed learning.)

Second, work hard. There's no substitute for applying your efforts to your job. No one wants to hire or keep a lazy employee. All jobs become boring in one way or another at some time, but you'll need to work your way through those times with the same energy and effort you show in the interesting and exciting moments. (Tim *briefly* discussed work and working. He then proceeded to outline how hard work and knowledge of the job are the keys to success.)

Finally, you need to believe in yourself and your talent. I call it self-confidence. You must believe you can perform. You must approach each task with a positive attitude. Your actions, attitudes, and accomplishments are significant if you trust yourself. You can succeed at your chores if you believe in yourself!

The road to success is difficult at best. Everyone here today has made enormous sacrifices to provide you graduates with the opportunity to succeed. But your degrees today are no guarantees of success. Society expects much from you. You are the *intelligentia* of the modern generation. You are the experts in your field.

Your employers expect you to know your subject, remain abreast of new developments and work hard with all the information available. They'll provide you with the place to work, the opportunities for success, but you must make your own contribution. And don't forget that you must believe in yourself whether things are going your way or against you. Persevere!

I challenge you to be all that you and those who know you realize is possible. Can you meet that challenge? (Tim concluded with a restatement of his earlier formula for success.)

If you were to apply the criteria in table 14.5 to this speech, it would be easy to see that Tim systematically met each standard. He acknowledged the sacrifices and paid tribute to the parents and students. He recognized the movement of the students into the work force (the "rite of passage"), and the body of his speech consisted of a series of guides for success in their working careers.

Best of all, Tim's speech was brief. He spoke for only fourteen minutes, but everyone in the audience was "captured" with the clarity of his ideas. After the speech, relatives and friends of the graduates gathered outside the auditorium and several said, "That was one of the best commencement speeches I ever heard. It was short and his ideas were really clear and good. I wish there were more speakers like him around!"

On ceremonial occasions like this one, audiences want simplicity, clarity, and brevity. Too many commencement speakers forget those planning guidelines. If you will plan carefully, you will include those essential elements and have the basis for a successful commencement address.

Keynote Speech

Whether at a recognition dinner for outstanding employees or for the "kickoff" of a new sales campaign, the keynote is one of those special occasion speeches we commonly hear. Its purpose is to set a tone or "mood" for the meeting and the people attending. It may be inspirational, challenging, or it may serve to outline the nature of the problem and what is going to be done to deal with it at this gathering. The keynote "unlocks" or opens up the nature of the meeting. Nearly every business, educational, or service meeting uses a keynote speech to get things started.

Keynote speeches, like introductions, should be brief and clearly stated. One difference is important. *Keynotes are a major focus of the meeting.* Although listeners know much more is to follow, the keynote speaker does not play "second fiddle" to the rest of the program or to the next speaker. In fact, this speech may be the most important feature of the meeting. We know from studying conventions and conferences that it is essential to get off to a good start. The keynote speech aims to do precisely that. It establishes the mood for the entire session. To be successful in this role, you need to develop your speech in a way that is consistent with the criteria in table 14.6.

Note how several of these features are present in a portion of Pat Trapit's keynote speech at the annual meeting of salesmen for Shelter Paper.

> As I look around this room this morning, I see dozens of success stories seated around me. I see people who have learned how important Shelter and its products are to daily living. But their learning didn't stop there. You decided it was important that all those paper users needed to understand that we stand for quality and service more than any other company in our business.
>
> That's not an easy job, but who ever said that Shelter Paper looked for the easy market and the easy sales? We've been leaders because we've taken on the opposition head-to-head for years and always come out the winner. Your attitude, your work, and your success are the reasons we continue to be the leader in paper product sales for the thirty-fifth consecutive year.

We're not here as a mutual admiration society. You and I are at this annual sales meeting to find out why we've been successful, why we lost some of those sales we really should have made, and to be updated on the latest products and techniques in our business.

But this is important. We need to remember that we are winners. What company in this business can claim to have larger sales, better paid salesmen and managers, or a more efficient home office staff? Your answer to that question is the same as mine: None! And no one will even come close if we continue to think and act like the winners we at Shelter have become over the years. Yes, it's the power of positive thinking. We're the best and no one is going to take that position from us.

We work harder, and have a better product. But most of all, *we have the best people in the industry working for us.* When you have the best people and the best product, you're going to be a winner.

That's what we have here today. Winners sitting next to winners. Our margin of victory is greater today than ever before and that is because each of you has thought, acted, and sold positively.

As you study that keynote speech and compare it to the criteria in table 14.6, you will see that Pat integrated each of the criteria into his message. Obviously his speech was designed to "stroke" the successful salesforce in addition to outlining what would be occurring at the annual meeting. How would you grade his efforts? Note the conciseness of his speech compared to the keynote speeches we often hear televised at national political conventions. Pat's speech is an interesting example of the speech of tribute applied in an everyday business environment.

TABLE 14.6   Criteria for a keynote speech

1. Determine the purpose of the meeting.

2. Use that theme as the crucial part of your speech.

3. Show how important that theme is to the listeners.

4. Make the speech personal and geared to the common concerns of the listeners.

Summary

Speeches for special occasions have much in common with both informative and persuasive discourse. All are audience-centered and your success in these settings is largely determined by the carefulness of your preparation. Speeches of introduction, keynote speeches, and speeches of tribute, including commencements and eulogies, require you to develop a set of standards of behavior or accomplishment. Your speech consists, then, of using those standards as you identify the ways the person meets or exceeds those criteria.

TABLE 14.7 Summary criteria for speeches for special occasions

Speech of introduction
1. Brief (about 2 minutes)
2. Qualifications of speaker
3. Credentials in the topic field
4. Reasons for audience to listen
5. Thorough knowledge of the speaker

Speech of tribute
1. Reason for recognition
2. Standards for success
3. How a person or an organization meets those standards
4. Additional reasons for recognition

Commencement speech
1. Comment on nature of the occasion
2. Tribute to the contributions and the sacrifices of the graduates and the audience
3. Provide challenge or define role of graduates and methods for success

Eulogy
1. Identify your knowledge of the person
2. Recognize the "humanness" of the person
3. Identify ways the person was concerned with others
4. Restate the common character and concern of the person

Keynote
1. Determine the purpose of the meeting
2. Use that theme in the speech
3. Show importance of theme to listeners
4. Make the speech personal and geared to the common concerns of the listener

The speech of introduction is characterized by brevity while meeting the other standards we discussed. More than anything else, you should remember that if you are taking the role of "introducer," *the audience is there primarily to listen to the other person, not you.*

Special occasions require unusual speaker sensitivity in many ways. A eulogy is presented at a time of great stress for most of those in the audience, so great care must be taken to maintain the proper atmosphere. Consider Edward Kennedy's speech as an example. As a speaker, be careful in your selection of language and in the specific kinds of illustrations you use to show the character of the person.

Ritual situations like commencements require you, as speaker, to fulfill the situational expectations. Remember that the audience wants to be acknowledged for their accomplishments and sacrifices. They also want to hear a promise of good fortune for graduates, but only if it follows standard virtues of hard work and clean living.

Speeches for special occasions require different approaches from other types of public presentations we have discussed in this book. They share the need for effective and thorough preparation, knowledge of the audience, speaker understanding of the person or the occasion, and the other primary matters of good speaking we have discussed at length.

Introductory speech	*Commencement*	**Key Terms**
Tribute	*Keynote*	
Eulogy		

Discussion Questions

1. What special occasion speech have you heard most recently? In what category would you place it? Using the criteria we have provided, how well did it meet those standards?
2. Prepare a list of speeches of special occasion that you have heard. What was the predominant strength and weakness of each, and of the speeches in general? Were they stronger or weaker than other types of speeches you have heard?
3. Do you believe that prominent public figures tend to be more effective speakers in this type of public speaking? What basic strengths and weaknesses do they bring to the situation? Compare their characteristics to those of a college student in each of the categories of speeches of special occasion. Be prepared to defend your selection in class.

Selected Readings

Linkugel, Wil A.; Allen, R. R.; and Johannsen, Richard L. *Contemporary American Speeches*, 5th ed. Dubuque, Ia.: Kendall-Hunt Publishing Co., 1982.
This is a superior source for speeches of special occasion. Each speech type is explained, the criteria are included, and the major features of the speeches are outlined. This is perhaps the strongest contemporary work in this field of special occasion speaking and one of the most popular.

Vital Speeches of the Day. Southold, N.Y.: City News Publishing Co.
This is the premiere publication of contemporary speeches in American society. Published twice a month and found in virtually every college library, it is the outstanding source of contemporary public speaking, containing speeches in all areas of current national and international concern. These speeches often fit into the category of speeches of special occasion as discussed earlier. Any serious college student should be familiar with this source of current public dialogue.

15 *Speaking in Groups*

Outline

Objectives

After you have completed this chapter you should be able to:

1. Identify and explain the characteristic features of decision-making groups.
2. Explain why people need groups.
3. Describe the ethical responsibilities when participating in group decision making.
4. Compare and contrast task leadership and social leadership, and describe the role behaviors in each category.
5. Monitor group tension levels and determine the roles needed by the group on the basis of that monitoring.
6. Describe the four most common public formats for presenting a decision-making group's thinking, and if appropriate, contribute the kind of leadership necessary to present each of these formats.

PREVIEW

Because decision-making groups are prevalent in our society, you will certainly have many opportunities to participate in them. Your interactive skills can be very important to the group's success as well as to your own personal success. Group decision making is essentially a cooperative endeavor. As such, you accept certain ethical standards when you become a member of a decision-making group. Each person in a group can and should provide leadership and avoid self-centered behavior. You can learn what behaviors a group needs by monitoring its tension levels.

Ultimately, a group will have to present its findings. We describe the most common formats for public discussion. What they primarily have in common is that they are audience centered. Thus, the skills of public speaking described throughout the rest of this book are directly applicable to your participation in the group decision-making process.

It is often said that the business of business happens in groups. Certainly the lifeblood of many organizations—their decision-making processes—is heavily centered in groups. It is sensible, then, for us to include a chapter in this textbook about communicating in groups. When you leave college and enter the world of work and civic involvement, you will be surrounded by decision-making groups of all types. You will certainly want to become an effective participant. The purpose of this chapter is to describe the most important kinds of communication behavior required by decision-making groups. You will learn what you can do to become a more skillful group member.

Decision-making Groups

There are many different kinds of groups. Your family represents one type of social group. Your public speaking classroom experience might include an informal discussion group. Our focus in this chapter is on a special kind of small group called a decision-making group. The terms *group, small group,* and *decision-making group* are nearly synonymous. They refer to any collection of three or more individuals who share some problem or some common goal. Their interactions and behaviors mutually influence the members of the group.[1] They communicate with each other face to face. They are aware of each other's roles. The critical elements in this definition include (1) group size, (2) mutual influence, and (3) goal orientation.

Size

Two individuals (a dyad) cannot be a group because they cannot create the unique environment necessary for group processes. They cannot join together to exert pressure on a third person. At the other end, a group that grows to about eleven individuals has reached the outside limit of manageability for a decision-making group. Beyond this number, controversial issues tend to cause the formation of subgroups, often with opposing goals. This chapter is about groups of people ranging in size from three to eleven members. Almost all of the decision-making groups you will ever work with will fall in this range. Most of those groups will be about six members strong.

Mutual Influence

Our definition of a decision-making group makes clear that the interactions of individual members have an impact on the group. The members listen to and talk with each other. They attempt to change each other's thinking and feelings. They are, in short, mutually dependent upon each other.

Goal Orientation

A decision-making group shares some problem or some common goal. They feel some common need. They get together to help each other. If three to eleven individuals in a room do not experience a need to work together, they do not constitute a group as we define the term. You can put people into the same room, but you cannot turn them into a decision-making group unless the members have a common purpose. Individuals who do not need to work together have no need to listen to each other or to consider each other's ideas.

Need for Small Groups

Every organization is an organization of groups! Groups are everywhere. You will find them at work, at home, in church, in school, in service organizations, and in many recreational contexts. Group activity occurs because individuals want to share common interests.

People need groups for at least two reasons. First, groups collectively provide more resources than individuals. For example, a group can usually gather more information and process that information more completely than an individual can—approaching it from a variety of viewpoints and probing the substance of each member's thoughts more completely. Some tasks are more easily accomplished by a group than by an individual. For example, a group of scouts may volunteer to pick up litter along a certain stretch of roadway. That kind of job is called an "additive task." Groups perform additive tasks better than individuals do.

Second, decision-making groups generally tend to be better able than individuals to control error. It stands to reason that group members can double-check their work more readily and more accurately than individuals can.

The quality of thought generated by a group will typically be superior to the quality of thought of an individual, since the group members can usually bring to light far greater reserves of information. Of course, there will be times when the best-trained individual can make better decisions than a group—even a group that includes an expert! For instance, you would undoubtedly prefer a single expert to perform open-heart surgery. However, tasks that are additive or decisions that result in policy are generally better performed by a group.

Participating in Groups

The advantages of group decision making cannot accrue if individual members do not make certain commitments to the group. Every member of every group assumes four responsibilities just by joining the group. Every time you agree to engage in decision making with other people, you agree to give up some of your individual sovereignty so that the group process can work. You assume an obligation to live by certain ethical standards.

Do Your Best

You have something to offer a group. You have knowledge. You are sensitive and analytical. You think. You feel. You believe. You cannot change your strengths and weaknesses, but you do not need to. You are okay just the way you are and you can contribute to a group. Give your group the best that you have. Do not hold back.

Sometimes individual group members do hold back. For example, people sometimes decline to take a leadership role because they think someone else might want to do it or because they resent perceived manipulation by others. Anything worth doing is worth doing as well as you can. If you agree to involve yourself in a decision-making group, commit yourself—all of yourself—to helping that group make the best decisions that are available. If you give less than that, you violate a standard of excellence that is widely valued in our society.

Behave Rationally

Keep an open mind, listen to evidence and arguments, and withhold personal decisions until the evidence and the arguments are presented. Behaving rationally means putting your personal interests second to the best interests of the group.

We have known individuals who were not able to put aside their personal convictions long enough to listen to another group member's positions or ideas. They bring to the decision-making group their own private truths and their private agendas. For example, one of us once served on a committee appointed by the mayor to make recommendations about how the mayor's office could improve two-way communication between the mayor and the local community. A member of that group had an ax to grind. He tried to get the group to advocate support for improvement of the city-owned art museum. His idea, apparently, was that the museum provided the best "outreach" opportunity for the mayor. He did not want to talk about or listen to anything else.

Do not allow yourself to behave in this manner. Your responsibilities to the group require that you listen carefully with an open mind, that you consider all the information, and that you work to evolve the most sensible decisions that the group is capable of producing.

Rational behavior may sometimes require very great personal courage. It may mean setting aside personal animosity. It may mean agreeing to work constructively and positively with someone you do not like. It may require you to face and deal with rejection of your own ideas. Even so, rational behavior is absolutely necessary. If the members of the group do not achieve it, the group cannot be productive. You take on an ethical responsibility to rational behavior every time you agree to work in a decision-making group.

Play Fair

Group decision making is a cooperative activity. It is not a competitive event at which you champion your viewpoint. This means that every group member has the responsibility to seek and present all the ideas and evidence they can, whether or not the information seems contradictory. Every member of the group has a right to expect you to play fair, just as you have a right to expect every other member to play fair. Do not engage in debate in a group decision-making meeting. As a matter of ethical responsibility, you are constrained from competing with the other group members.

Listen Carefully and Participate Fully

When you have prepared carefully and have something important to say, you want other people to listen to you. You have a right to expect them to take you seriously, to listen carefully, to ask questions, to give you feedback, and to evaluate your ideas with an open mind. If they did less than that they would be mistreating you!

You have the same ethical obligations to other group members. You have a responsibility to listen carefully and to participate fully with them, and they have a right to expect it. Listen to what they are saying and to what they are *not* saying. Ask them questions, keep an open mind, and express your feelings and thoughts about their ideas. To do less than this mistreats your colleagues. It also has the potential of damaging the group's productivity.

In summary, we have said that participating in a group means that you have an obligation to do your best, to behave rationally, to play fairly, and to listen carefully and participate fully. These things are a matter of choice; it is up to you to set high standards for yourself and act accordingly. In a larger sense, these obligations are a matter of ethical responsibility.

Leadership in Decision Making

Decision-making groups cannot function without effective leadership. Decision-making groups need leadership in identifying and understanding problems and solutions. When the members of a group engage in talk about controversial issues, they often get off the track. Sometimes the group members do not know what to do next, so they require the guidance of one of the members. When an individual member places personal goals before the goals of the group, leadership is needed. The kind of leadership we are referring to is called *task dimension leadership.*

Group communication also has a relationship dimension. A group must be cohesive if it is going to be productive. The members must feel like a unit; they must want to pull together to accomplish their common goal. Maintaining that sense of groupness is a relationship problem that calls for leadership.

We want to make one important point clear: leadership is not the exclusive right of an appointed authority. Moreover, it is not something that can be conferred upon an individual. Leadership exists in an individual's ability to assess a communication situation and to provide the ideas and information that the group needs. Because this is so, we believe that *every member of every decision-making group can and should contribute leadership.*

You can make a contribution in leadership even if you are not designated as the chairperson. Indeed, your personal and professional success, your upward mobility in your organization, and your credibility in the eyes of your colleagues will all be enhanced if you learn to provide the leadership that a group needs.

Gerald L. Wilson and Michael S. Hanna described the characteristics of an effective group leader.[2] Effective group leaders are well informed and are able to adapt their leadership styles to meet the needs of the group; they are flexible. They usually adopt a "democratic" style—one that takes into account the interests and expertise of other group members and that values group processes over individual processes. They monitor and guide the group's activities with careful planning. Effective leaders provide direction and structure to the group's activities through skillful communication, and they are sensitive to the social tensions of a group.

Effective group leaders seem to know when to focus attention on task concerns, when to focus attention on relationship issues, and when to focus attention on procedures.

Characteristics of Effective Leaders

How is it that effective group leaders seem able to contribute just the right kind of leadership when it is needed? How do effective leaders operate? How might you behave during a meeting to increase your leadership contribution? These questions, in one form or another, have been asked by students for many generations. Some of the best answers appear in an essay developed by Kenneth D. Benne and Paul Sheats.[3] These scholars studied the role behaviors that were characteristic of successful decision-making groups and divided their findings into three categories. The categories include matters of (1) task and goal achievement, (2) group maintenance and identity, and (3) personal concern for individual members. Following is a discussion of these three categories of role behaviors. Study them; they tell you how to behave when you are in a group meeting. Remember, however, that these behaviors do not occur by chance; you choose whether or not to perform them.

Understanding Group Leadership

Since a role is a collection of behaviors, Benne and Sheats listed those behaviors that help groups achieve their goals. Take a look at table 15.1. Notice that *not one* of the group task roles listed requires that you be designated as a group leader. Every one of the behaviors can be contributed by any willing member, and all of the behaviors are necessary to the functioning of an effective decision-making group.[4]

Task Leadership

TABLE 15.1   Group task roles

ROLES	TYPICAL BEHAVIORS	EXAMPLES
1. Initiator-contributor	Contributes ideas and suggestions; proposes solutions and decisions; proposes new ideas or states old ones in a novel fashion.	"How about taking a different approach to this chore? Suppose we . . ."
2. Information seeker	Asks for clarification of comments in terms of their factual adequacy; asks for information or facts relevant to the problem; suggests information is needed before making decisions.	"Wait a minute. What does that mean?" "Does anyone have any data to support this idea?"
3. Information giver	Offers facts or generalizations that may relate to personal experiences and that are pertinent to the group task.	"I asked Doctor Jones, a specialist in this kind of thing. He said . . ." "An essay in *The New Yorker* reported . . ."
4. Opinion seeker	Asks for clarification of opinions stated by other members of the group and asks how people in the group feel.	"Does anyone else have an idea on this?" "Can someone clear up what that means?"
5. Opinion giver	States beliefs or opinions having to do with suggestions made; indicates what the group's attitude should be.	"I think we ought to go with the second plan. It fits the conditions we face in the Concord plant best . . ."
6. Elaborator-clarifier	Elaborates ideas and other contributions; offers rationales for suggestions; tries to deduce how an idea or suggestion would work if adopted by the group	"Do you mean he actually said he was guilty? I thought it was merely implied."

From Wilson, Gerald L., and Michael S. Hanna, Groups in Context: Leadership and Participation in Small Groups. *Copyright © 1986 Random House, Inc. Reprinted by permission.*

ROLES	TYPICAL BEHAVIORS	EXAMPLES
7. Coordinator	Clarifies the relationships among information, opinions, and ideas, or suggests an integration of the information, opinions, and ideas of subgroups.	"John's opinion squares pretty well with the research Mary reported. Why don't we take that idea and see if . . ."
8. Diagnostician	Indicates what the problems are.	"But you're missing the main thing, I think. The problem is that we can't afford . . ."
9. Orienter-summarizer	Summarizes what has taken place; points out departures from agreed-upon goals; tries to bring the group back to the central issues; raises questions about where the group is heading.	"Let's take stock of where we are. Helen and John take the position that we should act now. Bill says 'wait.' Rusty isn't sure. Can we set that aside for a moment and come back to it after we . . ."
10. Energizer	Prods the group to action.	"Come on, guys. We've been wasting time. Let's get down to business."
11. Procedure developer	Handles routine tasks such as seating arrangements, obtaining equipment, and handing out pertinent papers.	"I'll volunteer to see that the forms are printed and distributed." "Look, I can see to it that the tape recorder is there and working. And I'll also run by the church for the chairs."
12. Secretary	Keeps notes on the group's progress.	"I keep great notes. I'll be glad to do that for the group."
13. Evaluator-critic	Critically analyzes the group's accomplishments according to some set of standards; checks to see that consensus has been reached.	"Look, we said we only had four hundred dollars to spend. What you're proposing will cost at least six hundred dollars. That's a 50 percent override." "Can we all agree, at least, that we must solve the attrition problem—that that is our first priority?"

TABLE 15.2 Group building and maintenance roles

ROLES	TYPICAL BEHAVIORS	EXAMPLES
1. Supporter-encourager	Praises, agrees with, and accepts the contributions of others; offers warmth, solidarity, and recognition.	"I really like that idea, John." "Priscilla's suggestion is attractive to me. Could we discuss it further?"
2. Harmonizer	Reconciles disagreements, mediates differences, reduces tensions by giving group members a chance to explore their differences.	"I don't think you two are as far apart as you think." "Henry, are you saying . . . ?" "Benson, you seem to be saying . . . Is that what you mean?"
3. Tension reliever	Jokes or in some other way reduces the formality of the situation; relaxes the group members.	"That reminds me—excuse me if this seems unrelated—that reminds me of the one about . . ."
4. Compromiser	Offers to compromise when own ideas are involved in a conflict; uses self-discipline to admit errors so as to maintain group cohesion.	"Looks like our solution is halfway between you and me, John. Can we look at the middle ground?"
5. Gatekeeper	Keeps communication channels open; encourages and facilitates interaction from those members who are usually silent.	"Susan hasn't said anything about this yet. Susan, I know you've been studying the problem. What do you think about . . . ?"
6. Feeling expresser	Makes explicit the feelings, moods, and relationships in the group; shares own feelings with others.	"Don't we all need a break now? I'm frustrated and confused and maybe we all are. I'd like to put this out of mind for a while."
7. Standard setter	Expresses standards for the group to achieve; may apply standards in evaluating the group process.	"In my view, this decision doesn't measure up to our best. We really haven't even set any criteria much less tried to apply them."
8. Follower	Goes along with the movement of the group passively, accepting the ideas of others and sometimes serving as an audience.	"I agree. Yes, I see what you mean. If that's what the group wants to do, I'll go along."

Decision-making groups also require behaviors that build the cohesiveness of the group and strengthen and maintain the relationships among the members. These behaviors, listed by Benne and Sheats, appear in table 15.2.

Again, notice that not one of these behaviors requires that you be an appointed leader. You can and should contribute to the relationship dimension of group communication. Every decision-making group needs these contributions, and every group values the people who contribute them. Thus the group context provides you an opportunity to make important contributions to others and, at the same time, to show that you are a competent person and a valuable asset.

Benne and Sheats identified and listed a third category of behaviors: self-centered roles that diminish the performer's effectiveness and damaged the group's productivity. We list them in table 15.3 because we want you to know that they are fairly common. You can avoid them as a matter of choice.

We know that certain role behaviors are essential to every successful decision-making group, and we have said that you can and should contribute them. Still, we know that some people seem to be natural leaders while others seem to have difficulty asserting themselves. What makes the difference? People who succeed in providing the needed leadership in groups monitor the tension levels of the group during meetings. They determine on the basis of their observations what the group needs and what they should do.

You can sense the tension levels in a group meeting. Sometimes, especially during moments of conflict, the tension levels are almost tangible. At other times, especially during social moments, the tension levels are so low that they are not even noticed. Successful leaders have learned to become sensitive to the constantly shifting levels of group tension. They use their observations as a way of knowing what the group needs.

Figure 15.1 illustrates how this works.[5] The dimension at the left-hand side of the diagram is labeled "tension." Group tension ranges from "0" upward. The plus mark (+) indicates ever increasing levels of tension. The bottom dimension of the figure is labeled "time." The line of dashes in the figure represents the group's "threshold of tolerance" for tension. If the tension stays below that threshold, the members of any group are comfortable enough to work on their tasks. If the tension rises above that level, by definition, the tension is too great. It is above the group's tolerance threshold. The group has no choice when tension is that high; they must deal with the tension.

Social Leadership

Counterproductive Behavior

Providing Leadership

Working with Group Tension Levels

TABLE 15.3 Self-centered roles

ROLES	TYPICAL BEHAVIORS	EXAMPLES
1. Blocker	Interferes with progress by rejecting ideas or taking the negative stand on any and all issues; refuses to cooperate.	"Wait a minute! That's not right! That idea is absurd. If you take that position, I simply can't continue to work with you."
2. Aggressor	Struggles for status by deflating the status of others; boasts; criticizes.	"Wow, that's really swell! You turkeys have botched things again. Your constant bickering is responsible for this mess. Let me tell you how you ought to do it."
3. Deserter	Withdraws in some way; remains indifferent, aloof, sometimes formal; daydreams; wanders from the subject; engages in irrelevant side conversations.	To himself: "Ho-hum. There's nothing in this discussion for me." To group: "I guess I really don't care what you choose in this case. But on another matter . . ."
4. Dominator	Interrupts and embarks on long monologues; authoritative; tries to monopolize the group's time.	"Bill, you're just off base. What we should do is this. First . . ."
5. Recognition Seeker	Attempts to gain attention in an exaggerated manner; usually boasts about past accomplishments; relates irrelevant personal experiences, usually in an attempt to gain sympathy.	"That was a good thing I just did." "Yesterday I was able to . . ." "If you ask me, I think . . ." "Don't you think I'm right [Don't you think I'm wonderful]?"
6. Confessor	Engages in irrelevant personal catharsis; uses the group to work out own mistakes and feelings.	"I know it's not on the topic exactly, but I'm having a personal problem just like this. Yesterday, Mary and I had a fight about . . ."
7. Playboy	Displays a lack of involvement in the group through inappropriate humor, horseplay, or cynicism.	"Did you hear the one about the cow that swallowed the bottle of ink and mooed indigo?" To the only female in the group: "Hello, sweet baby, let's you and me boogie."
8. Special-Interest Pleader	Acts as the representative for another group; engages in irrelevant behavior.	"My friend Alan runs a company that makes a similar product. How about using his company? We might as well spend our money with people we know."

From Wilson, Gerald L., and Michael S. Hanna, Groups in Context: Leadership and Participation in Small Groups. *Copyright © 1986 Random House, Inc. Reprinted by permission.*

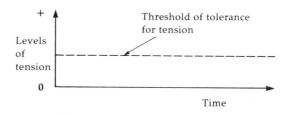

FIGURE 15.1 A Chart of Group Tension. Effective group leaders monitor a group's tension level to draw out the full resources of the group.

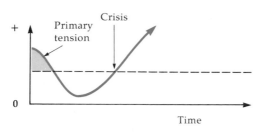

FIGURE 15.2 High Tension Levels. High tension levels need to be reduced by discussing the source of the tension. This often requires both candor and tact.

To illustrate how this works, let us imagine three different groups. One group will illustrate very high levels of tension; a second group will illustrate very low levels of tension, and a third group will illustrate optimum levels of tension. These illustrations are just that—illustrations. You will rarely, if ever, find a real group with clearly identified tension levels. Learning to monitor the tension takes patience. Don't be discouraged if it takes you a while. The payoff is well worth the price. Learning to become sensitive to tension levels in a decision-making group and learning what to do about them can help you make a dramatic impact on the success of your group, and on your own personal success as well.

Consider the case illustrated in figure 15.2. The tension levels are much too high. Follow the tension across the time dimension, beginning at the left-hand margin. The shaded area is called "primary tension." Primary tension is a common experience of groups. Every group experiences primary tension. It takes a while for a group to get down to business. Members seem to need to chat with each other—to joke, to talk about last night's baseball game, or to gossip about some local celebrity. They do this because they are experiencing primary tension. Primary tension is that feeling that you get when you enter a room for the party, only to discover that the person who invited you is the only person you know there.

In this case, the group eliminates primary tension easily, and goes along for a while working on the task. Then, at point C, the tension rises above the group's threshold of tolerance. They reach a crisis. The tension levels are continuing to rise. If the group doesn't do something soon, one of two things will happen:

1. The group may expel the member who is creating the tension, or
2. The group may disband.

FIGURE 15.3 Low Tension Levels. Low tension levels need to be raised if a group is to be productive. An effective leader will turn the discussion toward the group's procedures to reorient the group toward its tasks.

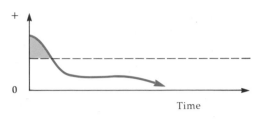

FIGURE 15.4 Optimal Tension Levels. Effective crisis management facilitates maximum group productivity. Members must be confident that their opinions will be heard and evaluated fairly.

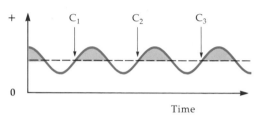

In any case, when a group is experiencing this much tension, it cannot be productive. The group must do something. Here is your opportunity for leadership. *When the tension levels are too high, perhaps because the group is in conflict, talk about the source of tension.* Is it disagreement over some goal? Is it disagreement over some procedure? Is it social conflict of some kind? Learning to talk about the tension wisely is a big step toward dealing with it.

Consider a second theoretical group. In figure 15.3 the tension levels of the group are too low. The tension levels have been taking a steady drop since the group first came together. Under these circumstances, the group cannot be productive. Leadership is needed, either because the group is enjoying themselves so much that they have lost sight of the task (a group can be too cohesive) or because the group is apathetic because its members are disinterested in the group activity or are not committed to the good of the group. In either case, this is another opportunity for you to provide leadership. The group needs to get moving on the task. *When tension levels are too low, talk about procedure.*

A third possibility exists. In figure 15.4 the group has eliminated primary tension without difficulty. You can see that they proceeded for a while before confronting a crisis, but they handled it well. Tension rose above the group's threshold of tolerance three separate times, and each time the group managed to work through the crises.

A group must experience this kind of crisis and crisis management in order to be productive. It needs to gain confidence in its ability to withstand the pressures of conflict and disagreement. Its members must know that they can say what they want to say without being fearful that the group will disband! Besides, there is a logical reason that tension is necessary for a productive decision-making group.

Any time a group is making progress, it is also making changes. All progress implies change, and change always introduces some level of tension. Repeated tension levels above the group's tolerance threshold are inevitable in a productive group. Part of what makes a group productive is that they learn how to manage the tension. This ideal situation, too, provides you an opportunity to contribute your leadership skills to a decision-making group. *When the tension levels are following a cyclical pattern, such as the one shown in figure 15.4, talk about the topic.*

In summary, what we have said is that you can learn to monitor the tensions that a group experiences. Based on your observations, you can identify what kinds of leadership the group needs. When the tension levels are too high, the group needs to talk about the source of the tension. When the tension levels are too low, the group needs to establish a procedure that will get it back on track. When a group is experiencing cyclical tension and release of the tension, the group has its best chance of success. When a group is working well, stay with the agenda.

When John Dewey published his ideas, in 1910, about how people think, he did not imagine that his ideas would have such a lasting impact on the theory and research of group discussion.[6] Nevertheless, his reflective thinking pattern almost presents a ready-made agenda that any group can follow. Over the years, speech and group discussion instructors have used and adapted the pattern of reflective thinking that Dewey described. One of the most useful variations on Dewey's thinking pattern was developed by Brilhart and Jochem.[7] To help you work with the pattern we have presented, we are including a full discussion outline based on the Brilhart/Jochem agenda.[8]

Working with an Agenda for Decision Making

I. What is the nature of the problem we face? (present state, obstacles, goals?)
   A. What are we talking about?
      1. Is the question or assignment clear?
      2. Do we need to define any terms or concepts?
   B. How much freedom do we have?
      1. Are we to plan and take action, or what?
      2. What sort of end product are we supposed to produce?
   C. What has been happening that is unsatisfactory?
      1. What is wrong? What is the harm? How do we know?
      2. Who is affected? How? Under what conditions?
      3. How serious is the situation?
      4. Have any corrective actions been taken? How did they work?
      5. What additional information do we need in order to understand fully the nature and extent of the problem?
   D. In general terms, what is the desired situation or goal we hope to achieve?

E. What factors seem to have caused this problem?
  1. Are we certain about any causes?
  2. What obstacles must we remove to achieve our desired goal?
F. How can we state the problem so that it includes the present situation, the desired situation, the difference, the causes, and the obstacles?
  1. Do we all agree on this statement of the problem?
  2. Should we divide our statement into "subproblems?"
    a. If so, what are they?
    b. In what order should we approach them?
II. What might be done to solve the problem (or first subproblem?) (Here the group brainstorms for possible solutions.)
III. What specific criteria should we use to evaluate our possible solutions?
  A. What absolute criteria must be met?
  B. What relative standards shall we apply? (List and rank these values and standards by group agreement.)
IV. What are the relative merits of our possible solutions?
  A. What ideas can we screen out because they are unsupported by facts?
  B. What ideas must we take out because our group members do not all support them?
  C. Can we combine and simplify our list of possible solutions?
  D. How well do the remaining ideas measure up to the criteria?
V. How will we put our decision into effect?
  A. Who will do what, and when?
  B. How will we check to be sure that we follow through on our agreements?*

Of course, when the group is actually working, members rarely will be able to follow such an agenda in precisely this order. Often, a member will jump ahead—a process called *reach testing*.[9] Others will follow. Someone may object on procedural grounds. Still another member may complain that an idea does not meet certain criteria. In short, a productive decision-making group resembles a cavalry charge in an old-time western movie. The horses are all going in the same general direction with the same purpose, but they are not following along in military precision.

Once its primary task is completed, a group is often asked to present its findings. At this point advocacy becomes important, calling into play your public speaking skills.

Presenting the Group's Findings

Surprisingly, the work of a decision-making group rarely ends with making a decision! Instead, the group usually ends up by presenting their findings to someone else—perhaps a management group or a single executive or a large gathering of people assembled to consider the group's ideas. In almost every case, a decision-making group will have to take on some form of advocacy in order to get its proposals adopted. Sometimes this report will be written, and at other times it will be presented orally. Sometimes the report takes both written and oral forms. Always, however, the goal is to present the group's work clearly and persuasively.

Figure 15.5 describes the relationship between decision-making discussion on one hand and advocacy on the other. Notice how this chapter relates to the earlier chapters on public speaking.

Identify the problem ⎫

Understand the problem

Establish evaluative criteria
for judging proposals

Seek alternatives to test

Develop a proposal

Prepare for advocacy ⎭

Discussion

Analyze the audience ⎫

Design the group report

Develop an action plan

Make the presentation

Implement the proposal ⎭

Advocacy

FIGURE 15.5 The work of a group is not finished until the group's conclusions are presented to a wider audience. Advocacy often becomes an important final phase of the group's work.

Written and Oral Reports

Written and oral reports of a group's findings are essentially similar. Each begins with a brief overview. Each presents the group's analysis of the problem. Each describes the criteria your group applied to possible solutions. Each offers a solution, then ends with a summary and an appeal for support of the proposal.

If the group has appointed a leader, that individual usually represents the report. If not, the group usually selects the individual member who is perceived to have the best communication skills. That person may very well be you. If you are selected, you should approach the oral report in the same fashion that you would prepare for any other speech. Your job will be clearly identified for you by the group. You will either inform and educate or persuade, or possibly both.

State the purpose of the report early and preview its main points. Review your group's analysis of the problem and the criteria you used to test the proposed solution. Describe the solution you are recommending. Support your ideas with the evidence and arguments that your group discussed. You may want to use visual materials as you make your presentation.

Be careful to adapt to your listeners and to the context. You surely will want to use language that is articulate. Finish with a summary and ask the listeners to adopt the group's recommendations.

At the end of the presentation, you may be asked some questions. Respond to those questions thoughtfully and honestly. Try not to deviate from the group's decisions during this period. Remember, you are not advocating your own personal point of view; the group's thinking is at issue.

It sometimes occurs that you and your group will be asked to present your ideas in a public discussion format. The remainder of this chapter focuses on the most common formats in which public discussion occurs.

Formats for Presenting a Group's Thinking

Public discussions differ from decision-making discussions in a fundamental way. A public discussion is held for the benefit of the listeners, and is not usually a forum in which group decision making occurs. Even when decision making does go on in a public meeting, the presence of the audience implies that the group will pay attention to the needs of the listeners. If you are asked to participate in a public discussion or to plan and present such a discussion, you will have to choose a basic format. The most common formats are the forum, or whole-house debate, the panel, the symposium, and the colloquium. Figure 15.6 illustrates these formats and shows you why and how to use them.

A forum is a public discussion that involves full audience participation. The most common example is the New England town meeting. People gather to propose and debate civic issues, and to make decisions about them. In its pure form, this kind of meeting includes impromptu or extemporaneous speeches from representative citizens. The people debate each other, ask questions, and make comments. Finally, a vote is taken on the issues, and decisions that affect the entire body are thus established.

Forum, or Whole-House Debate

More often, a forum will center on and be coupled with some other communication activity. A speech, a film, or a panel discussion may be used as stimulus material to "get the audience going." A chairman, or moderator, keeps the discussion moving in an orderly fashion.

The leader of such a forum has a difficult job. The task is to stimulate the group further, to assure that everyone who wants to speak has an opportunity to do so, to encourage as many people to speak as possible by making sure each individual presentation is brief. That is a difficult job when someone's emotions are aroused! The moderator's role is also to encourage, to recognize, and to clarify the various viewpoints so that the audience can make an informed and wise decision.

FORMAT CALLED	ARRANGEMENT SUGGESTED	REASON FOR USING	METHOD
Round table		To promote equality of feelings; maximize participation of all members; ensure as much spontaneity as possible.	Group discussion of problems and solutions for the purpose of making a good decision or sharing information.
Symposium		To present a variety of views in the form of short speeches or reports for the benefit of the audience.	Moderator introduces the panel; provides history of the issues at hand; presents each speaker in turn; monitors time; thanks the participants; ends the meeting with a brief charge to the audience or a summary of the issue.
Panel discussion		To conduct a semistructured discussion of issues on a topic for the benefit of an audience.	Moderator introduces the panel and problem and keeps the discussion flowing; restates often; controls (somewhat) equal and fair time allocation. Members are responsible for developing points of view and have some control of agenda.

FIGURE 15.6 Because public discussions are held for the benefit of listeners, careful consideration must be given to listeners' concerns and the role we hope they will play. (From Hanna, Michael S., and Gerald L. Wilson, *Communicating in Business and Professional Settings.* Copyright © 1984 Random House, Inc. Reprinted by permission.

If you are the leader of such a meeting, you might want to suggest some guidelines. Ask the members to be recognized before they speak. Establish and hold to a time limit for each speaker, and establish a method for assuring that the time limits are known and applied fairly. If a person has already spoken and others wish to talk, ask the person who has already made a speech to abstain while the others have a chance. Try to secure floor microphones and ask people to use them so that everyone in the audience can hear all the speeches. Keep the audience informed about the overall

FORMAT CALLED	ARRANGEMENT SUGGESTED	REASON FOR USING	METHOD
Forum		To encourage audience participation on issues surrounding a topic.	Moderator introduces the program and speaker, who presents a brief statement and interacts with the audience. Moderator participates to encourage audience involvement. A variety of discussion formats can be used.
Calloquy		To inform an audience through the use of planned questions designed to get unprepared responses from participants for the benefit of the audience.	Moderator introduces the speaker and panel of questioners, then regulates rotation and time. Sometimes summarizing, sometimes clarifying, moderator does not participate as a panelist.
Whole-house decision making		To debate issues as a body, then decide, using appropriate voting methods.	Moderator regulates the discussion and debate, attempting to get maximum input from both sides in order that members of the house may cast informed votes. Parliamentary procedure is commonly used to govern the event and facilitate orderly progress.

time frame of the meeting and the time remaining. Call for a different viewpoint if several of the speakers have said essentially the same thing. Finally, try to summarize the main ideas and positions presented on the various sides of the issues. If appropriate, clarify for the members what their actions will mean when interpreting their vote. For example, "If you move to this side of the house when I call for the vote, you will be voting to increase property tax support to the schools by one mil. If you move to this side of the house, you will be voting to keep the property taxes where they are now. Are we ready for a division of the house?"

Panel

A panel discussion is carried out for the benefit of the audience, too, but not with the audience. Panel members are usually experts, or reasonably well-informed people who share their points of view about a common question. The procedure is, typically, for a moderator to ask a question or questions and for the panel members to interact with each other in response to the question.

The moderator's job during a panel discussion is a demanding one. It includes developing the discussion question outline and distributing it to the participants, along with the ground rules that will operate. It is the moderator's job to pose questions, to maintain order, to summarize agreements and disagreements, and to keep the panel on track. The moderator, of course, also introduces the topic to be discussed and the members of the panel. In the end, the moderator summarizes the discussion, thanking the speakers and asking for questions from the audience. This also implies that the moderator will maintain progress and order during any question-answer period.

Symposium

A symposium is not a discussion. It is a series of speeches related to a central topic. Its purpose is to provide stimulus material or to inform. Sometimes a panel discussion follows the speeches of a symposium. Sometimes the symposium is followed by audience questions and panel answers or by audience participation in a forum. If you are ever the moderator of a symposium, you might want to review our coverage of the forum and panel discussions.

Colloquium

A colloquium is a format for public discussion that involves a panel of experts who are asked questions by an audience. The audience knows the general topic for discussion, and the members usually have prepared questions. Sometimes the format includes a primary question and a follow-up question. The experts respond to questions; they do not typically ask them. This format is useful for giving information, but it does not really allow the colloquium participants to interact with each other.

Each of these forms of public discussion can be used by groups to present their findings. Often they occur in combination. They are common enough that you may well have opportunities to participate in them. In every case, public discussions are presented for the benefit of listeners. It follows that if you want to be successful in this context, you will try to understand and adapt to these listeners.

Summary

Decision-making groups are everywhere. As a result, you will almost certainly have opportunities to participate in them. Your skill in doing so can make a significant contribution to your group's success and to your own, as well. Participation in groups means giving your best effort, behaving rationally, playing fair, and participating fully. These things are essential to a group. They imply that you must learn to be flexible and democratic, that you value group processes over individual enterprise, and that you plan carefully.

We listed the behaviors that are most common in successful decision-making groups, and we showed you how to work with the tension levels of a group. When those levels are too high, talk about the source of the tension. When they are too low, talk about procedures. When they are just right, stay with an agenda that will contribute to effective decision making.

A group will usually have to report its findings, either in oral form or in writing, or in both. We described what goes into a report and the formats for presenting a group's thinking: (1) forum, or whole-house debate, (2) panel, (3) symposium, and (4) colloquium. These public formats are different from decision-making groups because they are audience centered rather than problem centered.

Key Terms

Group	*Roles*	*Panel*
Decision making	*Tension*	*Symposium*
Leadership	*Forum, whole-house*	*Colloquium*
Participation	*debate*	

Discussion Questions

1. Make a list of the decisions you made this week on your own. Make another list of decisions you participated in making as part of a group. Compare your lists with those of one or more classmates. Do you find similarities and differences? What characteristic features separate the individual decisions from the group decisions?

2. Reexamine the group behaviors listed by Benne and Sheats. Mark each behavior: *A,* if you often perform the behavior; and *B,* if you seldom perform the behavior. What insights can you draw about your group participation skills from this exercise? You may wish to share your thinking with a group of classmates. If you do, try to answer this question as a group: How can an individual group member help others to perform needed roles more effectively?

3. Go to a public discussion event with a few classmates. After the event, discuss these questions:
   a. What kind of event was it? Did it follow a format described in this chapter?
   b. How would you evaluate the skill of the moderator? Why? What recommendations, if any, would you like to have made to the moderator before the meeting?
   c. What is your opinion of the oral communication skills of the participants? Why? What insights do your answers to these questions give you about your own choices of behavior?

Notes

1 Gerald L. Wilson and Michael S. Hanna, *Groups in Context: Leadership and Participation in Small Groups* (New York: Random House, 1986), 5. This chapter is based on that book.

2 *Ibid.*, 165–67.

3 Kenneth Benne and Paul Sheats, "Functional Roles of Group Members," *Journal of Social Issues* 4 (1948): 41–49.

4 These tables appear in this form in chapter 6, "Role and Role Emergence" in Wilson and Hanna, *Groups in Context.*

5 This idea was first presented by Ernest G. Bormann. *See* his *Discussion and Group Methods: Theory and Practice,* 2d ed. (New York: Harper & Row, 1975), 181–82.

6 John Dewey. *How We Think* (Boston: D. C. Heath, 1910).

7 John K. Brilhart and Lurene M. Jochem, "Effects of Different Patterns on Outcomes of Problem-Solving Discussion," *Journal of Applied Psychology* 48 (1964): 175–79.

8 John K. Brilhart, *Effective Group Discussion, 5th ed.* (Dubuque, Ia.: Wm. C. Brown Publishers, 1986), 308–10.

9 Thomas M. Scheidel and Laura Crowell, "Idea Development in Small Group Discussion," *Quarterly Journal of Speech* 50 (1964): 140–45.

Suggested Readings

Brilhart, John K. *Effective Group Discussion, 5th ed.* Dubuque, Ia.: Wm. C. Brown Publishers, 1986.
  This well-organized and easy-to-read book has been well received since it first appeared in 1967.
Harnack, R. Victor, and Fest, Thorrel B. *Group Discussion: Theory and Technique.* New York: Appleton-Century-Crofts, 1964.
  This classic work may be the best early blending of rhetorical theory and communication theory in the literature. Although it is more than twenty years out of date, its advice is practical and its research is solid.
Wilson, Gerald L., Hanna, Michael S. *Groups in Context: Leadership and Participation in Small Groups.* New York: Random House, Inc., 1986.
  You will not be surprised to learn that we think this is one of the best textbooks about group communication processes. We recommend it to anyone who wants a practical text that is well grounded in research.

SAMPLE SPEECHES •

The nine sample speeches here represent various levels of both polish and speaker experience. Students completing a first course in public speaking contributed the first three speeches. We have transcribed these speeches virtually word for word to convey an impression of how they actually sounded. While this approach has left some raw edges, be assured that these three speeches went into the gradebook as an A. The students who delivered these speeches obviously had worked hard in the course and were able to construct speeches that reflected their effort. You too can produce a speech of this calibre with some effort.

The next two speeches, " 'Buy' the People" and "Exercise," are the work of advanced students. The speeches were carefully crafted, fully written out, and then memorized. They were among the best speeches in a national competition where the primary emphasis was not on extemporaneous delivery. Nonetheless, these two speeches are superior models for the study of organization, argument, and support.

Frank Rhodes and Larry Gerlach, the authors of the next two speeches, represent yet another level of experience. They are successful professional people for whom competence in public speaking is an indispensible asset. Make no mistake, their personal success is partially due to their ability to speak in public.

Finally, Pat Schroeder and Mario Cuomo talk about matters that are very important to them personally. You can sense the strength of their convictions through their ability to organize and articulate their thoughts. (We have not provided marginal notes for the Cuomo speech in the hope that you will analyze it for yourself.) These two speeches illustrate in the clearest possible way the connection between public speaking and personal success; neither of these politicians would have risen beyond obscurity without sophisticated public speaking skills.

We hope that you learn from these speeches and that you also enjoy them. The topics here reflect our opinion that personal conviction and willingness to be provocative are attributes that make a speech attractive. You will find both of these attributes in this selection of speeches. In addition, you will note that each speech reflects the speaker's concern for the welfare or betterment of society. In a sense, all of these are public issues. Each of us is a member of society, so these topics relate to each of us. Learn and enjoy, and note the connections between public speaking and personal success.

See You in Court*

James W. Gibson, Jr.—Student, DePauw University

I'm here today to talk to you about the insurance crisis and, in particular, product liability and doctor malpractice insurance, and what needs to be done to resolve this crisis.

First of all, I would like to cite some cases that have come to my attention in doing some research on this topic. These two examples are taken from the CBS television program "60 Minutes." The first case that I discovered concerned a woman who sued a tool manufacturer because she injured her thumb while using a hammer. She claimed that the tool manufacturer should have placed a warning label on the handle of the hammer telling her to keep her other hand out of the way while using the tool. She won the case.

◄ Inductive approach in which sources of information are cited.

The second case that came to my attention concerned a woman who was in a hospital and fell asleep while smoking a cigarette in her hospital bed, set the bed on fire, and burned herself. She sued the hospital, claiming that the hospital should have put a sign, in view of the bed, warning her of the dangers of smoking in bed. She won the case.

Newsweek reported on a man who had a history of heart disease and who was overweight. He was attempting to pull start a Sears lawnmower and suffered a heart attack. He sued Sears, claiming that it was too hard to pull start the lawnmower: that was why he suffered the heart attack. He won the case and was awarded $1.4 million.

A final case that's of interest and concerns this topic also comes from *Newsweek*. It relates to two hot air balloon enthusiasts who apparently got caught in a rainstorm and had a wet balloon on their hands. They took the balloon fabric to a laundromat and placed the balloon in a commercial dryer, attempting to dry it. In the process, after it had heated up, the dryer blew up and injured them. They sued the dryer company, claiming the dryer company should have put some kind of label on the outside of the dryer, warning them. They received an award of approximately $1.1 million.

*Reprinted by permission of the author. James W. Gibson, Jr., receives full credit for this speech. His father was not involved in any way in developing it.

Now, exactly what is this insurance crisis and what kind of ramifications does it have? According to *The New York Times* on March 2, 1986, the current legal system has led to large awards, not because of producers' negligence, but because the producers can afford to pay.

Statistics are used ▶
effectively, but the years
compared are not the
same.

Some statistics that illustrate the magnitude of the problem today are reported in the January 27, 1986, issue of *U.S. News and World Report.* They show that in 1974, there were 1,579 product liability cases. Eleven years later, there were 9,221 cases of the same type filed in federal court. In 1970, there were only 7 million-dollar verdicts rendered. In 1984, however, there were 401 "million-dollar-plus" product-liability verdicts rendered.

The same source states that 20 percent of the cost of a common stepladder goes to pay for insurance. The problem has gotten so bad for doctors that obstetricians in New York have seen increases in their malpractice insurance rise to 16 percent of their gross income, on the average. For doctors, malpractice premiums exceed $2 billion in total.

An assertion is made ▶
without illustration or an
attempt at proof.

One of the reasons this problem has reached these proportions in business and industry during the last several years is that the courts on the state and federal level have greatly expanded the extent of producers' liability. Litigants no longer have to prove negligence on the part of the producer of a product. In many cases plaintiffs now win damages by linking products to health problems when there is no proof that the particular product caused harm. American manufacturers of products remain liable for their products as long as they are in use.

An effective transition ▶
from problem to solutions
in a problem-solution
sequence.

I've spent much time detailing a problem in business and in society today. Now, you ask, what is the solution? There is no easy solution. But obviously we need to find some answers before the problem gets out of hand.

The business sector and the doctors have reacted in quite a few different ways. Business, in response to increases in their insurance premiums of up to 1000 percent in a single year, have drastically reduced the amount of their coverage. In some industries the risk factor for liability has increased so much that some companies pay more in premiums than the nominal value of their insurance coverage. Other companies have just opted to discontinue the manufacture of some of their risky products.

Another option companies have resorted to is to introduce lawyers at every step of the production and planning process for new products. They also have involved lawyers to help them determine possible problems in older products. This can be extremely expensive. Doctors have started to screen their patients through a computer system, checking to see if the patient is a good risk, and whether they have a history of bringing malpractice suits against previous doctors.

Personalization of costs. ▶

This is costly to you and me. According to *Newsweek,* taxpayers in 1983 incurred $64 million in expenses. Sixty-four million dollars of our money went to pay for the paperwork necessary to handle the large volume of product liability and malpractice suits brought in state and federal courts.

According to Martin Conner, a Washington, D.C., attorney for General Electric, companies don't pay the price of product liability cases; consumers do. And the same thing could be said for malpractice insurance.

Many companies have resorted to self-insuring. Instead of taking out an insurance policy with an established company, they set up their own fund. They set aside a certain amount monthly, quarterly, or semiannually for insurance, or they anticipate that insurance expenses won't be large and they pay the cost out of operating expenses.

We also need to consider the no fault approach. It is similar to the one currently being used by sports equipment companies. This type of system, described in the March 3, 1986, issue of *Fortune*, would allow a settlement paying for all the medical and rehabilitation expenses needed as the result of an injury incurred while using a product, whether it be a hammer, a lawnmower, or a commercial dryer. It would also compensate the victim for the estimated future lifetime earnings lost. All this would be done in exchange for an agreement not to sue. In other words, this type of system compensates the victim for actual incurred expenses, but it does away with punitive damages.

◄ Examples of several potential solutions.

On the doctors' side of the problem, the most practical solution is to limit the amount of dollar award a litigant can receive. Without getting into the debate over the value of a human life, we need to consider this as a realistic option to be explored.

I'd like to give you an example to illustrate the complexity of this whole problem. A Chicago physician who is a friend of a personal acquaintance of mine recently attended a banquet. During the meal a man fell from his chair onto the floor and people began to scream for help. The doctor rushed over to see what was wrong. The man had stopped breathing and he had no pulse. The doctor immediately applied CPR to the man and revived him. An ambulance, which was called, took the man to a hospital, and he lived. After the man was discharged, he sued the doctor because in the process of administering CPR two of his ribs were broken. The physician recently said that in the future, if a similar situation developed, he would not respond to the cries for help. He would let the person die instead of rescuing him because of the potential for a lawsuit.

◄ An interesting and applicable example.

Ask yourself. Would you like to be the person in need of emergency medical help when this physician is the only one available? How do you know that won't be the case?

◄ A rhetorical question with solution choice left to listener.

This example illustrates the extent of the insurance crisis today. What we need now is a practical and equitable system that will quickly and effectively solve our problem.

I've tried to outline the magnitude of the liability and malpractice problem we face today and to suggest solutions that might work, but I leave the choice to you.

Ignorance Isn't Bliss*

Denise Tilles—Student, University of Missouri, Columbia

Effective use of a rhetorical ▶
question establishes
common ground.

Statement of purpose and ▶
assertion of personal
involvement enhances
credibility.

Have you ever said something to a person, only to realize you have completely put your foot in your mouth? Usually it is something unknowingly offensive about someone who is a friend, perhaps a test you did better on, or their religion. It's easy to say the wrong thing and it is just as easy to really hurt somebody. Today, I would like to speak to you about religious discrimination—how it feels to be discriminated against and what we all can do to try to be a little more sensitive.

An appeal to audience ▶
decency and the impact of
offensive remarks on the
speaker.

Some internal ▶
inconsistency followed by
an audience-involving
statement about personal
behavior.

It's hard for me to recall just how many anti-Semitic remarks I've heard in the last week alone. These recent comments are what prompted me to speak about this subject. Whether people choose to believe it or not, anti-Semitism is still very rampant in America today. I've never felt as if I was an overly sensitive person, but when an anti-Semitic comment is made, even if it's not directed at me, I just get confused. Sometimes I get really angry though I usually try to conceal my anger, or I just try to take it lightly and act as if that comment really didn't pertain to me. When I do this, I feel very low, like a liar or even a traitor. If a certain remark offends me, why am I not able to have the courage and pride to say so?

A reason why prejudicial ▶
statements create stress.

Obviously, the easiest thing to do is just to ignore comments that bother you. Sometimes this even works, but the hurt just wells up inside of me. Nothing is really solved by keeping silent, except saving face and not letting people know that I am Jewish. On more occasions than I'd care to recount, girls in my own sorority have unknowingly made anti-Semitic remarks to my face. I even have a difficult time telling them, my own sisters, that I'm Jewish and that what they've said has hurt me. Most of all, what I really want to say is to just think about what you say and to whom you say it.

An example involving the ▶
variables discussed earlier.

This thought brings to mind a sticky situation that happened during sorority rush. During a rush party, a girl I was speaking with happened to mention that she was unable to attend every rush party because she had to take placement tests. I replied that that was too bad. She said it was all right; she was only missing the "gross" sororities—the Jewish sorority and other horrid ones. I momentarily had to fight the urge to punch this girl, but instead I tried to watch the skit. I felt so angry, so flustered, that I almost started to cry. I escorted her out after the skit and told some of my sisters what had happened. After I told my story, some of them waited, as if to say—is that all? At this point I was even more exasperated. All I could do was wonder why.

---

*Reprinted by permission of the author.

The only reason I can think of why prejudice exists is sheer ignorance. Perhaps prejudice is perpetuated within families. I must admit that my father has a personal vendetta against Chinese drivers, and that is no better than someone stereotyping Jews as tightwads. However, prejudice does exist. People are not going to be able to understand every single culture, religion, or country. It is easy to make fun of or put down something that you really know nothing about. I know this because I'm just as guilty of prejudice as anyone else. The question is, what can we do to be a bit more sensitive towards prejudice?

◄ Movement from the effect (prejudice) to the possible causes.

Obviously, I don't have a definitive solution for prejudice. If I did, there would really be no need for this speech. I think that one way we can all begin to combat prejudice is within ourselves. Try to imagine how a black person feels when they're called a "nigger"; a Chinese person, a "chink"; a Jew, a "kike." I could go on forever with prejudicial generalizations, and more than likely, all of you have been discriminated against in one way or another. So you probably understand: it hurts, plain and simple.

◄ A call for listeners to identify with people who are objects of prejudicial statements.

I don't have any wild hopes of erasing all prejudice within this classroom with just one six-minute speech, but I hope I've stimulated some thought and empathy in each and every one of you. If I have, great. If I haven't, I suppose that's fine too. However, the message I'd like to leave all of you with is simple: Think about what you say and the potential effect it may have on others.

◄ A call for audience interest and thought about the effect of prejudice.

Walk in Another's Shoes*

Karen A. Pils—Student, University of Missouri, Columbia

Just for a moment, let me put you all in an unpleasant hypothetical situation. Pretend you have just been notified that the mother of one of your friends has died. You are stunned and saddened, and want to comfort your friend as he or she is grieving.

The ways you offer sympathy may vary depending upon your religion, but if you are like most people, you will visit the mortuary, mail a sympathy card, send a cake or baked dish to the family, or make a donation to a charity or organization in honor of the deceased. Then you leave the funeral home stating those famous last words, "Call me if you need anything," knowing that your phone probably won't be ringing.

◄ A Hypothetical situation is used for the introduction.

I'm not here to denounce any of those actions. I think everything I have mentioned is a kind, loving, and supportive thing to do for someone in need during a trying time.

*Reprinted by permission of the author.

Effective use of rhetorical ▶
questions focuses on the
prevailing problem.

I am here, however, to ask you a question. What about a week or two later? You will go on with your life, busy with your own family and problems, but what about your friend? They, too, will continue with their life, but they will be wearing the scars of their loss. As they struggle back to their jobs and activities, the pain and sorrow won't be as obvious, but it still remains. The grief they openly expressed during the eulogy or burial will be turned inward, but the hurting is all the same.

Series of parallel questions ▶
focus attention on the
momentary concern.

Why is it, then, that we bombard grieving people with visits, overflow their homes with food, flowers, and cards, and ring their phone off the hook, all at a time when they are so beside themselves that they can't think straight?

Why is it, then, that a few days later when the food is gone and the flowers have wilted and these people feel so alone, that we forget about them and what they've been through?

Why aren't we there to lend a shoulder to cry on when our friends are faced with the morbid task of cleaning out their loved one's belongings or sending thank-you notes to all those people who were so thoughtful but are now nowhere to be seen?

Statement does not follow; ▶
no previous reference was
made to the American way
of life. The next statement
is an expression of the
basic problem.

Even though it is an American way of life, doesn't it almost seem ludicrous that we swarm these people at a time when they really can't enjoy our company? Then, when holidays or other heart-wrenching reminders roll around, they are left alone and sad, with only memories to keep them company?

Now I am as guilty of this as anyone. Just thinking back, I can remember many instances when I have been warm and supportive when a friend has been faced with a death or tragedy, only to forget about it and them a few days later.

Personal reference and ▶
experiences.

In my senior year of high school, the star of our soccer team was killed in an automobile accident. His family always had parties, and they had a lake house that we were welcome to use. The boy was very well liked and popular so, naturally, the funeral home was packed with people and flowers. There was a special prayer and speech said for him at school, the cheerleaders sent a cake to their home, and the team canceled their games that week. But later, his parents sat in the bleachers at the games in a daze, all alone. They were so nice to us, but I never again stopped by their house.

Recently, I was home for Easter. When I was at church, I saw a neighbor girl across the aisle whose fiancee was killed in a freak spring-break accident. I sent her a card when I heard about it, but I bet she would have liked me to call her that weekend when I was home.

Another strong emotional ▶
appeal.

The reasons we act this way are usually because we say we're too busy or we feel funny. Well, both excuses might be true, but I know when my mom and dad die, I'll want my friends around, even if it's just to make small talk and pass the time. I'm sure you'd feel the same.

I'm not asking any of you to be a psychiatrist or act as clergy, but I do encourage you to give a little time or thought to someone who is hurting. I don't think any of us is too busy to make a phone call or write a note. If you feel funny, remember, it's the thought that counts. When you are thinking to yourself, I bet this Christmas will be hard on Mrs. Smith, invite her over. Statistics show that most depression occurs at the holiday season. Is it asking that much to invite one lonely person to your home? Or, when you say, "this would have been Johnny's nineteenth birthday," mail his parents a "thinking of you" card. This Sunday is a good time to start. It's Mother's Day, which might be a very sad day for those people who have lost their mothers. Perhaps call them to see how they are or plan to meet them for lunch that week.

◄ A plea for action and interest.

◄ Specific directions for listener reaction as a result of problem description.

Remember, death is a tragic event that we all have to face. Losing a loved one, whether it is a parent, sister, or best friend will be so traumatic that it may take years to recover. Please don't forget about these grieving people in a few days.

◄ A strong emotional ending.

"BUY" THE PEOPLE*

John O'Connor—Student, Loras College, Dubuque, Iowa
Coached by Vaughn Gayman and Don Stribling

Many have said we as Americans are very lucky. We live in the land of the free and the home of the brave. The American dream exists here—that is, anyone, regardless of race, color, creed, or financial standing can accomplish anything in life they choose, including perhaps, a prestigious seat in the United States Senate or House of Representatives. I don't think so.

Economist John Galbraith, speaking at Grinnell, noted with alarm, "Politicians' commercial appeals on TV are the latest assault of money in democracy. This abbreviated horse opera gives access to the man with money." Representative Henry Reuss, Wisconsin, appearing on "Meet the Press," said, "Campaign contributions are out of hand. Unless we do something meaningful about them, they will corrupt and ruin the republic."

◄ Use of contemporary authority helps to establish theme.

I spent last spring in Washington, D.C., as an apprentice reporter. I had thought my elected representatives represented me . . . would respond to me without go-between . . . that my vote meant something to them. What I found, instead, was disillusionment.

◄ Credibility is established.

I now believe our Congress represents the will of people with single special interests, whose year-round presence in the capital, whose parceling out of Political Action Committee . . . PAC . . . money has a major

*From O'Connor, John, "Buy the People," given at the Interstate Oratorical Association, Mankato, Winning Orations 1984. Reprinted by permission.

Clear statement of thesis is ▶
followed by statistics to
identify the problem.
influence on laws and regulations, and this is why. *Time* magazine counts
over 2,500 trade associations and professional groups with offices in Washington. One thousand eight hundred of these are the national headquar-
ters for their organizations. They never leave Washington—you and I can't
get there to express an opinion. *Time* estimates these 2,500 organizations
employ 87,000 people; spend $4 billion a year for one purpose—to get their
special way. One former lobbyist calls this "a new branch of government."

These lobbyists have a right to their presence in Washington, but through
their nationwide PAC contributions, direct undue influence in far-off
congressional districts. In fact, says Ann McBride of Common Cause, "The
PAC contribution becomes part of the lobbying campaign."

Use of specific instances ▶
inductively builds the case.
Representative James Leach, Iowa, calls his home state "the quintessen-
tial playground of PAC committees." He observed one Iowa candidate getting over $40,000 for one campaign, with just $1,000 of that from his own
district. Seventy-eight PAC sources aided the winner . . . 17 bet on the
loser. In a year's time, one Iowa congressman drew $160,000 from PAC
coffers . . . his losing opponent, $49,000. PACs can pick winners.

Dr. Herbert Alexander, UCLA, a national authority on PACs points out,
"In 1960, the total congressional election costs were $175 million. By 1980,
they had multiplied ten times . . . to $1.2 billion." Senator Proxmire, Wis-
consin, who spent just $177 campaigning, objects. He says, "I am outraged
at the colossal amounts of money poured into election campaigns. I think
it is scandalous and corrupting. Special interest money in campaigns is one
of the reasons the federal government has gone out of control."

This newest and most powerful source of money was originally thought
to be the answer to the problem. The Political Action Committee, now
known as PAC, was to be limited to a $5,000 contribution per organization
and $1,000 per individual. How twisted this plan has become!

January 16th of this year, the *Chicago Tribune* reported, "In 1972,
Congressional candidates got 14 percent of their money from PACs . . . 17
percent from the party. By 1980, party contributions were the same, but
the PAC cash had doubled."

In 1980, House Minority Leader Robert Michel of Illinois spent $130,000
to be elected. Two years later, $680,000, of which 70 percent came from
PACs, from such non-Illinois civic-minded giants as Grumman, the big defense contractor, the National Rifle Association, and the American Dental
Association. Columnist Sylvia Porter notes that 3,000 PACs spent $240 mil-
lion on last fall's congressional races. She says they were "hunting laws
they disliked and congressmen who voted for them. Something must be
done before the 1984 election."

On December 18, 1982, the *Des Moines Register* reported 215 congressmen who voted for a UAW-backed bill got $1,300,000 in UAW PAC
money. The 188 who voted against the bill got $72,000. Of the 65 house
members who got the most UAW PAC money, only one voted against the
bill. Money buys influence, but there is light at the end of the tunnel.

Four Senators repulsed all PAC money—Hart, Proxmire, Boren, and Rudmond, with Rudmond saying, "PAC is a scandal that is waiting to happen. Most PACs are organized by business to fight labor money." Congressman Tom Tauke of Iowa offers a conservative, but deadly agreement—"Most congressmen," he says, "are not influenced in a substantial way, but the public perception is that Congress is being bought." If that's the perception, people feel powerless, and they won't vote. Just last month, at a Washington, D.C., symposium sponsored by Harvard University, former President Ford said people are trading their right to vote for the growing power of PACs. He said, "Voter participation is disgustingly low." Only Congress can change the system, but you and I can change Congress.

◄ Excellent use of contrast shows potential alternatives.

Reformation in Congressional election campaign funding will have to be stimulated by the voters. No congressional representative in his or her right mind is ever going to shoot Santa Claus. Dr. Alexander, the PAC specialist, would remove present limits on funding by political parties, saying, "Congress' original intention in setting up the PACs is now proved wrong . . . the PACs are taking the place of the former responsible parties." Only parties can determine candidates, policies, issues, platforms. As the parties shrink, the PACs grow fat . . . immune, unknown, and threatening.

◄ A clear and specific call for the solution is given.

Senator Hayakawa calls the PACs nothing but huge masked bribery operations. He would limit contributions to no more than $100 a person, allowing each donor to designate recipients and be identified. He has another suggestion . . . since radio and TV stations get a free federal license, let them provide free time for federal elections.

Sylvia Porter suggests a $500 limit on personal contributions, with no large donations from top executives, one of the present motives for PAC existence. Fred Wertheimer, head of Common Cause, suggests $2 of public money for every $1 of private donation . . . making the single contributor of real importance.

◄ Use of authority figures supports further potential remedies

I believe we should use the broadest possible approach as a beginning and sort out the most worthwhile remedies as they fail or succeed. Let's continue the income tax checkoff, but put real effort into making it large and more general. . . . Let's work toward limits on out-of-district congressional PAC power . . . let PAC contributors designate where their money goes and not permit one person or a small board determine how PAC money is applied. Let's make limited federal funding available to parties and independents, enough to make them invulnerable to pressure groups but not enough to make running for office a profitable enterprise. Let the voters know before an election what PAC money is coming into their district and not after a contest ends.

◄ Clear statement of goal is followed by implications of noncontrol.

Control the costs of campaigns or they will control us. Put local funding back into focus. Give the campaigns back to the candidates and the votes back to the voters. Our congressmen did not invent this new style money machine and most would like to put away their beggar's tin cup.

Use of a pun provides an ▶
unusual and effective
conclusion.

Mr. Lincoln . . . you once told us government was "by the people". . . .
I don't think you could have imagined who is now doing the "buying" for
us.

Exercise*

Deidre Wallace—Student, Bradley University, Illinois
Coached by George Armstrong and Gary Dreibelbis

Exercise—it's the latest thing, and anybody who is anybody is doing it.
Whether it be for that perfect body or just to add ten years onto your life,
exercise is the cure-all for any physical problem. Well, just ask Jane Fonda
or Richard Simmons or Linda Evans or Jim Fixx. Well, maybe Jim Fixx isn't
the right person to ask. Fixx, the author of the book *The Complete Book of
Running,* died of a heart attack while jogging. To think that vigorous activity will always lead to that supreme body is a bit naive. Because there

Thorough statement of ▶
misconceptions includes
specific pro-and-con
examples for the
introduction.

is another side to exercise that Jane Fonda won't tell you about, that Richard
Simmons won't tell you about, and that Jim Fixx can't. That's the side of
pain, exhaustion, injuries, and in some cases even death. You see, we've
too often been told that pain is a necessary part of exercise—do it till it
hurts. Not true. According to Dr. Howard Hunt, chairman of the Department of Physical Education at the University of California, exhaustion
doesn't mean your body's weak—it means it is overtaxed. Before we can
begin to solve this problem, we must realize that exercise can be dangerous
for both the beginning athlete and the experienced; we must understand
why so many Americans fall prey to these dangers; and finally, we can look
at some solutions that will get us back on the right track towards healthy
exercise.

Before I go any further I would like to clarify my position on exercising.
I'm not suggesting that exercise properly or in moderation is bad or un-

Excellent statement ▶
clarifying thesis so there
can be no
misunderstanding.

healthy, and I'm not suggesting that we should all abstain from any type
of physical activity. However, according to a March 1984 issue of *Current
Health Magazine,* over a million people each year huff and puff their way
through workouts without even knowing that they may be heading for
trouble.

Many of the problems caused by exercising are just not knowing the
proper way of doing it. And it is usually the overly eager beginners that
fall into this category. Understand, these problems don't have to stem from
some strenuous exercise such as weight lifting or marathon running. It can

*From Wallace, Deidre, "Exercise," given at the Interstate Oratorical Association, Mankato,
Winning Orations 1985. Reprinted by permission.

be as simple as stretching. Stretching is a very natural thing to do and basically what these books and programs are all about. The problem is that we no longer limit ourselves to gentle beneficial stretching. In efforts to become oversized gumbies, we tend to overstretch to help loosen and relax our muscles. But we are not loosening them; we're tearing them. Dr. Richard Dominquez, medical director for the Sports and Rehabilitation Institute in the state of Illinois, says that there are more injuries as a result of stretching than as a result of stiffness. Even the most common stretching exercises have resulted in injuries—sit-ups, toe-touches, and deep-knee bends are just a few. Both sit-ups and toe-touches put enormous strain on the ligaments in the back and deep-knee bends put enormous pressure on the cartilage in the knee. But probably one of the most dangerous stretching exercises can be found in Jane Fonda's workout program—The Yoga Plow. Now, you may not recognize the name but I'm sure most of us have done this before. The plow is when you lie on your back and flip your feet over your head and touch your toes on the floor behind you. By doing this the circulation is often cut off to the brain and has resulted in strokes. I'm sure you understand why I don't demonstrate.

◄ Clearly, the beginning of identification of the breadth and nature of the problem.

Even the exercises that seem the most harmless have resulted in injuries. A 1980 issue of *Changing Times* states that injuries worthy of emergency room treatments for that year were suffered by 448,000 cyclists, 61,000 players of tennis, and more than 65,000 swimmers. And of course, we can't forget the most popular form of exercise today—running—unfortunately creates the most problems. That same issue of *Changing Times* states that over 60 percent of all runners complain about one injury or another, and after reading the article I can understand why. It states that as a 120 pound person jogs, there is actually 360 pounds of shock on each leg in every stride.

◄ Effective use of statistics and specifics for support.

But as the beginning athlete becomes more advanced, their problems seem to shift. They no longer stem from unawareness, but rather obsession. Many aren't satisfied with exercising in moderation but feel the need to take their workouts to the extremes. And this overexercising can throw our entire system out of balance. A June 30, 1984, issue of *Science News Magazine* reported that the repeated jarring of the internal organs while running can break down the intestinal lining and has resulted in internal bleeding. And now the *Journal for the American Medical Association* states that many women suffer from nonexistent menstrual cycles and joggers' infertility. In fact, 83 percent of all pre-menarchal trained athletes suffer from nonexistent cycles. Dr. Colm O'Herily tells about the cases of two women who regularly ran twenty miles a week. After a period of time, both women's menstrual cycles ceased. So, he prescribed a fertility drug, but it didn't help. Finally, he asked his patients to lay off the track work. And after eight weeks and half the dosage, both women had become pregnant.

◄ Use of authoritative sources reinforces arguments.

But probably the biggest question since Jim Fixx's death is the effect that exercise has on our heart. You see, we have this misconceived notion that not only can exercise help strengthen a healthy heart, but it can cure any heart problems we might have. Not true. Stanford University School of Medicine says that "Habitual exercise does not guarantee protection against sudden death before or immediately following exercise." And Fixx is the prime example. Hours before his daily run, Fixx complained of exhaustion, tightness in his throat, and chest pains—and yet he still ran. In fact, Dr. Kenneth Cooper, founder of the Aerobics Center in Dallas, Texas, and a consultant to the United States Air Force, had urged Fixx just eight months prior to his death to come in and have a heart function evaluation through a treadmill stress test. But for reasons unknown, Fixx refused. But he is not alone. Stanford University analyzed the medical histories of eighteen individuals who died while running. Sixteen out of the eighteen people died of heart-related problems. Why?

Why do we continue to push ourselves to these extremes? Well, at a recent seminar at Cornell Medical College, psychiatrists agreed that many exercise programs are potentially addictive and this negative addiction is increasing among exercisers.

The problem is growing, and we have no one to blame but ourselves. We've become so engrossed in this entire fitness craze that we have lost sight of what is really important—our health. We can often find short-cut schemes to help us shape up quickly. And we can find those schemes on any shelf in any bookstore. Well, think about it. Are we not being constantly bombarded with ways to shape up or trim down? There are workout programs by Jane Fonda, Christie Brinkley, Richard Simmons, Linda Evans, and now the latest Garfield the Cat. Now, who in their right mind would trust their health to a cartoon character? But then again, who is Jane Fonda to tell us what type of workout programs we should be doing? These exercise programs are geared toward the masses, not the individual, and they are not directed towards health but rather profit. Physical fitness has become a highly commercialized, glamourized, profitable business. And let's face it—there is not one exercise program that can do everything for everybody. Once we turn off that tape Jane Fonda is gone, and all we have left is ourselves and the problems that we have created. We are lacking in responsibility to ourselves not to let our obsessive vanity and these attractive life-styles blind us to our medical needs.

It's time we do something for ourselves, but this time let's do it right. First, we must not overestimate the qualifications of these people who write these books and programs. They're not experts, they're not doctors, and many are not qualified to tell us what type of exercise program we should be doing. We should take the initiative to find out which exercises are beneficial and which ones to avoid. Furthermore, we must learn to discipline ourselves both physically and psychologically. Like the dieter who has to discipline himself not to eat that extra piece of cake, exercisers must learn

Acknowledges the two-sided nature of argument.

Use of motive appeal of physical attractiveness and peer status is part of problem statement.

to discipline themselves not to run that extra mile. Plus, we must listen to our own body's warning signals and when pain hits, stop. But probably the best way to assure ourselves of a proper fitness treatment is to see a professional. By having a physical checkup, the doctor will be able to tell us what type of exercise programs are suitable for our specific, individual needs. And if complications do arise, the doctor will already know our workout schedule and be able to help us with these problems.

◄ Call for general and specific solution activity by listeners.

You see, exercise can be an enjoyable activity, as long as we remember that the chief goal is to improve our well being. Once exercise becomes an end in itself, it places our health in jeopardy. Now maybe someone should put that on a cassette tape.

The Role of the Liberal Arts in a Decade of Increased Technology
AN ENDURING VALUE FOR SIX REASONS*

FRANK H. T. RHODES—President of Cornell University

Delivered at the Harpur Forum, State University of New York—Binghamton, Binghamton, New York, March 29, 1984

Your warm welcome is particularly heartening because, given the recent barrage of education reports, I sometimes worry that people's eyes may begin to glaze over at the mere mention of a talk on education. You may remember Horace Mann, the nineteenth century educator, and his foolproof method for dispersing any mob. Rather than read the riot act, Mann would simply announce a lecture on education. He was confident that not a soul would remain.

That is even more true when the subject is liberal arts education, for in an age of high technology and scientific advance, the liberal arts are often viewed as sleepy backwaters of the academy, harmless enough perhaps, yet somehow on the sidelines of the action, detached and irrelevant to the problems of the real world. Liberal arts professors have become the Rodney Dangerfields of academe, commanding less respect and often less money than their vocation-oriented colleagues.

◄ Historical perspective is related to current achievements—common ground thrust.

Faith in science and technology, on the other hand, has become almost a secular religion, as achievements in those fields have become ever more spectacular. As a writer for the *Washington Post* observed a few years ago, "Had the automobile developed at a pace equivalent to that of the computer during the past twenty years, today a Rolls Royce would cost less

*This speech is reprinted by permission from *Vital Speeches of the Day*, April 15, 1984, p. 532

than $3, get three million miles to the gallon, deliver enough power to drive the Queen Elizabeth II, and six of them would fit on the head of a pin."

From penicillin to plastics, from digital watches to dial telephones, from radial tires to robotics—the advances of science and technology are unmistakable in our daily lives, while the influence of Shakespeare's sonnets, or the music of Mozart, or the philosophy of Kant is much less obvious. And it is the material aspects of our culture rather than the philosophical or aesthetic ones that seem to dominate today.

Not surprisingly, undergraduate enrollment in high-demand specialties, such as business and engineering, has increased dramatically in recent years while the number of students willing to major in such esoteric areas as classics or philosophy has declined. Students and their families, having paid a small fortune for a college degree, want to be sure of a return on their investment.

Statement of thesis. ▶ At the risk of sounding quaint, strange, impractical—let me suggest that a broad foundation in the liberal arts is the best career education available in a decade of increased technology. It is the best education. Period. . . . Let me stress that I am not arguing against professional education; I am arguing against narrow vocational training. The first is large, expansive, having the spirit of the liberal arts, setting skills as means within larger ends; concerned with not "the job," but with life and with the social goals the profession promotes and the ethical standards it demands. The second is narrow, restrictive, developing specific skills in preparation for routine tasks sometimes very technical or scientific; it involves knowledge for specific ends, raising no questions of larger significance, impervious to social context, oblivious to moral choice. A liberal outlook may be nurtured within the context of professional education. It soon withers in the presence of vocational training.

Labels major arguments ▶ I see the liberal arts as of enduring value for *six* reasons. Let me tell you
and their supporting   what they are. *First*, they provide skills and encourage attitudes that are
materials.   vital in whatever career we pursue. The ability to write and speak with clarity and grace; to understand times and cultures other than our own; to appreciate the sources not only of institutions but also of our beliefs and values; to apply them humanely in our daily lives, and to explore the human experience in all its richness and ambiguity: These are the aims of the liberal arts, and they are applicable not to a single vocation but to the whole range of human endeavor, for as John Gardner has observed, their purpose is to shift to the individual the burden for pursuing his or her own education.

Quotation provides ▶ Although students with strong technical skills still have the edge, at
support.   least initially, in the job market, many companies are beginning to look for students with more breadth. As a New England Telephone recruiter said recently, "We need managers who can deal with diverse situations, and liberal arts students are perfect for that because they've had a diverse education."

Second, our economic survival as a nation depends on our international understanding and our sensitivity and skills in living and working across national boundaries. . . . A comprehension of other countries and cultures brings its own rewards but it will also bring better performance in international trade. Our economy is becoming more and more internationalized. In 1950, about 5 percent of our GNP was involved in international trade. In 1980, it was 17 percent and growing rapidly. Over 70 percent of all our own products here in the American market now face foreign competition.

Third, vocational skills rapidly become obsolescent. Breadth of understanding and broadly applicable knowledge are important in this era of high technology because we cannot predict with any certainty what specific skills will be needed to perform a specific job even a decade from now. Already many mid-career engineers, in what should be their most productive years, are finding their skills inadequate to deal with technological advance. And doctors, a decade after graduation, open themselves to malpractice suits if they continue to use some of the equipment and techniques considered state-of-the-art when they were in medical school. But it is not just within the confines of particular careers that obsolescence erodes skills. Whole careers are becoming obsolete. No narrow vocational training will prepare our students for that. . . . Lifelong learning has to be based on a broad and strong general foundation of undergraduate studies.

◄ Irony to verify an argument.

Such practical justification of the liberal arts, however, reminds me of a cartoon by Michael Maslin that appeared in *The New Yorker* (April 6, 1981) some years back. It shows a middle-class man, in a middle-class living room, watching a middle-class television set. On the screen is a large pot, and a voice behind the pot says, "How much would you pay for all the secrets of the universe? Wait, don't answer yet. You also get this six-quart covered combination spaghetti pot and clam steamer. Now how much would you pay?" And indeed, knowledge is still considered most valuable when it is linked to something directly useful.

◄ Humor as relief and for partial support of an argument.

My *fourth* point is the most useful reason of all for the liberal arts. Life is empty without them. Attempts to justify liberal education solely on the basis of applicability to the world of work miss a more basic truth—that a job is not a career, only work and money. A career is work that enlists our best efforts because we value the ends the work is intended to advance. We select our careers, but our careers shape us, determine much of what we do and what we are, satisfy us or frustrate us.

And it is here that the liberal arts gain new significance, for through them, we can learn to discriminate between the meritorious and the meritricious, to determine which endeavors are worthy of our best efforts and which are specious, and ultimately we can learn to know ourselves, socially and culturally as well as individually.

Reference to authority for ▶
further support of
position.

"Through the humanities we reflect on the fundamental question: What does it mean to be human," the Rockefeller Commission on the Humanities noted some years ago. "The humanities offer clues but never a complete answer. They reveal how people have tried to make moral, spiritual, and intellectual sense of a world in which irrationality, despair, loneliness, and death are as conspicuous as birth, friendship, hope, and reason . . . they stretch our imagination, and they enrich our experience. They increase our distinctively human potential."

. . . As Reinhold Neibuhr has observed, "Man is the kind of creature who cannot be whole except he be committed, because he cannot find himself without finding a center beyond himself . . . the emancipation of self requires commitment."

Fifth, science and technology, in a narrow sense, are amoral. But their application involves profoundly moral issues.

Increasing scientific specialization has substantially altered our view of life. Numbers have grown stronger, words weaker, and the division between the world of the scientist and that of the humanist has become a yawning chasm. The complexity of important issues—from nuclear power plants to the effects of pesticides on the environment—demands that as many people as possible be able to separate the technical issues from the political and moral ones.

. . . We must ensure that all citizens can participate in a rational discourse on technological issues, informed by the perspectives of both the scientist and the humanist. For from the scientist we learn what is possible, but from the humanist we learn what is acceptable, and so define the boundaries beyond which human dignity is imperiled.

The two worlds may seem antithetical, but they desperately need each other, for, as Jacob Needleman has observed, "There is a point where the gathering of knowledge merely spins round and round on one level and where the only real breakthrough is to a wholly different species of knowing, integrated with feeling. All the data and theories in the world do not by themselves magically add up to a new quality of knowing."

But there is a *sixth* reason why liberal education must seek to reunite the sciences and the humanities, and that concerns the way in which great science, great art and great literature are done. Science is not self-sustaining.

. . . Scientists do spend their lives chipping away, bit by bit, at a small part of a particular problem.

Yet the truly great discoveries, the great leaps in understanding, have often been guided not by the systematic methods of scientific inquiry but by the scientist's vision of beauty and art and sense of the mystical. As Einstein once observed, "The most beautiful and most profound emotion we can experience is the sensation of the mystical. It is the sower of all true science. He to whom this emotion is a stranger, who can no longer wonder and stand rapt in awe, is as good as dead."

The liberal arts, I submit, are a vital part of undergraduate education, because

—they nurture skill and attitudes essential in any career

—they provide an international perspective

—they produce self-motivated learners and so enable us to overcome the obsolescence of vocational skills

—they add a dimension of breadth, beauty, and significance to all of life

—they promote an informed citizenry, able to evaluate and judge the complex choices of our changing society

—they provide the dynamics for the continued growth of science.

◄ Internal summary of implications of thesis.

They are necessary components in the education of all, whatever their vocation. They are necessary, but not sufficient. For there is an alarming gap between the pretensions of the liberal arts, and their performance: between the professions of the humanists and their behavior. The role of the humanities is to explore experience in all its wholeness, its contradictions, its ambiguity, its richness.

. . . But if the humanities fail to challenge our vision of life, if they fail to explore the ethical dimensions of our existence, if they fail to confront the confusion, the discontent, the uncertainty, the nobility and the glorious potential of our humanity—they have failed us. For that is their goal: without it, all else is shallow. For ultimately, as Agnes Arber has written, "biology is intelligible in physiochemical terms, but it is not explicable in those terms." Ultimately, life, our life, is more than a process, more than adaptational response, however perfect, more than molecular interaction, however subtle. It is to ponder that elusive, larger whole that the liberal arts exist.

What is needed is not just "liberal arts" as an entry in the college catalog. What is needed is that men and women, distinguished in the disciplines, devoted to their teaching, and committed in their living to the spirit of the liberal arts.

So in this decade of increased technology . . . let us reassert the priority and the ultimate value of the liberal arts.

◄ Call for acceptance of thesis as the conclusion.

. . . The determined, hopeful, and forward-looking perspective is the ultimate reward of a liberal education, and upon it rests not only our personal well-being, not only our economic strength or our capacity to survive as a democracy, but also the creativity and the humanity upon which the future of our species and this planet depends.

Telecommunications and Sports
THE FUTURE OF SPORTS IN AMERICAN SOCIETY*

Larry R. Gerlach—Professor of History; University of Utah

*Delivered at the Warren P. Williamson Symposium, Youngstown State
University, Youngstown, Ohio, October 25, 1983*

I'm sorry we're late, it has been an interesting morning. . . . Before I begin my remarks, I would like to let you know where I am coming from in terms of interest in sports. I was on my way to Cooperstown by way of the New York Yankees when I discovered as a freshman at the University of Nebraska that I could no longer throw or hit a curve ball. I then bent upon a career in football and I was going to play, believe it or not, with the Detroit Lions. Except as a freshman at the University of Nebraska, I got hurt. I was not injured, I was only hurt. People kept beating the hell out of me, and I decided that what I would then do is turn to history.

Humor is used in the introductory remarks.

. . . My remarks today will constitute remarks, not a paper. . . .

Each spring I teach a course entitled, "The History of Sport in America." The course draws extremely well with 300 or 400 students. It is the only course I teach where the students come convinced of the importance of the subject at hand and are deeply interested in exploring the topic at great length.

The first day of class I ask two questions: What is sport? What is athletics?

. . . I am perplexed that without exception my students who cover sports for the local campus newspaper have no idea as to the nature of that about which they write. And I am absolutely amazed that the forty or fifty varsity athletes in class have no intellectual comprehension of the activity which brought them to the university in the first place and which constitutes the driving force of their collegiate lives.

The speaker sets the tone and direction for the rest of the speech.

Sport, I am convinced, is the best-known yet least-understood phenomenon in American society. . . .

Sport is an extension of play involving two or more persons. Sport turns on games and contests which are highly organized, competitive, characterized by the established rules, but like play, sport has as its primary purpose fun for the participant.

Athletics on the other hand, derives not from play at all, but from work. Athletics, as they have been referred to from the ancient Greeks on, refers to intensely competitive confrontation between especially trained performers whose primary objectives are: a) spectator entertainment and b) victory. Although the game involved in sport and athletics may be the same as, for example, basketball, the two activities are worlds apart in terms

Effective use of definition.

*Reprinted by permission of the author.

of purpose and attitude. And to make this very complicated thing exceedingly simple, I would simply call your attention to the obvious difference that we understand between intramural sport and intercollegiate athletics.

. . . Two fundamental and basically irreconcilable, philosophical conflicts color our involvement with sport. First, while we extol the amateur sportsman we insist that our performers be professional athletes. Second, we want sport to be fun and to be purposeful. Today in trying to determine the sort of role or why the emphasis on sport in American society, I would like to look at that second phenomenon.

. . . Surely our emphasis on sport in modern America stems in large measure from the basic fact that Americans view sport as a serious, purposeful enterprise related to the fundamental well-being of society at large. We still hear ad nauseam such mindless prattling as "sport builds character" when the very actions of the lords of sport give lie to that simpleminded rhetoric.

. . . Just as television is responsible for the creation of the modern sport industry, television has contributed fundamentally to the problem of modern sport. The impact of television is many fold.

First of all, promotional. The enormous capacity of television to reach people has sold sport. If TV moguls devote so much programming time to sport, then sport must be important. If television devotes virtually an entire day to covering the Super Bowl, then that contest must be important. And by extension, sport itself must be very important. I would suggest that sport is regarded as being much more influential in our society than it really is because of the attention that television pays to it.

◄ Beginning of "signposts" to cue the main ideas.

The second is financial. Television with its national marketing capabilities has brought unbelievable wealth to the world of sport and created nothing short of a sport industry. The result has been an extraordinary proliferation of sport franchises and leagues—the major leagues, baseball, the National Football League, the NBA. When I was a kid, that is in the 1950's, there was no resemblance to these institutions today. . . .

◄ Speaker continues to follow through on cueing as he does for all main ideas.

Television, third, has fundamentally intruded on sport by directly affecting the contests themselves. Baseball's league championship series and night-time World Series, football's absurd playoffs, and the hyperbolic Super Bowl, even the NCAA's utterly reprehensible mass post-season basketball tournament is due to television payoffs. Contests start at times that conflict fundamentally with common sense and the interest of performers because of television payoffs. My friend Bear Bryant says, "I'll play anytime, anywhere, if the price is right." Basketball now incorporates TV timeouts in a way that fundamentally affects the strategy and execution of the game. The New York Jets defeated the San Diego Chargers earlier this season thanks in part to a referee's concern about a TV commercial. . . .

The point is that television does not merely broadcast games; television manipulates the games.

Fourth, television broadcasts a distorted image of sport. . . . Television is not concerned with sport but with professional athletics. Television made the National Football League. Television made the National Basketball Association. Television made the golf and professional tours. At the time of WWII, there was no stable NFL, there was no systematic professional basketball in this country, there was no golf tour, there was no tennis tour. And today when most Americans think of sport they think of professional televised sport. And it is not surprising, I think, that the sports that are televised are the ones that televise best. The coverage of sport in your local newspaper is a far more accurate view of American's interest in sport than the broadcast schedules of the national networks. . . .

Fifth, television promotes a perverse concept of athletism as the norm in the sport world. The pros have become the models, and the value of the pro game becomes the values of the sport generally. I think that is obvious to anyone who has watched youth or high school sports and those youngsters slavishly imitating the pros. The athlete is a conspicuous minority among the inhabitants of the sport world, yet the athlete sets the tone due to television. Moreover, the incredible hype of television promotes a larger than life concept of sport in which winning triumphs over participation.

. . . As to the future of this, the pro games will go on albeit in somewhat diminished form. I think we can put up with only so much shlock, so much pimping, so much hype, and frankly so much bull. Ratings are down for Monday Night Football whether it is Monday Night Football on Monday, Monday Night Football on Wednesday, Monday Night Football on Thursday, Monday Night Football on Friday, Monday Night Football on Saturday or Monday Night Football on Sunday. Television has made sport almost a caricature, a grotesqueness of cheap commercialism where the broadcast all too often overshadows the contest. . . .

The greatest impact of television has been on intercollegiate athletics. Television in the next decade promises to accomplish what university presidents, athletic directors and coaches have been trying to do for the last 100 years, namely, destroy intercollegiate athletics as an academic amateur sports enterprise. The open professionalism of intercollegiate athletics will, if nothing else, end the rampant corruption and blatant hypocrisy that currently afflict the collegiate sport establishment.

In 1873, Andrew D. White, president of Cornell University, responded thusly to a request by Cornell footballers to travel to Michigan for a game. "I will not permit thirty men to travel 400 miles merely to agitate a bag of wind." Three years later John Bascom, president of the University of Wisconsin, responding to student and alumni pressure for increased athletic programs as entertainment, said, "If athletics is needed for amusement, we should hire a few persons as we do clowns to set themselves apart to do this work."

Well, in the intervening years, university presidents learned about the money to be made from intercollegiate sport if not directly then indirectly

Specifics for support and ▸ some ridicule.

through alumni donations and so on, and 100 years later, my friend, Bear Bryant, made the following statement, "I used to go along with the idea that football players on scholarships were student athletes which is what the NCAA calls them, meaning a student first, an athlete second. We are, of course, kidding ourselves trying to make it more palatable to the academician. We don't have to say that anymore and we shouldn't. At the level we play, the boy is really an athlete first and a student second." When men like Joe Paterno of Penn State and Tom Osborne of Nebraska agree to play a kickoff classic in August in East Rutherford, New Jersey, after publicly arguing that game was against the best interest of the program and their players, the collegiate sport scene is in sad shape.

◄ Use of authority and example provides support.

. . . Sport accurately reflects American society, its frustrations, its fantasies, its cultural values. The arena is at once apart from and a part of everyday life . . . My son asked me about the comment he hears always that sport is simply children's games played by adults. He said, "Is that right?" And I think that is right and I think that is why sport plays such a very important role in our society.

. . . Four reasons: Sport is pure. Sport is the only nonideological cultural activity in our society, or any society. . . . Sport is only a kinetic enterprise. There is no value represented as two athletes line up to run 100 meters. It is pure. It is innocent. It is basic.

◄ Beginning of conclusion summarizes the speaker's position.

Second, sport is elemental and elementary. It involves confrontation between obvious good guys—my team—and obvious bad guys—your team. That conflict is cleanly, finely, and clearly resolved through the use of physical force. . . . One defeats opponents literally by beating them and that is the basic mechanism of conflict resolution. . . .

Third, sport is simple and simplistic. It is the cultural activity in our society that is wholly intelligible to the lowest common denominator in society. My thirteen-year-old can discuss basketball on an equal basis with me. . . . It is intelligible, too, and embraceable by all elements in the culture.

And fourth, sport, to continue the childhood metaphor, is fantastic. Sport turns on illusion, on fantasy, on dreams whether dreams of future glory or nostalgic remembrances of glories that once were or might have been. I think it symbolic that the relationship between journalism, particularly broadcast journalism, and sport is so evident and that the majority of TV addicts, Star Wars freaks, fairy tale fanatics and sports fans in this country are children. Sport represents in large part the maintenance of childlike innocence and values in a harsh, cynical adult world.

. . . In my youth there were perceived heroes, perceived exalted values to sport participation. As a youth, I viewed sport as a blissful refuge from everyday life. . . . Fantasy has always been an essential, perhaps the essential, element in sport. If sport loses its illusions and becomes part and parcel of reality, I fear very much about the future of sport in American society.

Great Expectations
FROM ABIGAIL ADAMS TO THE WHITE HOUSE*

Pat Schroeder—United States Representative from Colorado
Delivered at the Landon Lectures on Public Issues, Kansas State University, Manhattan, Kansas, March 19, 1984

Political and economic currents rarely move straight ahead, like a train on a track. They meander, double back and cross over before finally building up enough pressure to force permanent changes in the political landscape.

The 200th anniversary of feminism in America was celebrated in 1976 without much particular fanfare when we honored Abigail Adams as the first American feminist. Abigail Adams was the Tom Paine of the colonial women's movement. She lobbied George Washington and Thomas Jefferson to emancipate women in the Constitution. Here's what she told them:

> *Interesting use of ▶ quotation establishes mood and thrust.*

> If particular care and attention are not paid to the ladies we are
> determined to foment a rebellion and will not hold ourselves bound
> to obey any laws in which we have no voice or representation.

Women did not issue their declaration of independence until almost seventy-five years later, at the famed Seneca Falls convention in 1848. . . .

Women gained property, occupational, educational and political rights, and in 1920 won the long-sought right to vote. They had great expectations for a strong women's party or, at the least, an immediate and significant feminist impact on American politics.

History of women's ▶ struggle gives general and specific perspective.

But the movement ran out of *political* steam. Many women thought the battle was won and their interests turned elsewhere. The Depression hit, followed by World War II, the Cold War and the Korean War.

After World War II, the GI Bill sent thousands of mostly male veterans off to college. The marriage rate increased, followed by a baby boom. The average marriage age for women dropped clear past twenty and down into the teens.

In the 1950s, The Model Woman was cheerfully waxing the kitchen floor in a white clapboard house in suburbia. All was well, or so it seemed.

In 1960, *Redbook* magazine featured an article, "Why Do Young Mothers Feel Trapped," and asked their readers to write in with their stories. Over 24,000 mothers did. All was not well.

Betty Friedan's book, *The Feminine Mystique*, came out in 1963 and sold two million copies over the next 20 years. The mystique was "the problem that had no name"—the problem that had prompted 24,000 letters from *Redbook* readers.

*This speech is reprinted by permission from *Vital Speeches of the Day*, May 15, 1984, p. 472.

Friedan focused attention on the identity crisis many women experienced, the lack of fulfillment, the mystery that being a woman was enough, and she gave it a name.

Ten years later, in a 1973 epilogue to her now famous book, Friedan explained that the solution was "suggesting new patterns, a way out of the conflicts, whereby women could use their abilities fully in society and find their own . . . human identity, sharing its action, decisions and challenges without at the same time renouncing home, children, love, their own sexuality."

. . . What were the changes in society that moved us this far, and where are we headed?

Over the past several generations, while political feminism rose and fell, there were major social and economic changes going on in America.

Some, like the migration of Americans from rural to urban areas, are well known.

Others are less known, or are seen as recent trends. In fact, however, they have been building for decades.

For example, female participation in the salaried work force has been steadily increasing *for the past century*. It is not just a post-World War II phenomenon.

In 1890, only 5 percent of married women and 20 percent of all women were in the salaried work force. . . . *By 1980, half of all women in America were in the work force.*

"My wife doesn't work," the former boast of many American men, was wrong on two counts. She either worked at home, in an unsalaried job, or she worked outside the home in a salaried job. In many cases, she did both.

Look at education: over the past century, the number of undergraduate degrees awarded to women climbed slowly but inexorably. *In 1870,* 15 percent went to women. . . . *By 1970,* the gap was narrowing again. *In 1980,* women received 49 percent of all undergraduate degrees. . . .

The percentage of doctorate degrees awarded to women in the last 10 years has almost doubled—from 16 percent up to 30 percent. . . . as women have made great strides in education their economic fortunes have stagnated. Because of job segregation and pay inequities, the wage gap between men and women has widened.

Contrary to what one might expect, the wage gap is about the same regardless of educational level. Women, high school drop-out or college graduate, receive less than 60 cents for every dollar earned by an equally educated man.

In my opinion, the single most important women's issue in the 1980s will be comparable worth—equal pay for jobs of comparable value.

A history lesson. Just over twenty years ago, in 1963, Congress passed the Equal Pay Act requiring businesses to pay equal wages for equal

◄ Effectively interpreted statistics establish the scope of the problem.

work. . . . The fight to pass that law went on for years. Employer organizations argued it would cost them too much money and was improper government interference.

The equal pay fight was just the beginning. The simple fact remains that occupations filled with women—nursing, teaching, and secretarial—are generally low paying.

Comparable worth does not mean pay men less, nor does it mean pay women more. It means pay PEOPLE what they are worth. In many cases it will mean paying women more.

Now the naysayers argue that there are no standards—no one can determine what a job is worth. . . .

No, the problem is not lack of standards. *The problem is that there are standards and the standards are wrong.*

When a nurse or a high school math teacher with a college education is paid less than a liquor store clerk with a high school education, there is something wrong with our wage standards, not to mention our values.

. . . The real cause of the wage disparity is that most women's jobs— 80 percent of all women are in twenty-five job categories like nursing, teaching, service and office jobs—are not highly valued. Can someone explain to me why cutting a lawn is more valuable to society than teaching kindergarten?

In the first successful, major comparable worth lawsuit in the U.S., the federal case decided in Seattle last month, the judge found that there were standards, and the state of Washington violated them. There was a 20 percent disparity between jobs held largely by women and jobs held largely by men.

. . . The startling rise in the number of female heads of household and poor elderly women has feminized poverty. Divorce is a pivotal factor. Although there are indications that the divorce rate may have plateaued in recent years, between 1920 and 1980 it more than tripled.

And if it has leveled off, it's a rather high plateau—more than 50 percent of marriages contracted today will end in divorce, separation or desertion. The economic effect of divorce on women, especially those with children, is nothing short of disastrous.

Less than half the women who retain custody of the children receive their full, court-ordered child support. Almost one quarter receive nothing.

A California study of 3,000 divorced couples found that one year after divorce, the woman's income had dropped 73 percent while the man's had increased 43 percent! It is little wonder, if present trends continue, that by the year 2000, the poor in America will be almost entirely women and children.

The anti-ERA lobby talks a lot about women needing to be "protected." But that's exactly the point of the ERA: inequality is no protection. Whatever the standard—wages, pensions, child support, survivors' benefits— women come up short.

Numerous specifics further ▶ establish the range of the situation.

Arguments from the other ▶ side of the issue are presented.

It is no wonder that the ERA has become an economic issue. The gender gap, the difference between how men and women tend to vote, is largely based on economic issues. Inequality is an economic issue.

. . . These trends are reshaping American politics because our political system accommodates itself to shifting currents. Women have adjusted to the new interest by male politicians in women's issues, and men have adjusted to the increased role of women and women's concerns in politics.

For example, the Congresswomen's Caucus, which I cochair and helped found in 1977, admitted congressmen in 1981 and changed its name to the Congressional Caucus *FOR* Women's Issues. Over 100 men joined and the total membership is now 129, making it one of the largest caucuses in the Congress.

. . . The Economic Equity Act—a package of tax, retirement, insurance, alimony and child support, day care, and regulatory reforms to improve the economic security of women—now has 131 cosponsors in the House and 32 in the Senate.

The sudden burst of talk about a female vice president may very well make possible what no one thought probable as recently as one year ago. There is a "why not?" spirit to the question. And why not a women as president?

◄ Specifics show how much progress has been made.

More importantly, the new feminist awareness in politics makes it more likely that the presidential and vice-presidential nominees, male or female, will be committed to social, political and economic equality for women.

The real immediate impact of the gender gap, however, is that women have the power, in numbers, to provide the margin of victory for the next president. If you find that hard to believe, ask the governors of New York, Texas and Michigan, who were all elected in 1982 with the women's vote.

The number of female elected officials has been slowly increasing, especially at the local and county levels, which serve as farm teams for higher office. At the congressional level, however, the increase has been glacial.

Successful female congressional candidates averaged about 9 during the 1940s; 14 during the 1950s; 12 in the 1960s; 16 in the 1970s; and is running about 20 in the 1980s. At these increments, women will have reached parity in the House—half the seats—in about 400 years!

Since 1971, when the National Women's Political Caucus began keeping tabs, the number of women mayors has increased from 7 to 76, state legislators from 362 to 992, and members of Congress from 15 to 24.

. . . Politics is a game of inches and angles. Women are putting a 5 percent to 15 percent edge on issues of interest to them, increasing their numbers among elected officials, and becoming a leading political indicator, drawing men to their standard.

◄ Reference to the introduction gives further emphasis to the conclusion.

The female force in politics, exhorted by Abigail Adams in 1776, and predicted with the right to vote in 1920, has come to pass.

Speech to the Police Conference
of the State of New York*

Mario M. Cuomo

Presented During the Campaign for the Governorship of New York, Albany, March 24, 1982

I'm pleased to be here. Peter [Reilly, president] made it sound as though I were doing you a big favor by coming, and I'm not. You do me the favor by having me.

I'm pleased to have this opportunity to talk to you today for a few minutes. The reason I need to start early and get out on time is that the Governor has a meeting at ten o'clock with just the legislative leaders. We have trouble again on the budget—it has not been put together. We're trying desperately hard to avoid the kind of debacle we had last year, when we were forty-two days late—at which time, when asked about a budget not coming in on time for three years in a row and how I felt about that, I said, frankly, "I feel very bad, because it's another symptom of a society that's gone lawless."

We all talk about violent crime and the increase of violent crime; we all know about that. But if you look around, it's happening everywhere. In every part of our society there's a loss of discipline, a lack of respect for authority, for the rule, for the necessity to defer to the rule. And here is a legislature and a whole government assembled in Albany whose principal function legally is to get the budget done on time. And three years in a row we didn't live up to the law, while at the same time we were trying to tell the people of this state that they must. So the budget debacles are a serious problem that goes way beyond the $30 million it cost us last year to be late. And that's what we'll be talking about at ten o'clock this morning.

I wish that I could talk to you about libraries and education and economic development and the things I would do with money in this state if I were the governor—if I were the king. All the wonderful things we've not done that we'd want to do.

We have a whole generation of people in wheelchairs who will never live a reasonable existence because we can't figure out how to transport them. We have senior citizens in Clinton County and Essex County literally stealing from free lunches so that they have something to eat at night. We have 14 percent of the population unemployed in Buffalo. We have problems of every kind that we ought to be directing our attention to, and

---

we're distracted by another problem that we have to talk about whether we want to or not.

I don't like saying it, because it's a disgrace that we have to say it, but the biggest problem in this society today, the one that comes before all the others, is the problem of keeping law and order.

Some time ago a fellow—Teddy White—wrote a book, *In Search of History*. He was talking about Chungking in 1939 and the Communists and why it was that communism was so appealing to the Chinese at that time. White said, "It's because the first obligation of government is to keep people safe from one another and from the hordes, from the attackers, and they did that."

We're not doing it in this state. It's never been worse. We talked about it at the last convention. I've talked about it ever since. I've talked about it for seven years, and it gets worse every year.

I've talked about being born and raised in the 103rd Precinct in South Jamaica. You know, that was supposed to be a tough community in those days. Everybody fought. You had gang wars and someone might even stick you with a knife occasionally. But it was nothing like what it is now. The violence is sick, it's deep, it's penetrating, it's irrational, and it's everywhere.

What do we do about it as a society? Well, I'll tell you. I said in my announcement—and again I say it reluctantly because I'd rather not have to deal with this as the first priority—that when I become governor, the first priority for me will be to do everything we possibly can to bring down the grotesque crime rate. And this is a pledge I made to my family and to myself as well as to you. Because crime has struck us the way it has struck everybody.

I'm a lieutenant governor. I have state troopers; I'm protected. I know every cop in New York City, I think—I taught a lot of them. I knew them when they were sergeants, and now they're inspectors. I even knew Sid Cooper, who is in charge of internal security for the New York City Police Department and became chief inspector.

I and my family should be safe in New York City. Yet my daughter got attacked twice by the same guy down the block from our house at four-thirty in the afternoon, in broad daylight. We haven't caught him yet. We have his picture, or we think we have his picture—we have the police artist's rendition. We've got everybody looking for him, but we haven't caught him. At four-thirty in the afternoon both times, down the block from my house, in a "good" community—a beautiful girl, eighteen years old.

Now she'll never be the same, unless God is very, very good to us. And we're on our knees thanking God that she wasn't badly hurt; that she wasn't raped; that nothing worse happened to her; that she didn't get killed. So I feel it—and we feel it—the passion. If my son ever got his hands on this guy—forget my son, if I ever did, I cannot predict how I would behave. I'm not a saint, and I'm not God. And if you stood that person in front of me and said, "There he is," I don't know what I would do.

So I'm not shocked that a whole society that sees this day after day—that sees police mowed down, that sees nuns brutalized, that sees old women raped—should say, "My God, you've got to do something about this. And you've got to make the ultimate response, you've got to give us capital punishment. Give us something tough, if only because we must say to this world, 'We will not live this way anymore!' " I understand that. I understand the feeling. People have had it for a long time in the history of civilization.

But I think we have to do something more basic about crime. I think one of the problems with that feeling is that politicians have used the death penalty to eclipse more important questions, more important things that need to be done.

I think basically what we have to do—and every penologist will tell you this, and everybody who ever wrote a book on criminology, and everybody who was ever on the street—is this: we've got to convince potential criminals that we're going to catch them, convict them, and can them. And that we're going to do it for sure. They've got to know they're going to pay a price.

The percentage of arrests for crimes committed is down. I don't care what the book says. You ask anybody who will tell you the truth in New York City or in Buffalo—for crimes committed, the percentage of arrests is way down. It has to be. There are a lot of crimes we don't even pursue anymore. Burglary in New York City: who in the heck investigates a burglary in New York City? Who has the police? Who has the forces to investigate burglaries? If you're lucky and the car is going by and you see a guy going through the window, then maybe you'll be able to make the arrest.

We have to catch them; they have to know they're going to get caught. We have to convict them; they have to know they're going to get convicted. And we have to can them; there has to be a place where they pay a price. It's not happening now. Now they know that the chances are we're not going to catch them. And if we do catch them, the chances are they won't get convicted. Twenty-six arrests and no trial—the death penalty is not going to frighten that kid because he knows nothing is going to happen to him.

I talked to an attorney yesterday from South Jamaica, my old community, who told me to bring these kids in to the judge for sentencing and tell them, "Take the stuff out of your pockets. No hash, none of that stuff, because you may go to jail, and if you go to jail, they'll search you and find the stuff." But the kids bring it anyway. Why? Because they're not going to go to jail, and they know it. They go in with the stuff in their pockets and they come out of the damn place with the stuff still in their pockets. And you think you're going to change that by saying "We're going to have the death penalty"?

If they do get convicted, we have to have a place to put them—a prison cell. We have to do something with them when we get them in Auburn for nine years. What do you do with them? Should we teach some kind of skill, give them some kind of shot, do something about getting them a job when they get out?

Well, these are hard questions. We need more police, number one. And more state troopers. New York City is down about ten thousand police since 1972. Ten thousand fewer police than in 1972. Is the death penalty going to change that?

We need better prosecutorial capacity. We need more judges. We blew nineteen indictments in Brooklyn because there were no court clerks ready—the cop was ready, the witness was ready, the D.A. was ready, and the judge was on time, but they didn't have clerks.

We need prison cells—yet we lost the argument last year for the Prison Bond Issue.[1] For all the people screaming for the death penalty and outraged at violence, when it came time to put some money up for the prisons, they wouldn't do it.

Will more police and judges and clerks and prison cells cost money? Of course they will cost money. But what I'm saying to you is that everything worthwhile costs money, and this has to be the number one priority.

After you agree to spend the money, you have to learn to spend it more intelligently. You have to *manage* the system. You know what we don't have in this state? With all the police we have, local and state troopers, D.A.'s everywhere, prosecutors everywhere, an attorney general's office, the Feds you have to tie into, rehabilitation programs, parole, probation— we have no single place where all of that is coordinated statewide. Does that make sense? I don't think so. We coordinate everything else. We coordinate education. But there's no single place in state government where criminal justice is coordinated.

This year, for the first time, the Governor, in response to that need, has asked Tom Coughlin of Corrections to put together a panel and at least start talking. But there has to be more than talk. There has to be a working, coordinative mechanism. We're just getting started in New York.

Now let me talk about my position on the death penalty. The truth is that I don't believe it works; that I remember this state when we had it; that I don't believe it deters; that I don't believe it protects my daughter or my mother. I believe it is a "copout" and I believe that the politicians have used it for years to keep from answering the real questions, the questions like these: How come we're short some ten thousand police? How come the state troopers are paid so little in this state, where they're supposed to be so important? How come we have run out of prison cells? How come probation and parole are not all that they should be? How did we get here? Politicians don't want to deal with those questions. So they deal with a nice, simple question—the electric chair—and that gets everybody off the hook.

Now, to those of you who want the death penalty, and I assume that's most of you, I want to say at least this: "Look, if you want the death penalty, at least don't let them con you. Insist on cops, insist on prosecutors. Insist! Don't let them buy you cheap." Hey, if I were a policeman, what I would want is a cop to my left and a cop to my right. You ask the fellows in New York City who are ten thousand short or the troopers upstate—in Herkimer County one night, there was one trooper on duty in all of Herkimer County—ask them what they'd like. I think "more police" is an answer they'd give you.

In the end, the people will decide for better or for worse what they want. I hope they will come to agree with me. I hope with all my heart that they will agree with me, because as much as I love and respect you, I think on this issue you're wrong, and I feel that deeply.

That's all that I feel on criminal justice that I can tell you in ten and a half minutes. If you have any questions, now or later, I'd be delighted to address them.

I'll add only this. I intend to stay in this race until the very end. I intend to be governor of this state. When I am, your concerns—what you need, what you are, what you represent—will be very, very important to me. There won't be anything more important. I pledge that to you. And I don't think you've ever heard anybody say about Cuomo that he didn't mean it when he said it—and he didn't live up to his word.

Thank you.

Notes   1 A bond issue of $500 million for prison construction was defeated by the voters in 1981.

Using the Library

In this section we provide you a quick overview of what a library is, how it functions, and how you can best take advantage of it. The world's knowledge is stored in libraries; it is yours for the asking, but you must know how to ask for it.

Many students think of the library as a very forbidding place—a place where they are supposed to be quiet all of the time and where books are stored for a few intellectuals. Nothing could be farther from the truth. A library is not a warehouse of materials for the exclusive use of a few individuals.

Departments within the Library

Think of a library as you would a department store. If you enter any large department store, you know that you will find a variety of specialty departments—women's wear, men's wear, housewares, electronics, linens, cosmetics, and the like. Although department stores are not all laid out the same, they are usually similar. That is, you generally know which department to enter to find what you are seeking.

All libraries are pretty much the same, too, though they may be larger or smaller, and they may be organized somewhat differently. When you enter a library, you can expect to find the following departments—and perhaps others.

Circulation Department

The circulation department is usually responsible for maintaining the bookshelves in a library, and for checking out all materials that circulate. Books, of course, are circulated, and in some libraries, so are records and tapes, portable computers and software, and VCRs and videotapes.

Many faculty members reserve library materials or personal materials for their students. Most of these materials usually are not checked out to students for more than an hour or so, but some materials may be checked out for a specific number of days.

Most libraries have temporary reserve collections and permanent reserve collections. Temporary reserve materials flow in and out of the reserve department according to the needs of the institution—what classes are being taught and what research projects are under way, for instance. The permanent reserve collection is usually comprised of very rare or valuable materials that the library would be unable to replace. This material may be housed with the temporary reserve materials or in a related area called the rare books and materials section.

A library usually has a card catalog or a listing of reserve materials, and a reserve desk where you will find someone who can help answer your questions about the collection.

Reserve Readings Department

The library reference department houses a broad range of reference works that usually do not circulate—for instance, dictionaries, encyclopedias, almanacs, handbooks, college catalogs, directories, telephone books, and many general and specialized bibliographies, abstracts, and indexes. Here you may find such works as the *Readers' Guide to Periodical Literature,* the *Social Sciences Index,* the *Applied Science and Technology Index, The New York Times Index, Who's Who,* and *Current Biography,* providing they are not housed in the serials and periodicals department.

The reference department should be your first stop when you visit the library, since the reference librarians can direct you to all the wonders in the other collections. Become acquainted with the reference librarians and ask them for help, because they can save you countless hours of work and frustration. You will find them eager to assist you. They are paid to help, and they take it as a matter of professional pride and responsibility to help you. You cannot offend a reference librarian by asking for information.

Reference Department

The government documents section in your library houses federal, state, and local materials, some of which circulate and some of which do not. Here you will find a broad range of materials generated by the government as part of its work. The government documents section is one of the most difficult collections in the library to access because of the extensive and broad interests of the governments. It is also one of the most useful sections of the library.

You can learn how to use the catalogs and indexes that provide access to the government documents without too much difficulty. Usually the department has a brochure designed to provide this instruction. You will

Government Documents Department

never learn everything there is to know about this wonderful collection of materials. Even the most competent researchers must ask the government documents librarians for help, but that is okay. The librarians know the collection well, and they want to assist you.

Serials and Periodicals Department

The serials and periodicals department provides assistance in finding information in periodicals, newspapers, and other serial publications. Some are stored in bound volumes and some on microfilm. Some—especially the most recent issues of magazines, journals, and newspapers, for example— are stored on racks near or in a reading room. In this department you will find a serials reference desk. Become acquainted with the persons working at that desk; they can help you with your research.

Not all libraries house serials and periodicals in one centralized location, however. Some divide the collection according to appropriate subject area. Help in finding materials located in libraries organized in this way would come from staff people in the appropriate subject-area location.

Microform Department

The microform section of the library may be found in the serials and periodicals department, in a separate department that houses materials on microform, or integrated with the print materials, especially in subject-divided libraries. Microform materials include back issues of newspapers and magazines, for example, and such wonders as ERIC, the "Library of American Civilization," and the "Library of English Literature." Usually these materials do not circulate, but you can make photocopies of most of them with the help of the librarian.

Instructional Media Department

The instructional media department houses a wide variety of audio and visual materials (records, tape recordings, foreign language lessons, plays, films, 35-mm filmstrips/slides, videotapes, photographic archives, and so on). Some of these materials circulate and some do not. Still, you are welcome to visit the instructional media department and use the materials you find there. Notice that in some libraries the media holdings are restricted to class-related use and are not intended for entertainment. Some departments have both types of holdings. Learn the policy at your library.

To facilitate the flow of materials between libraries, a system has been set up that allows one library to borrow materials from another to fulfill the requests of library users. These materials must be classified as circulating items and they may be borrowed for only a limited period of time. There are special forms to fill out for different types of materials. Learn to use them, but first check your own library to be sure that it does not have the materials you need.

Interlibrary Loan Department

Some libraries have a database searching department or division, or a database searching unit within the reference, periodicals, or interlibrary loan departments. Wherever it is housed, the function of this unit is to provide computer searches for you in specific subject areas. The data bases for these searches provide citations, with or without abstracts or summaries for materials on your subject. These materials usually consist of periodical articles, books, and documents.

You must be very specific when asking for a database search. Be sure you know some important key words or phrases in the subject area, and be sure you have done a manual search in your locality before requesting a database search. The service can be rather expensive and it is sometimes quite time-consuming, especially if you are not specific in your request. This service is an enormously helpful and powerful addition to the more traditional functions that libraries provide.

Database Searching Department

Large libraries often develop specialized collections, and some even house those collections in separate facilities for the convenience of their most frequent users. For example, if you have a medical school at your institution, you will almost certainly find a medical or biomedical library. Law schools usually have a law library, and journalism schools often house a branch of the library specifically for their students. You will want to know which specialized collections your library holds and where they are located, especially if they are outside the main library.

Specialized Collections

Once you have located the different departments of the library, you need to know how to use them. Sources of information you may need are located in a variety of reference tools within the library. You will find general and specialized indexes, a card catalog, and a broad range of bibliographies.

Identifying Materials in the Library

General and Specialized Indexes

The word *index* refers to any alphabetized listing of names or topics. An index provides access to periodical articles by subject and in some cases by author or title. An index also provides complete bibliographical information (author, title of article, name of periodical, volume and issue number, date, and pages) needed to locate the article. Indexes are a useful source in forming a working bibliography.

Consult the card catalog or computer data base under the subject "indexes" to discover those that are in your library, or ask the librarian to make suggestions. General and specialized indexes come in a variety of formats. Look at each index to discover how to use it. You should not have any trouble learning the system for each one, and you will be glad you did.

> *Pointer:* Each index includes a range of serials and periodicals. Find out which ones your library owns, so that you will not waste your time listing entries, only to discover later that your library does not subscribe. You may not have time to use the inter-library loan system.

An abstract is similar to an index, but it usually summarizes each item included in its various issues. Like indexes, abstracts have many formats. Ask the librarian for help in using them; it will be very worthwhile.

The Card Catalog

A card catalog is an index of materials in a given library or collection. The materials are described and classified in such a way that the user can refer to an entry, then easily find the material. In some libraries the traditional card catalog has been replaced with a computerized data base or public access on-line catalog, but since there is no standardized computer-access system, you will have to learn how to use the one in your library. Ask for help; the computer system will be easy to use once you have learned the system. Moreover, most computer-access systems are menu driven; that is, all you have to do is read what is on the screen and follow simple directions.

Card catalogs list authors, titles, and subjects alphabetically—usually in separate catalog sections, although many libraries intermix all three. If a book is co-authored or is listed under more than one subject, you may find several cards for the same work. The listings by author will include the authors, editors, compilers, and translators of the work. If you want to know what works by a particular author are owned by the library, consult the author cards, looking up the author's last name first. If you know the title of a work but not the author, consult the title cards. Entries by title leave off the articles *a, an,* and *the* when they appear as the first word of the title.

The subject catalog may be your most useful research tool. If you know the subject you want to research, you can open the catalog and find every work the library has on that subject. Since libraries generally use an authorized source for the subject headings (they do not make up their own

```
DS
774       Spence, Jonathan D.
.S59        The gate of heavenly peace: the Chinese and
          their revolution, 1895-1980
          / Jonathan D. Spence. -- New York :
          Viking Press, 1981.
          xxii, 465 p. : ill. ; 24 cm.
          Bibliography: p. [423 ]-444.
          Includes index.



            1. China--History--20th century.
            2. China--History--1861-1912. I. Title

WMA       23 NOV 81        7555180   WIM8at        81-65264
```

FIGURE A.1 An Author Card.

subject headings), it is best to consult that source first to make sure you are looking in the subject catalog under a recognized or correct form of the subject. For example, if you want to research "speaking" as a subject, you will not find it listed in the subject catalog. The Library of Congress Subject Headings book would tell you to *see:*

Debates and debating
Elocution
Extemporaneous speaking
Lectures and lecturing
Oratory
Rhetoric
Voice

Then, if you look under "debates and debating," you will find additional related subjects to explore.

Study the card headings and subheadings carefully. You will notice that the subject cards cross-reference other entries in the same catalog system, and also in other cataloging systems used by your library. For example, some libraries include works that are cataloged using both the Dewey Decimal system and the Library of Congress system. The samples in figures A.1, A.2, and A.3 are in the Library of Congress system. If your library uses both systems, you may have to do some looking before you find what you want.

```
                    The gate of heavenly peace

        DS
        774      Spence, Jonathan D.
        .S59       The gate of heavenly peace : the Chinese and
                 their revolution, 1895-1980
                 / Jonathan D. Spence. -- New York :
                 Viking Press, 1981.
                   xxii, 465 p. : ill. ; 24 cm.
                   Bibliography: p. [423]-444.
                   Includes index.


                   1. China--History--20th century.
                   2. China--History--1861-1912. I. Title

        WMA      23 NOV 81        7555180   WIM8at        81-65264
```

FIGURE A.2 A Title Card.

```
                    CHINA--HISTORY--20TH CENTURY.

        DS
        774      Spence, Jonathan D.
        .S59       The gate of heavenly peace : the Chinese and
                 their revolution, 1895-1980
                 / Jonathan D. Spence. -- New York :
                 Viking Press, 1981.
                   xxii, 465 p. : ill. ; 24 cm.
                   Bibliography: p. [423]-444.
                   Includes index.


                   1. China--History--20th century.
                   2. China--History--1861-1912. I. Title

        WMA      23 NOV 81        7555180   WIM8sc        81-65264
```

FIGURE A.3 A Subject Card.

It will be most helpful if you know the general categories and sub-categories in each system. Refer to figures A.4 and A.5 to compare the general categories of each of these systems. You will notice immediately that the older Dewey Decimal system is far less precise than the newer Library of Congress system.

		A	General Works—Polygraphy
		B	Philosophy—Religion—Psychology
		C	Archeology—General Biography
		D	History and Topography (except America)
		E	America—American History
		F	Local History—Latin American History
000–099	General Works	G	Geography—Anthropology—Sports
100–199	Philosophy	H	Social Sciences—Business
		J	Political Science
200–299	Religion	K	Law
		L	Education
300–399	Social Sciences	M	Music
		N	Art—Architecture
400–499	Language	P	Language and Literature—Drama
500–599	Pure Science	Q	Science
		R	Medicine
600–699	Technology	S	Agriculture—Plant and Animal Husbandry
700–799	The Arts	T	Technology
		U	Military Science
800–899	Literature	V	Naval Science
		Z	Bibliography and Library Science
900–999	History		

FIGURE A.4 Major Categories in the Dewey Decimal System.

FIGURE A.5 Major Categories in the Library of Congress System.

We want to stress the need for writing down the complete call number from the catalog card for a particular book when you use the card catalog. The call number is located in the upper left-hand corner of the catalog card. Using the example from Figure A.1, you would need to write down:

DS
774
.S59

This is the book's address in the library. To be casual about this important matter can cause you a good deal of lost time in the stacks. For instance, to write down "DS774" is something like saying "I live on Maple Street. Pick me up at 6 P.M." Just as there may be dozens of houses on Maple Street, there may be dozens of books with the classification number DS774.

Bibliographies

After you use the card catalog, you may want to extend your reading list still further. A bibliography is a reference work that lists other books on a subject. There are bibliographies on almost every subject! For example, you might find a book by Ruth M. Walsh and Stanley J. Birkin, titled *Business Communications: An Annotated Bibliography* to be useful.[1] Refer also to the *Bibliographic Index: A Cumulative Bibliography of Bibliographies!*

Collecting Materials

Now that you have some idea of what is located in the different departments of the library and how to use the library, you are ready to begin your research. Once you have made it this far, the difficult part of "library research" is behind you, and the excitement of the discovery begins.

Develop a Working Bibliography

Once you have identified a subject, begin developing a list of materials that might be useful. Do this systematically: include one bibliographical entry per note card in the format that you will use later.

> *Pointers:* Include only one entry per card.
> Use a standard card size for all entries.
> Consistently follow a single bibliographical style.

The following examples of note cards (figs. A.6 and A.7) are based on the *MLA* (Modern Language Association) *Style Manual.*

Evaluate Your Sources

It is very important that you be able to know if the information you have located is worthwhile. If you want to produce information that you and your receivers can depend on as accurate, then you must judge the quality of the source.

Primary or Secondary

Some works are *primary* sources. That is, they are basic materials that have not been edited or annotated. Manuscripts, diaries, newspaper articles, and some books fall into this category. *Secondary* materials are characterized by interpretation and evaluation. They are edited and often reflect a particular viewpoint. Thus, whether material is from a primary or secondary source can make a big difference to the accuracy of the source.

Objectivity and Bias

Some works are strongly biased while others remain objective. Clearly, the quality of a source is influenced by its bias. For example, if you read a book like Betty Lehan Harragan's *Games Mother Never Taught You,*[2] you are reading biased material. If you were to use this work as a resource on the topic of "Sexism in American Business," you would need to know that the author's point of view is not objective.

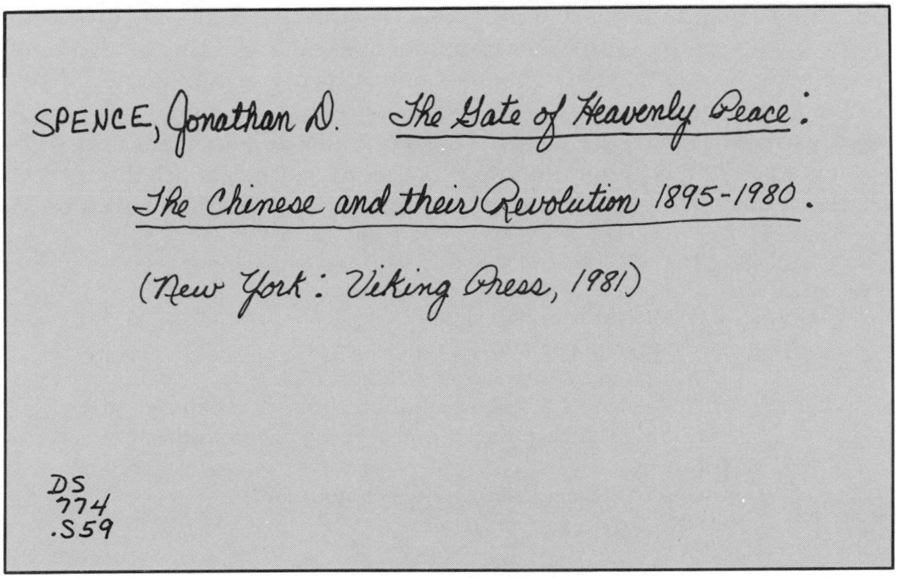

SPENCE, Jonathan D.   *The Gate of Heavenly Peace:*
The Chinese and their Revolution 1895-1980.
(New York: Viking Press, 1981)

DS
774
.S59

FIGURE A.6 Bibliography Card for a Book.

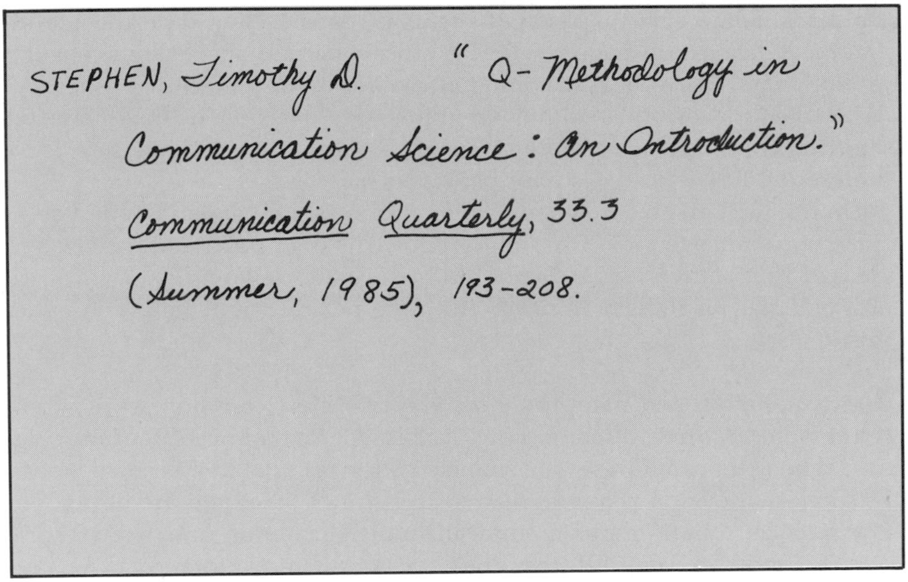

STEPHEN, Timothy D.   " Q-Methodology in
Communication Science: An Introduction."
Communication Quarterly, 33.3
(Summer, 1985), 193-208.

FIGURE A.7 Bibliography Card for an Article.

Author
Qualifications

An author's qualifications to write about a subject can make a big difference in the quality of the source. For example, the authors of this book are not qualified to write a textbook about economic theory or human neurology. You would want to check such things as degrees, professional credentials, work experience, and the like, if your argument is important and if the evidence you find is important to the argument. You can check the author's qualifications by looking him or her up in biographical dictionaries or encyclopedias. *Ask the reference librarian for help.*

Gather Your Materials and Take Notes

Pointers: Use note cards or half sheets.
Use one note per card, and one card per note.
Use a standard note-taking system.
Include complete bibliographical information on each card, including the page number on which you found the information.
Include a subject heading on each note card.
Double-check everything for accuracy.

Use Note Cards or
Half Sheets

The size of the note card you elect to use is a matter of preference. Some scholars prefer smaller cards as a way of keeping their notes short. Others develop a preference for larger cards so that later they can edit directly on the cards. Some even prefer half-sheets of paper. They type the bibliographical data except page references on several half-sheets at once using carbon paper. Then they take longhand notes on one sheet at a time.

Let the kind of notes you make guide your decision in this matter of selecting the size of your note cards. However, once you have selected a preference, live with it. *Use only one size of note card.*

Do not use full-size notebook paper for notes! Full sheets invite you to make your notes too lengthy and to follow the organizational pattern and ideas of your source. If you do not limit your notes severely, you run a risk of accidental plagiarism. Writing one note per card will help you avoid this.

Use a Standard Form
of Entry

Direct quotation and paraphrase are the two most common ways of entering notes. A direct quotation (fig. A.8) is an exact replication of the original. When you paraphrase, you summarize the original in your own words. Be sure you develop a system that clearly shows what you are doing. For example, put quote marks around all quoted material, and write "paraphrase" on a card (fig. A.9) that does not carry direct quotation.

A Final Word about
Plagiarism

Plagiarism is taking the ideas or the language of someone else and claiming it as your own. If you do this intentionally, it is outright stealing—one of the most serious offenses in the academic community. People and their careers have been ruined because they plagiarized the work of others.

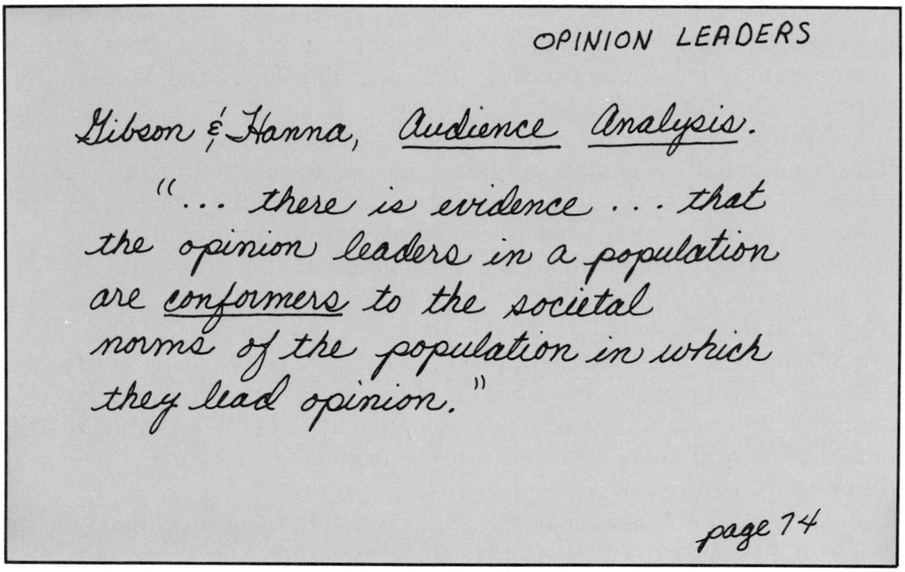

FIGURE A.8 Note Card: Direct Quotation.

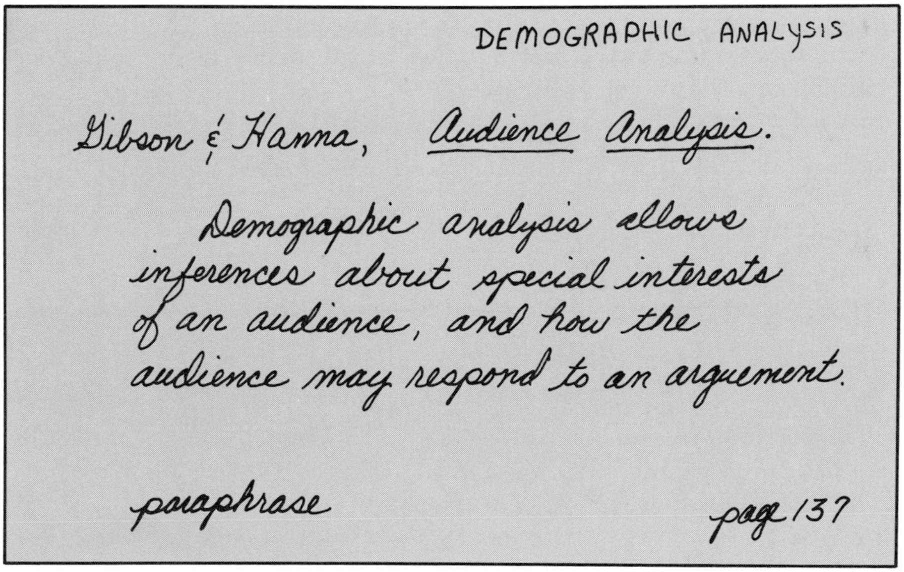

OPINION LEADERS

Gibson & Hanna, *Audience Analysis*.

"... there is evidence ... that the opinion leaders in a population are *conformers* to the societal norms of the population in which they lead opinion."

page 74

FIGURE A.9 Note Card: Paraphrase.

DEMOGRAPHIC ANALYSIS

Gibson & Hanna, *Audience Analysis*.

Demographic analysis allows inferences about special interests of an audience, and how the audience may respond to an argument.

paraphrase

page 137

Plagiarism can also happen by accident! Some very honest and well-intended students have plagiarized without knowing it. This is because they used another person's ideas or language, but failed to give the other person credit *because they did not know how.*

Crediting the source is a matter of form and style, as well as of integrity. If, unintentionally you do not follow a correct form of entry or if you do not indicate by the way you record information that the ideas or the language are not your own, then you have plagiarized unintentionally.

Some students believe that the way to give credit is to include a superscript (footnote or bibliography number) at the end of a paragraph—or a page—and include an entry in the notes at the end of a paper. They follow this format whether they are quoting material directly or paraphrasing. This approach can be misleading; there is a better way. If you quote materials, set the quotation apart from your own material with quotation marks, indentation, or the like. Ask your professor which style sheet you should follow, and then follow it faithfully.

If you are paraphrasing materials, your wording must show that you are doing so. In a speech, you would say something like, "To paraphrase John Marshall . . ." If you are writing an essay, you would indicate paraphrased material by writing something like, "In his 1985 essay, John Marshall suggested . . ." In the written form, you would then include a footnote to show where you got the quotation you are paraphrasing. The superscript would appear next to the first mention of the name, as in "John Marshall.[24]"

Notes

1 Ruth M. Walsh and Stanley J. Birkin, eds., *Business Communications: An Annotated Bibliography* (Westport, Connecticut: Greenwood Press, 1980).

2 Betty Lehan Harragan, *Games Mother Never Taught You: Corporate Gamesmanship for Women* (New York: Warner Books, Inc., 1977).

Glossary

A

Abstraction   The process of deriving a general concept from specific details; a partial representation of something whole.

Accessibility   Criterion for judging visual supporting materials.

Accommodation   Situation in which individuals who are experiencing interpersonal conflict refrain from overt expression of the conflict.

Action, appeal to   Final appeal in the conclusion of a speech that is designed to elicit action.

Action continuum   Theoretical spread of possible positions that audience members can hold between action in favor and action against a position.

Active listening   Process of paraphrasing another person's ideas or statements, including the provision of feedback about nonverbal messages.

Adaptive   Act of adjusting to listeners and/or audiences.

Affection   Positive regard for someone; fondness for; love.

Affiliation   Attachment or unity on basis or terms of fellowship.

Agenda setting   As an effect of media, the focusing of attention and discourse on certain issues or problems that are perceived as important. As a group activity, the process of determining and arranging the subject matter for discourse.

Alliteration   Act of repeating a sound in two or more stressed syllables for auditory effect.

Analogy   A form of support that uses similarity between features of two or more things to provide a basis for comparison.

Antithesis   Opposition or contrast of one idea to another idea. For example, "Give me liberty or give me death."

Apprehension   *See* communication apprehension.

Approach-approach conflict   Conflict over mutually exclusive but equally attractive outcomes.

Approach-avoidance conflict   Conflict resulting when outcomes from an act or decision are perceived as both desirable and undesirable.

Appropriateness   Degree of suitability for a particular purpose, occasion, or audience.

Aristotle   Ancient Greek philosopher (384–322 B.C.) who wrote, among other things, *Rhetoric* and *Poetics.*

Articulation   Movement of speaking mechanisms (tongue, jaw) to form the sounds of speech.

Attention   The act of directing or concentrating the mind on a single thought or point of focus.

Attention-getting devices   Part of speech used to attract and heighten attention and interest of listeners.

Attitude   Feelings, disposition, or manner of behavior toward some object, phenomenon, or event.

Audience   The receivers of messages: in speech, the group of listeners; in writing, the readers.

Audience analysis   Process of identifying and understanding the characteristic features of an audience.

Avoidance-avoidance conflict   Conflict that results when avoiding an undesirable outcome will yield a different undesirable outcome.

B

Balance   A sense of psychological well-being in which we perceive the world as harmonious and consistent.

Barrier (or breakdown)   Interruption in the flow of communication attributed to some structural defect in the communication process. This is a controversial idea among communication scholars, who perceive it as inconsistent with a "process model" of communication.

Belief   A statement that something *is.*

Bodily action   In speech, use of gestures, posture, eye contact, and so forth to communicate ideas and to reinforce spoken words.

Body of a speech   Major portion of a speech in which the main ideas are developed and supported.

Brainstorming   Procedure for generating a large and diverse idea base quickly; often timed.

C

Cause-effect   Organizational pattern that flows from the causal fabric to its effect.

Central idea   Sometimes called a thesis, the single most important idea in a speech.

Certainty   In logic, the position that what is being observed could not have occurred by chance. A 100 percent level of confidence. Certainty also refers to an attitude that is closed-minded, thus not considerate of alternative positions or view points. The opposite of certainty, from this perspective, is "provisionalism."

Channel   The means of transmission; the vehicle through which messages are sent.

Channel capacity   A measure of the maximum amount of information that a communication channel can handle at any given moment.

Circular   In a communication event, the flow of ideas from the source to the receiver, and back to the source when the receiver responds.

Code   A system of signs and symbols used to transmit messages between people. Sometimes used to suggest a system of symbols for translating messages from one form to another.

Cognition   The act, power, or faculty of apprehending, knowing, or perceiving.

Collective expectation   A standard applied to behavior to discover if it classifies as a norm.

Combination   To unite; to bring into close relationship, as a single unit. Placing events or phenomena together.

Commemorative speech   A special occasion speech for the purpose of praising or honoring.

Communication apprehension   The unpleasant feelings some people experience when they find themselves in a communication situation, particularly a public speaking situation. At one time, communication apprehension was commonly referred to as "stage fright."

Communication power   One of the criteria for judging the quality of visual material. The degree of potency and memorability of visual or other symbolic material.

Comparison and contrast   A rhetorical device; an analogy. A form of support in which two things are compared for some persuasive or informative purpose.

Conclusion   The end of a speech or essay. The purpose is to focus the thinking and feelings of the audience on the main idea of the speech.

Conflict, interpersonal   A form of competition. A situation in which one person's behaviors are designed to interfere with or harm another individual (expressed). Disagreement or opposition of ideas or opinions (unexpressed).

Conflict, intrapersonal   Condition or status of emotional tension. *See* approach-approach, approach-avoidance, and avoidance-avoidance conflict.

Conformity   Behaviors produced by an individual that are uniform or consistent with the expectations of a social system and are least likely to produce negative consequences or influence from the other members of the social system.

Connotation   The affective value or meaning of a word. The emotional associations an individual user brings to a word.

Conservative   Cautious; moderate; without flashiness. Ideas and concepts that are not extreme to the general population.

Content and relationship dimensions   The notion that language refers to both the world external to a speaker—the objects, phenomena, and events outside the individual (content dimension)—and to the relationship existing between the speaker and another individual (relationship dimension.)

Context of communication   The physical, social, psychological, and temporal environment in which a communication event occurs.

Credibility   The believability of an individual. Perceived worthiness of a source.

Credibility gap   Tendency of people to disbelieve one another. The difference between the image of integrity an individual attempts to project and the perception of integrity that another holds of that individual.

D

Data bases   Collections of information that have been organized for use in a variety of ways. Usually applied to computer-based information filing and retrieval systems.

Decision   A choice among available or imagined alternatives.

Decision making   The process of choosing among alternatives, or arriving at a decision.

Decode   The process of deriving message value from a code.

Decoder   The mechanism or agent that decodes. In public address, the listeners decode the speech; the speaker decodes the listeners' feedback.

Deduction   Organizational pattern that flows from a generalization to a particular case—for example, all people die; therefore, you will die.

Definition   Form of support. Formal statement of meaning or significance.

Demographic analysis   Use of demographics to draw inferences about an audience's attitudes, beliefs, prior information about a subject, and so forth.

Demographic profile   Statistical data of a population describing its vital and social features; for example, sex, age, and socioeconomic status.

Denotation   The associations attributed to a word by members of a speech community. The "dictionary definition" of a word. The features of meaning of a word that are usually accepted by native speakers of a language.

Description   Use of language to picture some object, phenomenon, or event.

Dialect   A variety of a language that differs from the standard, or general usage.

Dichotomy   Division of an idea into two mutually exclusive groups. For example, good—bad.

Direct evidence   A physical object that may be used as evidence to support an argument or idea.

Dyadic communication   Communication between two people.

E

Emotion   An affective state in which fear, joy, anger, and the like are experienced. Generally considered to be the counterpart of logic. Speakers often seek to arouse some emotion in their listeners as a means of securing agreement or action.

Empathy   Experiencing what another person experiences; feeling what another person feels.

Encoder   The component of the communication process in which information is translated from one form into another: in speech, to translate ideas into spoken words. A telephone mouthpiece serves as an encoder as it translates spoken sounds into electrical impulses.

Equality   The attitude, reflected in communication choices, that each individual is inherently a worthy human being. Equality encourages supportiveness. The behavioral opposite of superiority.

Ethics   The branch of philosophy that studies moral value—rightness or wrongness.

Ethos   The perception of an individual's character; for example, an audience's perception that a speaker is honest, knowledgeable, and of good will and intention.

Evaluation   The process of making a value judgment about some person, object, or event.

Evidence   Facts, objects, or testimony that may be used to support claims or draw inferences.

Evolution   The history of an object, idea, or event; the enduring changes.

Examples   Form of support that uses one of a number of things to show characteristics of the whole number. An instance used as an illustration.

Explanation   Form of support; exposition. Act of making clear by describing or interpreting the details of an object, plan, or purpose.

Extemporaneous   Style of speech delivery that uses careful preparation and notes, without memorization or a manuscript.

Eye contact   In speech making, use of vision to establish rapport with listeners and to study nonverbal cues of listeners for feedback.

F

Facial cues   Changes of movements of the face, such as blinking the eyes or frowning, or very subtle and rapid changes in muscle tone of the face—sometimes called "micromomentary" changes.

Fact   In speech, a proposition that something is true and verifiable; form of support that displays an accepted truth to verify an assertion.

Fallacy   A logical error, sometimes deliberately misleading or deceptive, that renders an argument unsound.

Feedback   Messages sent from a receiver to a source, which have the effect of correcting or controlling error. Feedback can take the form of applause, yawning, puzzled looks, questions, letters, increases or decreases in subscription rates, and so forth. In groups, feedback sometimes is used by members to teach an individual his role or to extinguish the behavior of a deviant member.

Field of experience   The image of the world that an individual holds as a result of interacting and communicating with it. The field of experience is dependent upon language (how you talk about the world—the things you say to yourself and others) and such things as memory and forgetting. Thus, an individual's field of experience is unique.

FIRO   Fundamental Interpersonal Relationship Orientation. Analytical system developed by William Schutz for examining and understanding human relationships, based upon need for inclusion, control, and affection.

Flexibility   Viewing ideas and relationships as changing and requiring adjustment of personal viewpoints.

Forgetting curve   A model that traces the amount of material retained or forgotten over time.

Forum   A large group meeting designed to encourage audience participation on issues surrounding a topic. Typically, a moderator introduces a topic and a speaker, who presents a brief statement and then interacts with the audience. The moderator encourages audience participation and involvement.

Frame of reference   The psychological "window" through which an individual views the world. For example, an individual committed to a religious orientation may apply the precepts and perceptions of that religious orientation to all of his or her observations and perceptions.

G

Game   A simulation, with rules governing the behaviors of the participants. In game theory, games may be played in three forms: win-win, win-lose, and lose-lose.

Gatekeeping   The act or process of filtering messages sent. Some messages are allowed to pass intact, some are distorted, and others may be eliminated altogether.

Generalization   A general statement or principle.

General purpose   The broad intention that motivates a speech: to inform, entertain, persuade.

Gestures   Bodily movements that express ideas or reinforce spoken messages or convey ideas independently of speech.

Goals   Objectives; effects; aims; end results sought.

Grabber   Jargon term used to indicate the first idea presented. Its purpose is to "grab" the attention of the listener.

H

Hierarchy   An arrangement of needs, goals, or achievements based on their rank, class, or importance.

I

Illustration   Form of support that uses examples to clarify or make intelligible.

Image   In speech, the mental representation, idea, or form. A description of something. For example, listeners form images of ideas based on what a speaker says and how he or she says it.

Impression formation   The process of forming images of a speaker or the speaker's ideas, on the basis of verbal and nonverbal messages.

Impromptu   A style of speech delivery without preparation or prior planning; speaking "off the cuff."

Induction   Organizational pattern in which ideas flow from specific instances toward a generalization—for example, John died, Mary died, Helen died, and William died; therefore, all people die.

Inference   A guess; a judgment based upon observed data about the meaning of that data.

Influence   Ability to produce effects in others by persuasion or power. In communication the effects typically are the result of persuasion rather than power.

Information   In information theory, available data. The more the available data, the more the information and the greater the certainty. More commonly used to mean anything that reduces uncertainty.

Information overload   Condition in which the amount of information is too great to be processed. Occurs typically in groups, when the number and complexity of messages are too great to be dealt with.

Information processing   Using perceptions to transform data into information, usually followed by action upon those perceptions.

Innovative   Unusual or creative. The ability to make or introduce something new, or to introduce or influence change.

Interact   Two acts by group members that occur in sequence and are related to each other.

Interference   In listening, an act, fact, or occurrence in which physical or semantic noise combines with the speaker's presentation in such a way that it reduces the effect of the presentation.

Internal summary   A short review or recapitulation of some part of a message.

Interdependence   A relationship between elements or people, such that each is influenced by the other.

Interpersonal communication   Communication between or among people, characterized by give and take. Distinguished from public communication by its personal nature, as opposed to the impersonal nature of public communication.

Interpersonal needs   Motives that produce affiliation. The reasons for establishing a relationship. In William Schutz's system, inclusion, control, and affection.

Intrapersonal communication   Communication within oneself.

Introduction   The beginning part of a speech, the purpose of which is to get attention, state the speaker's thesis, and prepare the listeners for what is coming.

Involuntary   Done without choice or will. Often an act that occurs instinctively. In listening, for example, paying attention to some distracting stimulus, such as a sudden cry from the congregation during a sermon.

Issue   A question that is central or critical to an argument. Issues may be of fact (something is), value (something is good), or policy (something should be).

J

Jargon   Technical language evolved by specialists so that they can communicate more accurately and efficiently about their interests or concerns.

Jumping to conclusions   Reaching a decision, judgment, or inference prematurely. It often involves ignoring information that does not reinforce existing information or beliefs.

K

Kicker   The last statement(s) of a speech. A kicker seeks to focus listener attention on the central idea, or to produce an upbeat feeling.

L

Language   Primary message system. A body of words, plus rules for their use, that ties people together into a speech community.

Leveling   A communication phenomenon in which messages are distorted by reduction of details, intensity, or complexity when they are repeated in a series.

Listening   The active process of receiving aural stimuli.

Logic   Reasoning. Having to do with cognitive processes. In persuasion, the process of deriving conclusions from evidence and arguments presented.

M

Main ideas   Most important assertions of a speech. The key or critical arguments. The major claims to be developed and supported.

Manuscript   A written document. A style of speech delivery in which a written document is read aloud to a group of listeners.

Mean   A statistical average.

Median   The point of division between equal parts. The middle number of a given sequence. The average of the two middle numbers in an even-numbered sequence.

Mediation   Conflict management technique in which disputing parties agree to negotiate with the help of an arbitrator. Usually understood to be binding.

Memorizing   A method of preparation and delivery of a speech in which the speaker commits all major ideas and supporting materials to memory and delivers them word for word. Not recommended as a method of delivery.

Memory   Ability to retain and recall impressions and experiences. One of the classical canons of rhetoric, the others being: invention, arrangement, style, and delivery.

Mental set   Psychological orientation, produced by prior events or perceptions, that contributes to bias in perception or comprehension.

Message   Any sign or symbol or any combination of signs or symbols that function as stimulus material for a receiver.

Metaphor   Comparison of things to other things or concepts. Often used as a form of support for ideas in a speech or essay.

Method of topics   Organizational pattern that follows the natural divisions of a topic. For example, the human body includes several systems: skeletal, circulatory, respiratory, muscular, nervous, endocrinal, and so forth.

Mode   In statistics, the most frequent occurrence of a value—for example, the most frequently achieved score by class members on a given test.

Model   A physical representation of an object or process. Models may be visual or verbal, and may be two- or three-dimensional.

Modification, nonverbal   A cue or message sent, nonverbally, to modify the meaning of the verbal message.

Motivated sequence   Organizational pattern developed by Alan H. Monroe: attention step, need step, satisfaction step, visualization step, action step.

N

Narrative   A story of events or experiences; an account used as a form of support.

Noise   Any source of interference or distortion in message exchange. Noise exists in the process to the extent that message fidelity is damaged. Three broad categories: (1) physical, or channel noise, (2) semantic, or psychological noise, and (3) systemic, or system-centered noise.

Nonverbal   Without words.

Nonverbal communication   Process of sending and receiving messages without words.

O

Objective   The purpose, goal, or intended end result of a speech.

Occasion   In public address, a particular time characterized by certain circumstances—for example, an event, ceremony, or celebration. Nearly synonymous, in speech making, with "context."

Openness   In language, the phenomenon that allows native speakers to talk about matters that they have not discussed before, and to understand talk they have never heard before. In relationships, the willingness of an individual to receive and consider ideas from another.

Operational definition   A definition by example.

Opinion leader   A person whose opinion molds public opinion. In a group, an individual whose ideas influence the direction or decision of a group.

Oral style   Language characterized by short words, repetition of ideas, and use of contractions. *See* style.

Organization   A human system designed to achieve some set of specific goals and characterized by a recurring sequence of events, such as a fiscal year.

Outline   Written phrases or sentences showing the structure, or arrangement and relationships, of ideas.

P

Parallelism   Comparison of the nature, tendency, or direction of two things in order to show the likeness, agreement, or similarity between them. As a figure of speech, use of similarity in the structure of related sentences—for example, "Ask not what your country can do for you. Rather, ask what you can do for your country."

Paraphrasing (listening)   Repeating in one's own words the ideas of a speaker.

Paraphrasing (testimony)   Repeating in one's own words the ideas of a witness.

Pause   A temporary stop in the flow of speech, made for emphasis.

Perception   The process of becoming aware of stimuli that impinge on the five senses.

Personal evidence   Evidence generated by a human being, such as the spoken opinion of an expert, or a document.

Persuasion   The process of influence. The process of changing attitudes, beliefs, and behaviors.

Physical noise   *See* noise.

Physiological reaction   Bodily reaction to perceived threat. In communication anxiety, it usually involves perspiration, "butterflies" in the stomach, and nervous movements of the arms and legs.

Policy   An assertion characterized by *should* or *ought* that suggests or advocates a course of action. An officially determined course of action.

Planning outline   A working document in which a speaker develops the structure and relationships among ideas, arguments, and evidence.

Positive feedback   Feedback that reinforces behaviors for the purpose of increasing the likelihood that the behaviors will recur—for example, nods of agreement, or laughter in response to an anecdote.

Positive reinforcement   Increasing the likelihood of a particular response by rewarding it.

Process   Ongoing activity. Continuous changing in the pursuit of a goal.

Propositions   Assertions of positions—for example, fact = something is; value = good/bad; policy = something ought to be.

Pronunciation   The act of pronouncing words. The result of the act of pronouncing words. A basis on which listeners make judgments about speakers—for example, "His speech tells me he's a redneck."

Provisionalism   Behavior suggesting an attitude of open-mindedness, tentativeness with respect to a conclusion. Opposite is certainty.

Psychological reaction   The internal response of a listener to what he or she perceives—for example, a listener may think, "I need this information."

Public speaking   Act of delivering an address to an audience.

Purpose, general   Entertain, inform, change belief, convince, stimulate to action.

Purpose, specific   The particular goal of a speech. The effect sought. Usually stated in terms of the observable behavior a speaker wishes from some listener.

Q

Quotation   Form of support that uses the exact language of a witness, usually an expert, to establish the credibility and acceptance of an idea.

R

Reasoning   Act of forming judgments, inferences, or conclusions from evidence and arguments.

Receiver   A person or thing that takes in messages.

Reciprocity   Assumption that people will respond to behaviors with similar behaviors.

Redundancy   In information theory, a measure of the predictability of a message. The greater the redundancy, the greater the predictability and the less the uncertainty. In public address, providing the same idea more than once, and through more than one channel.

Reflective thinking   A pattern, or sequence, of logical thought that provides a convenient organizational pattern for analysis: (1) identify the problem; (2) define and delimit the problem; (3) develop evaluative criteria against which to test alternative proposals; (4) seek alternative solutions to propose and test; (5) develop a final solution to advocate.

Reflexiveness   A feature of all languages that allows language to refer to itself. Language for talking about language is said to be self-reflexive.

Rehearsing   Practicing for a public performance or presentation; involves the polishing and refinement of ideas, but not their memorization.

Reinforcement   Increasing or strengthening the likelihood of a response.

Reliability   A measure of the extent to which independent observers agree. A measure of the extent to which a measuring instrument will measure the same phenomenon in different cases.

Research   Systematic study of a subject to discover or revise facts, opinions, or images of the subject.

Response   Behavior that results from some stimulus, such as a speech.

Rhetorical question   A question that implies its own answer, which is asked for persuasive effect.

Risk taking   Willing to attempt an unconventional approach to idea generation and development.

Role conflict   Conflict felt by an individual when the expectations of one role do not seem to fit the expectations of another role.

Rule of thirds   Principle of design for two-dimensional visual aids: the visual plane is divided into thirds, both horizontally and vertically, and the major components of the design are located at the intersections of the dividing lines.

S

Selective perception   Unconscious process of sorting through available stimuli and selecting those to be perceived.

Self-awareness   Consciousness of one's physical and intellectual self.

Self-concept   The image of oneself that has evolved out of interaction with significant others over time.

Self-disclosure   Revealing oneself—one's thinking, feelings, beliefs, and so forth.

Self-esteem   Liking for oneself; self-respect.

Self-fulfilling prophecy   Process of making a prediction come true—for example, predicting that a group experience will be exciting, then fulfilling the prediction by experiencing the group as exciting.

Self-reflexiveness   Ability of something to refer back to itself. Language is self-reflexive. People can be self-reflexive.

Semantic noise   Error introduced into a communication event due to peculiarities in the use of language. Sometimes called psychological noise.

Scapegoating   Placing blame on some outside cause, such as an individual or agency.

Simile   Figure of speech that compares unlike things—for example, "The ship of state government."

Simplicity   One of the criteria for judging visual supporting materials. Basic, neither complicated nor complex.

Situation/context   Terms used interchangeably. The immediate surround of an event. The environment in which an event takes place. The presence of variables that may influence a communication event.

Situational perspective   A perspective that relies upon examination of a situation in order to guide decisions about appropriate leadership.

Slang   Very informal use of language that is typically vivid, vulgar, and socially taboo.

Social dimension   The relationship dimension of group communication, having to do with such relational matters as cohesiveness.

Source   The origin of an idea or a message.

Space   In public address, the basis for a pattern of organization that relies on geographical relationships.

Speaking outline   A document used as notes during the presentation of a speech. Its components include one-word reminders of major ideas, and often meta-notes as reminders to the speaker of something planned.

Specific instance   Form of support. Account or description of a particular case in point, used to support some claim that what is true of one instance is true of a whole class of similar instances.

Spontaneity   Characteristic of interaction in which individuals speak freely and straightforwardly without editing or developing strategies of control. Encourages supportiveness. Opposite is strategy.

Stability in perception   Phenomenon of the perceptual process that renders perceptions of people and things relatively constant or consistent with previous conceptualizations of those people and things.

Stage fright   Communication anxiety. Fear of performing or speaking before a group.

Statistics   Form of support. A shorthand method for summarizing a large number of cases or examples.

Stereotype   Application of a fixed set of characteristics about a group to an individual member of that group in such a way that the uniqueness of the individual is ignored.

Stimulus   Data to be perceived. Anything in the experiential field that arouses an individual or impinges upon the perceptual mechanisms of that individual.

Strategy   Application of a plan to control another. In interpersonal communication, strategy fosters defensiveness. Opposite is spontaneity.

Structure   The arrangement of components of a system—for example, a speech outline.

Style   Use of language in a speech or essay.

Subpoints   Arguments or assertions that are related to but subordinate to main ideas.

Substitution   Using nonverbal messages instead of words to regulate another individual during a communication event.

Success   Favorable end of an effort toward a goal.

Summarize   In listening, a technique for increasing accuracy in comprehension and memory of what a speaker says. A brief recapitulation of what has been said.

Superiority   Attitude or opinion that another individual is not equal to oneself. Opposite is equality.

Suspension of judgment   Reluctance to jump to conclusions about ideas or positions. Often called "holding your fire." *See* jumping to conclusions.

Supporting material   Any verbal or nonverbal material used to develop or establish the credibility and acceptance of some part of a speech.

Supportiveness   Category of behavior identified and described by Jack Gibb that implies or suggests an interpersonal attitude characterized by candor, freedom of fear, and a sense of equality. Behaviors that yield a sense of supportiveness include description, problem orientation, spontaneity, empathy, and equality.

Symbol   Anything that arbitrarily stands for something else. Symbols do not usually bear any natural relationship to the things for which they stand—for example, a flag bears no natural relationship to the country for which it stands and a word bears no natural relationship to the thing it represents.

Symmetry   In communication, any response that mirrors the antecedent stimulus.

System   The sum of all the components of a thing, plus all the relationships among those components, joined to form a single entity and interdependent in such a way that any change in the system affects the entire system.

T

Target audience   The particular set of receivers for which a speech has been designed. The group from whom some particular behavior is desired. May be a subgroup in a larger audience.

Task dimension   The part of a communication event having to do with objects or ideas, as opposed to relationships.

Testimony   Form of support. Written or spoken statements, usually by an expert, used to establish credibility or acceptance of an idea or claim.

Theory   The foundation of an explanation or description of any complex phenomenon. Sometimes described as a complete set of if-then statements that serve to allow explanation or prediction.

Thesis statement   Statement in the introduction of a speech that gives the most important point, or purpose, of the speech.

Time   In public address, a pattern of organization based upon some sequence of events.

Transition   Unit of speech designed to move the listeners from the consideration of one idea to the consideration of another idea.

Triangle of meaning   A theoretical model developed by I. A. Richards showing the relationships among an object, phenomenon, or event; thinking about that object, phenomenon, or event; and the symbolic representations people generate about their observations.

Trust   Confidence in another person. Belief that the behavior of another person can be predicted.

V

Value The worth of something. The characteristic or quality of a thing that renders it desirable. In speech, a kind of proposition characterized by judgmental terms such as *good* or *beautiful*.

Variable Something that can increase or decrease in some dimension, as in the variable worth of the American dollar overseas. Something that can have different values.

Visual aids Form of support. Use of visual material to establish credibility or acceptance of some claim.

Vocal cues Any variation in rate, pitch, force, or articulation of speech intended to suggest meaning or interpretation of the spoken words.

Vocalized pause A pause characterized by habitual phonation, as when a speaker says, "uh."

Voluntary Willingly and with mental consent. Usually involves the giving of attention to an idea that, for one reason or another, is appealing to the receiver.

W

Written style Characterized by lengthy sentences, polysyllabic words and minimum repetition of ideas. *See* style.

TROUBLESHOOTING GUIDE

Public speaking activity can continue throughout your lifetime. In school, at work, and in social, civic, and religious organizations, you will have many opportunities to give public speeches. We have encountered many people who wanted a quick reference work to refresh their memory about what they once knew about public speaking, or to give them information they never had about managing a public speaking situation. This book will serve as a helpful tool when those situations arise—helpful beyond the level provided by most public speaking textbooks.

At times the typical index, including the index in this book, may not be a useful problem-solving tool because it is not problem oriented. To find solutions to your problems, you would ordinarily have to read through many sections of a book. Something more is needed; therefore, we have developed this *troubleshooting guide*. It is a problem-oriented index based on the kinds of questions that speakers most often ask about how to solve the problems they confront when called upon to give a speech. Make a habit of using this guide. We are confident that you will find *Public Speaking for Personal Success* a helpful resource for many years to come.

How to use this troubleshooting guide

◄ State the problem you are experiencing out loud or in writing.

◄ Think of key words that describe the problem you have stated. Key words are listed alphabetically in the following directory.

◄ Locate those key words in the problem-solving index.

◄ Find a question similar to the one you have asked, then turn to the referenced pages of the text for an answer.

◄ If you do not find relevant key words in this directory, refer to the index at the back of this book to locate information related to your problem.

DIRECTORY

PROBLEM CATEGORY AND QUESTIONS	LOCATION OF ANSWERS
A	
Aggressiveness	
People tell me that I am aggressive. What do they mean?	243–44
People say I am too aggressive. Is there anything I can do to change that perception?	244
People say that I am shy, but I do not feel shy. What do they mean?	244
Anxiety	
I am worried that I cannot succeed as a speaker. Is there any help or hope?	42–43
I feel afraid even when I think about giving a speech. What can I do to prevent this feeling or, at least, deal with it?	20–21, 36–37
Why am I afraid of giving a speech?	30–31
Is there anything wrong with me because I am fearful of giving a speech?	19
Assertiveness (See also Aggressiveness)	
How can I be more assertive?	244
Attending and Attention (See also Listening)	
Sometimes when I am trying to listen, I cannot concentrate on what is being said. Is there anything I can do?	57–58
Sometimes I find myself drifting off instead of paying attention. Is there anything I can do to prevent this?	55–58
How can I get attention from my audience when they are getting tired?	141–47

PROBLEM CATEGORY AND QUESTIONS	LOCATION OF ANSWERS
Audience Adaptation	
My listeners are relatively unsophisticated about my topic. What should I do?	290
How can I know if my topic will be appropriate for my audience?	98–100
I have a good idea, but I am not sure how to tie it into the interests of my listeners.	34–35, 76–83
Audience Analysis (See also Demographics)	
I would like to develop a questionnaire to test the audience position on my topic, but I do not know how to begin. Any suggestions?	80–83
Is there a way to analyze my class as though it were a real audience?	80–83
I do not know anything about my audience. How do I begin an audience analysis?	65
How do I actually perform an audience analysis?	68–75
C	
Communication Anxiety (See Anxiety)	
Communication Process	
How does public speaking fit in to the communication process?	17–21
Comparison and Contrast (See also Support)	
How do comparison and contrast work as supporting material for a speech?	194–95, 277
When should I use comparison and contrast as supporting material?	194

PROBLEM CATEGORY AND QUESTIONS	LOCATION OF ANSWERS
Conclusion	
When I come to the end of my speech I have trouble finishing it. What should I do?	147–51
Credibility	
I want my listeners to trust me and have confidence in me. What can I do to enhance my own credibility?	288, 295–99, 326
How is it that people can tell a lot about me by the language I use?	239–45

D

Definition of Terms (See also Meaning Agreement)

What should I define and what can I leave undefined? Why?	192–94, 239
How do I actually present a definition?	266–67
Delivery (See also Visual Aids)	
Is it ever okay to read a speech from a manuscript?	159
I am thinking about writing out the speech and memorizing it. Is this approach okay, and what are the risks?	158
How do I actually give the speech? I am prepared, but what about delivery?	167–72
What is the best way to use visual materials when I am giving a speech? Are there any pointers about delivery?	222–23

PROBLEM CATEGORY AND QUESTIONS	LOCATION OF ANSWERS
Demographics	
I know that demographics are important to audience analysis and marketing research, but what should I look for?	71–73
What should I do with the demographic information that I collect about an audience?	73

E

Evidence (See also Support)

What is a good definition of evidence?	183–84
What are the various kinds of evidence and their strengths and weaknesses?	185–96
Where can I find evidence?	184
How can I know if the evidence is any good? What tests can I apply?	184

G

Group Leadership

I am supposed to organize a decision-making group. Are there any guidelines that will help me select the participants?	324–25
How many people should I involve in a working group?	325
I am in a good group. I want to help us make maximum progress on our task. Any advice?	326–28
My group seems bored to death. No one seems to care about anything. Is there anything I can do?	336

PROBLEM CATEGORY AND QUESTIONS	LOCATION OF ANSWERS
What are the differences between written and oral language?	156–57, 246
What language technique can I use to make my speech vivid and interesting?	271–73
Leadership (*See* Group Leadership and Group Participation)	
Listening (*See also* Attending and Attention)	
People sometimes do not listen to me, and I sometimes have a problem listening to others. Why is listening such a problem?	50–52
Logic	
Something seems wrong with the logic of this speech, but I cannot figure it out. Any ideas?	299–300
Is there a difference between *fact* and *belief*?	179–81
M *Meaning Agreement* (*See also* Understanding)	
Sometimes my listeners think I mean something quite different from what I intended. What is the problem? Is there a solution?	239–43
Sometimes people misunderstand the words I use. What is the problem?	231
Moderator	
I am supposed to be the moderator of a panel. What should I do?	344
We are planning a whole-house debate, and I will be the moderator. What should I do?	341–43

PROBLEM CATEGORY AND QUESTIONS	LOCATION OF ANSWERS
Motivation (*See also* Persuasion)	
What motivates people to do what they do?	291–95

N

Narrow and Focus

People tell me not to "bite off more than I can chew"—to narrow and focus my topic. How do I do that?	100–103

Notes

What is the best way to make and use notes?	161–62
Can I use my outline for speaking notes?	131–34

O

Organization of Ideas (*See also* Outlining)

Is there a surefire way to organize the ideas for my speech?	35
What are the most commonly used ways of organizing speech ideas?	108–9
I want to give a speech about a problem that needs to be solved. Is there a best way to organize such a speech?	112–14
I want to talk about a topic that is really interesting to me, but I'm not sure how to organize it.	119
When do I put the problem first, and when do I put the solution first?	116
I have lots of evidence and examples that prove my idea is right. What is the best way to organize this material?	122

PROBLEM CATEGORY AND QUESTIONS	LOCATION OF ANSWERS
I want to propose some changes, even though there really isn't anything wrong with what we are doing now; I just think my idea will make things better. How can I organize such a speech?	116
I want to stimulate my listeners to action. How should I organize this speech?	123–26
Outlining	
How do I make an outline for a speech?	127–31

P

Participation (*See* Group Leadership and Group Participation)

Persuasion (*See also* Organization of Ideas)	
How do I give a persuasive speech?	286–91
Is it okay to tell the listeners what I want from them?	291
I want my audience to feel they need my proposal. How can I set up such a need in my listeners?	291–95
Is there anything that affects the staying power of a persuasive message? I want my listeners to be persuaded for a long time.	300–302
Should I tell my listeners what I want them to conclude?	290–91
Should I present only one side of the argument, or should I present both sides?	289–90
What emotional appeals can I use to persuade my listeners?	287–88, 301

PROBLEM CATEGORY AND QUESTIONS	LOCATION OF ANSWERS
Practice	
What is the best way to practice a speech without memorizing it?	163–64
R	
Remembering	
I am worried that I will forget what I want to say and lose my place in the speech.	43
Reports, Group	
I am supposed to report my group's findings to management. What should I do?	340–41
I am supposed to report my group's findings at a meeting. What should I do?	341
S	
Shyness (See also Aggressiveness)	
What are the symptoms of shyness?	243–44
Speech Situations and Problems	
I have to give a speech soon. Does this book present an overview of what I have to do?	38–39
What should I do when I am called on for an impromptu speech?	159–60
I am going to give the commencement address at my *alma mater*. What should I do?	316–18
I will deliver the eulogy at a friend's funeral. What should I do?	313–16
I must give a speech of introduction.	308–11

PROBLEM CATEGORY AND QUESTIONS	LOCATION OF ANSWERS
I have been asked to give the keynote speech at a conference.	318–19
I am supposed to give a speech to praise someone. I do not want to overdo it.	311–13
Stage Fright (*See also* Anxiety)	
I think I am suffering from stage fright. What are the symptoms?	36–37
Style (*See also* Language)	
People tell me that I ought to work on my interactive style. What do they mean, and what should I do about it?	246
Supporting Material (*See also* Comparison and Contrast)	
Is there a way to tell if a statement needs support?	179–83
What are the common ways to support an idea?	184, 273–77
How can I use comparison and contrast as supporting material for a speech?	194–95, 249–50
How can I differentiate between a good example and one that is not? How do I use examples wisely?	195–96
What is the difference between an illustration and a story?	143–44
Is there a set of dos and don'ts for using statistics as supporting material? Is there a test for the quality of statistics as supporting material?	188–91
What is the best way to use quotations?	185–273
When should I quote a source directly, and when should I paraphrase?	192

PROBLEM CATEGORY AND QUESTIONS	LOCATION OF ANSWERS
T	
Tension and Conflict	
Tension is so high in my group that they are not getting anywhere. Is there anything I can do?	333–36
Topic (See also Narrow and Focus)	
I am supposed to give a speech and I have no idea what I should discuss. Any suggestions?	33–35, 93–100
I am worried that my topic will not be interesting to my listeners.	42, 94–95
U	
Understanding (See Meaning Agreement)	
V	
Visual Aids (See also Delivery)	
What is a visual aid?	202
What should I support with visual materials?	208
When should I use visual supporting materials?	203–8
How do I select visual materials?	211–14
How do I judge the quality of a visual aid?	214–21
I want to be sure my visual is well balanced. What criteria can I apply?	216–21
How can I suggest action and tension with a visual aid?	215–16
How can I suggest calm and peace with a visual aid?	215–16

CREDITS

Photographs

Chapter 1
Page 2: © Roy E. Roper/EKM-Nepenthe; **page 7:** UPI/Bettmann Newsphotos; **page 10:** Courtesy of Chrysler Corporation; **page 15:** © John Bird; **page 20:** © P. Davidson/Image Works, Inc.

Chapter 2
Page 28: © James Shaffer; **page 40:** © Jean-Claude Lejeune.

Chapter 3
Page 46: © John Bird; **page 56:** © Jean-Claude Lejeune.

Chapter 4
Page 52: © Nancy Anne Dawe.

Chapter 5
Page 86: © Nancy Anne Dawe; **page 99:** © James Shaffer; **page 101:** © Bob Coyle.

Chapter 6
Page 106: © Joan Menschenfreund/Taurus Photos; **page 123:** AP/Wide World Photos; **page 124:** Courtesy of Remington Products, Inc.; **page 126:** © Nancy Anne Dawe; **page 132:** © James W. Gibson.

Chapter 7
Page 138: © Patsy Davidson/Image Works, Inc.; **page 147:** © Michael Siluk; **page 150:** © Nancy Anne Dawe.

Chapter 8
Page 154: © James Shaffer; **page 170:** © James Shaffer.

Chapter 9
Page 176: © Nancy Anne Dawe; **page 193:** © Mark Antman/Image Works, Inc.; **page 194:** AP/Wide World Photos.

Chapter 10
Page 200: © Nancy Anne Dawe; **page 216: a,** © Jean-Claude Lejeune, **b,** Courtesy of Pontiac Motor Division, General Motors Corporation.

Chapter 11
Page 226: © Art Pahlke; **page 230:** Courtesy of The National Broadcasting Company; **page 232:** © SCALA/Art Resource, NY; **page 233:** UPI/Bettmann Newsphotos; **pages 234, 235, 237, 238:** © James Shaffer; **page 240:** © Jean-Claude Lejeune; **page 245:** © Alan Carey/Image Works.

Chapter 12
Page 256: © Tim Jewett/EKM-Nepenthe; **page 265:** © Alan Carey/Image Works, Inc.; **page 273:** © Michael Siluk.

Chapter 13
Page 280: © Jeff Smith; **page 298:** © Howard Dratch/Image Works, Inc.

Chapter 14
Page 306: © Nancy Anne Dawe; **page 313:** © H. Armstrong Roberts.

Chapter 15
Pages 322, 339: © James Shaffer.

INDEX